Missionary to the Mountain West

BISHOP TUTTLE

Missionary to the Mountain West

Reminiscences of Episcopal Bishop Daniel S. Tuttle
1866–1886

Daniel Sylvester Tuttle

Foreword by Brigham D. Madsen

University of Utah Press
Salt Lake City
1987

Originally published as Reminiscences of a Missionary Bishop.

Copyright 1906 by Thomas Whittaker.
Reprinted May 1977 by the Helena Letter Shop, Helena, Montana 59601.
Reprinted 1987 by the University of Utah Press.

Photographs in this book are courtesy of
Utah State Historical Society

Library of Congress Cataloging-in-Publication Data
Tuttle, Daniel Sylvester, 1837-1923.
  Missionary to the mountain West.

  Reprint. Originally published: Reminiscences of a missionary bishop.
New York: T. Whittaker, c1906.
  Includes index.
  1. Tuttle, Daniel Sylvester, 1837-1923. 2. Episcopal
Church—Bishops—Biography. 3. Anglican Communion—
Bishops—Biography. 4. Episcopal Church—Missions—
Montana. 5. Episcopal Church—Missions—Utah.
6. Episcopal Church—Missions—Idaho. 7. Anglican
Communion—Missions—Montana. 8. Anglican Communion—
Missions—Utah. 9. Anglican Communion—Missions—Idaho.
  I. Title.
BX5995.T8A3 1987   283'.3 [B]   87-8225
ISBN 0-87480-305-5

To
the memory of
my dear wife,
except at whose request they would never
have been written,
and
without whose love and help they would not
have been worthy to be written,
these reminiscences
are
reverently dedicated

FOREWORD

When I first read Daniel S. Tuttle's Missionary to the Mountain West (previously published as Reminiscences of a Missionary Bishop) as a graduate student at Berkeley, I was struck by its readability, humor, interest, and the excellent insight portrayed by a young minister of the gospel into the events and personalities which characterized the frontier "virgin soil" of early Montana, Idaho, and Utah. Now, many years and a lot of other "reminiscences" later, I am more than ever convinced of its significance as a valuable contribution to the early history of the northern Rocky Mountain region.

Daniel Sylvester Tuttle, a native of the state of New York, graduated from Columbia College in 1857, second in his class, and then completed his ministerial education at the General Theological Seminary in 1862. Assigned by the Episcopal Church as pastor at Morris, New York, he so distinguished himself that, much to his surprise and one year short of being the required age of thirty, on October 5, 1866, he was elected to be the missionary bishop in the new territory of Montana with jurisdiction also in Utah and Idaho. One of the factors which brought him to the attention of his superiors was his physical strength, commanding presence, and obvious leadership ability, qualities certainly needed for opening a mission in the rough mining camps of the Northwest. An incident which he later related in his reminiscences emphasized his courage and humanity and the good judgment of those who chose him for the assignment. He was riding in a stagecoach when "a so-called doctor . . . by manner and act was insulting to a colored woman in the coach. . . . I reproved him, and when he repeated the offense, I shook him soundly. At the next station, he got out and slunk entirely away from our sight."

Leaving his wife and infant son in New York, he started for his missionary labors in the West in May 1867, arriving at the terminus of the Union Pacific Railroad at North Platte where he and another tenderfoot companion bought rifles and practiced "shooting" so as to be able to defend themselves against Indian attack. He also made out his will while at the frontier town of Denver. But as one follows his experiences in the mountains, it becomes obvious that Bishop Tuttle, who had never been farther west than Niagara Falls, adapted rather quickly to western life. By the time he reached Salt Lake City, he had had his first experience riding in a rough stagecoach. In his memoirs he describes at length and with great interest his experiences during the next nineteen years as he traveled over 40,000 miles in the jerkies and mud wagons which passed for passenger coaches in his missionary region. His tribute to the hard-driving Jehus who steered their six-horse teams over rocky roads and snow-filled gulches reveals his sympathy and understanding of them, "I have never known a more true, self-respecting, heroic class of men. . . ."

Tuttle was responsible for Episcopal missionary work in the 340,000 square miles of territory in Montana, Utah, and Idaho where there was a scattered population of 150,000 and where the largest settlement, Salt Lake City, had only 20,000 residents. Over the next nineteen years of his term as missionary bishop, he held services in fifty-

Bishop Tuttle

two towns in Montana, fifty in Idaho, and nineteen in Mormon Utah. Bishop Tuttle started his labors in Virginia City, the capital of Montana. Here, he was introduced to the accommodations of the Planter's House, where there was no lock on the door, "no wash bowl or pitcher in the room. Every morning we go down to the office to wash, wiping our faces on the office towel." During the first sixteen months of his western labors and before his wife and son joined him in Montana, his letters home constitute perhaps the most interesting part of his reminiscences as he recounts his introduction to western manners and life.

By September 1869, Tuttle established a residence in Salt Lake City where his family lived for the next seventeen years while he spent much of his time being bounced around in stagecoaches on the rutted roads of Montana and Idaho. When at home, the Bishop recorded that he "did not feel either elated or despondent at the thought of crossing swords with the Mormons." In his initial meeting with Brigham Young, Tuttle described the Mormon Prophet as "pleasant and courteous and far less coarse than when he is speaking in public. I did not detect any violation of grammar or of good sense or of good taste on his part during our call." In a later evaluation of Young, Tuttle revealed the respect which he came to hold for the Mormon leader and the Utah Saints and which was mutually returned by them for the energetic and wise Episcopal Bishop whom they came to like and admire very much. Tuttle wrote of Young, "Shrewd, practical, industrious, energetic, temperate to the degree of abstemiousness, he was conscious of fitness to rule, and others unhesitatingly accorded him leadership. Persistent of aim and firm in will he was, and yet he knew how and when

Bishop Tuttle

wisely to bend or yield." These attributes could well be assigned to Daniel S. Tuttle himself who was lauded by the Mormon Deseret News on his departure from his bishopric for a new field in 1886 as "Kind, courteous and urbane, yet dignified and firm in his demeanor, he has made friends among people of various shades of opinion."

Daniel S. Tuttle's reminiscences constitute a valuable resource for anyone investigating and writing about the early history of the three states he covered as a roving missionary. And a general reader will get nothing but downright enjoyment in traveling with the young bishop as he describes his adventures and the picturesque places and people he meets. Bishop Tuttle won the hearts of those he met in Idaho and Montana as well as among the Mormon people. The miners and mountaineers of these territories "tested his manhood" and liked what they saw. As solemnly pronounced by Mr. William Bunkerly: "He's full jeweled and eighteen karats fine. He's a better man than Joe Floweree; he's the biggest and best bishop that ever wore a black gown. . . . He's a fire fighter from away back, and wherever he chooses to go a brimstone raid among the sinners in this gulch he can do it, and I'll back him with my pile. He is the best bishop, and you hear me howl." To those interested in the West of the Montana, Idaho, and Utah region of the 1860s and 1870s and in the life of an important and interesting religious leader, nothing more need be said; Bill Bunkerly said it all.

Brigham D. Madsen
University of Utah

Preface

The life and work of Daniel Sylvester Tuttle was significant.

He came to Montana when the Gold Fever was rampant. He traveled by stagecoach and horseback to minister to people in the name of Christ in communities which are now but memories. He established churches in camps which are now thriving communities.

From Montana he traveled to Idaho and Utah. When Bishop Brewer was elected to the Montana jurisdiction Bishop Tuttle moved to Salt Lake City, Utah, where he carried on his ministry with vigor.

His final move to Missouri took him away from the western field where he had labored so well.

It is with gratitude to God for the life and work of Daniel Sylvester Tuttle that the Spiritual Life Commission of The Diocese of Montana offers this reprint of his Autobiography.

A special word of commendation must go to The Rev. Canon Victor G. Richer for his work in bringing this project to completion.

+Jackson E. Gilliam
VIIth Bishop of Montana

PREFACE

My dear wife preserved no little of memoranda of my life in the Rocky Mountains. Once and again she importuned me to gather it together into a connected recital.

When in 1889 we had settled upon having a summer cottage on Lake Michigan, I yielded to her request and began these " Reminiscences." I could give to them only my summer vacations. Pressing duties of life allowed me no other time.

I finished them in 1904. I have only two motives in printing them.

First, to accede to the wishes of one dear to me, whose desire I want all the more to comply with since she has been taken from my side.

Second, to pen an honest record out from a tenderly grateful heart of how kind and good and helpful to a brother man were those who were wrong in belief and those who were wild and wicked in conduct of the men whom he knew and loved " in the mountains."

The Rev. G. D. B. Miller has added to his life of faithful help to me the great kindness of supervising the printing and publishing of this volume.

DANIEL S. TUTTLE.

St. Louis, Mo., April 9, 1906.

CONTENTS

Reminiscences of Bishop Tuttle

CHAPTER I

INTRODUCTORY

As I write this, in July, 1889, I have been a bishop more than twenty-two years. For almost twenty of these years I was a missionary bishop, and it may not be amiss in me to write down somewhat about these twenty years.

I was a member of the class of 1862 of the General Theological Seminary, New York City; among my class-mates being Bishops Robertson, Jaggar, and Walker. Twelve of us were ordered deacons in the Church of the Transfiguration, June 29, 1862, by Bishop Horatio Potter, the Rev. Dr. Littlejohn preaching the sermon. In the afternoon I preached my first sermon in St. Peter's, New York.

In the second class below me in the seminary was George W. Foote. His father, the Rev. George L. Foote, was the rector of Zion Church, Morris, Otsego County, N. Y., and earlier in the spring had been pros-trated by a paralytic stroke. In taking thought for his father and his father's parish, and casting about what to do, young Foote came and asked me if I would, on graduating, go and help his father. His mother's maiden name was Tuttle. Indeed her father and mine were first cousins. I knew, therefore, of the family as kinsfolk, though personally I was acquainted with young Foote only.

July 10th, I received a formal request from the Morris vestry asking me to come and " fulfil temporarily the parish duties of the rector, Rev. G. L. Foote," and I at once went to Bishop Potter to ask what he wished me to do. I had a double reason for going. First, he was my bishop; secondly, for two years and more as private tutor I had been teaching his sons, and I knew he felt a personal interest in me.

In reply to my question regarding his wishes he said, " Go to Morris. It is one of the best rural parishes in the diocese. The farmers from a great sweep of country round about are loyal churchmen. I attended a vestry meeting there lately, and was much gratified by the earnestness and intelligence manifested. The prostrated rector needs you. Go."

Accordingly I wrote to the vestry my acceptance of their invitation. I accepted not without reluctance, however, for I had been counting on a vacation and rest of at least two months before taking active duty in the ministry.

For five years, including two years between college and seminary (in one of which I was also a teacher in Columbia College Grammar School), and the three years of the seminary course, I had been busied in giving private lessons in classics and mathematics. And vacation times, also, were filled with teaching. I thought, therefore, that I had earned a real rest, and I wanted to take it. But the bishop's words were enough, and I gave up my desire. July 19th, therefore, found me at Morris. Mrs. Foote gave me a home in the rectory, and Mr. Foote allowed me in cash one-half of his modest salary of $900.

Mr. Foote's paralysis confined him to his room, almost to his bed; his speech was also much confused, though his mind and thoughts were clear. He lived, however,

until November, 1863. This year and a-half with Mr.
Foote and under him was of the greatest value to me.
He was preëminently a pastor, ever ready to " rejoice
with them that do rejoice, and weep with them that
weep." And he could " reprove, rebuke, exhort with all
long-suffering and doctrine." People who knew him in
his vigor told how, in joy and in sorrow, in the home and
the school and the mart, in feasting and in the sick room,
with a wonderful tact never at fault, he would ever con-
trive to let fall some thought wholesome for spiritual
guidance.

I can but think that among Americans this power of
the pastor is the greatest for good that a clergyman can
possibly wield. I do not forget that by ordination there
has been made over to him his priestly prerogative, *i. e.*,
authority divinely given and historically transmitted for
ministering the sacraments. I have no desire to under-
estimate the power that earnestness and eloquence do
certainly give in preaching the Word. Yet I remain
fixed in the conviction that the most wide-reaching and
long-lasting results for good, the American clergyman
wins as pastor. If children love him, and women respect
him, and men have full confidence in him ; if the happy are
happier to welcome him among them, and the sorrowful
lighter in heart, more hopeful of the future, and stronger
for duty, by his coming, if he is a prophet among them
in the true sense of the word, that is, one speaking for
God and the realities of the world invisible, then, it seems
to me, the daily life and pastoral converse of such a man
of God with his flock will contribute far more to their
spiritual advancement than any special efforts he can
make as priest of the Church or preacher of the
Word.

From the troubled utterances of Mr. Foote on his sick

bed and in his chair I received instruction of the best sort in pastoral theology.

" Do not yourself forget," he said, " and,—not failing to be cheerful and kindly and interested in what interests them,—do not let others forget,—that you are a minister of God appointed to serve among them."

In after years I had occasion to note the wisdom of the advice, for in the mountains I knew more than one minister who weakened his good influence or quite wrecked his usefulness by not having heard and heeded such advice. These clergymen knew that to be stiff, angular, distant, reserved, was not right for them, but they went too far in the opposite direction of affability and good-fellowship. Multifarious sociability displaying itself in cigar smoking, story-telling and boisterous hilarity, though practiced from a good motive, wrought them harm. In the inmost better nature of the rude mountaineers, and in the memory of their boyhood days, was fixed the image of the godly pastor. They took it ill, and with honest resentment, that the respected image should be obscured and disfigured by what appeared to them unseemly and undignified ministerial behavior.

" Do not be afraid to urge people to come to confirmation," said Mr. Foote. " Timid ones need encouragement. Scrupulously sensitive ones need help against their doubts and shrinkings. Children, when old enough, especially those in Christian homes, are to be asked to come, almost as a matter of course. And most people will be found waiting to be spoken to by the pastor. Few, of themselves, and by their own motion, will come to him and ask to be confirmed."

Experience has proved to me the wisdom of these words. Especially have I found good results in speaking upon confirmation to calm, thoughtful, reserved men.

Had I waited for them first to speak to me, the waiting would have had no end. Two classes only ought not to be urged. First, those who have no motive in "joining the church" but the social prestige they may secure; and second, those who look upon confirmation as a process of what is popularly called "whitewashing," and who desire it for that purpose. In these two cases, instead of urging them to come, prudence and kindly firmness are to be used in motioning them back.

"In visiting," was Mr. Foote's advice, "be unfailingly courteous. Notice the children. If there be any deformed or feeble-minded or strangely affected person present, speak to him or her exactly as to the rest. Betray no surprise and make no comment. Make it seem sure that one equally with another is under your care and pastorship."

What of good is in the *nil admirari* rule of cultivated society is covered by these words of Mr. Foote. Not to notice, at least not to show that you notice, marked peculiarities in those you meet; not to allow in one's self display of uncontrolled passion or emotion; not to give boisterous expression to approval or disapproval of persons and things; not to disturb one's own and another's equanimity by rashness of contention, or uneasiness of excitement,—all these are excellent rules. But to admire nothing, to be surprised at nothing, to wonder about nothing, after the severe manner of some demigod, and to choke back enthusiasm and repulse animation seem to me conduct altogether too unnatural to be pleasant, too self-satisfied to be wise, too calculatingly narrow to be noble, and too unsympathetic to be right wholesome.

"Here, in our rural region," said the rector, "you will be asked to preach funeral sermons. Do not refuse. Frequently you will have before you those that at no

other time will come within hearing of the voice of the
minister of God. With God's blessing you may drive
home to them wholesome truth. Say little of the dead,
but improve the opportunity to urge upon the living
thought about righteousness, temperance and the judgment to come. So you will avoid offense that might be
given by seeming to show contempt for an old custom
of the country, and you can with good effect improve
the occasion to preach the Word."

I have found it good to follow this advice. The
Prayer-Book service for the burial of the dead is of itself impressive and sufficient. If choice be fully left to
me I use it only. And in many places in the mountains
I was shown by one or another miner, or lawyer, or
business man, a copy of the Prayer-Book with the information that they had used it in reading the burial service
in the days before any minister had come among them.
Not a little one among the blessings bestowed by the
Prayer-Book is this of affording simple and fit guidance
and help to a frontier people in reverently and religiously
laying by the sacred bodies of the dead. To me just
setting out for my work as a young deacon, Mr. Foote's
two hints were worth everything. By heeding them I
was saved from giving offense to persons through refusing to preach " funeral sermons " ; more offense to truth
by dwelling upon elaborate details concerning the one
dead ; and further offense to taste and reverence by har-
rowing and playing upon the emotions of afflicted friends.

" Have confidence in your vestry, give respectful attention to the views which they may present. Let them
know that you trust them. Coöperate with them, and
seek to induce them to coöperate with you. Open the
vestry meetings always with the Creed, the Lord's
Prayer, and a Collect or two ; " this also I was advised.

My relations with vestries have always been kindly and satisfactory, and I think mutually helpful. I confess I have never found in myself ready sympathy with the outcry against vestries that voices itself in our church papers. Perhaps Mr. Foote's counsel about " coöperation," and " respect," and " trust," started me on the course where least friction lies. Doubtless my first experiences with a vestry were well calculated to make me an optimist about all vestries. They were men good and true with whom I knelt and took counsel in vestry meetings in Morris. Ten of them there were, and all earnest communicants. Three only are now living. Six were farmers and four merchants. They were evenly divided as Democrats and Republicans. Two of the former were of the extreme " copperhead" kind, one of the latter had been for years an out and out abolitionist. And we were in the midst of the heats and strains of our Civil War. I myself was a Republican, and in the early summer of 1861 had been vigorously drilled in military tactics in a company of Home Guards, which met evenings in a room under the Fifth Avenue Hotel, New York City, and in Madison Square; of which company I was chosen a sergeant. What a tribute to the wise soberness of the Church that men like us, differing intensely in political views, could be united in her fold and earnestly loyal to her, throughout the war !

So predisposed I am to think favorably of vestries and to welcome trustfully coöperation with the laity, I perhaps can hardly venture to call myself unprejudiced in what I think and say touching the usefulness and value of that type of parochial organization which obtains in the American Church.

Of such parochial organization I honestly avow myself an approver and a supporter. Negatively, because

I do not know of any better system of local church management to put in its place. Positively, because I think there are equities and excellences in it. " But," some one says, " have tithes; get people to pay tithes, and then pew rents and subscriptions and vestries will not be needed." Well, I believe in tithes. I am a friend to tithes, and I am glad and grateful to be permitted to say that since I was eighteen years of age I have put by the tenth of my income, keeping it in, and using it out of, the " Lord's purse." And I grant that if all could be persuaded to the same course, there would be no need for pew rents and subscriptions. But I do not so clearly see that there would be no need of vestries. Is not the coöperation of laymen needed and wisely used in such matters as buying lots, and building churches and keeping them in repair, and meeting and providing for, in an honest, businesslike way, the constant expenditures necessarily incurred in sustaining the ministrations of the church? Does not the pastor occasionally need advice and counsel? In making and carrying out his plans does he not want to know how they strike the people, and to have their excellence rated from the people's point of view? How better than through a vestry can he get the coöperation, and the counsel, and the standpoint for looking wisely, that he needs?

Another one says, " Have a central treasury." (By this is generally meant, I think, a diocesan treasury, the bishop, I suppose, to be the comptroller of it.) " Pay all clergy out of it, as senators and congressmen are paid out of the treasury, then vestries would not be needed to ' hire ' their minister, forsooth. The bishop, according to his will and wisdom could send and pay his clergy, as ought to be the case."

The allusion to the United States Treasury imparts not

much strength of argument. For that treasury is filled
by taxes imposed by law, the payment whereof is enforced by penalties. But church taxes must be voluntary.
The difference is in a nutshell, but it is a big difference.
How then, is the question, is the central treasury to be
filled? It may be answered, "by tithes." The tenths
would indeed, I grant, if faithfully paid fill it well and
keep it full. But until that measure of faithfulness be
reached, how shall it be filled? It might be answered,
" Let all the payments now made to the parish treasurer
be sent instead to the central treasury. That is all we
ask. Then the bishop could allot to the clergy each his
portion equitably, and the gross inequalities and painful
uncertainties under which we now suffer would cease to
exist."

This answer goes on the supposition that there would
be readily paid into the central treasury the aggregate of
all that now is paid into the parish treasuries. Is this
supposition a reasonable one? It appears to me that
under this plan two classes of givers would not give as
much as now, and that it is doubtful if the third would
give more. First, there are those who give from local
interest and pride. They are glad for the church to be
built, the services to be sustained, and the minister to be
supported, and they will help, because it is all for " our
town," its advancement and improvement. One who
has had experience knows that this local public spirit
can be counted on for a good deal in sustaining the
ministrations of the church. But, it is safe to say, not a
penny of such giving could be had if it were known that
it was to be carried out of the town and deposited in a
central treasury.

A second class of givers are the fixed church folk who
look upon the parish as their spiritual home, and the

pastor as their spiritual guide, whose hands they are to uphold and whose wants they are to supply. It needs no course of reasoning to demonstrate that this class would give less for a general treasury than they will in providing the immediate parish expenses in which they are personally interested, and for which they feel themselves directly responsible. Duty, honor, a laudable pride, gratitude and affection conspire as inducements to give in the latter case. In the former only sense of duty and honor could be relied on to operate actively, and it must be highly educated and well developed sense of honor at that.

The third class of givers are the faithful ones who regard themselves as having their goods in stewardship, and who like to give where and when and how they think God would have them give. These are the thoughtful and intelligent and considerate and earnest men and women. I venture to affirm that they know that often harm comes from large giving. So knowing they learn to be careful. They frequently refrain from giving large help to parish treasuries lest such giving break down the vigorous self-help of the other people of the parish, weaken its Christian wholesomeness, and work its pauperization. So they send the most of their money to the hospitals, and schools and missions. One may, therefore, claim that they would be likely to hesitate to send large gifts to a central treasury for fear of the influence they might have in weakening the healthful life blood of self-help.

To my mind it is clear that a central treasury could never succeed in getting so large an amount of money as do the parish treasuries for meeting the needs of the church. But suppose it could even secure a larger amount, a well filled treasury is not always a blessing.

The nation has of late been struggling with an honestly distressing anxiety over a surplus in its treasury. The fulness of supply in the treasury is to be dispensed in no haphazard way, if its law of administration and current of distribution are to do good, not harm. Is it said that the bishop is undoubtedly the fit administrator and distributor? Shall he, without dispute, be the comptroller? Ah then, more painfully uneasy than ever shall lie the head that wears a mitre. He to have the key of a well filled treasury, and with his right hand in it to reward the faithful of his clergy, to encourage the humble, to restrain the eager and ambitious, to rebuke the domineering and proud, to advance the hard-working and well-deserving, to press back the indolent and the self-seeking, and to put up with the inefficient and the shirks! All this would put his wisdom to such a test and the people's loyalty to such a strain that both he and they would in no long time, I venture to say, gladly withdraw from such a condition into the comparative freedom of their present relations.

Until something better can be suggested to take the place of the present parochial organization, I may be pardoned for being, in the interest of good order, its firm supporter.

And some things, I apprehend, may be said positively in its favor. It is an obvious truth that the clergy are not the Church. They are only part of the Church. "The visible Church of Christ," says Article XIX, " is a congregation of faithful men, in the which the pure Word of God is preached, and the sacraments be duly ministered according to Christ's ordinance, in all those things that of necessity are requisite to the same." The " faithful " have a right then, and it is their duty, to take counsel together concerning their well-being and their on-going

as a spiritual community. The parochial organization
furnishes opportunity for such counsel. It is claimed
that in the primitive Church the laity had no part or lot
in such counseling. It makes little matter whether this
claim be well supported or not. Changed conditions
surround the Church in America. A course eminently
fit for us might have been quite unsuited to the primitive
Church. As our preface to the Prayer-Book has it,—
" It is a most invaluable part of that blessed liberty wherewith Christ hath made us free, that in His worship, different forms and usages may without offense be allowed,
provided the substance of the faith be kept entire; and
that in every church, what cannot be clearly determined
to belong to doctrine must be referred to discipline; and
therefore, by common consent and authority, may be
altered, abridged, enlarged, amended, or otherwise disposed of, as may seem most convenient for the edification
of the people, according to the various exigencies of times
and occasions."

Now, I take it, whatever religious body wants to win
its way among Americans, and has the faintest hope of
ever becoming " the American Church," must take heed-
ful care to observe two American watchwords, " local
sovereignty," and " no taxation without representation."
On issues outlined by each of these watchwords the two
mightiest wars of the nation have been waged. The
South failed, as I think it deserved to fail, in fighting for
the former. In the logical estimate, sovereignty must be
national, not local. But in practical every-day matters,
and short of that " estimate," when the life of the nation
comes distinctly into view, he greatly mistakes who judges
otherwise than that Americans are intense believers in the
prerogatives of local sovereignty. The War of the Revolution, in its sturdy success, set the seal of abiding ap-

proval to the other word, " no taxation without representation." Our parochial organization is framed on the line
of these American maxims and is in touch with American
ideas. So it is fitted, as on vantage ground, to influence
American citizens and win its way in American communities.

I am aware that under the system there emerges in the
parish every now and then the lay pope, male or female.
And doubtless out of it are begotten harmful ideas about
" hiring " and " dismissing " ministers. Yet, I am of the
opinion that, spite of these drawbacks, the parochial
organization is a healthy and helpful adjunct to the right
sort of American church life.

If the bishop would take pains to do two things, perhaps
complaints about it would not be so frequent. These are :

I. To urge upon vestries payment, regular, and in
full, of the salary pledged to their pastor. The uncertainty of income is, I am convinced, a more unsatisfactory
feature of clerical support than the smallness of income.
People are quick to mark a fault in a clergyman's careless-
ness in meeting pecuniary obligations. If he incurs debts
that he cannot pay, if he is not scrupulously careful to
meet exactly, in time and amount, his promises to pay,
then ensues for him a loss of character and influence in
the community to a degree that almost no other faults
of conduct entail. Now, if the bishop meeting each
vestry shall plainly remind them that, as they well know,
a clergyman is adversely talked about and disesteemed
who does not promptly meet his business engagements,
and then ask them as plainly how the pastor is to be able
to pay his debts unless the dues to him are promptly
paid, I think very many cases of heedlessness and
thoughtless neglect would be in the way to be quickly
mended.

2. To call the attention of vestries to the manifest injustice involved in a forced speedy dissolution of the relation between the pastor and themselves. In business ethics it is not deemed fair to cancel an engagement between two without first serving reasonable notice to each. Therefore a notice of three months, or six months, or a year, according to circumstances, should be given to the clergyman in cases where the conclusion has been thoughtfully reached that a change must be made. There is, I venture to assert, a love of fair play in American minds that can be counted on. There is regard for business rectitude and honor among American men that can always be appealed to.

If the bishop somewhat in these ways will address his remonstrances to the American sense of justice and honor, through the parochial organizations, my word for it, in very many cases there will be shame and repentance and reformation in the matter of slovenly payments of dues to clergymen, and there will be a wholesome shrinking from the curt " dismissals " complained of.

In securing local lay coöperation, mission " committees " are to me the same as " vestries." In the case of each, authority may be devolved upon them, and responsibilities exacted.

Besides Mr. Foote's wise counselings, other things in Morris fitted me for the future. On August 23, 1862, I was elected assistant minister of Zion Church. During the year and a-half of Mr. Foote's continued rectorship, I could not but notice that small amounts of salary due were sent in to Mr. Foote from time to time, by the treasurer, as they came into his hands. I took heed of the fact, and marked in connection with it that the parish was such an one as could promptly meet its engagements. On November 18, 1863, on Mr. Foote's death, I was chosen rector at a salary of $800 per year. I accepted, and in my letter of acceptance stipulated that I should be paid promptly and in full at the end of each quarter, giving notice that I should charge interest in a regular business way upon any deficiency that then existed. I may remark that I never had occasion in all my rectorship at Morris to charge up one penny of interest. I received seven calls elsewhere while at Morris. Among them, to the rectorship of Quincy, Illinois, and Binghamton, Ithaca, and Oswego, New York. The salaries offered in these four places were respectively $1,000, $1,400, $1,000, and $1,500. But I did not want to leave Morris; I felt it a duty and a pleasure to stay. On December 29, 1865, the vestry of Zion Church made my salary $1,000. September 12th of the same year I married Harriet M. Foote, eldest child of the late rector, who was four years younger than myself.

Morris made and kept me strong physically. In college and seminary I had been used to exercise in a gymnasium. So under the horse-shed of the church I put up a pair of parallel bars and continued my exercise. Throughout the summer, nearly every afternoon, I went for a swim in a large mill-pond near. I had my own horse (dear old " Jersey," my heart gratefully recalls your fidelity and good service as I now write), for getting about my large parish, and I took complete care of him myself. So, with God's blessing on an original good constitution, and with habits maintained, of exercise and of an hour at least spent every day in the open air, it has come about that in twenty-seven years of ministerial life I have been absent from duty in church from sickness only two Sundays.

Socially, Morris was a helpful school. Half a dozen old families were there, whose members were the inheritors of the excellences given by birth, good breeding, education, culture, ancestral traditions. Then in the business folk of the village and the honest working farmers of the large country parish I had opportunity to mingle with, to know, and to learn from, all sorts and conditions of men.

As a writer and preacher of sermons my advantages were manifold. Only one sermon a week was needed. For morning service the whole country round came to church. The horse-sheds were densely populated. At noon was a short intermission; and baskets and buckets provided a modest lunch, eaten under the umbrageous maple trees in the beautiful churchyard. After that came the Sunday-school, accompanied by evening prayer, and a talk of a few minutes, generally upon some collect or rubric or office or Article of the Prayer-Book. This was all that Zion Church demanded. In the evening it was my custom to go for missionary work to some one of six points in the neighboring region.

What better schooling could a preacher have? Only one sermon a week called for. I began writing that on Tuesday morning, and all of Tuesdays and Thursdays and some time Fridays, from morning till 5 P. M., the time of my outdoor exercise, I would be busied in my study. Mondays I read novels, and snoozed and went to bed early. Saturdays I did the thousand and one little things necessary to be ready for Sunday's work, including the holding of a Bible class in the church in the afternoon. Wednesdays, "Jersey" and I would be off visiting. I seldom if ever wrote upon my sermon at night, and quite as seldom did Friday afternoon come without finding it entirely finished. I am convinced that a young deacon should never undertake the preparation of more than one sermon a week. If there must be two for the church services, let him read one out of print, would be my advice. " Why not extemporize," some one asks. I answer, extemporizing is a practice fraught with great risk to the young man. If he prepare for his second sermon an extempore one, to make it what it ought to be, he must give as much time and anxious care to it as he would to a written one. If he do not, unstudious habits of life, unthoughtful ways of reasoning and teaching are begotten and nourished, to his great harm in after years. As between preaching with manuscript and without I am on the side of the manuscript. This is especially true for the young, because of the dangers I have adverted to. But it does seem to me young men could be taught to *preach* the written sermon rather than to *read* it. The true preacher is both an orator and a teacher. He does not neglect the helps that go to make up the former. One of the greatest of these is the power of the eye. To *preach* his sermon well, therefore, it is requisite that he be sufficiently familiar with its thoughts and words to be able to look up and off from the manuscript, once in a while, into the eyes of those listening. Painstaking care in reading over the sermon beforehand, and practice in looking into people's eyes from the pulpit are the things needed. For the young man, painstaking care in preaching the sermon beforehand is of great value. Beyond my swimming-pond at Morris was an island, away from houses, reached by a long slab over the stream, and with a beautiful grove upon it. Between two trees, almost joined together at the root, I set up a rude pulpit board, and there every Saturday I spread out my sermon for the next day, and preached it, loud and full, with the birds for listeners. The exercise helped my voice. Emphasis took to itself right inflections. Eye and hand and bodily posture

familiarized themselves with their duties and adjusted
themselves to the ways of most efficient work. Then
every Sunday morning, complying with Mr. Foote's
desire, I read over the sermon aloud to him in his room
before going to church. It may well be believed that in
the pulpit, body, mind, memory and eyes, were thoroughly
at home with that sermon, and I was free, with God's
help, to throw earnestness of heart into it, and quite as
free to hurl what force was in it into the listening ears
and watching eyes of the congregation. All my life I
have kept up the habit. I have never preached a sermon
from the pulpit that I had not beforehand read over aloud,
or, as it were, preached, in the grove, or my study, or
some upper room. For myself, I do not of choice preach
extempore. Nor do I think I make at all a success at it.
Yet a kind of ambidextrousness, gotten by these talks on
Sunday afternoons in Morris, has alway stood me in good
stead.

One sermon per week thoughtfully written and painstakingly preached, enough Sunday afternoon talking
practiced to give facility in that line, missionary jaunts of
Sunday evenings to widen a young man's horizon and to
put him to his mettle as the persuader and instructor of
many men of many minds in different congregations;—
was this not all, I repeat, right good schooling for a
preacher?

As pastor, the hints, suggestions, directions, guidances,
I received from Mr. Foote were as well-springs of abundant
helpfulness to me. And the large country parish was a
field of practice of unspeakable value. There were two
hundred communicants in it, more or less. During my
pastorate of five years I presented one hundred and
twenty-two for confirmation, baptized one hundred and
forty-one, married twenty-three, and buried fifty-five. In

the Sunday-school and in the Bible class of Saturday
afternoon were two brothers, who came some miles from
the country to attend, sons of Mr. Norris Gilbert, the
senior warden. The younger one attracted my attention
from the first Sunday. He was fourteen years old, large-
eyed and bright-eyed, quick to answer at catechising, an
untiring listener at the " talks." This was Mahlon N.
Gilbert, now assistant bishop of Minnesota. Mr. Foote,
when coming to the parish two or three years before, had
also been singularly attracted by him. Going up to him
one day after Sunday-school, in the kind way Mr. Foote
had with children, he said, placing his hand on his head,
" You are a right good listener, my boy ; it interests me
to look at you when I am speaking ; I hope you will
grow up to be one of these days a minister yourself to
help us in the church." The thought was first put into
the boy's mind then and there. Behold its growth and
fruit! Ought we older ones not to bethink ourselves how
a word in season uttered to a boy or young man may be
the starting point for securing him for the work of the
sacred ministry? Subsequently young Gilbert studied
Latin and mathematics with Mrs. Tuttle and myself;
went to Fairfield Academy and Hobart College ; came to
Ogden, Utah, and was the first teacher in our school
there ; traveled with me in a long visitation in Montana ;
came East to Seabury School, Faribault, for his theological course ; returned to Montana, and as deacon served
at Deer Lodge and built St. James' church. Then he
became the greatly loved rector of St. Peter's, Helena,
whence he was called to Christ church, St. Paul. I cannot tell all the story of how the lines of my life's history
have become closely woven with his, or how my heart is
gladdened as a loving father's over the great good work
for the church that he is doing in these later days.

Five other boys who were under me in Zion church are now clergymen, H. L. Foote, A. C. Bunn, R. Mansfield, D. W. Duroe and L. C. Washburn. My immediate successor in the rectorship, Rev. N. S. Rulison, is now (1889) the assistant bishop of Central Pennsylvania. Dear old Morris! Most true and loyal in devotion to the church thou hast always been. My heart ever goes back to thee in warm and grateful memories for all thou wast to me, and for the good equipment thou didst furnish me with, against needs of subsequent years. Almost a generation has come and gone since we were together, though once I thought to live and die in the peacefulness of thy beautiful valley, and be buried where "the forefathers of the hamlet sleep." My love for thee was a first love. I went to thee in my youth. My love for thee is an only love. I was never to have another parish to be tied to, in the sweet and strong bonds of special pastoral care and fixed home life. In unfeigned sadness I know I left thee. In sorrowful regret I think thy people parted with me. Is it a wonder that to this day my spirit is filled with rest and with thankfulness at thought of thee, of the five years of life I gave to thee, and the five years of experience and helpful preparation thou gavest me?

CHAPTER II

ELECTED BISHOP 1866

OUR first child, George Marvine (named after a dear old friend of my schoolboy days in Delhi, New York), was born September 21, 1866. The Annual Convention of the Diocese of New York was to meet on Wednesday, the 26th. I wanted very much to attend but, inexperienced father though I was, I knew it was not wise or kind for me to run off from a baby five days old. Yet mother and child got along so nicely that my wife said, " Go." On Wednesday, therefore, I started, awakening the quick indignation of the ladies of the parish by doing so. It then took a day and a half to get to New York City from Morris, for we were forty miles from the nearest railroad. I arrived, however, in time to be present at the latter half of the Convention. I was the guest of Dr. Sabine, father of the Rev. W. T. Sabine, one of my seminary classmates. Young Sabine afterwards found himself famous from his alleged refusal to say the burial service for the funeral of George Holland, the actor, and for his waiving off the friend, who came to request his attendance, to " The Little Church around the Corner."

I remained in New York City after the Diocesan Convention for a visit of a week or two, attending the consecration of Bishop Williams of Japan, in St. John's chapel, on Wednesday, October 3d. Friday afternoon I was out making some calls. When I came in a little after five o'clock, Dr. Sabine himself answered the door-bell. He said, " Smith and Walker have been here to tell that you have been appointed Bishop of Nevada." These were seminary classmates of mine, and one of them, a good deal of a humorist and joker, so I laughed at the story and at what I deemed the joke, and went to my room to dress. Within half an hour the servant came up to say that Bishop Potter and another gentleman were in the parlor. In much trepidation now, I descended, to find Bishop Potter and Bishop Lay awaiting me. The latter I had never met. Bishop Potter introduced me to him and then said to me, " Have you heard anything strange in the way of news to-day?" I answered, " Yes, Dr. Sabine awhile ago told me that some classmates had come here with a story that I had been elected Bishop of Nevada." " Well," said the bishop, " what if the story should be true?" " Why," I answered, " I can only say that I am but twenty-nine years old, and shall not be thirty until the 26th of January next." Then there was silence. The two bishops talked together in a low tone. At last Bishop Potter said: " We are here, a committee from the House of Bishops, to announce to you your election by the House this day to be a missionary bishop. Of course you must be thirty years old before you can be consecrated. But the restriction does not, we venture to say, apply to the election. Go back to Morris and go about your duties there until your birthday is past, and God be with you!"

Uttering some kind words to me, they soon withdrew and left me to wrestle with my surprise as best I could. A first duty was clear, to send a telegram to the mother of our two weeks old baby, lest the startling news reaching her from other sources might do her harm. Then, considering a little, I settled into repose of thought. I said to myself that when the Standing Committees come to act upon my nomination and learn how young and unknown I am, (I am sure I was absolutely unknown to any of the members of the House of Bishops, except Bishops Potter and Whitehouse), they will decline to confirm, and there will be an end of it. So I quietly stayed some days longer in New York. By inquiry I discovered that the missionary district to which I had been appointed was not Nevada, but " Montana, with jurisdiction in Idaho and Utah."

Up to this time (1889), there have been in the American Church eight foreign missionary bishops and twenty-seven domestic, thirty-five in all. Of these I was the fourteenth. The missionary district to which I was assigned was arranged and newly constituted in the same meeting of the House of Bishops in which I was elected. Nevada and Arizona made another field, to which Bishop Whitaker was appointed in the General Convention of 1868.

The metes and bounds of missionary districts in our own country are now fixed and definite, as they were not altogether at first.

In 1835, although Bishop Kemper was appointed to be the missionary bishop of Missouri and Indiana, yet for nineteen years, until he became the diocesan of Wisconsin, his field was really all that is now comprised in the states of Missouri, Indiana, Iowa, Nebraska, Kansas, Minnesota, and Wisconsin. We may say that it was only thus limited because farther west none but Indians then lived.

In 1838, Bishop Polk was made missionary bishop of Arkansas, but his field was really all the Southwest, and he became the diocesan of Louisiana in 1841. In 1844 Bishop Freeman was definitely appointed to " Arkansas and the Southwest." In 1860 Bishop J. C. Talbot, likewise, was appointed to the " Northwest." What a field !

Bishop Scott, in 1854, had taken Oregon and Washington, but there was left for Bishop Talbot all now comprised in Nebraska, Wyoming, Colorado, Utah, Nevada, Dakota, Montana, and Idaho, to say nothing of New Mexico and Arizona ; or perhaps they might more suitably fall under the "Southwest" to which Bishop Lay had been sent in 1859. Bishop Talbot, however, did missionary work in Nebraska, Colorado and Nevada. He passed through Wyoming and Utah, but did no work in them. Perhaps he was in Dakota, but I think not. I know he never was in either Montana or Idaho. No wonder in the General Convention of 1865 that the House of Bishops felt called upon to subdivide the enormous field of the Far West. Bishop Randall was given Colorado, Wyoming, New Mexico, and, I think, Montana and Idaho. But he never saw these last named territories. To Bishop Clarkson were assigned Nebraska and Dakota. In the special meeting of the House of Bishops in 1866 a further rearrangement was ordered, and Montana, Idaho, and Utah were made a missionary district, and I was elected to take charge of it. I have lived to see many other subdivisions.

To my mind it was one of the most important steps ever taken in the American Church, when in 1835, under the energetic leadership of the elder Doane, these two truths were set forth and emphasized: First, that the Church is herself the great missionary society, and that every one baptized is therefore a member of the one as of the other. Secondly, that bishops are the proper "missionary" officers, and under bishops, specially and directly, missionary work should be carried on. The operation of the latter principle put Kemper into the field in less than a month after the close of the General Convention, and has given to us his thirty-four successors, missionary bishops. I marvel that it took the American Church fifty-two years to realize the importance of this principle, or at least to put it into practice. For the one hundred and seventy-six years between the settling of Jamestown, in 1607, and the close of the Revolutionary War, in 1783, did she not herself languish for lack of a bishop of her own to live in her midst and give her watchful care? Men loyal to her and loving her, like Washington himself, never had an opportunity in their youth to be confirmed; and so by scores and hundreds from want of the accustomed rite failed to become regular communicants. Of the young men of the soil, only one here and another there could hope to become clergymen, for the uncertainty and expense of a voyage to London for examination and ordination, and that, be it remembered, not by steamer, were obstacles quite insurmountable. Not a few clergymen in England embarked for the colonies, in the case of each of whom success at home was a diminishing quantity, or reputation, from one cause or another, was an endangered thing. Other clergymen came over who were well-meaning and of fair ability, but who, without old standards to keep them up, and old disciplines to guide them, steadily sank, in character, or efficiency, or aim. It is obvious how readily things could go from bad to worse with no eye and voice of a bishop to warn and no immediate ecclesiastical discipline to correct and restrain.

When the American nation became independent in 1783, and the American Church, by securing three bishops of her own, became independent in 1787, these same evils were to reproduce themselves in the region where bishops were not, and on the frontier. Sufferer that she had been for one hundred and seventy-seven years from being deprived of bishops, we wonder that

the American Church did not now at once set herself to
provide for her need, especially for supervising her out-
lying missionary activities. Yet it was not till after
thirty-two years, that the first bishop was sent West.
Chase, of Ohio, went in 1819; and thirteen years after, in
1832, Smith of Kentucky. It was forty-eight years before the first missionary bishop was sent out; that was
Kemper, who went in 1835. Perhaps three reasons may
be suggested for this seeming inattention and inactivity
on the part of the Church. First, Americans had got on
for nearly two centuries without bishops. It would not
be strange that even church folk should grow to have a
much weaker impression of their value, through this prolonged absence of their persons and disuse of their functions. Secondly, in people's minds bishops were associated with the nobility and the monarchy of the old
country. They were determined to have none of the
latter; and naturally an unwillingness to welcome the
former was bred and strengthened. It was not easy to
make bishops, or when they were made to induce the
people to greet them cordially and mind them heedfully.
It took fifty-eight years before the thirteen original
States secured bishops for themselves. Delaware and
Georgia did not obtain theirs till 1841. Of course the
missionary waste places must suffer until the settled communities could be supplied. It may be remarked that
the second war of 1812, waked anew the old-time animosities against red-coats and tories, and all other things
British, and therefore against bishops.

Thirdly, for the first half century of our national life the
energies of the people were taxed to solve pressing financial problems : to redeem and retire the Continental currency; to pay and bond the debt incurred by the war;
to set on foot methods for creating and developing the

commerce of the country. The people of the infant
states were by no means rich. To send out missionary
bishops would require the coöperation of the united
church, and the dioceses were only as yet feeling their
way towards concerted action. The sending would also
entail considerable cost, and the church was too feeble as
yet to support it.

It is easy, it seems to me, to point out the eminent fitness of doing missionary work by missionary bishops.
What was the practice at the beginning? Were not the
apostles " missionary bishops," proceeding immediately
after the day of Pentecost to do missionary work in
Judea, and Samaria, and Galilee and Western Asia, and
Northern Africa, and Southern Europe? Were not
Paul and Barnabas the same, starting out first and foremost to do missionary preaching and missionary pastoral work themselves, and then returning over their
route to instruct and strengthen the churches and to
ordain elders to serve in them?

With Apostolic sanction and practice in favor of
missionary bishops, there need be adduced nothing more
to strengthen the argument. Yet it may be well to observe the practical benefit, accruing to adherence to the
Apostolic plan. The missionary bishop, moving over his
entire field and acquainting himself with it, knows where
to place a presbyter in residence this year, and another
next year, and another the year after, far better than can
a secretary of a missionary society with headquarters in
a city of the Atlantic coast. With the prestige and authority which his office undeniably gives him, the bishop
can rouse the interest and evoke the efficient coöperation of the people in the field. He is a fixture among
them, as a presbyter would not be. He belongs to them;
they are responsible to him. They must meet him for

praise or blame at regularly recurring times, and they are ashamed to show themselves utter failures in their relation with him.   So is secured one of the most important elements of best missionary work, viz., the wholesome habit, on the part of the people in the field, of sturdy self-help.   Obviously, the inducements will be manifold to the presbyter to join with his people in drawing for his mission all he can from the central atlantic treasury. But the bishop will strive to moderate this eagerness because he needs the money for other points.   Besides he knows the blasting effect upon the growth of a parish of a subsidy to it from the outside too long continued. Also, as he goes about, he can now and then fix his eye on a boy or young man well fitted to enter on studies looking to the sacred ministry, and can wisely guide his steps.   The sons of the soil will make the best sort of missionaries in the future.   And what better society for the increase of the ministry can there be, to secure the help absolutely needed by the young men, and to supervise them in life and study and conduct, than the bishop himself?   When he visits the Eastern centre of church strength and influence and generous giving, the authority of his office, the experience in his work, and the responsibility attached to his position as the commander-in-chief in the field, to which he is strictly held in the thought of the church at large, eminently fit him to give information, to arouse interest, to direct sympathy, and to get help.

After my election, I returned to Morris and " went about my business," as Bishop Potter had advised. Thoughts of withdrawal from Morris and of investment with Episcopal authority for work in the Rocky Mountains did not sorely press, for I deemed them events unlikely to happen.   Nevertheless there soon came from the presiding bishop (Hopkins) a letter courteously but plainly asking that I make and announce my decision concerning acceptance. When I was obliged to face this all-important question, I found affection and loyalty to my dearly loved parish, and deep consciousness of my own unfitness from the inexperience and crudity of youth, strongly impelling me to stay where I was. But I could not hide from myself that duty and obedience to the Church commanded me to go. Therefore, after all indulging of honest expectations that " nothing would come of it," I found myself writing on January 22, 1867, four days before I was thirty years old, my letter of acceptance to Bishop Hopkins. Soon I preached to my people a sermon announcing my decision, reading to them from the pulpit a letter from Montana I had lately received. The letter was from Virginia City, the capital of Montana, and was signed by Governor Green Clay Smith, Chief Justice H. L. Hosmer, and other officials, proffering to me a hearty welcome, and promising efficient coöperation when I should come among them. The presiding bishop's reply to my letter of acceptance was as follows :

"Burlington, Vt., January 28, 1867.
" REV. AND DEAR BROTHER :
    " On my return from the consecration of Bishop Neely in New York, I found your very interesting letter of the 22d instant, and I read it with the deepest feeling of thankfulness for the truly Christian spirit which it displayed; that spirit of humility and simple reliance on the Lord, which is the best warrant for His effectual blessing.
    " I shall proceed without delay to address the Standing Committees, and when the canonical majority have sent in their testimonials, no time will be lost in preparing for your consecration. As you decline to suggest any other names, etc., I shall enclose your letter to your attached friend, who presented your name, with the highest encomiums, to the House of Bishops, viz., Bishop Potter, and

request him to arrange the details to which I shall then be ready to give the presiding bishop's authority.

"With my earnest prayers that the Holy Spirit who has called you, as I trust, to this weighty administration, may in all things direct, sanctify, and abundantly prosper your labors in the Church of our glorious Redeemer, I remain,

"Your faithful and affectionate
"Brother in Christ,
"JOHN H. HOPKINS.
"REV. DANIEL S. TUTTLE."

Then I set myself to work to learn somewhat of the field I was to go to. I did not grasp the topography of it; my ideas concerning it were very hazy. Any expert traveler could have laughed at me more loudly than I laughed at some friends in after years. These said to me, "Well, if you must be banished to those savage desert regions, we are right glad that at any rate you can have your two brothers-in-law and your old friend Mr. Goddard with you." As a matter of fact, one brother-in-law, Rev. Mr. Foote, was in Salt Lake City, more than four hundred miles away from Virginia City, where I lived; another, Rev. Mr. Miller, was in Boise City, four hundred miles from Mr. Foote, and eight hundred from me; and Mr. Goddard was a hundred and twenty-five miles from me, five hundred and twenty-five from Mr. Foote, and nine hundred and twenty-five from Mr. Miller. We were quite safe from troubles likely to arise from questions of metes and bounds of parishes, or of intrusion of one pastor into the curé of another.

When I got it into my head that Montana and Nevada are not the same place, nor exactly in the same region, indeed that they were a thousand miles apart, I turned to the files of the "Spirit of Missions," and also made inquiry of Bishop Randall, and in other quarters, to find out all

I could about Montana, Idaho, and Utah.   Evidently, it
was virgin soil that I was to be sent to till.   No clergyman of the church had even so much as set foot in Montana.   Bishop Talbot had passed through Utah over the
stage-line, on his way to visit Nevada, but had never held
a service in the former territory.   Bishop Scott, who had
taken charge of Oregon and Washington in 1854, had
once gone a little way into Idaho and held a service ; and
the Rev. St. Michael Fackler from Oregon had come up
to Boise City, Idaho, in August, 1864, and remained as a
missionary till   October, 1866, building a little frame
church in Boise, costing $2,150.   Leaving Boise, Octo-
ber 1, 1866, Mr. Fackler soon afterwards sailed from
Portland, Oregon, for the East.   During the journey he
died, and was buried at Key West.   A few months after,
Bishop Scott also sailed from Portland to the East, and,
by a singular coincidence also died on the way, or at least,
three days after entering New York harbor, July 14,
1867.   Therefore, in this great field, of approximately
350,000 square miles in extent, with 150,000 inhabitants,
there was not one clergyman of the church, and there was
only one place in which church work had been done and
a church building erected.   It was clear that if possible
some missionaries must be secured to go with me.

Rev. George W. Foote, Mrs. Tuttle's brother, the same
who had been instrumental in bringing me to Morris,
was rector at Otego, ten miles distant from Morris.   Rev.
G. D. B. Miller, engaged to be married to a younger sister of Mrs. Tuttle, was rector at Butternuts, six miles
distant.   Rev. E. N. Goddard was at West Burlington,
twelve miles distant, and had charge of many of the missionary points that I was interested in and had served
when I first came to Morris.   These three men said they
would go with me.   Mr. Foote secured also, as another

helper, a young deacon just graduating from the seminary, whom he knew well, Rev. T. W. Haskins, nephew
of the well-known rector of St. Mark's, Williamsburg (or
East Brooklyn).

Meanwhile the presiding bishop had appointed, May
1, 1867, as the time, and Trinity chapel, New York, as
the place, for my consecration.   Bishop Hopkins, himself was to preside ; Bishops Potter and Neely were to present, Bishop Randall was to preach, Bishops Odenheimer
and Kerfoot were to assist, and Rev. Drs. S. R. Johnson
and Morgan Dix, presbyters, were to attend.

At Oxford, Chenango County, N. Y., lived Hon. Henry
R. Mygatt, an eminent lawyer, and an earnest and generous churchman.   He was a " gentleman of the old
school," the embodiment of courtesy and culture.   I met
him first in his own home, stopping as I did a little while
at noon in June, 1864, when on my way to Greene to exchange with the Rev. Ferdinand Rogers, D. D.   Mr.
Mygatt was small in height and size.   But nothing else
about him was small.   Dignified in manner, indomitable
of will, an able and successful lawyer, untiring in industry and energy, unfailing in urbanity, devoted to the
church and her missionary work, he was one of my
staunch friends for counsel and help in my early years.
Through him it was, though I did not know it, that the
letter previously spoken of had come to me from Montana, for Chief Justice Hosmer was his kinsman and personal friend.   On my visit to Oxford to deliver my missionary sermon he put two hundred and fifty dollars into
my hands.   In many ways, as will appear hereafter, he
made smoother the path for my entrance into my new
field of work.   I saw him last in 1874, when semi-paral-
ysis had laid its hand on him and had ended his professional usefulness.   Not long after, he died.   Only a very

humble tribute of expressed gratitude can I render to his memory in return for all the generous kindness that for years he showed me. The touching story has been told me of the characteristic way in which he withdrew from his professional career. Doubtless indications had warned him that his strength was failing. One day in court he was pleading an important case. Suddenly he was conscious of inability to think logically. Quietly he turned to the associate counsel and asked him to take his place and go on with the case. Then, as quietly, he gathered his papers together, carefully tied them, and waited for some little pause in the proceedings. When it came, he took the bundle and his hat, and turning to the court with a kindly smile said, " Good-bye, your Honor," finally drawing near the judge and shaking hands with him. In the same way with characteristic grace and courtesy he bade good-bye to his associates and opponents of the bar, and to the officers of the court, not even forgetting the crier. Then, while a solemn hush pervaded the entire court room, for most of those witnessing well knew what it meant, he opened the door and passed out, leaving behind him forever the work of his profession which he dearly loved, and in which with stainless integrity he had won distinguished success and honor.

At Cooperstown, Otsego County, N. Y., lived and still lives Mr. G. Pomeroy Keese, a zealous and intelligent churchman who has been another of my kind and generous helpers. With him, in his home, was his grandmother, Mrs. Pomeroy, sister of Fenimore Cooper. Though of advanced age she was yet strong in clearness of intellect and energy of character. I remember and value highly the advice she gave me. " Use, wisely and well, what is given you for missionary work. Do not lay it by. Do not hoard it up. Use it as soon as you prudently can for God's glory and the good of souls. God will provide. His rule is to give us daily bread." It is of much importance that men and women be taught the privilege and duty of constant giving, and be trained into the expectation and habit of constant giving for missions.

At New Berlin, Chenango County. N. Y., lived Mr. Horace O. Moss. He, with Mr. Mygatt, was one of my earliest counselors and helpers. And for all these years he has been a loyal and generous supporter of the missionary work. He has been a lay deputy to the General Convention from Central New York ever since it was made a diocese; he also represented Western New York before, and he is, I think, next to Governor Baldwin of Michigan, the deputy of the longest continuous service in the House. He is one of a class of Americans that all thoughtful citizens wish could be multiplied a hundredfold among us, a man of leisure, wealth, culture, patriotism, and devoted philanthropy, making and keeping his home in the country.

His rector, during my first years at Morris, was the Rev. Richard Whittingham, younger brother of the Bishop of Maryland. He was a man of marked ability, unworldly aims, and earnest devotion. I learned much from him, and association with him raised greatly my own tone of life.

In the parishes round about me which I visited I received many a cordial " Godspeed," and received gifts of between five hundred and six hundred dollars. At last the day for my withdrawal from Morris came. On the morning of April 28th, being the Sunday after Easter, I preached my last sermon. I may be permitted to quote from it.

" Four years and nine months ago I first came among you. The parish register shows that during these five years fifty-five adults and eighty-seven children have been baptized, in all a hundred and forty-two. A hundred and twenty-one have been confirmed, and sixty-one have been buried. The parish register tells another tale also that, I think, will surprise you. In these five years thirty-one of the communicants of this parish have died, seventy-three have removed, and fifteen have been transferred, making a total of one hundred and nineteen communicants whose names have been erased from the list since I have been among you. One hundred and nineteen communicants gone in less than five years! It is a startling story, is it not? But remember that most of these are helping the church, and working for Christ and living for heaven, wherever they have gone. Remember, also, and remembering, thank God, that in your own dear, old parish, as I have reported to you to-day, two hundred and forty-two communicants yet remain.

" I leave the past. I lay my record down of those washed here at this Holy Font, and fed at this Holy Table, and laid to their earth-rest on the sides of yonder hill.

" I lay the record down, praying God for Christ's sake, begging you for your love's sake, to forgive what of unfaithfulness there has been in my ministering among you.

" For a moment let us face the present. I can but think that God is putting upon you and me a hard trial this day, in asking us to sever the bonds which bind us so lovingly together. But He sends the trial. I brought it not upon myself. You brought it not upon yourselves. Let us strive in prayer to Him to strengthen our faith, to see and know and realize that He sends this trial as all trials out of His abounding mercy and goodness and love. And look, are there not things in it to move our thankfulness? Back with the tears, and look and see!

" Here is the church rousing herself to her missionary work, and girding herself to march forth and occupy for her Master and Saviour all the fields of our Great West; here is your own parish providing a bishop to go forth to work where never a bishop has gone before; here am I standing face to face with you this day ready to proclaim this truth,—a truth known and precious to you and to me,—that when we part, I to go, you to stay, we part loving each other, esteeming each other, forgiving each other, with no sharp thoughts of hate needing to be softened, no differences needing to be adjusted, no misunderstandings needing to be explained. These are things, I say and I want you to feel, to thank God for; and these things, I further say,—if we will now resolve to look away from self, and up to God, and through the future, and on to heaven,—these are things for us to take courage from.

"A word more, brethren, about the future,—your future and mine.

"First, your future. Thanking God for the past and the present, dear brethren, take the courage that He surely offers to give you for the future. Ye are a strong parish. Ye have been a strong parish in the past, and ye are going to remain, I trust and believe, a strong parish in the future. Strong in the Lord and in the power of His might. Strong, not merely to take care of yourselves and provide things decent and comfortable for yourselves, but strong to help others; strong to do work for Christ, to do good to souls, within your parish and outside of your parish, within your county and outside of your county, within your diocese and outside of your diocese. Suffer me as your departing pastor here to press upon you one word of exhortation. Strive, dear brethren, ever and earnestly strive, to be at unity among yourselves. Brethren of the vestry, I beseech you, it is my last requést to you, pray ye and work and help each other as in God's sight to endeavor always to have unity of spirit in the bond of peace among you. Differences ye may have. They are not wrong, if only they be differences about ways and means, and not differences of spirit and principle. But frown down upon all differences of the latter kind which go to breed divisions ; and in my last words, I beg you, as you value peace, as you love souls, as you would serve God acceptably and go to Him one day, to be conciliatory when you are in majorities, to be patient and cheerful when you are in minorities, that so the blessed bonds of peace and love among you need never be broken. The same things would I say to you all of the congregation. May I hope that you will think sometimes of these four maxims that I leave with you. 1. Love God and try to serve Him day by day. 2. Forgive each other much. 3. Make allowances for each other. 4. Think more of the hour of your death and of your own wilfulness and waywardness in God's sight, and less of the things of the passing days and of the sins and faults of others round about.

" Well, God help you all, in that future, long or short as He willeth, God help you all for Christ's sake to walk in the ways of peace and holiness and charity and for-giveness ; and if ye do so, never shall my soul fear but that my old loved parish will remain strong and blest unto the latter days.

" And my future. Ye know that it is a strange unknown future to me, do ye not ? Ah, I could tell you a long tale of how I shrink from what is coming to me, the cares and toils and anxieties, and fears lest I may be grossly unfit for my responsible position.

" And I could add to the tale told the expressions of

my sorrow in leaving forever the quiet, rural, peaceful home that I have found among you.

"But these things I will not dwell upon. It is not well. My future I am trying to leave, without over-anxiety, trustfully in God's hands. May the shaping of it be of His goodness, and the walking in it of His grace. In view of it I ask of you two things : first, that on your knees, before God, our Father and Guide, you will pray for me that I may be helped, strengthened and sanctified in my work. Secondly, that you will remember me in your offerings. In your offerings of money, giving to me and my work what God puts it into your hearts to give ; and in your offerings of personal service. If there be teachers here who will come ; if there be boys here who in the future will take upon themselves, through God's blessed guidance, the sacred ministry of the church,—I desire here earnestly and affectionately to ask and entreat you to come out to my help and support in that wide field given me to care for, yonder towards the setting sun."

"Beloved brethren, in bidding good-by to you I am bidding good-by to the only flock of which probably I shall ever be the immediate pastor. I came to you first, when I had been but a few days in deacon's orders ; I go from you to work elsewhere, but I do not go to another flock. I do thank God for the five years' life He hath given me among you. I do take courage from these years past to meet the future years. Beloved, I hope ye also are willing and ready to thank God and take courage. God reward you with His kindness as ye have been ever kind to me and mine ! God bless you with His good-ness ! God help me in His mercy ! God save us all in His love for Christ's sake and bring us together home,— to that home, offering permanence and rest, the view whereof even now mightily helps us to thank God and take courage!"

On Easter Day I had broken the bread and given the cup for the last time to my people. There were a hundred and thirty-nine communicants. On Monday morning, April 29, from the hillside as we rose out of the beautiful valley of Butternuts to go to the railroad at Oneonta, through eyes that could not keep clear for vision, I took my final look of the dear old country church that had ceased to be mine own, and of the peaceful parsonage home that had been the happy shelter of me and my loved ones during my first five years of experience as a minister. Peace, rest, love, happiness—these had been mine there. Is it any wonder it was in sorrow that I turned away? Yet I knew and felt the truth of Keble's words; and with God's help, I was honestly walking on the way to prove them:

> " Think not of rest : though dreams be sweet,
> Start up, and ply your heavenward feet.
> Is not God's oath upon your head,
> Ne'er to sink back on slothful bed ?
> Never again your loins untie,
> Nor let your torches waste and die,
> Till, when the shadows thickest fall,
> Ye hear your Master's midnight call ! "

CHAPTER III
(1867)

PREPARATIONS

My face was now turned towards the new sphere of duty opening wide before me. On the afternoon of the day I left Morris, at Portlandville, Otsego County, N. Y., I united in marriage the Rev. Mr. Miller and Miss Mary T. Foote. At the same time and place the Rev. Mr. Goddard and Miss Mumford were married by Rev. Mr. Pidsley, pastor of the bride, and rector at Portlandville. Mrs. Geo. W. (Pidsley) Foote was present. Mr. Foote had already set out for Utah, accompanied by Mr. Haskins. They left New York City together on the 5th of April, and arrived in Salt Lake City, after detentions and perils from floods and snows, the one on the 3d, and the other on the 4th of May.

After the wedding, accompanied by Mr. and Mrs. Miller and Mr. and Mrs. Goddard, we pushed on to New York, where we arrived Tuesday morning. On the night boat from Albany down were the Presiding Bishop and Mrs. Hopkins. The presence and greetings of this distinguished and venerable couple were a benediction. I had, several years before, in New York, heard Bishop Hopkins preach in St. Bartholomew's Church, corner of Lafayette Place and Great Jones Street, and he seemed to me a Greek philosopher transformed into a Christian apostle, talking. With Mrs. Tuttle and the baby I went to Dr. Sabine's house to stay. At this house, 46 West 23d Street, nearly seven months before, I had been apprised of my election. Wednesday, May 1st, the Festival

of St. Philip and St. James, we repaired to Trinity Chapel,
where I was consecrated Bishop of Montana. Of those who
officiated at my consecration, only Dr. Dix is now alive.
I may be pardoned for recording here some of my memories of my fathers and brethren. Dear old Dr. Roose-
velt Johnson, amiable, benevolent, beneficent, saintly,
the obliging, unwearying friend of all of us students of
the seminary, whether we were worthy or worthless;
ready and willing to go to no end of trouble for us in
things little and great. I never knew a more unselfish,
lovable man. Yet, like St. John himself, whose strong
lines of character won for him the name of a " son of
thunder," Dr. Johnson's amiability was not softness, nor
weakness, nor sentimentalism. A right shrewd man he was,
with out-flashings of delicious wit and humor, and I have
known stern words fall from him of reproof and rebuke
like blows of a sledge hammer, where violation of principle was concerned. Although a very learned and able
man he was not strict enough in his lecture room to spur
us students to the best diligence. But the example of his
meekness, charity, forbearance, loving-kindness, simplicity, godly sincerity, holiness, sank deep into the hearts
of us all, the seeds of preciousness unto fruits of blessing.
In the great time of awakening, many and many shall
they be who shall rise up and call the dear old doctor
blessed.

Bishop Odenheimer struck me as a man of power and
learning and independence. In proof of the last named
quality I recall that he alone of all the House of Bishops
would not sign the declaration concerning regeneration
prepared by the Bishop of Maryland, in the General Convention of 1871 at Baltimore. He argued well in debate
and could drive home his point, but he then weakened
its force by unwise repetition. It was like hitting a nail

well on the head and putting it to its place, and then
hammering away at it till you break its head or split the
plank, thus marring or destroying the binding power.

Bishop Kerfoot was earnest, warm-hearted and true,
and full of energy. But he had been a schoolmaster and
not a parish priest and in his energy he was often impatient. He was disinclined to recognize efficiency in
the *laissez faire* method of dealing with things that vex.
The impulsiveness of his nature threw itself with force
into whatever he was aiming at or advocating and made
him seem to be, what doubtless in his heart he did not
mean to me, dictatorial.

Bishop Randall was not a young man when in 1865 he
was sent out to Colorado, then the " Far West." But
any who heard his missionary addresses saw that his force
of manner had not abated, nor his fire of eye dimmed.
In fact youthful vigor rather than elderly caution characterized his work as bishop. Swayed by the excitement
of the times and the region, he erected church structures
with fervid enthusiasm. Some of them were in mining
towns, the permanency of which can never be assured.
These would be in danger in after years of being left to
the owls and the bats.

Of Bishop Horatio Potter I ask to be allowed to speak
as a son of his father. For two years before going to
Morris I had been tutor to his sons, spending the summer
vacation with his family at Essex, on Lake Champlain.
For a week or two each summer, as he could catch the
time, he also would come to Essex. In external demeanor he was stately and cold. We young people
honestly stood in awe of him. Yet even we perceived
in him a vein of delightful humor. And in his heart
there was abundance of thoughtful kindness and loving
great-heartedness. Totally differing from Bishop Ker-

foot he had strong faith in the curative power of *laissez faire*. And who shall say, in his way of guiding the great diocese of New York in times of confusion and great trouble, that this faith of his was misplaced? He was bishop for thirty-three years. During fifteen years he administered the whole field of what are now the three dioceses of New York, Long Island, and Albany. Pale, slender, white-haired as he was, we were amazed that year after year he could fulfil with such marvelous fidelity his long list of appointments. His devotion to duty was unfailing; his systematic industry untiring. In the House of Bishops he was noted for wisdom of counsel. He was not a parliamentary leader. He was not the man to take in charge a proposition and press it through the House. But if there was a drift among his brethren towards the adoption of an unwise course, no one could with more clearness and force point out the evil of the way and the loss at the end. He was not fitted like his brother, the bishop of Pennsylvania, and his presbyter, Dr. Muhlenberg, to call out large gifts from his laity for church objects. He seemed to shrink from putting any pressure of this sort upon his people. Yet his was no small contribution to the solidity and enduringness of unity and strength in the great diocese of New York, making it a reservoir for other people, by the thousands, to draw from for their needs. Faithful, laborious, sagacious, philosophic, large-minded, far-sighted, high-souled, holy,—all the church and all the world agree that he was these. Suffer me to add also that he was loving-hearted, kindly, tender. Of human instruments undoubtedly his hand did most to place me where I am. Ever after, his hand was a father's helpful hand to me. As a grateful son I ask to record my humble tribute to his memory.

My first sermon after consecration I preached on Sunday morning, May 5th, in St. Paul's Chapel, New York City. Here I had been a parishioner for several years when in college and the seminary, as well as a teacher in and the superintendent of its Sunday-school. I remember the monthly visit to us and the sermon of the venerable Dr. Berrian, rector of Trinity. Then Dr. Francis Vinton took the head of affairs at St. Paul's, and after him Mr. Dix. My more immediate pastor, during all the years, had been Mr. Dix. To the nation old St. Paul's is historic. Hither Washington repaired for worship after his inauguration as president in Wall Street in 1789. To me the old church is dear. I worshiped here for six years of my young life. From it and its Sunday-school I went to my deacon's work at Morris. When changes in the interior were made some years ago, the wooden cross over the old altar was sent to me; it now stands over the altar in St. Paul's, Virginia City, Montana. A teacher in the Sunday-school, Miss Jane Mount, in her will left me $10,000 for building a church. Her surviving sisters added nearly as much more; and so St. Paul's Chapel, Salt Lake City, a beautiful stone church costing almost $20,000, was built. By the same ladies a parsonage right by its side, and also a rectory at Ogden, Utah, have been provided. Loving and healthful associations with old St. Paul's are therefore interwoven with the warp and woof of my life. A little cross for the watch-chain made out of the wood of the pew in which Washington worshipped is one of my souvenirs.

Sunday, May 12th, and a day or two thereafter, I spent at Rochester at a delegate meeting of the Board of Missions. Here for the first time I met Rev. B. Wistar Morris, who was to be called not long after to be the

bishop of Oregon; I met also Bishop Wilmer, of
Louisiana, and Mr. Wm. B. Douglas. Ever since I have
been bishop the last named has been a steady and generous giver to my missionary work. His home is at
Rochester, and out from it I am sure, steady streams of
benefaction have been flowing for many years to the out-
posts and by-fields of the American church.

Bishop Wilmer of Louisiana was a character quite
unique. In him wit, humor, pathos, humility, breadth,
logic, poetry, saintlikeness, and absent-mindedness, were
wondrously blended. Speeches of his in the House of
Bishops would convulse the members with laughter, while
not even the suggestion of a smile could be detected on
the speaker's face. Bishops will recall with me how in
Baltimore in 1871, in a debate upon Sisterhoods, he said,
"Sisterhoods,—I honestly confess I do not like them.
They seem to me strangely suggestive and provocative
of anything but harmony. The only Sisterhood I read
of in Holy Scripture is the one at Bethany. Dissensions
in it were marked, and one is tempted to wonder if their
sharpness might not have worried the brother's life out
of him and brought him to a premature grave, since the
grace and power of our blessed Lord were taxed to
secure harmony." By this time the official preserver of
order, the aged presiding bishop (Smith) had succumbed,
and laughter ruled supreme save in the frame of the
speaker himself. It was said that it was the earnest
straightforwardness of Bishop Wilmer in urging upon
the late Mr. A. T. Stewart the grave responsibility resting on him as the steward of great wealth that set the
latter upon the plan of providing a cathedral and school
and bishop's house for the diocese of Long Island. In
Rochester I was charmed and moved by his eloquent
addresses; and I do not forget the tender feeling with

which he came up to me personally and said, " God bless you, my young brother, in the work you go to do. Life, growth, hope, promise, they are all there. Think sometimes of us your older brethren, who are almost in the ashes of despair, in a region of desolation, amid a people scattered and peeled." It was his description of the South at the close of the Civil War. In the twelve years after, we are glad to believe, he lived to see much of recuperation and revived hopefulness.

At Rochester, also, I met for the first time Mr. and Mrs. William Welsh of Philadelphia. The American church has known no more indefatigable worker for her interests than Mr. Welsh. The superintendent of the immense Sunday-school at St. Mark's, Frankford; the preacher of lay sermons there Sunday after Sunday ; the devoted member of the Board of Management for the hospital and the faithful visitor of the sick lying therein ; the untiring worker on the floor and in committee in Diocesan and General Coventions ; the diligent philanthropist in efforts to protect and civilize the Indians ; a watchful custodian of the interests of Girard College ; a sturdy upholder, in days of need, of honor and righteousness in the conduct of the municipal affairs of Philadelphia,—his earthly life was filled to the full with loyal and earnest service of God and his fellow men. My grateful memory recalls how in many and many an instance he stood by me, a helpful and generous friend. Since his death, his wife and daughter have not ceased to go steadily on with his famous Bible class work at Frankford. Mrs. Welsh, with a vigor amazing in one so old, teaches a large class of men,—almost a hundred of them —every Sunday. Miss Welsh has two Sunday classes of young men and young women, with nearly two hundred in each of them. For twenty years and more they have

called themselves, I am pleased and proud to tell, the
" Bishop Tuttle Boys," and the " Bishop Tuttle Girls,"
and have been my helpers in the Utah missions. I still
visit them yearly if I can. Some, married and with children of their own, still loyally stay in the classes. A
more staunch body of supporters than they my missionary life has not known.

In going to Rochester I was accompanied by the Rev.
Dr. Twing. In after years we were in the habit of calling him the " Archbishop," as so many of us missionary
bishops were his attachés when he was secretary of the
Board of Missions. We all grew to love him. He never
failed in kindness and consideration. The doctor was a
power of strength to every missionary bishop. His whole
heart was in the missionary work of the church, and his
stalwart frame was a true indication of how big his heart
was. At times, when I was visiting No. 22 Bible
House, the vigor of his salutatory embrace would not stop
short of lifting me clean off my feet. His excellent
characteristics of fitness for the post he occupied were
enthusiasm, fervor, devotion, sustained energy, loyalty,
catholicity of spirit, fidelity. It seems to me that to him
more than any other one man is due, under God's blessing, the infusion of the missionary warmth and zeal that
the American Church has rejoiced in during these later
years. It was his crown of earthly glory to be a leader
in the blessed work of lifting the church up into a higher
sphere of unselfish missionary activity than ever she had
known before. Nineteen years of duty of the most faithful sort in the missionary cause he spent, ere he passed to
the " rest that remaineth to the people of God." I always
received inspiration from the example of his life and the
warmth of his friendship.

Before starting for Rochester, as I was one morning

passing through the halls of the Bible House, Rev. Dr.
Dyer called me to his desk and after some words of
kindly greeting said : " Mr. Wolfe has entrusted to me
one thousand dollars, which he desired to give you for
your field, and I am ready at any time to pay over to
you this sum." I then went to Mr. Wolfe's house on
Madison Square to thank him for his gift, and also for
the large consignment of " Mission Services " he had provided for my use. This " Mission Service " he had himself compiled. It consisted of the " Morning Prayer "
and " Evening Prayer " of the Prayer-Book, with a part
of the communion service, and some " Selections of
Psalms," and some hymns. Supplied with these pam-
phlets and taking care to announce pages and to give some
directions about responding, I have almost never failed to
have a good and satisfactory church service, even in
places where no church folk were in the congregation.
When all the rills are counted that have gone to swell
the force of church activities in our frontier life, let not
Mr. Wolfe's " Mission Service " be forgotten. The sum
Dr. Dyer transmitted to me was not my only gift from
Mr. Wolfe. More than once afterwards he sent me a
check for one thousand dollars. When I bought at
Ogden, Utah, the " Old Tannery," where the Memorial
Church of the Good Shepherd is built, the necessary fifteen
hundred dollars of purchase money was furnished by him.
John David Wolfe, what a noble giver he was ! Not pro-
fuse, but prudent. Not careless, but thoughtful and
prayerful. Almost every day of his later life it was
much work for him to examine discriminatingly and to
determine faithfully what applications he ought to consider favorably, and where to bestow his benefactions that
they might do most good, or at least be likely to do no
harm. After the father's death, the daughter, Miss

Wolfe, strove to follow in the same line of effort to decide righteously and to give wisely. But what to the father's trained business habits presented itself as a daily duty, to be got through without much wear and tear, to the daughter came as a burden hard to bear and wearisome in its inexorable recurrence. The earth was made glad and the Church was made strong by these two givers in more places and ways than will ever be known, save in the last day of disclosure of all things.

At Trinity church, Rochester, May 15, 1867, I confirmed two women, presented by Rev. Dr. Van Ingen. This was my first confirmation.

May 17th, I went to Scarsdale, West Chester County, N. Y., and with Rev. Dr. Twing held a missionary service. Rev. W. W. Olssen, now (1890) an honored professor in St. Stephen's College, was the rector.

Dr. Olssen is one among the forces giving direction to my life. In 1853 I was ready to go to college, but had not money enough. To supply the need I resolved to teach for a year. Through one who had been as a father to me in all my boyhood, Rev. T. S. Judd, rector of my native parish, Windham, Greene County, N. Y., I secured the position of assistant teacher in a boys' school which Mr. Olssen had started at Scarsdale. At that time I intended to go to Hobart College. Mr. Olssen was a graduate of Columbia College, New York City, and he persuaded me to plan to go there. He also helped prepare the way for me to go, and in the fall of 1854 I entered the sophomore class.

I was a green country youth of sixteen when I came under Mr. Olssen's influence. The gentleness of his character, the holiness and unselfishness of his life, the vigor of his intellect, and his scholarly attainments, impressed me from the first. He had graduated at the head of his class in Columbia. In classical and mathematical learning he was one of the very few I have known who seemed completely ambidextrous.   It was a recreation to him either to solve the longest mathematical problems, or to turn some nursery rhyme like,

> " The three little kittens
> Have lost their mittens "

into Greek verse. His intellectual worth is equaled only by his modesty. Consequently, even through the books he has written and the work he has done, the world has not yet found him out. What a specimen of crude awkwardness I must have seemed to him and his accomplished wife, who was the youngest sister of Bishop Whittingham. In July, 1853, a week or two after having been confirmed at Windham by Bishop Wainwright, I came to Scarsdale. My first communion I received at the hands of Mr. Olssen.

Through the interposition of Mr. Olssen I secured from the Society for the Promotion of Religion and Learning of the Diocese of New York free tuition in college, and a small grant of money yearly besides. In the main, however, I paid my way through college and the seminary by teaching during vacations and by services as a private tutor.

Mr. Olssen loaned me some money for college. My dear and only brother, Lemuel, gone twenty years since to the rest of Paradise, loaned me more. He was a blacksmith, unmarried, older than I, and had laid by something through hard work. My heart bounds with warmest beats of brotherly affection when I recall how generously and cheerfully he gave over to me whenever I asked him. Some elder brother in such a case might answer, and with good reason : " Your choice is an easy walk of life.

My money has come by the hardest sort of work ; you must not ask me to give it out." Neither by word nor by look did he answer like that, and in the deepest part of my nature, where esteem and affection make their home, dwells the grateful memory of my loved brother. I had the greatest happiness of laying my hands upon his head in confirmation in 1868.

I may mention that when I graduated from Columbia in 1857, I was under engagement to Mr. Frank Lyon to go to Demopolis, Alabama, for a year or two to be tutor to some boys in planters' families. In a month or two, however, a letter came from the Demopolis people regretting that they must cancel the engagement, as the hard times of '57 pressed them too sorely. I was in debt and wished to teach in order to pay my debts ; and now I knew not what to do or which way to turn. It was in September. In despair I tried to get an engagement to teach a public school in a country district, but I failed. I was dispirited ; life looked to me very dark ; the disappointment about the Alabama engagement seemed to me the sorest I had ever been called on to bear.

Yet in the event how kind to me was the leading of God's Providence. Had I gone to Alabama, the few years spent there would doubtless have plunged me into active participation in the sad difficulties of the Civil War.

In October I went to New York City to visit some kind friends, the Wilsons, in Brooklyn, who had invited me. I answered advertisements for teachers, and I worried all my friends in letting them know I wanted an engagement. Discouragement doubly deep was settling down upon me, when, one day, a request came from Dr. Anthon, my college professor in Greek, that I would call to see him. He told me of a boy who wished private

lessons in Latin and Greek. Here was a ray of light.
The doctor knew I was overjoyed, and feared I would
not be shrewdly wise, and said, " What are you going to
charge?" "I don't know," I answered. I would cheerfully have taken anything that was offered. He added,
" Don't charge less than one dollar an hour for your
work."

This, my first pupil, was Henry Bolton, now, I think,
professor of chemistry in Trinity College, Hartford.
Soon another and yet another were added to my list,
and, before the year was out, I was busy teaching in this
way eight and even ten hours a day. In two years my
debts were all paid and I had money for books and
against needed support during the three years of seminary life that in 1859 I entered upon.

Among my pupils of this period, or belonging to a
time somewhat later, were the sons of George Law, the
son of Moses Taylor, the son of Dr. Alexander Stephens,
the brother of Bishop Riley, the sons of Bishop Whitehouse and of Bishop Potter, Mr. W. S. Dana, afterwards an
officer of the United States Navy, Mr. Cortlandt Palmer,
Mr. Cortlandt de Peyster Field, Mr. William Jay, Mr. J.
Hooker Hamersley, Mr. David Lydig, and the son of
Mr. Pell of St. John's Square.

Three of these have been special helpers in my subsequent work. Mr. Hamersley and his family built the
Memorial Church of the Good Shepherd in Ogden, Utah,
at a cost of $11,000.

Mr. Field has been all my life one of my dearest and
most helpful of friends and wisest of counselors. Mr.
William B. Potter, now professor of mining and miner-
alogy in Washington University, St. Louis, and member
of the Standing Committee of the Diocese of Missouri, is
also of the greatest comfort to me, standing steadily and

sturdily by my side when the evening of life is beginning
to fling shadows in my face. I have always been a lover
of boys, and these men will simply remain " boys " to me.

Fresh from my work as tutor in Latin and Greek and
mathematics, I was amused at my reception by Rev. Dr.
Turner of the General Seminary when, in the fall of 1859,
I presented myself to him for examination for entrance.
I was a stranger to him. From a summer country sojourn and clad in an indifferently-fitting suit of gray, I
presented myself one morning in his study and made
known my request. " Have you read St. John's Gospel
and the Book of the Acts in your Greek Testament ? "
he asked. " No, sir, not particularly, of late, I think ——"
Then in his quick, nervous way, with the sibilant suction
of the lips and the shrugging of the shoulders that all his
old pupils will remember, he broke out with, " Indeed,
sir, and why not ? These are the requirements. Why is
it that young men will present themselves to us for entrance into the seminary without having done what is
required, and without an adequate knowledge of Greek ? "
Nettled and resentful he passed a Greek Testament to me
and bade me translate. He directed me to various passages,
and added some questions of grammar and construction.
Then, in a much milder tone, he asked where and when
I graduated, and with kind words, a most cordial grasp
of the hand, and a welcome to the seminary, dismissed
me. Ever after, he was one of my kindest friends. When
I was a senior in the seminary he did me the honor to
ask me to look over his published works in the matter of
Greek renderings, and see if anything in the way of improvement suggested itself to me, remarking modestly that
in his earlier years he had not had the advantage of a thorough drill in the niceties of Greek. I did as he requested,
and on receiving my suggestions he wrote :

"Seminary, October 19, 1861.

"*Mr. Daniel S. Tuttle,*

"DEAR SIR:

"I am much obliged to you for your kind note containing important corrections and suggestions. Those on the volume on Genesis cannot be carried into effect, as no additional edition is intended. That on Hebrews 7 : 18, 19, is very important. I have placed it in my note on page 97 and expressed a favorable opinion of it. If another edition is printed, I shall modify the note and probably speak in decided preference of it, which the usage of μὲν and δὲ seems to require.

"I remain, very truly yours,

"SAM'L H. TURNER."

The contrast between my readings in Greek and my browned skin and farmer-like dress caused Dr. Turner to rate me higher than I deserved. He talked of me to his fellow professor, Dr. Johnson. Dr. Johnson was, as it were, chaplain to Bishop Potter. Then came a call to me to be tutor to the bishop's boys, and there followed in time the nomination to the Episcopate. Out of the depths of my bitterly-felt disappointment, God's Providence ordered these things in place of what, had I gone to Alabama, might have been a far different chain of events. My life has been crowded with lessons like this, to teach me not to repine at present disappointments, but to summon cheerfulness of acquiescence in them, as being surely sent and meant by God's Providence to be blessings rather than ills.

My dear friend Mr. Mygatt did most for me in the specific way of preparation for going West. Chief Justice Hosmer was (although I did not know it till after I had gone to Montana) an old friend of Mr. Mygatt, and therefore it was the latter who secured the forwarding of that letter of welcome to me from Virginia City.

United States Senator James W. Nye, of Nevada, at Mr.
Mygatt's request, secured me a trip pass over the stage
line to Salt Lake City and to Virginia City. In those
early days a ticket for the same distance cost four hundred dollars. In sending me, on May 3d, the pass from
Oxford, Mr. Mygatt writes: " I would like very much
to have you meet the senator. He may give you useful
information of the West. I read to-day of the solemn
services of Wednesday. Mrs. Mygatt and myself were
sad because we could not be present. I thought of you
every hour in the day. I expect to hear that our St.
Paul's parish was well represented. Our rector, Mr.
Tuttle (Warden), and Messrs. Van Wagenen and Clarke,
expected to be present."

I wrote to Bishop Randall for advice. He answered:

" Boston, February 1, 1867.
" I think you shd. be in Montana by the first of June,
or soon after. Take with you every article of clothing
which you may need for a year, or until you return East,
as the prices are fabulous. Yr. baggage should be shipped
as freight and sent on some weeks before you leave.
Passengers are allowed twenty-five pounds of baggage.
All over this is charged for, at the rate of fifty cents a
pound. Matter sent by express is not much lower. Of
course you will not take your family with you at present ;
—at least it would not be advisable. As to companions,
get as many clergymen as you can find,—and take them
along. Leave one by all means at Salt Lake City, where
there is a remarkable opening for our services at this
time. I have received lately an urgent letter in respect
to this matter. A delay may lose to us this opportunity
for years. This town is represented as a very pleasant
place of residence. You need not wait for your consecration before you cast about for a good missionary,
not to the Mormons, but to others *among* the Mormons.
I suppose that an open attempt to convert Brigham

Young's followers w'd be followed by very unpleasant consequences.

"The Rev. Mr. Fackler, the missionary at Boise City, Idaho, I am grieved to say, died a few weeks ago on his way to the East, after an absence of many years. He died at his post ministering to victims of the cholera, and was buried at Key West. He was a noble missionary. A ch. was built and a parish organized by him. A man is much needed to fill that vacancy.

"That God will strengthen you for, and most abundantly bless you in, your work, is the prayer of
"Your affectionate brother in Christ,
"GEORGE M. RANDALL."

Through his friend, Judge Samuel Nelson of the United States Supreme Court, Mr. Mygatt also procured for me most helpful letters from the secretary of war to Generals Sherman and Augur and others. The general letter commendatory was an autograph as follows :

"War Department,
"Washington City, May 8, 1867.
"To all officers in the military service of the United States in the territories of Montana, Idaho and Utah :
"This note will introduce to you the Rt. Rev. Bishop Tuttle, who is about to visit his Episcopal charge in the above mentioned territories.

"I commend him to your kind courtesy and attention, and request that you will afford him such facilities of transportation for himself and his personal effects, and such protection as he may need, and as may be in your power consistent with the service.
"Yours truly,
"EDWARD M. STANTON,
"Secretary of War."

In sending the different letters to me the secretary added with his own hand the following :

" DEAR SIR :

" At the request of Mr. Justice Nelson I enclose some letters for your use to military commanders and officers in the West, which I hope may be of service to you. You will observe that I have requested them to furnish you facilities for transportation as far as may be consistent with the service. In consequence of the military operations now in progress, it is not likely that they can give you much assistance in this particular, and especially not for books or any bulky articles, as the whole means of transportation is probably required for military stores. I would also respectfully suggest the doubt of expediency in your starting as soon as you propose, or until further information of the state of the Indian hostilities shall be obtained.

" Wishing you a safe journey and every success,
" I am truly yours,
" EDWIN M. STANTON."

Mr. Warren Hussey wrote me from Salt Lake City. In after years Mr. Hussey prospered in his business and became rich ; then lost, and became poor. But whether rich or poor he was always an earnest, true, generous, faithful friend to me and to the church. I confirmed him and his wife in the first confirmation class presented in Salt Lake City. During his entire residence there he was senior warden of the parish. To him, more than any other layman resident, was due the prompt and vigorous upbuilding of our work in Utah. Mr. Hussey now lives in Spokane Falls, Washington. My memories of him are of the warmest and most grateful kind. It will be noticed that Mr. Hussey, from his business associations, and perhaps from the reactionary state of mind induced by resentfulness at unfair statements and unjust dealings, is inclined to take a favorable view of the Mormons.

"*Banking House of Hussey, Dahler & Co.,*
"*Salt Lake City, March 13, 1867.*
"*Rev. Dan'l S. Tuttle, Morris.*
"DEAR SIR:
"Your valued favor of the 11th February forwarded me by our mutual friend, Rev. H. B. Hitchings, is duly at hand, and for and in behalf of the friends of the church here I will try and answer your inquiries to the best of my ability.

"I am quite intimate with Prest. Young and have very frequently heard him express himself concerning other churches coming in here; and am very sure they will meet a hearty welcome from him, *under certain circumstances.* He is not at all prejudiced against other religions, but is most in favor of his own of course. Have frequently heard him say that the Mormons were not the only people to be saved. Other denominations would also be redeemed, but they must all, his and every other Christian Church, work and pray, practice and live the religion they profess, etc., etc. They *do profess to live and practice their religion* to greater perfection than other denominations, and have great grounds for making such assertions. In a conversation had with Prest. Young since receipt of your letter he has only reiterated former statements, and assured me no minister, nor any one else, who w'd come here and mind their own business, need have the slightest fear of being disturbed by Mormons.

"There are very few communicants here, some ½ Doz. or so to my knowledge. Other Gentiles who are not communicants, however, would be very glad indeed to see a church established here, and are willing to aid in supporting a minister, provided he is the right kind of a man.

"I was out with a subscription paper yesterday afternoon and readily raised a subscription of over $1,200 for the support of a minister one year and can increase it to $1,500 or more. A large amount would be required to support a married clergyman. Rents and living are high, and it is very expensive traveling here. If any one comes it must of necessity be a single man. The latter can obtain a good room and excellent board here at $22 per week, including lights, fuel and washing; and at $1,500 per year could get along very nicely indeed. While it would require almost this amount merely to rent a house for a married clergyman. All are anxious for a clergyman at once, and the sooner a start is made the sooner we will get under headway, and the more liberally we can get subscriptions. There is no other church in operation here now but the Mormons. The Catholics will be here during the spring or summer, and probably the Methodists; and the first here will get most support.

" Your best route to come out either to Salt Lake or to Montana will be by Chicago, Omaha, and out to terminus of the railroad (now some two hundred and fifty miles west of Omaha) by rail, and from there here by stage, stopping at Denver awhile to rest and recuperate. From railroad terminus to Denver is nearly two days and nights by coach; and from Denver here some five or six days and nights, time depending on condition of roads. From here to Virginia City, Mont. (four hundred miles), three or four days and nights by coach. Even if you do nothing here, your route to Montana is via this place and we trust we shall see you anyway.

" This comes somewhat near answering your inquiries, and in addition to doing so I desire to give also my ideas of our wants here. Prest. Young and the Mormon Church are, in my opinion, the worst lied about, if I may use this expression, of any people living. Parties here who are at enmity with them, and others who desire large government contracts, are exceedingly anxious to bring about if possible a collision between them and our government, in hopes of bringing on another Mormon War. No abuse seems too low to heap upon them by these friends of Christianity; no story too big to tell and publish to the world. The Mormons would be a very different people from any I ever saw to *like* such treatment. They seem to be just foolish enough to desire *justice* done them if possible, and that the truth is enough to tell at all times.

" Prest. Young said to me, he did not expect anything

of this abuse and detraction from an Episcopal bishop. ' They are men of education and better sense; they are gentlemen, and any gentleman is welcome here, no matter what his creed,' were about his words.

"The supporters of your church here will be Gentile business men generally,—men who are daily mingling, in business and socially, with the Mormons and their leaders, and who are determined to live here in peace and harmony and do justice to all; and they are utterly and absolutely unwilling to give money and support to any minister who will come here and get himself and friends into trouble. Our minister, if we are so fortunate to get one, should be a young man of ability, and a good Christian; a man willing to work for his cause and build up his church on its merits and not expect to tear down an opposing cause to build on. Such a man will undoubtedly prosper here, I think, and receive a general support from the Gentile population. I trust you will pardon my long digression from your inquiries, when I say that it was upon my promising to write you as I have that parties were induced to subscribe to a minister's support as they did. ' We are willing to give, but we want a man to come here who will preach the gospel, and attend to his discreet duties,' was the usual answer to my soliciting subscriptions. Such a man if he possesses fair ability and is a good Christian, I feel must succeed. I think the Sabbath collections, aside from amt. subscribed for a salary, will give quite a revenue, above paying all expenses for rents, fuel and lights, as the audience will be large aside from church members, especially if we get a smart, able man. The better the man the more can be raised for him. I shall continue soliciting and raise the amount as high as I can.

"Hoping it is God's will that we may meet you here in June, and that all will work for the good and advancement of His cause and the improvement of His creatures,

"I am sincerely yours,

"WARREN HUSSEY."

CHAPTER IV
(1867)

THE JOURNEY WESTWARD

THE morning of May 23, 1867, found me at breakfast at the Delavan House, Albany, with Mrs. Tuttle and our eight months' old boy George, facing the sadness of a long separation. At eight o'clock the Albany & Susquehanna train pulled away from the platform, bearing mother and child back to Morris. They stood on the platform of the rear car until out of sight. I could not well see them for tears, and these would have flowed even more copiously had I known all that the good-by meant. It was in my mind to go to my field, and then in the autumn come back after my family and get some added missionaries for help. But the field was found to be one so imperatively needing my presence that I did not come back till September, 1868. So really the good-bye of that morning meant sixteen months of total separation.

In the afternoon Rev. Mr. Goddard, Mrs. Foote (wife of Rev. G. W. Foote, who was already in Salt Lake), and Miss Sarah K. Foote (Mr. Foote's youngest sister, fifteen years old), joined me. At 6 P. M. we took the train for the West, picking up Rev. Mr. Miller at Medina at 5:20 next morning.

I was launching out into the unknown in more senses than one. I had never as yet been farther West than Niagara Falls. We passed through Canada on the 24th. This is the Queen's birthday and all the country was in holiday attire. We reached Chicago at 7 A. M., Saturday 25th, and stayed till Tuesday. I dined twice with Bishop Whitehouse, preached on Sunday morning at the

Cathedral, and was entertained by Mr. and Mrs. Barter, parishioners of the Cathedral. Sunday I took tea with Dr. Rylance and in the evening preached for him at St. James.'

I had been tutor, as I have stated, to the boys of Bishop Whitehouse. Bishop Potter and he were the only members of the House of Bishops, so far as I know, who knew anything personally of me at the time the House elected me bishop.

Bishop Whitehouse was a man of immense learning and of varied and extensive accomplishments. For wide-reaching erudition and acuteness of intellect he was conspicuous. I will not say there was not warmth of spirit and heart to go with the former qualities. The speeches of the bishop in the House of Bishops did not persuade and convince as from his scholarship and ability one would suppose they ought to have done. It was also against them, perhaps, that they did not clothe themselves in short sentences and Saxon words, which Americans best like. The same seeming lack of all-round sympathy militated against the bishop's influence in a special degree, in the active, vigorous, almost frontier town Chicago was during his Episcopate. My own description of the town in a letter to my wife after first coming into it was, "Chicago is a second New York. The same bustling activity, and restless uneasiness appear everywhere. The same prevalence of high prices and wild speculation. The streets and signs and stores look like New York. They tell me, there are here now, 200,000 or 250,000 inhabitants."

Into this restless throng the bishop did not throw himself with any glow of ardor or cordial liking. He was kind, true, courteous, high-minded, always the gentleman. His Western people thoroughly respected him, and were justly proud of him. But they did not take

him into their hearts and bury him therein under a
warmth of affection, which is a bishop's most precious
earthly reward.

We left Chicago at 3 P. M., May 28th, and reached
Omaha at 9 P. M. of the 29th. The latter was a town of
near 10,000 inhabitants, dating its origin from the Pike's
Peak excitement of 1859. Council Bluffs, Iowa, opposite it, is the older town. At or near it, as the name imports, had been held many councils with the Indians.
Not far from it was " Winter Quarters," as the Mormons
called their settlement, into which they moved for tem-
porary sojourn when they left Nauvoo in 1846 and before their first detachment pushed on to Salt Lake in
1847. In coming from Chicago, from Boone to Council
Bluffs we had ridden uneasily on the recently completed
and still unballasted western part of the Chicago and
Northwestern Railroad. In getting across the Missouri
River, from Council Bluffs to Omaha, the kinds and degree of discomfort were unspeakable. The river, itself
turbid and sullen, well deserved the name the natives
give it, " The Big Muddy." The ferry-boat was flat,
rude, unclean, more like a raft than a boat; the approach to it on the Iowa side was a steep bank of sticky,
slippery black mud, down which we all walked or slid as
best we could, our baggage and blankets being pushed
and hurled after us in indiscriminate confusion. The
same kind of paths of departure from the deck existed on
the Nebraska side, where vigor and vigilance were put to
the sharpest test to surmount the muddy acclivity. The officials and attendants and transfer agents were the most ex-
asperatingly " know nothing " and seemingly " care nothing " set of men ever seen ; and so, confusions and delays
innumerable greeted the bewildered " tenderfoot " now
first entering the gate city of the " Far West."

The Omaha church folk were very kind to us. Bishop Clarkson was absent on a visitation in his immense missionary field, then consisting of Nebraska and Dakota. But the rector, Rev. Mr. Van Antwerp, billeted us upon his people. I was sent to Mr. Woolworth's, Mr. Goddard and Mr. Miller to Mr. Hall's, and the two ladies to Mr. Yates'. In all these twenty years, in going to and coming from my Rocky Mountain field, Omaha has been my half-way house, and her people have proved most kind and helpful and hospitable. Usually I have stopped with my dear old friend, Mr. Woolworth. His unswerving loyalty and generous devotion to the church all these years have deepened and strengthened the great personal esteem and affection of my heart towards him. To my wife I wrote: " Mr. Woolworth is a native of Homer, N. Y.; an old parishioner of St. Peter's, Albany, under Bishop Potter; a communicant of the church; and the best lawyer in this State. He is a most kind and excellent host. His wife wears glasses and does a great deal of her own housework. In fact, the ' monstrum horribile' of procuring house servants is as great here as with you. For very indifferent help they pay here $5.00 a week. Mrs. W.'s three children, Charlie, Jeanie (Mrs. W. is Scotch), and Norah, are pleasant and pretty. Norah today is quite sick, feverish. As I sit here in the parlor writing, in her mother's room near she is talking and muttering in feverish dreams. The W.'s have buried two children and they are a little alarmed about this one. There are no trees here, and no rocks, and I feel lonesome. A few hills behind us, however, relieve the lonesomeness somewhat. The streets are very muddy, and the whole town new, formless, and dirty. They say they suffer here greatly from high winds, and in summer time almost intolerably from dust. This morning, church was open for Ascension Day services. Mr. Miller and I read service."

Three days after, on Sunday, June 2d, I wrote: " I have come home to a very sad house. Little Norah Woolworth, two years and a half old, and one of the brightest of children, is dying, probably, of brain fever, or congestion. She has been very precocious, and has been probably doomed to this, to speak humanly, by her active brain. The mother has not left her bedside for three days and nights, and will not leave her. Last night I prevailed on Mr. W. to take some sleep, and I myself sat up till 2 A. M. I have had prayers with the parents and for the child and the tears flow freely from the eyes of us all. I sympathize with them deeply; I feel my own loneliness and separation from dear ones; I think it may possibly be God's will that you and I shall bury our boy too before he be five years old, and the sobs come in thinking he may go away, while I am far, far off. But, ' Be still, and know that I am God!' I am trying cheerfully to leave all in His hands. I preached this morning my Ascension sermon. There were fifty-two communicants, more than half of them men. Yesterday I called at General Augur's headquarters. The general has gone on West. Perhaps we shall see him as we go on. He is a communicant of the church. They told me at headquarters that the hazard of the route was not greater than usual. In all places where Indians threaten, an escort of eight or ten men is sent with every stage. We shall, therefore (D. V.) push on to North Platte and to Denver, to-morrow at 6 P. M.; arriving at North Platte at 8 A. M. Tuesday, and at Denver on Thursday or Friday."

On Monday June 3d, at 6 P. M., we left Omaha on the Union Pacific Railroad for North Platte, the terminus of that road, some three hundred miles out on " the plains."

We reached there 9 A. M., on Tuesday. I wrote immediately to my wife: " I am standing up here in the office to write to you. We arrived two hours ago. On coming to see about the five seats in the stage, for which we telegraphed Friday last from Omaha, the agent asked me, ' Do you wish to go on this morning ? It is my duty to inform you, that no stage came from the West yesterday, and that the report is that the Indians captured said stage (no passengers in it) and killed the driver.' I said, ' Wait then till I've gone over to military headquarters, and come back.' At the tent over which the flag was flying Colonel Lewis told me that the Indians said to the outward driver yesterday that he might pass then but could not pass to-day. I inquired, then, among the dozen or more men waiting here and they said they would not go on this morning. Therefore, for our band my decision is that we stay here for the present; until day after to-morrow, at least, when Wells, Fargo & Co. will send out two coaches. These will keep together, and there will be fully twenty armed men along. If necessary we three will get rifles. General Sherman has gone forty miles on west with some excursionists. He is expected back to-night. When he comes, I shall present my letter to him from Secretary Stanton, and then I know he will give us an escort if he has any to send. Trains and camps are thick on the plains all around, and hundreds and thousands of men are waiting here to push on. All will be well with us. We are in the loving Father's hands and under His protection,—

> " ' God of our fathers, by whose hand
> Thy people still are blest ;
> Be with us thro' our pilgrimage,
> Conduct us to our rest.'

" At Mr. Woolworth's, dear little Norah died yesterday

morning. It would have touched your heart, dear, to hear Mr. and Mrs. Woolworth thanking me with streaming tears that I was with them in their sorrow. Bishop Randall, when he went through two or three weeks ago, lost his valise. I have it now with me and shall carry it to him, God willing."

We really stayed five days in the crowded, hastily constructed, high-priced hotel at North Platte. We could get only one bedroom appropriated to us, so the two clergymen slept on their blankets on the office floor. Each night after the ladies had retired I lay down on the floor in their room, with a blanket and a pillow, my revolver under the latter. The novelty of sleeping on the floor or on the ground wore off in after years, for hundreds and hundreds of my night rests have been taken that way.

It is extremely difficult for me now to take myself in thought back to what I was and what I felt then. They were days of strange experience to me. I had never before been west of my native state of New York; now I was far west, at the terminus of all railway travel, and the limit of civilization. I had never seen Indians, save a few peaceful Tuscaroras at Niagara Falls; now the plains all round me were inhabited by thousands of these hostile men. Emigrant wagons and ox-trains and mule-trains before this were quite unknown to me, and such things with their accessories filled North Platte to the full. The tents and flag, the uniform and accoutrements of the United States military service presented in the encampment yonder were also new to me; for though four years of Civil War had been lately raging my lot had been cast in scenes remote from internecine activity. Only thirty years old as I was; by no means an especially brave man but rather naturally inclined to be prudent and shrinking; with such a non-belligerent body-guard as two clergymen and two young women, for whose safety indeed I was to be largely responsible,—I am quite sure that nothing but the abiding thought that I was in the way of duty, and the deep sense of God's near and wise overruling Providence, kept me steady and carried me through all that then confronted me.

Extracts from North Platte and Denver letters to my wife tell some things better than descriptions written now could tell them.

"*North Platte, June 5, 1867.*

"Here we are yet, safe and sound. I have just come in from the platform, whence one stage-load of men has started off. They were all armed to the teeth, most of them with two revolvers and one sixteen shooting rifle each, so that if every shot tells, each man can kill twenty-eight Indians. Still they think that possibly they may come back instead of going on. Meanwhile we remain here until to-morrow. I am really of opinion that now is as safe as any time to go on, but we shall try to be exceedingly prudent. General Sherman did not come back with the excursionists who returned this morning. He has gone still further on to Fort Sedgwick, and General Augur also. General Myers, in command here, says that six hundred cavalry are daily expected. If they come they will at once be detailed to guard the route. A paper was started yesterday here, semi-weekly or daily, twenty-five cents per copy; a glass of cider or ale costs twenty-five cents, lemons sell two for twenty-five cents; meals are a dollar each. I presume our expenses here must be nearly five dollars a day, each. There is a Dr. Taylor here, a professor in Iowa Medical College, going to Denver to make mineralogical investigations. He has been in military service and is an intelligent man of middle age. There is also a General Hay waiting to go on. I watch what these men say, and when they go, hope to go with them. They did not seem inclined to join the coach of this morning."

" *North Platte, June 6, 1867.*

" Here we are yet. No stages or mails through from Denver yet. Probably a stage-load started off westward from the other side of the river this morning, but we have heard nothing definite of it. It seems probable now that we shall wait for a day or two until we can go on the Union Pacific Railroad, fifty miles further, and then get by mule train twenty miles to Fort Sedgwick, and that from there the military authorities will give us escort. Rumors last night were that Baker's Ranch, sixty miles from here, has been attacked and Baker killed. This morning we have as yet heard nothing. We wait for definite, substantiated reports. All the men I have learned to value and trust in most are waiting too."

" *North Platte, June 7, 1867.*

" I am sitting in a room, No. 7, and have quite a newsy letter to write to you. Mr. Goddard, and Nelly (Mrs. Foote), and Sarah are here, and also Rev. W. A. Fuller, of Nevada, Colorado. Hereby hangs a tale. Mr. F. is now telling his story to them all. I resolved not to write to you till after the Western stage should come in. Three coaches came in this morning from Denver, in one of which were Mr. Fuller and Mr. Godbe. Mr. Godbe is a Mormon from Salt Lake City. He saw George (Rev. G. W. Foote) not long ago, and tells Nelly that George has a very pretty house for them all secured, just in the heart of the city. Now for Mr. F.'s story. He left Denver last

Friday. On Saturday he was riding, the only passenger, with two leaders of stock riding behind. Suddenly he heard the firing of guns and the shout of the driver to his horses, and saw the driver fall dead. Then the coach horses ran, and the two leaders of stock put spur to their horses and ran back. One of them was shot dead. The other escaped and has come on to-day. Mr. F. saw that the horses were running and got out of the coach on the box, the Indians meantime firing at him. He shows us a hole in his coat sleeve that is the nearest they came to him. Meantime the off horses ran faster than the nigh ones and the coach began to go in a circle. The lines had fallen down upon the tongue. So Mr. F. got down upon the tongue for the lines. Just then the coach went into a deep slough and shook him into the mud, the wheels just missing him. Most of the Indians went on after the coach. Mr. F. rose to see yelling Indians coming after him. He says he gave himself up for lost. Yet, looking towards the river he thought, as he is a good swimmer, he'd try the last chance. He started, and the Indians after him. By this time another band had caught the coach, and as it is a law that what the Indians first lay their hands on is their own prey, all rushed to secure the horses. Besides, they doubtless thought they could afterwards secure Mr. Fuller. He of course hurried to the river, tore off his clothes, plunged in, swam to an island in the stream, and looked around to reconnoitre. He saw two men running towards the river and beckoning to him, and thought them Indians. But soon he discovered that these were two soldiers that were out from the fort. They were looking for deserters. So he swam back to them, mounted with them, and rode hurriedly to the fort. The ranchmen say they can't understand how in the world he escaped. They cannot see why the Indians

spared him. God's loving Providence saved him for His
work, I doubt not. I have kneeled down and thanked
Him for His goodness in sparing this servant of His;
and I am much cheered and strengthened to go forward
in the way of duty that He shall unfold. Mr. F. has no
boots on, and not one particle of baggage. I have given
him a linen collar, and have offered to advance him money,
but this he has. Wells, Fargo & Co. have given him a
present, as they call it, of a hundred and thirty-five dollars. Mr. F. advises me to push on now, or else to stay
for three months. He thinks the risk now between here
and Denver quite small. The railroad authorities and
stage agent mean to take us on Sunday next to the
end of the road, and then fill five stages with thirty or
more well armed men of us, and so push on, perhaps
with a cavalry escort also. The driver of Mr. F.'s stage
was scalped and tomahawked and terribly mutilated; and
the mail-bags that came from the West this morning are
all in shreds. The letters were scattered on the plains by
the Indians. Last night we had a most terrific wind and
rain-storm here. It blew down tents and buildings, swept
gravel and dust into all the rooms, and blew much rain
into some. I have not had off my clothes, and have
hardly been without my revolver, since we have been
here. With Mr. Godbe is a Mormon woman. She is
not very beautiful. He is a bright, intelligent, affable and
easy gentleman."

"*North Platte, Noon, Saturday, June 8, 1867.*
"We have this morning held a council of war. The
conclusions are these. Mr. Miller puts back to the East.
The ladies and Mr. Goddard and myself press on to Denver to-morrow morning. Matters may arise between
now and tomorrow to change our plans; but these plans

now are as I have said. Should we hear rumors that make it exceedingly imprudent for us to push on, we shall not go. The railroad cars will take us to-morrow, however, forty or fifty miles on, and then we shall be near Fort Sedgwick. At Fort Sedgwick I hope to find General Augur, and I think we shall be able to procure an escort. Nelly and Sarah were ready to go back if I said the word, but I could not say it. I hope through God's grace I have decided as He would have me do. So much would be lost for Him and for the church were I to put back. Pray for me that I may rest and move and act under His guidance and protection. I send you a paper published here, by this mail. It says hard things about the coming Indian War. Much is true, but much also is greatly exaggerated. I am trying to do what is prudent, as well as what is right; and all I wish to leave in our loving Father's hands.

" I have been out and purchased two rifles for Mr. Goddard and myself, at twenty-seven dollars each. This afternoon we shall go out and practice shooting with them. The party starting out to-morrow will consist of more than twenty cool, strong, well-armed men, besides ourselves ; most of them Westerners familiar with the plains and living in Denver. If we were not to go now with this strong party we might not have as good a chance in months. At Denver, if there be trouble between Denver and Salt Lake, as I have no doubt there is, we will remain until it be prudent to push on. Mr. Miller will stay here till we are off, for fear we may yet deem it wise to send Nelly and Sarah back.

" Now, dear, I have told, and do tell you all, absolutely all the worst. You know that out of duty to God and His church, and out of love for you and the boy, I will be careful and thoughtful, and not rash. But I cannot decide otherwise than to go on. God will protect us, and escorts will be with us, doubt not! Mr. Fuller said that going now we would go with the minimum of risk. The Indians are inhumanly cruel, it is true, but it is also true that they are exceedingly cowardly, and they rarely attack a thoroughly well-armed party. Now, dear, with the tears rolling down and with a promise to write you whenever there is bad news, not to be so careful to send you good news as bad, and commending ourselves to the protection of the " God of our fathers," I say good-by for a little while. Give my love to all dear friends in quiet old Morris. How I do now appreciate that one word *quiet !* "

" *North Platte, Saturday, June 8, 1867.*
" I am happy to state to you that Mr. Miller has decided to go on with us. I have bought a rifle for him, and he goes on. On the whole I am very glad ; glad for ourselves that we can keep together and have his help ; and glad for him, as I think he would have been unhappy and Mary would have been unhappy, had he returned. We are getting ready to leave here in the cars to-morrow morning. It will be a strange Whitsunday for us. Nineteen men, all well armed, go. We hear no bad reports to-day. Besides us nineteen men, there are also sixteen soldiers under a lieutenant, going with us as far as Fort Sedgwick."

" *Denver, June 12, 1867.*
" Kneel down, dear, and thank Almighty God through the loving Saviour for His mercy and goodness to you and to me and to all ours. I have done so, with a full and tenderly touched heart. We are all here, safe and sound and well, and in good spirits. Only all are tired

and sleepy; N. most so; I least so; Mr. Goddard with a bad cold and cough; S. avowing that she will sleep the first month after her arrival in Salt Lake; Miller philosophic; myself dreadfully sunburned, as I rode on the outside of the stage most of the way, day and night.

" We left North Platte at 10 A. M. on Whitsunday. At 9 A. M. I gathered our little party and a few others up in the room of Mr. and Mrs. Reed (Mr. R. is the superintendent of the Union Pacific Railroad); I read the morning service entire, except the lessons and the commandments, and we commended ourselves specially to the protection of our Heavenly Father. At North Platte no religious services of any kind are held on Sunday. Men work and trade and buy and sell just as usual, and gamble and quarrel more than usual. It must be one of the wickedest places on the face of the earth. I should gladly have had full services there had I stayed on Sunday. Well, starting at 10 A M. we rode for sixty miles westward on the first passenger train that had gone further than North Platte. Then getting out, we crossed the Platte River in two or three squads on a flat-boat that was towed by wading and swimming men, helped by two men working oars.

" The current of the Platte is swift, though it runs through a level country, and the waters are muddy, mostly snow water from the mountains. We all got safely across the river and into the stages (four of them) by about 5 P. M. We carried about twenty-five rifles (all breech loading, and some shooting twenty balls without re-loading), thirty revolvers, and nearly four thousand rounds of ammunition. We arrived at Julesburg, about forty miles distant, at midnight, having had nothing to eat but a sandwich each, since breakfast. At J. we took supper and pushed on till about 2 A. M. I rode all the first afternoon and night and into the afternoon of Monday on the outside of the stage. We passed through Fort Sedgwick about 3 A. M. on Monday, and I hunted up the officer of the night. From him I heard that Generals Sherman and Augur were both there. I had hoped to see General Augur and get an escort if possible ; but at so early an hour I could not well rouse the general up, and had to content myself with leaving my card for each. A mounted man on a fleet horse, well acquainted with the Indians and their ways, went before and beside us, as a scout, to watch the ravines and bluffs and secure us against surprise. In the afternoon of Monday, through a dangerous part of the way, two scouts accompanied us. It was a strange thing to feel that we were riding through an enemy's country, and that only the sharp eyes of yonder easy riding scout and the constant protection of Almighty God were saving us from being surprised at almost every turn by Indians, hundreds of whom, doubtless, were just beyond the distant bluffs, less than ten miles off, their scouts, of course, constantly watching us. I never before experienced such a feeling. It would have made you smile grimly to see Mr. Goddard with me on the stage top, each of us carefully holding our rifle, and me with a carbine pouch slung over my shoulders carrying fifty balls. Let me say, once for all, we have come over " the plains ! " On them are no trees or shrubs or bushes ; you can see for miles and miles in every direction. Here and there are mounds or bluffs and gulches and ravines, and from these the Indians make their attacks.

" Well, thanks be to God, the only Indians we saw were two or three squads on their ponies riding after us, but on the other side of the river. Fortunately the Platte is now so swollen that they could not easily cross after us. We saw where the driver was killed, and where

Mr. Fuller escaped; and where horses and a passenger
had been killed, etc., etc.   Doubtless the Indians watched
us all along, but they knew we were fully armed and
would not attack us.   We arrived here at 6:30 A. M., to-
day (Wednesday), having ridden day and night, much to
N.'s fatigue; and having eaten at very irregular and long
intervals, much to poor S.'s intense disgust.

"We saw the Rocky Mountains in the very early
morning, a hundred and fifty miles distant.   A most
majestic sight they were, seeming like silvery clouds of
sharpest outline resting along the horizon.   I see them
now from my window, though I cannot just here have a
sight of the two highest points, Long's Peak and Pike's
Peak.   I am fifteen miles from the base of the first range.
The first range is of dark, rough, picturesque piles, not
unlike the Catskill range, only greatly higher, and not
wooded.   Lying back of this first range is the Snowy
range, here and there hidden behind the first, here and
there rising in cliffs and points and bluffs, far above the
first.   This Snowy range is now entirely covered with
snow (including of course Long's and Pike's Peak).
This morning the Snowy range looks like whitest,
thickest, clearest-cut clouds, resting all along the horizon,
save where they are shut out by the frowning first range.
Each Snowy peak, white and glistening, has a few dark
shades over it, owing to wooded ravines and shadows
cast.   Did you ever look at the moon through a tele-
scope?   I think the Snowy range looks to me this morning most like that, silvery, clear, with dark spots and
seeming hollows.   From Denver we can see two hundred
miles of the north and south stretch of these magnificent
ranges.   Isn't it wonderful?

"Your letter telling me of the dear Morris home and
enclosing the pansy is received.   God bless my dear

Morris parish! God bless the old house and yard and church where we were married, and where we lived, and where baby was born and baptized! God bless Mr. Rulison, my successor at Morris (now the assistant bishop of Central Pennsylvania). Please tell the people how happy I am that they move so vigorously and lovingly and that they do all they can to help him."

" *Denver, June 14, 1867.*
" Last evening, with Bishop Randall and Mr. Hitchings (the rector at Denver), I attended a Mite Society. The rest were invited but declined. There were fifty or more present, I think, and their conversation, so far as I noted, was unusually sensible and intelligent. There was a freedom from ' airs,' and a directness of manner among them that was marked. And they are very little impressed by dignitaries. We two bishops attracted very little attention. At least I did, very little. All were civil, courteous and polite. But there was a self-respect which allowed none of them to attempt any flattery or fulsome eulogy. I think you would be struck as I was, by this coupling of true civility with an entire freedom from ' toadying ' of any kind, and with the frankest and loftiest self-respect. Some very pretty young ladies were present, and many young gentlemen, but most of the assembly consisted of young married couples. It seemed to me that Bishop Randall had to be introduced to as many as I. This, doubtless, is owing to his being away a good deal. Ah, dear, you and I must live among our own people and identify ourselves with them, as soon as we can, no matter how rough they are or how many comforts we must forego. I feel already that I shall spend but little time at the East next winter; only enough to come to bring you on. It will be best, and

right, and is needed and required by duty, that I stay as much and as long as possible in our own field.

"How long we are to stay here I don't know. Under God's Providence it depends, first, on the Indians; second, on Wells, Fargo & Co. The Indians have been stealing a hundred horses and murdering a dozen men between here and Salt Lake. At present Wells, Fargo & Co. will not send stages. Meantime we bide here, paying, I'm afraid, at this hotel (The Tremont) four dollars a day board for each one of us. We are in God's hands, and striving to be prudent we leave our future in His hands. Every day I report at the stage office for facts and news, whereupon to form plans. N. and S. had thirty-two pieces washed, costing them six dollars, I seven pieces, which cost me a dollar fifty."

"*Denver, Sunday, June 16, 1867.*

"In St. John's Church this morning Rev. Mr. Kehler took the service to the lessons. Mr. Hitchings read the lessons, Bishop Randall, in his cassock (his robes have not come yet and some of the congregation thought his cassock was a new device of ritualism that he had brought back from the East) read the ante-communion service, Mr. Goddard, the epistle, Mr. Miller, the prayers, and I preached my Trinity sermon from ' Hold fast the form of sound words,' which I think I wrote for Morris in 1863. Mr. Miller also, in behalf of eight or ten of us present, read the Thanksgiving for " Deliverance from our Enemies," in consideration of our safe return from the Platte.

"Yesterday, a coach arrived here from Salt Lake, coming through with perfect safety. On it was Mr. J. J. Tracy, agent of Wells, Fargo & Co., and superintendent of the stage line, a churchman. We have not seen

Mr. T., but we are sure he has come through, because at
our hotel this morning was left a letter from George
(Rev. G. W. Foote), for N., marked ' Politeness of J. J.
Tracy,' and dated within, June 7. He was worrying
somewhat about us, and hoping that we were staying
back at Omaha.

" Mr. Frank Palmer, the Denver partner of Mr. Hussey,
has called on N., and she finds in him an old Herkimer
(N. Y.) acquaintance. At least she knows his family at
H. very well, and his wife, who was a Miss Maggie Gray.
When P. assured Messrs. Miller and Goddard that he was
married fifteen months ago, left his wife in less than two
weeks, and has not seen her since, they took heart and concluded that they were not the most ill-used men on earth.
Mr. P. has now perfected arrangements for her to come
on, and she is to leave Herkimer for Denver (D. V.) to-
morrow. P. has been baptized by Mr. Hitchings and
expects to be confirmed with the next class.

" Bishop Randall is afraid that the Indian troubles, and
the exaggerated stories about them, will keep back his
clergymen (Whitehead, now bishop of Pittsburgh, Crow,
and Winslow), who are coming from the East. I have
made diligent inquiry since I came here and I think it is
now perfectly safe for travelers in coaches, from North
Platte here. Three coaches come every other day,
and the Indians do not and dare not attack them. If
you have opportunity, please spread this news on my
authority. It would be a great pity if Bishop Randall's
missionaries should not come on. He needs them now.
You know how we laughed at that part of the bishop's
report speaking of his ' army of one, and likely to be two,
provided the first one does not get away before we get
back.' Well, the first one did get away, as Bishop R.
laughingly said to me last night. Mr. Fuller left Ne-

vada, Colorado, and was on his way East before Bishop R. got to Nevada with Mr. Byrne, who succeeds Mr. Fuller.

"The *Spirit of Missions* for June is before me. There is a sentence in the editorial very touching to me. Look it out. This is it: 'His was willingness to labor patiently and quietly for results.' Quietness,—it's a dear, dear word to me. Always associated now with you, dear, and with Morris, and with heaven. God knoweth how gladly I would lay down all the honors of my position and go back to my loved quietness, my blessed obscurity. But God knoweth, too, that I mean to try to do what He bids, with His help and through the Saviour, never ceasing to look forward to the quietness coming hereafter."

"*Denver, June 18, 1867.*

"Well, here we are yet, and by what Mr. Tracy told us yesterday here we are to remain for a week yet. This morning Wells, Fargo & Co. have recommenced sending out daily stages with passengers to Salt Lake, and our turn would come to go to-morrow. Mr. Tracy, however, while saying that for four or five resolute well-armed men the passage would be comparatively safe, strongly advises me to wait with our ladies for a week at the least. Mr. T. is a quiet, stern, iron-gray, shoulder-bent man, with the keenest of eyes, the quietest of ways, the deepest of voices. He says he was present at George's first service (in Salt Lake). He expected there would be about twenty present, there were one hundred and fifty. The second and third Sundays the attendance was thin, the weather being stormy, but nowadays the congregation is good and is increasing. 'I assure you,' he says, 'there will be no difficulty in Mr. Foote's building up a vigorous parish at once.' I told you about our meeting Mr. Godbe, a Mormon, at North Platte. Mr. T. assures us that Mr. G. has 'lots of wives.'

"Wasn't it wicked in him (Mr. G.) to say so politely to N. 'Mrs. Godbe will be most happy to see you when you reach Salt Lake City'? Mr. T., who has spent much time in Salt Lake City, says that he always accepts an invitation to visit a Mormon, but never calls without an invitation. As he was riding out lately with Mr. Jennings, a prominent and wealthy Mormon merchant, Mr. J. invited him to stop at his house and take a glass of wine. He accepted, and within met Mrs. Jennings No. 1 (Mr. J. has two wives). A few days after he was invited to dine at Mr. J.'s and accepted. When the party was assembled in the dining-room, he found it to consist of Brigham Young, the twelve apostles, and other dignataries; a splendid dinner was furnished. As they sat down Mr. J. requested Mr. Young to ask a blessing; Mr. Young, however, said he preferred to have the covers removed first. So they were removed. 'Perhaps,' added Mr. Tracy with a twinkle, 'that the president might see and know what there was to be thankful for.' But no ladies were at the table. Soon the door opened and Mrs. Jennings No. 1 came in. As he had previously met her, Mr. T., of course, got himself ready to greet her, but much to his surprise she did not notice him or any one else, and no one noticed her. Moreover, she was very plainly dressed. She went to Mr. J.'s right hand and received her orders from him about the matters of the table, and in turn gave orders to Mrs. J. No. 2, who now came in. These two women, with some subordinates, then waited on the guests. You would have supposed them to be merely the upper servants of the house. That evening Mr. Tracy went to the theatre, and in the box next him were Mr. J. and his two wives. Mr. J. invited him to occupy a seat in his box, and there was entertained most politely by the two Mrs. J.'s, dressed most elegantly in silks and demeaning themselves as ladies. Strange, isn't it!

"This morning at breakfast we had to drink molasses in our coffee. Mr. Goddard, who never takes ' sweetening,' crowed and chuckled over the rest of us. Sugar is a dollar a pound, and little or none of it can be had anyway until Indians allow some wagon trains from the East to come in to supply us."

"*Denver, June 19, 1867.*

"I have this moment finished writing, signing, and sealing my will (I used my sleeve button for a seal), and Messrs. Hitchings, Miller and Goddard have signed it. Please read it and afterwards ask Mr. A. G. Moore to be kind enough to put it with the rest of my private papers in his bank. Mr. Goddard is now making his will, and Mr. Miller will make his also, unless he find satisfactorily that by the law of New York State his money would go to Mary in case of his death. We are doing all this, not because we apprehend death and destruction in our westward course, but because we think it no more than prudent and proper to do as we have done. I, especially, feel that it was incumbent on me to do as I have done, in view of the fact that I hold moneys in trust for the church. Mr. Jones, the agent here of Wells, Fargo & Co., says that Mr. Tracy left instructions for us to be sent through with special care by the stage going out next Monday morning."

"*Denver June 22, 1867.*

"It is just one month ago to-day since you and I set forth from New York City, and one month ago to-mor-

row since we parted at Albany. It has been a long
month and a strange month to me. Yesterday four carriage loads from here, including the two bishops and the
three parsons, went to the mountain on a fishing excur-
sion. We were more specially the invited guests of Mr.
Palmer. We got off about 5 A. M., and the ride up was
delightful. In our carriage were N. and S., Mr. Palmer,
a Mr. Fisher, a Mr. Clayton, and myself. We were in
Bishop Randall's carriage, before which the gentlemen
had placed a livery team. The prairies were covered
with a profusion of flowers, red, purple, yellow, white, and
dark and light blue; most beautiful flowers, too, bearing
the minutest inspection. We rode fifteen miles to Bear
Creek, on which we camped, and along which we were to
fish. I took a pole and a line and wandered two miles
up the cañon (as the ravine through which a stream flows,
or at some time has flowed, is called—pronounced can-
yon). The hillsides were jagged, rocky, precipitous, un-
wooded, except here and there by a stunted pine, and by
bushes of willow and alder along the peak side. The
creek was high and the water rushed, roared and foamed,
as the great torrent tumbled down in its flow. It was too
turbid and too rapid for good fishing. I, however,
caught three trout, Mr. Hitchings five, Mr. Fisher twelve,
and Mr. Palmer two. I enjoyed my tramping hugely,
and also the views I had. Yet we really saw only the
toes, as it were, of the foot-hills of the Rocky Mountains.
Some time after dinner, jumping was introduced, and
taking off my coat I beat them all at it, Mr. Palmer
coming in second best."

Mr. Goddard wrote to Mrs. Tuttle afterwards as follows:
" While on our delightful picnic at Bear Creek, the gentlemen of the party amused themselves a while with
jumping. The Colorado people jumped pretty well, but

the bishop took the palm by several inches against all competitors.	A captain of the United States army was with us, and as we were riding home got quite enthusiastic, exclaiming after speaking of the bishop's other excellences : ' Why, what a bishop ! Let him jump like that a little and he'll take those Montana men into the church at every jump. He'll only need to lift up his hand to originate a new Crusade.' "

" *Denver, June 24, 1867.*

" Well ! here we are yet. I rose at five and carefully packed everything and saw the others all up. Just as we were going to sit down to breakfast a black man came with a note from Mr. Jones, enclosing three telegrams that he had received from the division agents along the route to Salt Lake. I am thankful to say that these telegrams said nothing at all about Indians. They bade Mr. Jones not send any more passengers through for three days, because streams were high and two bridges at least had been swept away. They asked him to send on first a skiff fitted with rowlocks, that preparations may be made to row passengers across streams where bridges are gone.

" To-day being St. John's Day, the Masonic Fraternity have a procession, oration, etc. Bishop Randall and Messrs. Hitchings and Goddard are Masons. The bishop is to be the orator. Since we must stay, we are all glad to be here to attend. Mr. G. is quite elated and has asked N. to dine with him at the grand Masonic dinner at 6 P. M. Denver to-day is quite full of Indians—friendly ones, of course ; three or four hundred of them, men, women and children, trading skins, etc. The papooses, carried in sheaths on the backs of the squaws, are the funniest little fellows alive,—bright-eyed, stoical, never crying, always bobbing their heads about in observation."

" Denver, Tuesday, June 25, 1867.

" Mr. Jones hopes he will be able to send us on to-morrow, though he tells me that another bridge over the Boulder went yesterday. The skiff for the ' Medicine Bow' Creek started off this morning. Mr. Hitchings and I have just been out to see General Hancock, but we did not find him in. He arrived at Denver to-day and is encamped on the Platte, about three miles from here. The Masonic celebration went off nicely yesterday. The address of ' Sir Knight Rt. Rev. Bishop Randall,' so he was announced, was good,—extempore, rather long ; and the poem by a Mr. Carpenter, N. liked much."

" Salt Lake City, July 3, 1867.

" Thank God ! We are here, safe and well. We arrived at 7 P. M. yesterday, dirty and tired, but cheerful and well. We have just had dinner and now Mr. G. and I, in room No. 1 of the ' Revere House,' are writing to our wives. We left Denver 7 A. M., Wednesday, June 26th, in a stage, which we had quite to ourselves. We rode day and night until Friday noon, having for more than a hundred and fifty miles through the hostile country an escort of three cavalrymen. It seemed very strange to look out of the coach on moonlight nights and see the horses and armed riders galloping by our side. In less dangerous countries our escort consisted of only one rifle-armed man sitting beside the driver. Every night at dusk I felt very nervous, for dusk and daybreak are the favorite times to attack. But thanks to our merciful and loving heavenly Father we have been watched over throughout, and have not seen a hostile Indian from Denver here. N. and S. have stood the ride well, S. sleeping much, N. very little. The latter was very nervous about Indians, though she tried to conceal it. Her fears, sharp at night-fall, would keep her from getting the little sleep that the tumbling and rolling coach might perhaps in peaceful times have granted her. At North Fork, two hundred and thirty-six miles west of Denver, where we arrived Friday noon, we had to stop on account of the ferry being out of order from high water. We stayed over night. As there was only one house in the place, and that a board shanty occupied by the station-keeper and his wife, N. and S. slept in a stage that was fitted up for them, we three men sleeping on the ground, rolled in our blankets. Mr. G. didn't expect to sleep, but after all, did sleep very well. He confessed next morning that he had slept and that he felt much refreshed. By seven in the morning we were ferried over on a flat-boat, every bit of which had been sawed out by hand in a woody cañon forty miles off; and which, apparently worth twenty-five dollars, had cost the company a thousand dollars. Two ropes are stretched across the stream, and by pullies and by inclining the boat's side to the current, the movement of the water propels the boat across. Getting into the stage on the other side we entered on a route unknown to the driver. The old station had been washed away and the new one was placed farther up the Platte. Bumping and jouncing, and on no road whatever, we went over the plains, covered with bunches of grass and sage brush. Every now and then we had to get out, in order that a pick and shovel might be used to help us over little ravines. At one spot in crossing a little stream we found a formidable obstacle in the quicksand. The horses plunged into it and the first one sank to his back. After great difficulty we crossed it thus. There were two stages; all the men of the first stage, with us three, were ferried over on the back of a horse ; then the teams were doubled for each stage. Thus by yelling, and whipping, the coaches, the latter one containing N. and S., were dragged through. That morning we consumed six hours in traveling fourteen miles. Saturday night we reached Sulphur Springs and were told we could not go on till next morning for want of horses. Accordingly, N. and S. slept on their blankets on the floor of the station, and we three men made a bed for ourselves in the coach out in the yard.

Sunday, at 7 A. M., we started on. I read the church service for the day as well as the rolling stage would allow me, and I could not keep back the tears for thought of quieter Sundays. I read aloud, also, ' Jerusalem the Golden,' and Dr. Dix's ' Hours,' which book Mr. G. had with him. From Sulphur Springs we came very rapidly. In twelve hours we made seventy-five miles ; I remember one drive of thirty-seven miles which took us four hours and forty minutes. On that drive we had California horses, bronchos, I think they call them, wild and fleet. The driver would have to mount the box and get his reins in hand before the attendant could leave their heads. When these did leave, the horses would leap forward like wild animals, taking us on for miles whirling, bounding, and catching for support at whatever part of the coach we could. Monday afternoon we reached Fort Bridger. Up to this, though for three hundred miles we had been coming through the mountains, the face of the country was of the forlornest kind. Alkali plains, desert, sandy, white with soda ash ; red crumbling rocks on the right and left ; hillsides and defiles covered with only sage brush,—it is very, very forlorn. However, snow here and there to be seen was a relief, and I must not forget to record that constantly we saw flowers, white, red, pink, blue, that for delicacy and color would compare favorably with any of your exotics. I enclose one, of a number that Mr. Miller got out of the coach on purpose to pluck, as we came through Bridger Pass which is the pass over the summit of the Rocky Mountain range.

"When we reached Fort Bridger, however, which is about a hundred and twenty miles from Salt Lake, we began to see green valleys and clearly flowing streams with green banks, and were cheered by the change. At Fort Bridger were sixty or seventy wigwams of Indians. These were the Shoshones or Snakes, a friendly tribe. N. and S. talked with some of them while we were stopping for supper, and I went out with two bare-legged boys of them, who were practicing arrow shooting near by. While waiting for supper I heard my name called by somebody. I started up and a gray-whiskered man of pleasant speech introduced himself to me as Mr. Carter. He said he knew I was coming, for he had been in Salt Lake the week before, and had seen and heard Mr. Foote. I introduced him to the ladies, and they walked over with him to his store and house. I found he was Judge Carter (the richest man in Utah outside of this city, George says). At his house he made me take tea with him. He has a wife and two children there, and two daughters at Terre Haute, Indiana, in St. Agnes' Hall. At the table were three married ladies; and on my asking whether at Fort Bridger they had Sunday services, they said, ' No.' Mrs. C. said, ' I have been here six years, and in that time have heard but two sermons.' The judge said, ' I marry and bury; using the Prayer-Book service for burying.' I promised them that if I ever could in the future I would send them a missionary. If I can't do better I will go up myself and spend a week or two prospecting there, if the Lord please to bring me safe back from Montana. In Judge C.'s parlor were a piano, engravings, etc. There is a government fort with garrison there, Colonel Mills, whom I met, being in command.

" Tuesday, about noon, an ambulance met us and as it stopped the question came, ' Is Bishop Tuttle aboard ? ' I leaped out and found Major and Mrs. McClintock of Fort Douglas, which is near Salt Lake City, and General and Mrs. Chetlain, of the city itself. They said Mr. Foote was expecting us, and that they meant to return by Sunday. We now struck Mormon settlements. One Mormon woman rode with us several miles. I am quite sure she was one of the two wives belonging to the man at whose house we stopped to let her get out ; because when we stopped, though a woman was in the door of one wing, our fellow passenger did not go in there, but went to the door of the other wing, which was opened for her. Nearly all the houses of the settlements are built of sun dried brick, called adobe. This is nothing more or less than hard dry mud. We saw a few buildings of stone. The last twenty-five miles of the route here is the grandest and strangest. We came up and over and down the Wasatch range, whose tops are nearly always covered with snow, through the deepest gorges, down the narrowest ravines, by the side of the maddest mountain torrents. Hundreds of teams met us, going up after wood. Alas ! all the mountains here are well-nigh treeless, though the ravines of the last thirty miles are green and fresh from bushes and underwood. Wood for fuel costs twelve dollars a cord and has to be hauled twenty or thirty miles. Coal of fair quality, and moderate in quantity, is found forty miles off. On the Wasatch, Miller got out and made a snowball and brought it to us to feel of in the hot July day. I rode for the last thirty miles on the outside, through an abominable dust-storm. A stranger could not have told our faces from those of dusky Indians. Our first view of the Salt Lake basin was inferior, because we saw it through clouds of dust. We saw the basin, the River Jordan, the great Salt Lake, and the city, from the mountainside, an hour before we reached the basin. The Great Salt Lake, not as I supposed, is fully seventeen miles distant from the city. Distances look short, however, in this atmosphere. As Mr. G. and I sit writing at our open window I look out upon the snow-covered Oquirrh Mountains, which I have guessed to be fifteen miles distant, but which, instead, I am assured, are fifty miles.

" At last we got to the city. Driving to the office we found Mr. Haskins there. George was not there, however, not expecting the stage to be in so soon. Mr. H. was quite taken aback at sight of my cartridge pouch in front, my pistol behind, my trousers in my boots, and my dark features. He declares that he thought the driver had a brother of the reins and whip beside him, and did not recognize me at all. Leaving our baggage there, we all went in the stage up to G.'s house. Then we men left the ladies there and came here. First, we went to Clawson's bath rooms for a delicious bathe, which cost us seventy-five cents each. Then we came here to the Revere House to tea. Welcome was the sight of our meal, and Miller's mouth watered when a full pint of luscious strawberries was placed in front of each of us. O how good were the new potatoes, and green peas, and string beans, and fresh turnips we had for dinner to-day. After tea we all went up to George's and got our letters. I found four or five from you, and have received another this morning. Now I must stop, as we are all summoned to go out to the ' Church Association' (a quasi Church Mite Society), which meets this evening."

So at last I had reached my field. We left Omaha June 3d, and reached Salt Lake July 2d. We were one month en route, because of the Indian troubles, on a course traversed by stages generally in not more than eight or nine days.

My experiences in stage-coach riding are a vivid part of my Rocky Mountain memories. I have traveled more than forty thousand miles in that way. Most times I enjoyed that mode of traveling, many times I grimly endured it, a few times I was rendered miserable by it. Once only do I remember being quite unnerved by it. It was on the trip from Salt Lake to Boise City, which took about three days and nights of travel. Near all the way I was alone and in a "jerker" instead of a stage-coach. The latter, of Concord make, drawn by four, often by six horses, and carrying nine passengers within and five on the outside, was the Pullman car of early times. But the former was a small canvas-covered affair, seating four inside and one outside with the driver, and drawn usually by only two horses. This, when the wheels struck obstacles, did not have the easy roll and swing of the coach, but, as the name imports, jerked the passenger unmercifully on, or oftener off, his seat. To be alone in a jerker was to be in the extreme of discomfort. The vehicle not being steadied by a good load, and the passenger not being supported by contact with other passengers, the ceaseless unsteadiness drove away sleep, and wore one out in frantic efforts to secure some tolerable sort of bodily equilibrium. During the last fifty miles of that Boise trip I was more used up physically than at any other time I can think of in my life. I was past the point of grinning and bearing, or shutting the teeth and enduring. All the forces of resistance seemed to be beaten down and disintegrated. I was ready to groan and cry, and would have offered not a jot of opposition if the driver had dumped me down upon the roadside and left me behind under a sage brush. That experience made me understand the stories I had heard of the stage passengers who could not sleep, coming in after long journeys downright sick and even actually demented.

A funny story was once told me. One forenoon the coach rolled into Denver and the six horses came prancing up to the office of Wells, Fargo & Co. A large crowd was assembled, as the incoming and outgoing of the daily coaches were the great events for the town. At the stop, the only passenger quickly threw open the coach door, leaped on the ground, ran hurriedly across the street, and turning what the boys call a hand spring, stood on his head with his heels up against a supporting wall. Several men followed after him quite sure that here was another passenger crazed by a long, sleepless ride. One said to him in a tone of sympathy, " Why, cap'n, what's the matter ? " Slowly coming to a right-side-up posture, he answered, " Well, my friends, I'll tell you what it is. This standing on my head is the only one position which I haven't been in during the last twenty-four hours in yonder tumbling coach, and I wanted to make the thing harmonious and complete all around by carrying out the full programme."

Of the stage drivers I want to put on record words of grateful appreciation. The California and Rocky Mountain stage drivers of early days were a unique class of men. Their duty was only to sit on the box and drive ; stock tenders harnessed and fed the horses. Yet the drivers knew their own horses and had names for them, and they always took care to see that they were well looked after. Going round curves or down a mountainside, with his foot on the brake and the six lines in hand (often in one hand, if with the other he wished to use his whip), and with his eyes keenly watching the road as it stretched in front, the driver was such an example of marvelous skill as is a pilot in troubled waters. His one work was to watch and guide his horses. That he was often reticent, monosyllabic, was not strange, for it requires more thought than one might suppose to keep a heavily loaded coach right-side-up, and to see that each and all the horses do their fair share of work in the best way. It was a mistake to expect a driver to talk to one, or to talk too much to him. He had the important duty to discharge of carrying his passengers safely, and of sending forward the United States mail over his own route. In faithful and loyal effort to meet and do such duty I have never known a more true, self-respecting, heroic class of men than are he and his fellows. It was easy to sit in the post-office by a warm stove of a wintry night and find fault because the mail was not in on time, but had the grumbler been beside the driver who was coming in, in the sleet or the mud, had he seen how undauntedly he had met obstacles, how skilfully he had surmounted difficulties, how unflinchingly he had borne hardships, and how unsparing of self he had been in it all, fault finding would have died into reverent silence, or changed into grateful admiration for the driver's faithfulness and pluck. The old race of stage drivers, strong, taciturn, self-reliant, autocratic, haughty to men, but bright, brave, faithful, tender-hearted, true and kind to women and children, has largely died out. Increasing population, advancing civilization, multiplying railroads have banished them. Some of them have become farmers and stock raisers, some own livery stables, some are saloon-keepers, and some, alas, fill drunkards' graves. Scores and scores of them I have ridden by the side of, for days and nights, and they won my respect, my affection, my sincere esteem. They were rough men, most of them, I know. But they were true and kind as brothers to me. They were drinking men, many of them, I suppose. Yet only three of all that I have ridden with do I remember to have seen drunk when on duty. In one of these three cases I was the only passenger, in a night ride, and the night was dark and stormy. It was a time of anxious watchfulness, and several times I was down on the ground to find the road and help keep in it. In another case I and my four year old son were the only passengers. This was an afternoon drive. I mounted the box, tied my boy on and sat close beside the driver for steadiness and support, never, however, venturing to take the lines. That would have been an insult to him. Besides, a driver, even when drunk, would be quite as skilful in handling lines as would the best of us lubberly outsiders.

In the third case the stage was full of passengers, among them, Mr. E. L. Davenport, the actor, and his wife. At midnight over the coach went in a slough of deep mud. No one was hurt, but it was necessary to carry the ladies out to *terra firma*. I was among the tallest for wading and I bore Mrs. Davenport ashore. Fifteen years later she was passing through Salt Lake. I paid my respects to her and we recalled in a pleasant conversation the incidents of our midnight adventure in Echo cañon. Only twice have I been upset in stage traveling, and this Echo cañon mishap was one of the times. The other was in Port Neuf cañon, Idaho, and that too about midnight. Mr. Gilbert, afterwards assistant bishop of Minnesota, was by my side.

In Echo, as the coach went over, I was the under fellow of my seat. My two neighbors, scrambling to open the coach door which was now skyward, thought not of poor me. I was constrained to shout out, " We are safe, don't you see we have simply gone over, in the mud? Be careful of your feet, you are treading on us folk down here."

In Port Neuf, as we toppled over on a steep side hill, I was the upper fellow. Poor Gilbert was under, and my boot heels, as I trod ruthlessly on his head and face in my frantic efforts to get out of the coach door, left bruises on him, that gave him discomfort and me shame. As the upper man I had given no heed whatever to the indignant preachment I myself had uttered as the under fellow. Poor human nature!

The drivers were brave. Along the stretches of ten miles between the stations was almost never a habitation of any kind. At each station there was usually only one stock tender. The driver on these lonely routes took his life in his hands, he was singularly defenseless against either Indians or robbers; the latter of whom in his parlance, were " road agents." The team must at all hazard be kept in the road and controlled, so in the nature of the case he could not fight back. Riding into and through danger where one can do nothing active to resist it, is strong proof of real bravery. In the " boot" under where he sat the express box was carried, and in it often were thousands upon thousands of dollars in gold dust. Robbers knew this. With guns pointed at the driver they would shout: " Halt! Throw down your express box, quick!" There was nothing, then, for him to do but to comply, or to say, " I've all I can do to attend to the team." Then one of the fellows would climb up and get the box. The Stage Company and the Express Company never held the driver responsible for such loss of the box, knowing that all his attention must be given to the team, and that he could not offer active resistance.

One wonders that the box was not more frequently taken by robbers. One reason for the comparative infrequency of robbery was that the companies never spared pains or money to pursue relentlessly and prosecute every marauder. Every robber in the mountains knew that after he had made his attack, the hunt for him would never let up, and the penalty for his crime was inexorable. Another reason was that when much treasure was carried, one or two " messengers," keen-eyed mountaineers, quick to shoot and armed to the teeth with the very best of weapons, went along to protect.

The road agents had the manliness to respect the non-resistant attitude of the driver. They never, in malice, shot at him. In two or three cases I have known the driver to be killed; but this happened because, either not hearing or not caring, he did not halt when ordered to ; or else because the robber covering him with his gun, in nervousness and without meaning to do so touched the trigger.

Passengers usually got off easily. If the treasure box was heavy and full, they were let entirely alone and suffered merely a short detention. If the box, however, was rather empty, very likely the " agents " would insist on having the loose money and watches of the men. Women they never stole from. Resistance from passengers, covered as they were by one or more guns of the confederate assailants, meant bloodshed. One coach load of passengers in Port Neuf cañon, in 1865, resisting, were all killed.

In all my traveling I have not been on board a stage when it was attacked. Nor have I suffered any serious trouble as a passenger. Discomforts and annoyances, as a matter of course, I have had, but I never gave way to grumbling, and I think that this was the reason all the drivers took to me so kindly. Again my memory runs over with loving thoughts of the stage drivers. One in after years was my faithful gardener in Salt Lake, and sexton of our " St. Mark's Cathedral." Two closer grasping hands never met than his and mine, when on coming away I bade him a tearful good-bye. One in Idaho, who had gone to saloon-keeping, when I came round for a service, helped to get and prepare for me a hall. Early in the evening he came to me and said, " I'm going to church with you, bishop, to-night, the old saloon is locked up the tightest!" Still another, on a Sunday when the church services and a circus were rival performances in a mining town, came to me in the afternoon and said, " Bishop, I wanted to come to church to-night, but to be honest about it I must tell you I've decided to go to the circus. I liked the circus when a boy and I haven't seen one in years. But in your collection to-night I want to help. Take this, and put it in for me." As he went away he left in my hands a ten dollar bill.

The old stage drivers, dear personal friends they were. Good they did to me by their wholesome example of sturdy and unselfish fidelity. Would to God I had done them more good in persuading them to be loyal in service to the Master and Redeemer of their souls.

With fellow passengers I scarce ever had any trouble. On a few occasions, perhaps, I had a little with drinking people. Once a so-called doctor (he had graduated into his diploma from a hospital stewardship) by manner and act was insulting to a colored woman in the coach, who I knew had been the faithful servant of an army officer at Fort Shaw, Montana. I reproved him, and when he repeated the offense, I shook him soundly. At the next station he got out and slunk entirely away from our sight.

A story has been told of me, and been repeated in many papers, of some trouble I once had with a man for persisting in smoking in a stage-coach. This story, enlarged and embellished, is told of my bishop's experience in a Rocky Mountain coach. I may be forgiven the recital here of the actual facts.

When I was a student in the General Theological Seminary, New York City, I think it was in 1861, and in the senior class, early one autumn evening I got into a Fifth Avenue stage to go to Fulton Ferry, en route to Brooklyn to visit at a friend's house. As we went down the avenue, a lady, and later an elderly gentleman, got in. At the St. Nicholas Hotel, Broadway, two men entered, one tall, the other short, both smoking. Soon the lady giving evident signs of distress, I asked her if the smoke was disagreeable. She said, " Yes." I then said to the men, " Will you be good enough to stop smoking? This lady objects." The smaller man at once threw his cigar away. The tall one did not, but kept on smoking. I placed my hand on his knee and said firmly, " You must put up that cigar—you cannot smoke it in this stage." He retorted, " Are you boss of the stage?" I answered, " Yes, sufficiently so to assure you that you must not smoke here!" He then mutteringly quenched the light and put by the cigar. A little before reaching the ferry the two men got out. After getting on the ferry-boat I went out on the deck in front, as was my custom. Soon the two men of the stage came through the cabin and out on the deck near me. The tall one accosted me with, " So you were the boss of the stage, eh?" I turned away from him to another part of the boat. They followed me, and the same speaker coming near said something impudent. By this time my blood was up, and without a word I struck him with my flat hand in the face. My intention was to warn him to keep away from me. I was thoroughly astonished when I saw the effect of the blow. He staggered and fell and in falling involved his mate also, who was close beside him. The tall man lay sprawling, and his friend was half down. The latter sprang up and seized me. By that time I was thoroughly roused and I struck him a blow that landed him quickly as prostrate as the other. One does not know how hard he can strike with his fist when excited.

I had no intention whatever of knocking these men down, but only of giving a wholesome check to their impudence. I was quite as much astonished as they to see the quickness and completeness of their fall. One explanation, I suppose, is that at the gymnasium I had been taking boxing lessons for exercise.

Two deck hands now rushed upon me and said, " Stop this, we can't have any fighting here." I said, " I am not fighting, you need not hold me."

When we reached Brooklyn, the injured men hailed a policeman and made their charge. As I stepped from the boat this policeman seized me vigorously by the shoulders. I said to him, " You need not be rude—I am ready to go with you. Allow me to take this gentleman with me for a witness."

I turned to the elderly gentleman who had been with me in the stage, and who also was near me on the deck, and said, " You must go with me, sir, please, and tell exactly how this happened." He demurred and evidently was reluctant to comply with my request. But on my renewing my appeal and representing to him how necessary his testimony would be to make things clear, he consented to go. Off then I was marched to the nearest police magistrate. It was a unique experience. A hundred or more gamins and hoodlums, with the policeman, were my body-guard. I could hear them shout information to inquirers. " It's the tall fellow in gray. He knocked two fellows down aboard the ferry-boat."

When we reached the office the sergeant listened to the complaint. The tall man's eye was much swollen and the sight of it gave point to his accusation. When asked what I had to say, I only insisted that I had not struck in malice, but at first, at any rate, with the flat hand, to chastise impudence. I then requested that my friend, the elderly gentleman, should be allowed to tell the entire story. He did so, and when he had ended, the sergeant said to the accusers, " I shall not hold this man. He lives in New York. You must get out a warrant and arrest him and lay your charges there."

He asked me my New York address and then said, " You are discharged!" As I went forth, my gamin friends were good enough to give me a hearty cheer. I hurried to my friend's house and made my evening visit.

Next day I consulted a lawyer and put the matter in his hands. But no warrant was ever served upon me and no notice from New York officials came, nor from that day to this have I ever seen or heard anything of my two acquaintances.

This story, altered in shape or decorated in style, has gone the rounds in many a newspaper of the country. Universally the place of the occurrence is given as a Rocky Mountain stage coach, and the time of it my bishop's life in the West.

CHAPTER V

THE FIELD—UTAH

I was now in Salt Lake City, the largest town in the field, from which radiated the different stage routes over which I must travel. Technically, I was the " Bishop of Montana, having jurisdiction also in Utah and Idaho "— but practically there was no difference in my relation to any one of the three territories. Utah, Montana and Idaho constituted my field. In square miles and population (not counting Indians) it stood about as follows :

			Square Miles	*Population*
Utah,	.	.	105,000	100,000
Montana,	.	.	145,000	30,000
Idaho,	.	.	90,000	25,000
Total,	.	.	340,000	155,000

A sparsely settled region indeed, not quite one inhabitant to two square miles. And of the 100,000 people in Utah, I am quite sure there were not a thousand who were not Mormons.

Utah was made an organized territory of the United States in 1850. When the Mormons made their Salt Lake settlement in 1847 it was Mexican territory ; afterwards, in February, 1848, in the treaty of Guadaloupe Hidalgo, it was ceded to the United States. During these intervening three years the Mormons had organized for themselves the " State of Deseret," manufacturing for it a State Constitution, and asking Congress for

admission into the Union as a state. Brigham Young
himself led the pioneer band in, arriving in the Salt Lake
valley, July 24, 1847. In 1848 he returned to Iowa and
led another detachment to Salt Lake; but during all his
life thereafter (he died in 1877) he never once left his
Rocky Mountain home. For his capital city he chose
an excellent site, seventeen miles from the shore of the
Great Lake, on a sloping bench at the foot of the mountains, where the clear waters of City Creek, a bright mountain stream, issue forth from its cañon.

He planned for his town, streets of most generous
width, decreeing that the blocks for the most part should
be forty rods by forty in size. They were thus to contain ten acres each, and to be divided into eight lots, of one
and a fourth acres each. Ten rods front and twenty deep
would be the size of each original lot. Ample room this
would give for a good vegetable and fruit garden for each
family. For good vegetables and fruit Utah is noted;
the potatoes and beets, and the apricots and peaches are
among the best to be found anywhere.

Of Utah's one hundred thousand inhabitants, Salt Lake
City had twelve or fifteen thousand; Provo had three or
four thousand, and some of the other towns, like Ogden,
Logan, Brigham, Manti, and St. George, one thousand each.
Two posts of the United States army were in the territory; Camp Douglas, on the bench overlooking Salt
Lake City, three or four miles distant, and Fort Bridger
a hundred and twenty-five miles to the east. In these
posts were about three hundred soldiers. About two
hundred non-Mormons or " Gentiles " were in the service
of the Stage Company. In Salt Lake City were perhaps
two hundred and fifty other Gentiles, including merchants, of whom I remember five Jewish firms and two
others; lawyers, of whom I recall five, and bankers, two;

besides the United States officials, the governor, the secretary, the marshal, the assessor of internal revenue, the collector, and three judges. The postmaster was Mr. T. D. H. Stenhouse, a Mormon. I think the surveyorgeneral was also a Mormon. Scattered throughout the territory were perhaps two hundred and fifty more Gentiles, miners and traders, making a thousand in all. The non-Mormon religious history of the territory had been very scanty. A Roman Catholic priest from Nevada had been in Salt Lake City, but had contented himself with purchasing a lot for a future church, after which he had returned home. The Reverend Norman McLeod, a chaplain of the United States army, stationed at Camp Douglas, a Congregationalist, had in 1865 and 1866 preached for some Sundays in Independence Hall and started a Sunday-school. His were absolutely all the non-Mormon religious services ever held in Utah before our arrival. Of his Sunday-school Dr. Robinson was the superintendent. Dr. Robinson had married Miss Nellie Kay, the young daughter of a family that had apostatized from the Mormon faith. He had also lodged in the United States land office a preëmption claim to the " Warm Springs," situated a mile out from Salt Lake City. The city claimed this site, and upon Robinson's pushing his claim the Mormons became bitterly incensed against him. Brigham Young in the Tabernacle on a Sunday hurled anathemas at the " greedy and vile outsiders who come here to interfere with this people and rob them of their rights." Mrs. Robinson has told me the rest of the story; I give it as she gave it to me: " During the week succeeding that Sunday, and in October, 1866, one night we had retired early, the doctor not feeling well. Suddenly there came a knock at the door. I rose and went to it, and asked what was wanted. ' Is the doctor in?' I was asked. 'Yes,' I replied. 'A man on the next block has broken his leg,' I heard, 'and we want to get the doctor to come to him.' I went and told the doctor. He was loth to go, and wanted to send word that he was too unwell to do so. I interposed a plea for the wounded man, however, and he arose and went. At the door the doctor found two men and he had not gone with them more than two hundred yards from his own door before a pistol shot rang out and he fell, pierced by a murderous bullet. Passing friends found him and brought him groaning home, and soon after he died. It was a dastardly assassination, luring a victim to his death by taking advantage of the unselfish impulses of his benevolent heart."

No punishment of this world has followed this wickedness, no trace of the murderer or murderers, on which incriminatory action could be taken, from that day to this has ever been found. It suffices to remark that the machineries for pursuit, prosecution, and penalty were all in the hands of Mormons, and that they regarded Dr. Robinson as their deadly foe.

After this assassination the Rev. Mr. McLeod, who was visiting in the East, decided that it was best for him not to return. For the seven months elapsing before the arrival of Messrs. Foote and Haskins in Salt Lake, in May, 1867, Major Hempstead, a lawyer, kept up the Sunday-school, serving as its superintendent. At the very first opportunity, however, he turned it over to Mr. Foote, and the latter entered upon the charge of a Sunday-school of forty or sixty pupils, ready-made to his hands. He found only three communicants of our church in Salt Lake, Mrs. Hamilton, Mrs. Durant and Mrs. Tracy. For three years our own services were the only non-Mormon ones held in Utah. In 1870 the Methodists came, under Reverend

Mr. Pierce. Soon after, the Roman Catholics, under Father Scanlan (since made the bishop of Utah), began work. Later, and in the case of some, years later, and in the following order, came the Presbyterians, the Congregationalists, in renewed effort, the Lutherans, and the Baptists.

Our sources of growth were three. First, among the English immigrants into Utah were found not a few who had once been members and communicants of the Church of England. Some of these were disgusted with Mormonism and ready to apostatize from it, and there were instances in which these would revert with the eagerness of renewed loyalty to their old faith. Second, we were to win from the Gentile inhabitants all we could by commending the " Evangelic truth and Apostolic order " of the Church to them. Third, we were to gain confirmees and communicants from our parish school. In 1867, we admitted nine of the first class and five of the second. In 1868, of the classes, in order, respectively five, eleven, and six ; in 1869, two, six, and eight. Thereafter, a large percentage of the candidates for confirmation came from our parish schools.

In the summer of 1870, the Rev. J. L. Gillogly, a young deacon from the Berkley Divinity School, Connecticut, came to Ogden and began work in this second largest town of the territory, forty-nine miles north from Salt Lake. He and Mrs. Gillogly kept house first in a freight car that was fitted up for their use, holding services in the passenger room of the Union Pacific Railway depot. It will be remembered that the last spike of the railroad across the continent was driven in the autumn of 1869 ; though the Utah Central Railway connecting Ogden with Salt Lake was not built until January, 1871. In the autumn of 1870 Mr. Gillogly rented an abandoned saloon in Ogden and started his School of the Good Shepherd, with Mahlon N. Gilbert as the teacher. In 1875 the Church of the Good Shepherd, to the memory of Mrs, Catherine (Hamersley) Livingston, of New York City, was erected by friends, at the cost of $11,000. In Ogden, also, we were the pioneers. The Methodists were the first to follow; they came a year or two later.

At Logan, sixty miles north from Ogden, the Rev. W. H. Stoy began services and established St. John's School in 1873. Within a year or two the Presbyterians followed us, and then the Methodists. In Plain City, fifteen miles west from Ogden, under the guidance of Mr. Gillogy, St. Paul's School was started in 1873. Into this Mormon town no one but ourselves has ever come. In another Mormon neighborhood, Layton, once known as Kay's Ward, between Ogden and Salt Lake, St. John's School was started in 1886. I shall take occasion hereafter to speak more particularly of our six schools in Utah and their evangelizing work. In two Gentile towns of Utah, also, we have built churches, in Corinne in 1870, in Park City in 1888. Corinne was laid out in 1869; a little westward of it was where the Union and the Central Pacific Railway construction parties met and where the last spike was driven. It was thought that Corinne would speedily absorb into itself all the non-Mormon population and business of the Territory. The large mercantile firms of Salt Lake, such as the Walker Brothers, opened branch houses in Corinne, in preparation for the future transfer of all their business. We built a church of adobe, mainly from a gift of fifteen hundred dollars sent by Mrs. Minturn, of New York, in memory of her late husband, Mr. Robert B. Minturn. By her request it was called the "Church of the Good Samaritan." I think also a like amount was sent to the bishop of Oregon, and to the bishop of Nevada, and perhaps to some others, for "Good Samaritan" churches in their fields. Yet the event followed not the line of our forecast. Corinne now has two hundred and fifty inhabitants, and Salt Lake fifty thousand.

Some extracts from letters to Mrs. Tuttle will give my first impressions of Salt Lake.

" Salt Lake City, July 5, 1867.

" Salt Lake City is beautiful, as we last night saw it from the hill back of Brigham Young's house (these hills back we call benches). Streets straight and wide, rills of irrigating water running along the sides to refresh the growing shade trees, locust, cotton-wood, and soft maple, yards and gardens filled full of peach, apple and apricot trees, of grapes, and all vegetables ; the wide basin stretching away in the distance nearly fifty miles square ; the River Jordan two miles off, overflowing its banks ; the Great Salt Lake, like a sea, twenty miles away ; the snow-capped mountains bounding the basin on every side, all these make a beautiful view. Last evening at the theatre there was a " Fourth of July ball." Brigham Young was chief of the committee of arrangements. We did not attend, but a Gentile told me this morning that it went off pleasantly. Young and some of his wives were present, and bald-headed Heber C. Kimball was one of the most frequent dancers. I believe Foote and Haskins had invitations to the ball from Brigham Young. Almost every family here has a cow ; and all cows get their living free on the waste plains and pastures beyond the Jordan. A herd-man or herd-boy drives them all over the river every morning, and watches them and brings them back at night. For this he charges three cents a day per head. This morning as I rose, the herd-boy, dinner pail in hand, was driving more than two hundred cows along in front of the Revere House to cross the Jordan.

"Wednesday evening we all went to the meeting of the Church Association (George's Mite Society). It was held at the house of Mr. Gilbert, an intense anti-Mormon.

"The Gentiles here are not all united socially or religiously. There may be said to be three classes of them. First, the intense anti-Mormons, who say we are 'knuckling under' to the Mormons in our present course. Second, the moderate, indifferent people, without great prejudice, and without much energy. Third, those who are disposed to apologize for the Mormons and to think that in some things they are grossly misrepresented. Of this last class is Mr. Hussey, with whom many of the first class will not join in helping us on. Still, with steady work and good lives, we hope gradually to mould these classes, or what there is religious in them, into one."

"*Salt Lake City, July 7 (Sunday), 1867.*

"I have just come home from morning service. The services at Independence Hall were very pleasant. There was a congregation, I should think, of about a hundred. Mrs. Hamilton played the 'Mason & Hamlin' that the church people have purchased, and we had all the chants but the *Te Deum*. Mr. Goddard took the first part of the service, Mr. Haskins the latter. I read the ante-communion, and George the epistle, and Mr. Miller preached a capitally good sermon from: 'That My joy may be in you, and that your joy may be full.' The offertory alms amounted to $15.75. George gave notice of confirmation and communion for next Sunday.

"I dined with Mr. and Mrs. Hussey at their hotel (kept by a Mormon to whom and his wife I was introduced), last Friday, and in the evening rode up with them to Camp Douglas, two and a half miles away. Mr. Goddard is going up with Mr. Haskins to preach at camp, at 5 P. M. to-day.

" The Husseys have two children, Charlie and Katie. Mr. Tracy and wife and three children, Theodore, Mary and Willie, also board at the same place. Mrs. T. is a communicant of the church from Placerville, California, and has been here only about six weeks. Charlie and Theodore attend school. They have arranged to have Mr. Haskins take charge of the day school, spending an hour or more a day in it, Sarah, at thirty-five dollars a month, take the advanced room, and Miss Wells at twenty-five a month, teach the little ones. By to-morrow they expect to have as many as thirty-five scholars."

" Salt Lake City, July 10, 1867.

" Yesterday two letters arrived from you, of date respectively of 20th, and 23d of June. The shortest time in which letters can come from New York, I believe, is fifteen days. Your last one came in sixteen days. On Sunday evening Messrs. Goddard and Miller read service and I preached. A hundred and twenty-five persons were present. On Monday estimates were made concerning the day school. Expenditures for teaching for a year will be $720, rent $660. It is estimated that there will be a deficit of $1,000 in the funds for carrying it on for one year. I have told them to go on, and shall appropriate the one thousand dollars that Mr. Wolfe offers me to the meeting of this deficit. Mr. Haskins yesterday reported to me thirty-five scholars in attendance. They opened July 1st with sixteen. Mr. Haskins says that Sarah does very nicely and is much liked. We are hoping that Miss Wells, the other teacher (once a Mormon), will soon be baptized and confirmed. She came across the plains when she was six years of age. The Mormons entered this valley just twenty years ago the 24th of this month. They hold marked celebrations of the event every 24th of July. There are, therefore, young men and young women here who have never seen aught of the outside world, who have never witnessed Christian worship of any kind whatever, who have been taught (and from specimens here they may well believe) that all Gentiles are a cheating, blasphemous, licentious set of men. One great duty we have to do is, with God's help and blessing, to show these young Mormons by our lives and conversation that we are the pure, just, peaceable, and loving people that, if we are Christ's true disciples, we ought to be. Meanwhile, be it said, there seems to be less profanity, rowdyism, rampant and noisy wickedness among the young Mormons than among the youth of any other town or city where I've been. Drunkenness is a crime almost unknown among them. They exceed the Methodists in their expressions of equality and affection, in 'brothering' and 'sistering' everybody. The other day Haskins had occasion to ask a little boy in school for his name. 'Charlie Wright, sir,' he replied.

"'What is your father's name, my boy?' said Mr. Haskins. The boy, who is about eight or nine years of age, said: 'Brother Wright, sir.' Haskins with difficulty kept back a smile. He knew he had a Mormon boy there sure.

"Yesterday morning at six and a half o'clock Miller left us for Boise City. He will probably reach there tomorrow night or Friday morning. In a Boise paper of June 28th I found this paragraph: 'The Episcopal church of this place is being cleaned, curtained, and carpeted.' I am glad to believe, therefore, that the Boise

church people are getting ready to welcome Mr. Miller.
During this week George is having a chancel rail, a communion table, and a lectern put into Independence Hall.
Mr. Hussey and he are also talking of having the walls
shaded and the seats stained, to make the place churchly
and attractive.   Next Monday Mrs. Hamilton goes away
for a time, and Nelly will probably have to play at the
services in the interim.

"Yesterday, George, Mr. Hussey, and myself called on
Brigham Young. As we went up the street we met Mr.
Stenhouse, the editor of the *Telegraph* (Mormon paper),
and afterwards Mr. Hooper, late delegate to Congress.
Mr. Stenhouse is a fat and talkative man. He said to
me, ' You will find a great field for work in Montana,
sir, a hard field ; as Mr. Foote will find a hard work here.
Mr. Foote's will be harder too on account of us Mormons. He'll find us fixed and hard to be moved.' He
added, ' I haven't had the pleasure of attending your services, yet ; you have them at the same time as ours.' ' O
yes,' I said, ' so do bankers and business men have their
offices open at the same time. We must elect between
them.' When we came back from Mr. Young's Mr. S.
again met us. ' Did the president ask you to preach in
the Tabernacle ?' he asked. ' No,' I replied. ' Strange,' he
said, ' he must have been absent-minded ; he always is very
liberal and invites all to preach for him.' Then he went
on rambling, telling of a Bishop Jaynes and a Bishop
Simpson (Methodists), who had been here. Finally he
got to talking of a new house he is building. ' I'm building it for some of you Gentiles, Mr. Foote. It's on one
of the best sites in the city. I want you Gentiles to
have fine sites and comfortable houses, for we think you
are cut off from many of the sources of happiness that
we enjoy.'

" Mr. Young did some time ago invite George to preach in the Tabernacle, but George, very wisely I think, declined.

" Well, we went on to Mr. Young's, to his office. As we neared the gate he was coming out, comfortably dressed in white coat and vest and linen trousers, with turn-over collar, black cravat, straw hat, green goggles (used only for outdoor walks, to save the eyes from the glaring reflection of the sunlight), good watch-chain, umbrella under his arm, and light gaiters on his feet. He has a pleasant face and voice, is somewhat corpulent in person, is of medium height, and has gray eyes, sandy whiskers, and light brown hair, with only a few gray lines in it here and there. Mr. Hussey said, ' We were just coming in to pay our respects, President Young; Bishop Tuttle, President Young.' ' How d'ye do, Bishop Tuttle ? ' said the president. As he called me bishop, I answered, ' How d'ye do, President Young ? ' Then I added, ' You are going out, sir, and doubtless have an engagement. We'll call at another time.' ' Never mind,' he said, ' walk in now, I'll be glad to see you.' So we turned, he leading the way to his office. As we entered he introduced us pleasantly to three persons, calling me Bishop Tuttle every time. The persons were an older brother of his, a Mr. Calder, and one of the apostles, a Mr. Cannon. When we had seated ourselves the president asked : ' Are you just from the States ? ' ' Yes, sir,' I answered. ' I didn't know but that you might be from Montana,' he said. ' No, sir,' I replied, ' I shall go to Montana, God willing, next week.' ' From what State are you, sir ? ' said he. ' From New York,' I said, ' born and bred among the Catskill Mountains.' ' Ah,' said he, ' my father came from the Catskill Mountains. I was born in Vermont, but was brought up in Chenango County, New York.' George made some remark about the music, banners, and celebration of the 4th of July, which reminded him, he said, that we were in the United States. 'Perhaps so,' said Young, 'but they rather seem to me to be the Disunited States, for I see by the morning telegrams that the most rigorous military despotism is to be enforced in the South.' Turning to me, he said, 'Have you read the morning news?' I said, 'Not very minutely.' Then he went on for some time, speaking quite well on Mexican affairs, and on the execution of Maximilian and Santa Anna. We were in a room that resembled most a lawyer's large office, with iron safes, and tables, and pigeon holes by the hundred, filled with filed papers. On the walls were portraits of all the Mormon leaders. Young went to a desk, unlocked it, and took something out. Coming back he said : 'Have you seen any of the Green River gold?' (There is great excitement here about these mines, which, it is said, have been all along known to Brigham, but which only now he is allowing Mormons to open.) Taking the piece of gold, as large as my two fingers, from Young, Mr. Hussey said : 'It seems to be of fine quality.' 'The finest gold,' quickly rejoined Young, 'that I ever saw in my life.' Then checking himself, with the memory perhaps that he was (or that he ought to appear to us to be) a saint and a prophet, he added : 'But I am not a judge of gold, I know very little about it.' After a pause, leaning forward in his chair and fixing a keen eye on George he said : 'Mr. Foote, I want to ask you one question, and if need be, make an explanation. I am told that you have heard it said that I have taken the property of Amasa Lyman' (Lyman is one of the apostles, but is somewhat heterodox, and is now in ill-odor with Brigham. Some say he has started a schism and has left the terri-

tory) ; ' is it so ? ' ' No,' said George, ' I have heard no
such thing.' ' Two ladies told me that this report was
made and that you were present and heard it.' ' No,'
said Mr. Foote, ' I have heard no such report, perhaps
Mr. Haskins may have been the man, it was not I.' ' O
well,' said Young, ' I merely wanted to make explanation,
if you were the man.' There the matter dropped. As
we rose to come away and were shaking hands, Young
said to George : ' Mr. Foote, I want to say to you what
I said to the Catholic priest when he came here ; if you
hear rumors flying about touching me or this people,
come right here to me with them and I will always set
things right. That's the best way.' We were most
civilly and courteously treated in this call, but I was not
asked to call again. In voice and conversation and manner Mr. Young seemed pleasant and courteous and far
less coarse than when he is speaking in public. I did
not detect any violation of grammar or of good sense or
of good taste on his part during our call. He is so
powerful a man in everything here, and so unscrupulous
a man, I fear, in most things, that my policy will be to
have as little as possible to do with him. With his keen-
sightedness he must know, that if not in will yet in
reality, by our services and our school, we are putting
our clutches to his very throat."

" *Salt Lake City, July 14, 1867.*
" Wednesday afternoon I called on the Gilberts here.
They are Gentiles, living in a house which they bought
of Mormons, and the fitting up of which I observed. It
was built for a man with two wives. Entering the hall,
on either hand I found a sitting-room and off from it a
bedroom, while lying back was the long dining hall, suitable for the united family. Thus the Mormon houses,

many of them, are built. They are elongated structures, with several doors for entrance, and a suite of rooms for one family corresponding to each door. Somewhere behind, generally, is a dining-room, one for all. Sometimes, however, the Mormon man has his wives in different houses. One is in this little house, another in that, one in a corner of the yard, another in the next street, another in a farm house in the country.

" Last Thursday I rode out with Mr. and Mrs. Hussey. They board with a Mormon, Mr. Townsend, who has two wives. No. 2 is the active landlady. Mr. and Mrs. H. said to me, ' Mrs. Townsend No. 2 is very melancholy nowadays.' ' Ah,' said I, ' why ? ' ' Because Mr. T. is going to take a new wife,' they said. ' We shall probably soon have No. 3, a bride, in our house. No. 2 is in tears over it and yesterday called on Heber Kimball about it. To-day Kimball called to see her, and to-morrow she is going to see President Young.' ' Well,' I said, ' I feel sorry for No. 2.' ' I don't,' said Mrs. H. ' She is only being treated as she treated No. 1. Now she is in tears, while No. 1 is quite serene, or quite liking it that the sway of No. 2, like her own, shall be broken.' What women can be happy under such a system as this ?

" We rode three miles out to the Warm and Hot Springs. They are both sulphur springs. The Warm are about a mile and a half out, and baths, tubs, shower and plunge, are there provided. I have not yet tried them. The temperature of the water is ninety-five degrees, and would be to me, I fear, enervatingly warm. The Hot Springs are most remarkable; clear, limpid water pours forth abundantly from a hillside, through the chasm of rock, the temperature of it one hundred and ninety degrees. It is too hot for you to bear your hand in, and precipitates the sulphur with which it is impreg-

nated in the richest, clearest deposit of green I ever saw.
The particles of the precipitated sulphur cling to each
other and resemble long seaweeds in the bottom of the
current. This water, outrunning, makes a large lake,
that covers hundreds of acres, in which, as being so strong
of sulphur, no fish live, but over which I saw a pelican
and quantities of wild ducks swimming, as we went up.
It was a very strange sensation to me to put my fingers
into that limpid water, bubbling out from the chasm, and
to find it so hot that I couldn't hold them in it.

" Thursday I called on Mrs. Durant. She is a churchwoman, has been here some years, and is intensely anti-
Mormon. She assured me that the Mormon children,
on the sly, will swear wickedly, and that among each
other they are the most vulgar and obscene of all children. ' My little boy has often,' she said, ' come and told
me what the children say to each other, and their talk is
horrid. For this reason I have never let my boy (eight
years old) go to Mormon schools. At home, among
the Mormons, there is no discipline whatever. The
different mothers in the same family are quite jealous of
each other's interference over the children ; the father is
indifferent; so the children grow to be the most disobedient, undisciplined, ill-mannered of children.' ' Do
you know any of the Mormon women ? ' I asked. ' O
yes, my neighbors here are all Mormons, and some of
the women around me I like very much. They are most
kind and good. But my heart aches for them. There is
Mrs. Beattie in that neat cottage yonder, across the street.
Her husband has taken another wife and she has to submit to it. He and she are Americans ; they came from
St. Joseph, Mo., and are most respectably connected.
She is one of the best women in the world. Yesterday
among other things she said to me, ' I've lost all con-

fidence in man.' But that is all she would say. There's
Mrs. A., who used to be my neighbor; one of the best
and kindest women I ever knew. When she and Mr. A.
used to be here they were my best friends and quite
happy. I used to talk with her about polygamy, and she
vowed that she would take my advice and never let
Mr. A. take another wife. He and she used to argue the
question of polygamy night after night, sitting up till
after midnight. They moved away. Last week Mrs. A.,
visiting in the city, came to see me. She was a changed,
downcast, spiritless woman. In conversation she let out
to me that her convictions about polygamy had changed.
She thought it right, a divine institution, commanded of
God Himself; and believed that neither she nor her husband could occupy as blissful a place in the future world
without practicing it, as they would by practicing it. I
said, ' There, Mrs. A., don't say anything more. I know
why you are so changed and look so wearied and spiritless. Mr. A. has taken another wife, I see.' ' When a
man dies, how are the several wives and families supported?' I asked her. ' O,' she said, ' each woman has to
help support herself and her children by washing, sewing,
or teaching, and that too even when the husband is alive.
When the women get old and helpless they are often
destitute and actually beggars.'

"At 6:30 to-morrow morning Mr. Goddard and I start
for Montana. A large mail came in to-night, probably
bringing a letter from you; but it is not overhauled, and
off I must go leaving your precious letter to be forwarded
by George."

CHAPTER VI

MONTANA

For nearly fourteen years I was the Bishop of Montana, having jurisdiction, also, in Utah and Idaho. I was proud of the appellation. The experience of the fourteen years deepened the feeling of pride. Some of the dearest friends that my life has been blessed with live in Montana. I have always ventured the prediction that Montana will become the most prosperous and most populous of the states of the far Northwest.

In Montana, humanly speaking, I built on no other man's foundation. In Idaho Bishop Scott and the Rev. Mr. Fackler had preceded me. In Utah Messrs. Foote and Haskins were at work two months before I came. But in Montana, no clergyman of the Church before me had ever so much as set foot. For the first year I stayed and did a settled pastor's duty in its capital, living in a log cabin with my faithful cat " Dick " as my only companion. Ah, beautiful territory of the mountains! What buoyant years to us both were those we passed together. I recall most vividly their rude robustness, their unmeasured hopefulness, their astounding vigor, their audacious unconventionality! Even the errors and imperfections belonging to them we are not ashamed of. Neither the dignity of Statehood, now becomingly enwrapping you, nor the quiescent soberness of my own afternoon of life, is called upon to blush for them. We were young together. We made mistakes We did not always restrain excesses as we ought. But God did not desert us, and He has overruled for good. All thanks and praise be to His Holy Name!

Montana has an area of 145,000 square miles, and had a population of about 30,000 when I entered it. It had two large towns, Virginia City and Helena, and some smaller ones, Bannack, Blackfoot, Deer Lodge, Missoula, Bozeman and Fort Benton. It had been organized into a Territory of the United States three years before, in May, 1864. Before that its area was comprised in the territory of Idaho. Idaho was made a Territory of the United States in March, 1863.

Montana may be said to have first become a dwelling-place for white inhabitants in 1862. Lewis & Clark's famous expedition through it had taken place in 1805-6. In the years afterwards a few hardy explorers and some scattered hunters, trappers, and fur traders visited the region now embraced in its limits. In the '40s Jesuit missionaries to the Cœur d' Alene and Flathead Indians may have penetrated its borders. In the '50s some settlers were in the Hell Gate valley near what is now Missoula; and James Stuart and his brother Granville had come to Deer Lodge. But Montana as an abode for whites really dates from 1862. In the summer of that year gold was found upon Grasshopper Creek, near what is now the town of Bannack. The marked discoveries of gold of our western country have been as follows: California, 1849; Pike's Peak, Colorado, 1859; the Northern Mines of Idaho, known as the Orofino and Florence diggings, 1861; the Grasshopper diggings of Montana, 1862. And about the same time with the last, the Boise Basin diggings at Idaho City, Idaho. The Bannack mines were discovered by a party of Colorado prospectors who were on their way to the Florence diggings, but had been delayed or turned out of their course by impassable roads or discouraging reports. Earlier than the time of their discovery gold had been found near Deer Lodge. At this time all the present area of Montana east of the main range of the Rocky Mountains was a part of Dakota. All west was part of Washington. In the winter of 1862-3 there were three hundred and seventy-three men and thirty-seven women residents in and near Bannack ; and thirty-seven men and two women in and near Fort Benton, making four hundred and ten men and thirty-nine women in all, in that portion, now of Montana, then of Dakota, east of the mountains. In the same winter there were sixty-nine men and eight women in Missoula County, making one hundred and ninety-four men and twenty-six women in that portion now of Montana, then of Washington, west of the mountains ; a total population, in all, for Montana, of six hundred and four men and sixty-five women.

The early days of Montana were such as to try men's souls. The Civil War was raging and its tempestuous billows threw not a few lawless men as driftwood into the mountain wilderness. The mines of California, Colorado and Idaho sent not only their restless and hardy, but also their reckless and hardened, denizens upon stampedes to the new diggings. A mining community is eminently excitable, unruly, defiant, without fear of God or man. Add to all this that Yankton, the capital of Dakota, and so the centre from which restraint of civil authority must issue, was two thousand, two hundred miles away from the Bannack mines, and it will readily be understood what a fierce and turbulent cauldron life in Montana in the early days must have been. In the summer of 1863 rich mines were found in Alder Gulch, near the head of which Virginia City was built. So rich were the placers of this gulch that out of it one hundred and twenty millions of gold are computed to have been taken.

The year 1863 was a frightful one. The desperadoes were leagued together in a secret band for the purposes of robbery and murder. How thoroughly and efficiently they were organized was not known till afterwards, when it was disclosed that Plummer, the lawfully elected sheriff and the civil officer sworn to preserve order, was the actual leader of the band. He was a man of attractive address and polished manners ; in the language of the mountains " a perfect gentleman," and so won his way to the post of honor in the shrievalty. But his heart was black with the indulgence of all criminal passions, and when roused to anger or revenge he was a very demon. He was accounted the best and quickest pistol-shot in the mountains. A secret band of highwaymen, led by such a man, was a most formidable agent of violence and murder.

There were good men and true, however rude and wild, among the Montana frontiersmen. In the fall and winter of 1863 they began to ask themselves, " What is to be done ? " Robberies and murders were frightfully frequent. If the perpetrators were suspected and arrested, neither witnesses dared to testify nor jurors to convict. The evil-doers carried everything with a high hand, and the community was as a paralyzed victim under the reign of terror that prevailed.

Then a few brave men in Virginia City and in Bannack got together and said, " This must be stopped." They met and planned and counseled and the " Vigilance Committee " was formed.

The supporters of law and order knew that they were launching into conflict with most formidable adversaries. And they did not know how many or who of the people living in cabins by their side were linked with the secret band of the roughs. They were conscious of the fearful personal risk they were taking, but the crisis must be met, the determination must be made whether good or evil was to rule supreme in the community. Evil, thus far, had been high handed and had predominated; we must see now, said they, if it is to continue thus to hold sway.

They began with the arrest of George Ives, a well-known robber, and many times a murderer. They brought him to Nevada City, in Alder Gulch, a mile or two below Virginia City, on the night of December 18, 1863. He was accorded a trial, a most unique one. It continued for three days. Hundreds of resolute miners, gathered about, constituted the real jury and executive. Twenty-four of their number, chosen specially to hear the evidence and to retire to pass upon it, were a jury precedent. The judge to guide proceedings sat in a wagon, as his bench of justice. Two or three lawyers defended the criminal, two conducted the prosecution. All was done in the open air. At midday, as is often the case in the mountains, the bright December sun was as warm as that of October. Towards night a large fire of logs was built for comfort. The crisis had come. The struggle had reached its culmination. The strain of excitement was painfully intense. A special guard of scores of stern and fearless miners protected the court. But there were scores and even hundreds of desperadoes and their sympathizers in the crowd. Just at nightfall and as the moon rose, on the 21st, the twenty-four jurors retired. In half an hour they returned with their decision of " guilty," the vote having stood twenty-three to one.

The motion was made, " That the decision of the jury be adopted as our verdict." Counsel for the prisoner and many others attempted to interpose motions and acts of delay and postponement. Doubtless members of the secret gang intended by themselves and with their fellows to organize and push a rescue in the night. The miners determinedly passed the motion to adopt the verdict.

That done, the most critical time of all came. The execution of the verdict,—when shall it be, and by whom, and how? Delay and irresolution here would be fraught with unspeakable results of bloody contention. At that supreme moment one of the bravest deeds ever done by man was witnessed. Col. Wilbur F. Sanders, since United States senator from Montana, one of the counsel for the prosecution, young and of slender build, mounted the wagon by the side of the judge. Having recited that the prisoner had been declared guilty of the crimes of robbery and murder he ended his speech with these words: " I move that George Ives be forthwith hung by the neck until he is dead."

The daring young advocate took his life in his hands when he thus exposed himself in those evening shadows. Doubtless a hundred angry and desperate men were within a few feet of him, armed to the teeth, of quick and unerring aim, any one of whom would have been glad to shoot him down when speaking. But his very boldness cowed them and his promptness disconcerted them. The miners at once affirmed and adopted the motion, and Sanders' timely and intelligent bravery saved the bloodshed which a fierce contention begotten of delay would have produced. A gallows was impro- vised by means of a stout pine log run out from the end of an unfinished building. A dry-goods box served for the trap. Within fifty-eight minutes from the close of Sanders' speech the ghastly body of Ives was dangling

lifeless in the moonlight, and the abhorrent reign of violence and wickedness in Montana had received a determined check. Soon after Ives' death it was discovered
who the members of the blood-stained gang were. It
was learned that Plummer was actually their leader.

During the few months succeeding, the Vigilantes captured and executed no less than twenty-nine of these robbers and murderers, including of course their chief. The
self-constituted guardians of law and order acted with a
secrecy, a swiftness, and an inflexible determination to do
duty, that struck terror to the hearts of all the evil-doers.

To this day there is no historic record of who were
the leaders or members of the " Committee." Under the
circumstances it is wonderful how they were able to keep
themselves free from the sway of passion and revenge.
Of all the twenty-nine to whom they adjudged the penalty of death, there was only one, a man named Slade,
who had not been guilty of murder within the territory.
In every case save his, guilt would have been declared by
any jury impaneled under the provisions of the civil
law. Slade was hung because of his extreme viciousness,
his demoniac recklessness when in drink, his contemp-
tuous disregard of repeated warnings, and his savage defiance of authority and order. Plummer's gang had
slaughtered one hundred and two victims before the
community was roused to its effectual course of righteous
retribution. I do not see how the wholesome work could
have been done in any other way.

When Montana was organized, in May, 1864, the
righteous deaths of the score of dreaded miscreants, and
the hurried departure of other scores to regions better
suited for the plying of their nefarious vocation, left the
new territory well prepared for the regulations and re-
straints of civil law.

Three years after, I entered it, and for thirteen years I was quite familiar with all its inhabitants. I never heard the work of the " Vigilantes " alluded to by them in terms other than of gratitude and reverence. The saving of Montana to law and order in the critical time of 1863, was in morals a regeneration, and in commercial value the saving of millions of treasure to the future common. wealth.

I refer to my letters to Mrs. Tuttle for my first impressions of Montana.

" *Virginia City, Montana, July 19, 1867.*

" Mr. Goddard and I are here safe and well. We left Salt Lake at 6:30 A. M., on Monday last. and arrived here at 5 P. M., yesterday (Thursday). Throughout Monday we rode, much afflicted with heat and dust, through Mormon settlements. Their crops looked very fine. Some of their villages were very prepossessing, and everywhere we saw the delightful sight of streams of living water carried about their streets and yards and farms. These Mormons in the settlements outside of Salt Lake honestly believe that Brigham Young is a prophet inspired of heaven. They are ready to obey him implicitly in all things. While, therefore, I think his strength is breaking a little in Salt Lake City, I feel quite sure that there are thousands and ten thousands in the country ready to do all his biddings, and almost to worship him. On Tuesday, at 1:30 A. M., we entered Idaho Territory and all Tuesday and part of Wednesday rode through it. About 9 P. M. we arrived at Snake River, which, swollen, had carried the bridge away, over which we must be ferried in a flat-boat. A rope is stretched from one side of the river to the other, and two ropes from bow and stern of the flat-boat are attached to

it with pullies lying along the one rope. The bow rope
is taut and the stern rope more lax, so that the boat presents its broadside at an angle to the current. In this
way the current makes the propelling force and carries
us across. The Snake's current was the swiftest I was
ever on, except the 'Rapids' going to Montreal. The force
of it propelled us with astonishing rapidity. I was somewhat timid. Should the small bow-rope break (and a
terrible strain was on it), the boat would be swamped, and
we plunged into the raging flood. I was ready to fling
off my boots and coat at any time and try my chances
swimming ; though I confessed to myself that in such a
torrent, wide, rocky, steep-banked, my chances would be
little better than those of Mr. Goddard, who does not
swim. I was helped to my timidity by a remark of one
of the ferrymen, that the boat had got away from
them twice that day. But thanks to God for His love
and protection, we've been saved from and amidst all besetting perils.

"Within half an hour after crossing the Snake, and
while following along its valley, we were subjected to as
fearful an attack as has yet been made upon us. But
don't be frightened, the attacking party consisted of
about ten millions of mosquitoes. We had been warned
by a Jew riding with us out from Salt Lake, to provide
ourselves with 'bars,' and so strongly did he insist upon
the necessity of such protection that at Ogden City, forty
miles from Salt Lake, Mr. Goddard got a 'bar.' The
Jew was a Mason and so had influence with Mr.
Goddard as a brother Mason. I thought I could get
along without a bar, and so did not get one. But on
the Snake bitterly did I repent not doing so. Mr. G.
in gloves and bar bade defiance to the attacking battalions
and sat as quiet and serene as in his wife's parlor in Port-

landville. The little Jew laughed and chuckled from under his ponderous veil and said, ' Dat's de way, ye see, people tell oder people de trut. We preach to 'em about following dis and dat way, and dey don't believe us. Do de mosquitoes trouble you some, eh?'

"After a time we got out of the mosquito region. Soon I went bobbing about in sleep, and my hat went off and out the window. ' Hold up, driver,' I cried, ' I've lost my hat.' ' Whoa!' he said. I then went back and got my hat, and pulling it well over my brows thought I would now keep it safe. But bobbing and bobbing I must have been for some time in refreshing sleep after my late ' fight,' when, suddenly waking, I found my head cold. I shouted, ' Hold up, driver, where's my hat?' ' Whoa!' he cried; ' bother take ye, why don't you keep hold of your hat?' I went back rods and rods, but found no hat. So my dear old Morris hat is out among the sage bushes on the plains of Idaho! I tied a handkerchief about my head and came on.

"About 1 P. M., on Wednesday, we crossed the ' divide,' the summit of the main Rocky Mountain range, and entered Montana. It grew cold, and we found shawls and blankets not at all uncomfortable. By dark a cold rain set in and when we reached Beaver Head Cañon, at 9:20 P. M., the driver concluded that we had better wait till morning before pushing on. We were then fifty-seven miles from Virginia City. Accordingly, Mr. Goddard and I, after supper on pork and beans, lay down in our blankets on the station floor. I slept very soundly, Mr. G. not so well. Waking at 3:30 A. M., and getting up to be ready for an early start, we were astonished on opening the door to see rocks and trees and roofs and fields as white with snow as in midwinter. Two inches of snow were lying on the earth, and this was the morning of the 18th of July. ' Humph!' says sleepy Mr. Goddard, ' beautiful country this, isn't it ? '

" Montana pleases me more than the other territories for these two special reasons. First, there are trees here, many of the mountains and nearly all the ravines being plentifully covered with mountain pine. Secondly, there are plenty of living springs and streams of water, the freshest, coolest, purest, sweetest in the world. This is the best country for butter-making that can be found. Only here, since I left Otsego County, have I found sweet, delicious butter. The grasses are wonderfully rich and nutritious. A Dr. Cochrane from Brooklyn, whom I met last night, assures me that horses will work and keep in good order on the grass, as well as in other countries on a half bushel of oats, each, daily. It would do you good to see how sleek and fat and well-pleased all the cows and oxen look. If the grasshopper would only keep away, the wheat crop and oat crop of this territory would always be abundant. Potatoes are excellent in quantity and quality. Judge Hosmer says he has paid sixty cents a pound for potatoes. Now they are four cents a pound.

" We reached here, four hundred and fifty-four miles from Salt Lake, at 5 P. M., Thursday. For the last ten miles we came up Alder Creek, along which are gulch mines. On both sides of the creek the earth has been dug and thrown up and washed out, and it is still being so treated. Water in ditches and sluices is carried from the creek in all directions along the banks ; then the dirt is dug up and thrown into long boxes made of pine boards, and flowing water is let through them. The water washes away the dirt, and the gold particles, being heavy, are left on the box bottoms. The usual currency in all stores here is gold dust. Every little shop has its pair of balances and takes dust in return for goods, at eighteen dollars an ounce. Some dust is worth more, some less; but in buying and selling at stores this is the standard. At the banks they have tests for the dust, and will pay for it only its intrinsic worth, as tested. Dust here, as compared with greenbacks, is at fifteen per cent. premium. For instance, I went to a store and bought a hat. The price was $8, or $9.20 greenbacks. Every man carries a little buckskin pouch, and in that his money, that is, gold dust. There is a nugget here in the bank, found a few days ago, of solid gold worth about $420. It weighs nearly two pounds.

" We found log cabins and mining tents scattered along the gulch as we came on to Virginia City. Two little towns in the suburbs, Nevada and Junction, will have to be looked after by the rector who settles here. When we arrived, our first work was to get supper, our next to take a bath. The bath, with bootblacking and clothes-cleaning, cost me $2.25. Mr. G. had a shampoo, and his bill was three dollars.

" Virginia City is a town of numerous log cabins, perhaps a half dozen frame houses, a few stone stores, and a population, I think, of about two thousand, certainly not more. We stop at the ' Planter's House,' the Fifth Avenue Hotel of the place. Our bedroom is about twelve feet square, and in it are one double, and two single beds. Mr. G. and I occupy the double. As there is need, the landlord sends whom he will into the cots. No lock is on the door; no wash bowl or pitcher in the room. Every morning we go down to the office to wash, wiping our faces on the office towel. The nights are deliciously cool, and stowed under a sheet, two blankets, and a coverlid, we have most delightful snoozes.

" Thursday evening Mr. E. S. Calhoun, a young man,

called, bringing to me a letter of introduction from the
Rev. Dr. Washburn of New York City.   Dr. W. speaks
of Mr. C. as the son of one of the most prominent of his
church members.   On Friday I began calling some.   I
called on Mr. Calhoun, who is clerk in a store.   He
showed me the records of the ' Episcopalians ' here.   It
appears that an Englishman, Professor Dimsdale, began
reading service here more than a year ago.   He was a
good reader and attracted a little congregation, though
at first he made them smile somewhat, as, reading for
several Sundays from the English Prayer-Book, he
prayed most loyally for the Queen and entirely ignored
the President.   He afterwards fell into bad habits and
died here.   About six weeks ago the school-teacher, Mr.
Marshall, a Baptist, essayed to read service.   A churchwoman tells me he made most sorry work of it.   She
often had to interrupt and direct him in it.   No Church
clergyman, to the knowledge of these people, has ever set
foot within the limits of this territory before our coming.
The people here, however, in April last met together and
organized themselves as well as they could under the
name of ' St. Paul's Church,' electing eight vestrymen.
To-day they are improvising robing-room, lectern, seats,
etc., in an upper room, for our services to-morrow.

"I next called at the post-office on Dr. Gibson, the
postmaster.   Mr. Hussey had given me letters to him.
He, though a Unitarian, and his wife a Presbyterian, is
one of the new vestrymen, and he seems to be a most
kind and good man.   Mrs. G., coming two years ago,
was the first woman here.   Gold was discovered in June,
1863, and the first log house (tents had been used before)
was put up in August of that year.   For a long time
there were no floors in the cabins but mother earth.
Afterwards green raw-hides (buffalo, etc.), stretched on

pins and allowed to dry, were the Brussels carpet for the ' aristocrats.'

" I then called on Governor Smith. He is a stout, pleasant-looking young man, of about five-and-thirty, dressed in gray, and with ' hail-fellow-well-met ' manners. He is a Baptist and his wife a Presbyterian. She and his three little children have just come here to live.

" Since I began writing Judge Hosmer has called with Mr. Duncan, the Methodist minister. Mr. D. says that besides himself (he is only a local preacher), there is only one Methodist preacher in this territory, viz., Mr. Hough at Helena. The Presbyterians, he says, have not one man in the territory, nor the Baptists. The Roman Catholics have several priests, having established their Indian missions in the northern part of the territory nearly thirty years ago.

" In spite of all the drawbacks of this town, its cold, its present treelessness, its roughness, its log cabins, you and I, if it be God's will for us to live and work here, could be very happy. Kind hearts are here, cultivated women are here, intelligent society is here, some children are here ; and such a field for immediate faithful Church work as I never before saw. Now, I want to throw out a suggestion to you and to ask you a question. The more I think of it the more I feel as if it would be my duty to stay in my diocese this winter and do missionary work in Montana until I can get men to come. It seems as if, after visiting Bridger, September 22d, Salt Lake the 29th, and Idaho in October, I ought to come right back here and work, Mr. G. and I taking Helena and Virginia into our hands at once. Then, September 1, 1868, D. V., I will come East to attend General Convention ; and in November bring you and baby here. This also will save me the expenses of two trips ; all traveling expenses outside of my jurisdiction coming from my own pocket. From inclination I do not propose this, but from duty I may feel that I must do it. What do you think and say?

" A great work opens for the Church in this territory. I ought to have four men here at once, one here, one in Helena, one at Bannack and Argenta, and one at Deer Lodge. Think of it, only one Protestant minister now in all this territory!

" We are 6,700 feet above the level of the sea; 500 feet higher than the ' Tip Top House' on Mt. Washington.

" Chinamen do nearly all the laundry work, and do it very neatly, too. Chinese servants are quite in vogue; men, no women, are here. Rents are high, though not as high as heretofore. This hotel, primitive as it is, rents for $200 a month. A Masonic Hall of stone, to cost $22,000, is going up, the ground floor of which is to be rented to a mercantile firm for $4,000 a year."

The above account concerning ministers is not strictly correct. A Rev. Mr. Baxter, of the Methodist Church, South, had a Sunday-school and was gathering a congregation in Helena. And in the same town a Professor Campbell, engaged in teaching school, a Campbellite, or Christian preacher, some Sundays exercised his vocation. A Presbyterian minister, also, named Smith, had preached somewhat in Virginia City and had commenced the erection of a log church there. Before any satisfactory progress had been made, however, he had abandoned everything.

I was in Montana; in its capital city, a town four years old. Business buildings and residences were nearly all of logs. Almost every other one of the former was a saloon. Two or three of these latter were " hurdy-gurdy " houses, where women were in attendance for keeping up dancing

and all night revels. There was no church spire anywhere. The Roman Catholic priest held services in a
log structure surmounted by a cross, where a suspended
steel triangle served for a bell. There was a bend in the
Alder Gulch here and the town seemed flung down into
this crook. There were no vehicles in the streets such
as I had been used to. Instead, there were huge freight
wagons, from which goods were being discharged, that
had been dragged five hundred miles from Salt Lake, or
two hundred and sixty-five miles from Fort Benton on
the Missouri River.

The ox-teams—from six yoke of oxen to fifteen yoke
per wagon,—stood patiently or lay down chewing their
cud till the cruel lash of the " bull whacker " should rouse
and start them on; the sidewalks were crowded with
jostling men; while not a few on horseback, be-pistoled
and be-knived, passed along the street. Here Mr.
Goddard and I stayed for nearly three weeks, officiating
for three Sundays in an upper room that had been used
for one branch of the Legislature and was hence called
the council chamber. Our service of July 21st was the
first ever held by one of our clergy in Montana. For
Sunday, August 4th, we went over to Helena, one hundred and twenty-five miles distant, and there I left Mr.
Goddard, while I returned to Virginia City. At the
latter place I stayed till September 22d; then I went on
my planned trip to Fort Bridger, Salt Lake, and Idaho.
Sense of duty seemed to make it imperative that I should
stay for the winter and do work in Montana, and my
wife, doing as she has done all our married life, cheerfully approved of my decision, though it was to cost us
sixteen months of painful separation.

I give here some extracts from my letters of this period
from Virginia City :

" July 21, 1867.

" I have come up to go to bed, Mr. G. staying below a little to talk to a brother Mason. But I cannot get into bed without stopping to say a few words to you of my loneliness and homesickness. Mr. G., dear, good man, is as kind as kind can be, but for all, I do get lonesome and heartsick. Life seems less dear to me than when I was in our little rectory at home. If it were not that hour by hour the good God sustains me with the sweet consciousness that I am trying to do my duty as in His sight, I should be quite miserable. This morning I awoke crying from a dream that I was in my early boyhood's home, and that my dear mother, in bed, worn thin, grown blind, and dying, only able to recognize me by passing her hand over my face, was whispering, ' My own dear boy.' I have just written to her, telling her of my dream. I am three thousand miles away from you and her and from many dear ones. But after all I do not worry. God will, I know, for Christ's sake, take care of us and will bring us, if we are His faithful ones, to His home, some time.

" I have just visited a sick woman who sent for me. Her name is Donaldson ; she is the wife of a merchant here from St. Louis, a Campbellite ; she is far gone in consumption. It seemed grateful and refreshing to her to have me have prayers with her.

" Chickens here are two dollars apiece. My bill for five days at the ' Planter's ' was twenty-two dollars, twenty dollars for board and two for washing eleven pieces. We now are moved into a cabin owned by Mr. D. W. Tilton, the publisher of the *Montana Post*. The whole of the interior is one room, sixteen feet by twenty-four. There are two beds in the room. In one of these sleep Mr. Goddard and myself, in the other Mr. Tilton and

Mr. Godbe, brother of the Mr. Godbe whom I met at North Platte. A man comes in daily and shakes up rather than makes up our bed. Men rather than women do domestic work here. Mrs. Chapin, our landlady at the Planter's, said she was the only woman in the house. She baked all the pies, and had direct supervision of the chamber work, which was done by a Chinaman.

" I have had to buy a new tooth brush. It cost me a dollar fifty, and is no better than what we buy in Morris for thirty-five cents. I weighed myself last Saturday and brought down one hundred and seventy. I met Mr. Duncan this morning. He tells me he moves away to-morrow, one hundred and sixty-five miles, to Flint Creek. This leaves us in undisputed possession of Protestant Virginia City. No services but ours and the Roman Catholic will now be held here. Ought I not, as in God's sight, to preoccupy and hold this place ? "

" *Virginia City, Montana, July 27, 1867.*
" In the afternoon I called on Mrs. Meagher. She is one of the cleverest women, and most brilliant in conversation, that I have ever met. She is a fine looking woman too, with the blackest eyes and queenliest presence and prettiest face I've seen in the mountains. Her husband, Thomas Francis Meagher, the Irish patriot, was secretary of the territory and acting governor. A few weeks since he was drowned in the Missouri River at Fort Benton, falling into the water from a boat. His body has never been found. Mrs. Meagher was a Miss Townsend of New York City, and once of Orange County. Whether she became so before or after her marriage with General Meagher, she is a Roman Catholic. She will soon return to New York City, going down the river by boat from Fort Benton.

" I've made some inquiries about housekeeping expenses. Flour is ten to thirteen dollars a sack (*i. e.*, $25.00 a barrel), beefsteak is twenty-five cents a pound, butter is fifty cents, coffee and sugar are forty to fifty cents. Wood (four foot) is ten dollars a cord. These are not exorbitant prices by any means. I am sure one can calculate on keeping house with such prices without feeling that one must have at least $20,000 annual income. Servant-girls' wages would be high, I can assure you, forty or fifty dollars a month."

"Virginia City, Montana, July 30, 1867.

" Mr. Miller, under date of July 18th, writes very encouragingly from Boise, closing his letter with an amusing account of the walking powers of the English clergyman, Mr. Pope, who was with us at Salt Lake. I quote from his letter : ' I was just interrupted by the unexpected appearance of the Rev. Arthur F. Pope, Guilford, Surrey, England. If ever another Englishman comes, I will stick to my room. He proposed a " little walk," and we started out and went up through Oregon into Washington, around into Montana, down through Dakota, Colorado, Arizona, and up through Nevada home.' I have seen a Boise paper of the 20th, which speaks of Miller's first services, and publishes the apposite introductory remarks, which he made before the sermon. The editor speaks of him as if he was well pleased with him and the services ; he says he is a plain, sensible gentleman, free from those airs and affectations that stand in the way of usefulness of men from the East of any profession, when they come into the extreme West.

" Sunday afternoon I visited Mrs. Donaldson, and while I was there, two persons came in. One introduced the other to me as the Rev. Mr. King. Mr. K. is a Methodist minister from Colorado, who has come to take charge of Virginia City. He begins work next Sunday, and the Methodists talk of building a church at once. Mr. K. looks hearty and vigorous, but is, I should judge, almost too pronounced and noisy to suit thoughtful people. He has gone to Helena to see Mr. Hough, who is presiding elder of all this Western field."

"Virginia City, Montana, August 3, 1867.

" I have just called on Mr. Marshall, the Baptist, who has been our lay reader. I gave him a Prayer-Book, asked him down to our cabin, and by inquiry found out how he had managed. On the whole, for one totally unacquainted with our services, he got along very well. He said, however, that he always *read the absolution,* and generally one of *Henry Ward Beecher's sermons,* and closed service with extempory prayer! What think you and the old ' Zion' people of that? But he seemed very willing to hear and adopt my suggestions, and I am so well pleased with him that I have licensed him to read service here in my necessary absences.

" Of one perplexity the pastor of a Western parish is entirely freed. Here public opinion is, universally, in favor of the innocence and harmlessness and morality of such amusements as dancing and parlor card-playing. Therefore, if the pastor also himself believe them to be *per se* innocent, he need be not at all troubled lest indulgence in them by one part of his congregation be a scandal to another part. Were you to venture to suggest here, or anywhere in this West, as it seems to me, that it is wrong to dance, people would look at you with mingled feelings of amusement and pity.

" Yesterday Mr. G. and I took our first ride on horseback. We went to Christnot's Mill and Summit, a round distance of twenty miles. I laughed much at Mr. G.; he presented such a John-Gilpin like appearance on horseback. These California horses, that are most used, go at a break-neck pace. Well, we must learn to go horseback. It's the only mode of getting about here. We ascended several high points as we went along; dismounted, and used the opera glass for observation. I can't describe to you the beauties and grandeurs to be seen hereabout. I hope one day you will see them. Think of long, high ranges, stretching hundreds of miles away, with snow on the tops and sides, the peaks bare and bald, many of the slopes wooded, billows on billows, by the thousand, of hills between the ranges, green valleys with streams, deep gorges and cañons. Think of them all and arrange them in mental prospect in the most grand and beautiful ways,—and you have the views we saw yesterday. At Christnot's Mill we dined with Colonel McClure and his wife, from Chambersburg, Pa., who have lately come out, the colonel being a stockholder in the mill. I went through the mill and was delighted with it. An engine of fifty-five horse-power drives four sets of two heavy wheels for crushing the ore. Each wheel weighs twenty-five hundred pounds, and two, fixed on a vertical shaft, revolve horizontally in each tub into which the ore is cast. Water and quicksilver are in the tub, and the quicksilver secures the gold in an amalgam. Some of the gold particles escape through the sieve on the tub, and these are caught by quicksilver spread all along the plates over which the dirty water runs. Then the amalgam is afterwards gathered from the tub and the plates, and the mercury is driven off by heat, leaving the pure gold. That mill can crush a ton of ore an

hour, and each ton yields from twenty-five to forty
dollars worth of gold. The expenses of extracting are
about fifteen dollars a ton, so you see what a steady,
good profit such a mill can make."

August 6th, Mr. Goddard and I went by stage to
Helena, making the distance of one hundred and twenty-
five miles in twenty hours. Helena is another mining
town, flung down in Last Chance Gulch, where in the fall
of 1865 rich placer diggings were discovered. The stam-
pede had made it now to be a larger town than Virginia
City. Besides, it was much nearer to Fort Benton, and
as nearly all the heavy merchandise was coming to Montana, via the Missouri River and Fort Benton, the heavier
wholesale and commission business houses would naturally establish themselves in Helena. Virginia City stren-
uously fought against acknowledgment of the supremacy
of her younger sister, and in after years, by all the means
that she could lay her hands on, resisted the removal of
the capital to Helena. But in those days, before railroads
existed, one with half an eye could see that nearness to
the great Missouri River and its facilities of transportation settled the matter.

Sunday, August 11, 1867, when we entered it and held
the first services of the church, the town was not two
years old. Immediately after, I returned to Virginia
City, while Mr. Goddard remained for a month or two to
serve Helena. Then, induced by urgent calls from
home, he returned to the States by Fort Benton and the
Missouri River. In the summer of 1868, however, with
his wife and child, he returned to Montana, to settle in
Virginia City, there to do two or three years of most important and faithful work. In Helena we found, of Protestants,
two Methodist congregations worshiping, one being of
the Methodist Church, South.

Some further extracts from my letters may be given.

"*Helena, Montana, August 7, 1867.*

"I am to rise every morning at half-past six. This morning I was fifteen minutes late. Generally I read every morning before breakfast a chapter in the Greek Testament. I see by the New York telegrams that Prof. Charles Anthon is dead. I owe much that I am to him. In his death I have lost from this world a kind and tried and valuable friend.

"I'll finish and get this letter into the mail to-morrow morning. It ought to reach you, if the Indians allow, by September 1st.

"Helena is a town of about four thousand inhabitants, pitched, as you might expect, in the bottom of a dirty mining gulch. Fewer log cabins and more frame houses are here than at Virginia City; and this hotel (the International) is really quite comfortable and even genteel in its appointments. We have a room with a double bed just off the ladies' parlor, with a door window opening out upon a pleasant balcony. As I sit here writing, the most delightful balmy air is wafted into the window, though there also comes a confused din of auctioneers and teamsters shouting from the street below. There are here four banks, hundreds of stores, three schools, and three regular religious congregations. I called yesterday on the Rev. Mr. Hough, the Methodist minister, and was pleased to find in him a fellow townsman. He was born and his parents still live in Windham, New York, and for two years he was the Methodist preacher in Windham Centre. He and his wife keep house snugly. He says he writes to their bishops to send no unmarried minister to the West, and to send no man without his wife. Mrs.

H. says that a man and wife can keep house here as
cheaply as a single man can board."

" Helena, Montana, August 11, 1867.

"Anything but Sunday seems this to me, as I sit down
and hear feet moving, chains clanking, teamsters shouting more noisily than other days (because the miners
from the gulches all round come in to-day). A stalwart
negro, ringing a large hand bell, is shouting in front of
this hotel: ' Now, gentlemen, now's your chance. There's
a large stock of goods to be sold just below, in Bridge
Street, consisting of miners' equipments, picks, shovels,
dry goods of all kinds, and mountain trout and salmon,
etc., etc. Sure sale, gen'l'm'n, a man has left the stock to
be cleaned out at auction, whether he gets two cents for
it or not; now's your chance, gen'l'm'n.' A half dozen
teamsters are yelling together, like demons, at their oxen.
Indeed, anything but a calm, quiet Sunday is this. Before breakfast I went up to the post-office and out of the
one or two hundred stores along the streets only one soli-
tary one was closed. That was the ' First National
Bank.'

"Last evening there was a Democratic meeting in
front of this hotel, and the speakers were on the balcony
just outside of our window. It was sickening to see them
drink whiskey and hear the profanity and blasphemy of
their talk, as by twos and threes the speakers would retire
into the room just adjoining us. I feel sad for the country's future, ashamed of the American name. O Father
above, in mercy guide and rule our rulers ; in mercy, in
Thy purity and power, save our country !

"As I went by a hurdy-gurdy house on my way to
address the Sunday-school of the Methodist Church,
South, which meets in the schoolhouse where we held

services to-day, through its doors and windows flung
widely open I saw scores and hundreds of men, and ten
or a dozen women, dancing to the accompaniment of fid-
dles, and drinking and cursing ' between the acts.' Outside the door sprawled a man, dead drunk. Still there
are here, as the congregation this morning showed, many
gentlemen of culture and good breeding, a few accomplished Christian ladies, and some children.

" Now is the time for the Church to act. She must
occupy here at once. If Mr. Goddard does not stay
I shall send off a rousing call for a man to come at
once."

"Virginia City, Montana, August 21, 1867.

" I have just come in from listening to a long speech
from J. M. Cavanaugh, the Democratic candidate for
Congress. The election is to come off September 2d.
He is from Helena, and made on the whole a very fair
speech, stained, however, by a good deal of blackguard-
ism and blasphemy. W. F. Sanders, the Republican
candidate, lives here. We expect a speech from him
Saturday evening, the 31st. This morning I was much
disappointed at getting no letter from you. I took it,
however, quite cheerily, and came home and started,
prayerfully, a sermon from Psalm 107 : 8. I have done
somewhat at it, and hope, please God, to finish it next
Friday and preach it next Sunday. I miss my books
greatly, but mean to try to write a sermon a week without them, because I think it my duty so to do. God will
help me if I pray to Him, and try. Do you know that
never yet in my minister's life have I gone into my study
and commenced work on a sermon without kneeling
down and praying : ' O God, guide me and help me to
study, think, and write as Thou wouldest have me to do,

for Thy glory, the good of my fellow men, and the salvation of mine own soul.'

"I bought some paper for sermon writing this morning. It is just like this on which I write. I skip every other line for sermons. I bought four quires, and even accustomed as I am to high prices, was somewhat startled when the clerk said, 'six dollars, sir, greenbacks.' Each sheet, therefore, costs six and a quarter cents, and each sermon (usually seven sheets), forty-three and three-fourths cents for the paper. I have inquired also about some prices at the cabinet shop. The prices are : Six chairs (all the furniture of pine) $25.00 ; bureau, $70.00 ; washstand, $25.00 ; bedstead, $25.00 ; rocking-chair, $14.00 ; sewing table, $12.00 ; dining table, $18.00— total, $189, dust ; $236, greenbacks.

"I called on Mrs. and Miss Barber yesterday ; they are from Minnesota. They came here last October, having been five months on the way, constantly traveling by ox-train. Think of that ! Five months without ever sleeping in a house. Three hundred immigrants from Minnesota came with them.

"Let me tell you of how money comes in as well as goes out here. A little German boy not twelve years old earns $100.00 a month by taking care, at one dollar a week per head, of the cows that he takes out and herds throughout the day. But he is a remarkable little fellow, manly, trustworthy, honest, persevering, and a splendid little horseman, carrying his dinner out with him and remaining faithfully with the cows, day in and day out."

"*Virginia City, Montana, September 12, 1867.*
" Do you know what this day is ? It is the anniversary of our wedding day. My heart has been full of love and

longings, and my eyes not entirely free from tears to-day. Two years ago we were made one in God's holy sight, and in His Holy Church. To-night, when on my knees in prayer, I shall with God's help frame a petition out of the blessing ; and, thanking God for all His goodness to us, shall ask Him for the dear Saviour's sake to help us two, in weal or woe, in company or absence, so to live together in this life that in the world to come, *the home*, we may have life everlasting."

"*Virginia City, Montana, September 21, 1867.*

" To-morrow morning I start for Salt Lake, Fort Bridger and Idaho. I have been to say good-by to Mrs. Donaldson. She is very feeble and cannot last till I return. I am very sorry to leave her. She said : ' Brother Tuttle (her name for me), you have been a very kind friend to me. I don't know how I should have got on without you. Give my love to your dear wife. I do hope you will both be spared long to live together and to bring up your children. I thank you from my heart for all your goodness to me.' I said, ' We shall probably never meet again, Mrs. Donaldson, this side of the grave. May God help us both so to live and die that we may meet beyond, above ! ' She held out her skeleton hand, pressed mine, looked her thanks to me, and I came away in tears. Was it not payment and more than payment for all my painstaking efforts, to be so blessed by a dying voice ? What a tender, touching part of a pastor's life is this converse with dying friends, with departing souls ! How tenfold rewarded he is by the thanks and blessings they pronounce upon him as they pass away."

CHAPTER VII

IDAHO

IDAHO, the name of which in the Indian language, is said to mean " the gem of the mountains," was made an organized territory in March, 1863. When it was set off from Washington Territory it included all that is now Idaho, together with that part of Montana west of the main range of the Rocky Mountains. When I came to it in 1867 it had shrunk to about 90,000 square miles, and had a population of about 25,000. This population was for the most part distributed through three districts: (1) The north, in and about Lewiston, where gold mines had been discovered in 1861 ; (2) the southwest, in and about what is known as " Boise Basin," and in Boise City and Boise valley. Boise Basin was the mining region, forty miles distant from Boise City, discovered in 1861 or 1862, and sometimes called West Bannack, including afterwards the towns of Idaho City, Centreville, Pioneer, and Placerville. Boise City is on Boise River, and Boise valley is the farming district up and down the river. A mile or so from Boise City was Boise Barracks, with a garrison of the United States army. Old Fort Boise, a well known trading post of earlier years, did not then ex- ist. It was situated forty miles distant from Boise City, at the junction of the Boise River with the Snake ; (3) the southeast, where were many Mormon farmers who had immigrated from Northern Utah. The first few years I was there I held services only in what I name region No. 2, my visits being confined to the three towns of Boise City, Idaho City, and Silver City. Afterwards the three towns to visit grew to fifty, though I never held services in more than two towns of the Mormon district No. 3. In looking over my register I find that I have held services as missionary bishop in fifty-two towns in Montana, fifty in Idaho, and nineteen in Utah: total, one hundred and twenty-one.

In Idaho alone, of my three territories, had any Church work previously been done. Many of the early settlers at Boise City came from Oregon; consequently, about the year 1864 the Rev. St. Michael Fackler came from Oregon to Boise City and began church services there. He was a dear, faithful soul, a fine missionary and a godly pastor, and the fragrance of his memory lingers yet in Idaho as a holy inspiration. Under him a plain frame church was built in Boise City in 1866, costing about $1,500 in gold, which amount at that time meant far more in greenbacks. In the spring or early summer of 1867 he started for a visit to " the States," taking passage from California to New York by the Isthmus of Panama. At or near the Isthmus there was much fever and cholera aboard ship. Mr. Fackler, with assiduous kindness, ministered to the sick as pastor and nurse. Finally he was attacked by the disease and at Key West died. For this gentle, devout minister of God, though I never knew him in the flesh, my heart has always felt gratitude and love.

In his gentleness as a minister I think he made one mistake as a missionary. He served the Boise City people for nothing during his two or three years of residence among them, contenting himself with the allowance made to him by the Committee of Domestic Missions of No. 22 Bible House, New York. This mode of beginning Church work in American communities I hold to be a mistake. Giving for the gospel and the Church " is twice blessed; it blesseth him who gives and him who takes." To serve people as a missionary without training them from the first to give what they can is to deprive them of growth in one of the Christian graces; while, to accustom the people served, from the very first of their missionary service, to bear their portion of what may be called the tax ecclesiastical, is the wise way to adjust burdens and the healthful way to foster sturdy self-reliance and growth. Practically, however, it is the bishop who is to see to it that proper local support be secured for the missionary. And, virtually again, Mr. Fackler had no bishop. He was working within the jurisdiction of Bishop Talbot, but the bishop lived at Nebraska City, 1,500 miles, and a fortnight of day-and-night stage-coach riding, away from Boise.

Once Bishop Scott of Oregon essayed to visit Mr. Fackler while the latter was in Idaho. The bishop got as far as Boise Basin, where Mr. Fackler met him, and held services, I think, one each at Placerville and Idaho City. But he was taken ill, and without venturing the other forty miles on to Boise returned to Oregon.

Bishop Scott's thirteen years in Oregon were those of a long, hard struggle. He was hopelessly far away from the base of church supplies. Nor was the Church in America as generously alive to the providing of supplies as she has since become. He was crippled for lack of men and means for his work. He was left so much alone in his struggle as to feel that no sympathy for him existed anywhere. It seemed to him that no one in the Church cared what was done or what was not done in distant Oregon, and the isolation almost broke his heart. Then came the Civil War with its violent animosities, and where these had no place with its sore wrenchings and sad estrangements. A son of the South,

the bishop's heart was full of loving loyalty to his home,
and there was no room for doubt where his sympathy
lay. Therefore, notwithstanding the quietness and reticence he steadily maintained, he could not escape suspicion and dislike. So the years of his life in Oregon
were anxious and clouded ones. He lived them sustained
by faith, more than cheered by hope, supported by an
heroic devotion, rather than helped by sympathy and
encouragement. Yet he held steadfast from sense of
duty, until finally, as he was returning for a visit to the
East, death claimed him in New York harbor, July 14,
1867. The lines fell for him in hard places; but few
more faithful warriors for the Church Militant have there
been, and none with a record more completely unstained.

September 23, 1867, I left Virginia City to make my
first visit in Idaho. A day or two after I left, poor
Mrs. Donaldson died. I went direct to Salt Lake and
then eastward on the Overland route to pay my promised
visit to Fort Bridger. I spent Sunday, September 29th,
there, the guest of Judge Carter, holding services morning and evening in the Post Hospital. These were the
first religious services of any kind ever held there. Subsequently, by a survey ordered to settle the doubtful line,
Fort Bridger, which had been counted in Utah, was
adjudged to belong to Wyoming. This, therefore, was
the last as well as the first of my services at this post.

Sunday, October 6th, I spent in Salt Lake, then on the
9th I took stage for Boise City, a distance of four hundred
miles, the fare for which was $120. Mr. Miller wrote
me of a trunk that had come to him from New York
with the transportation expenses, eighty-nine dollars.
The freight bill on the boxes containing his modest
library was $308. I may mention that when Mr. God-
dard and I were in Virginia City a telegram of twelve

words sent by him to Mrs. Goddard in New York cost
$12.90. Such items give an idea of the cost of living
and of service in those early days in the mountains.
They go to justify the fairness and wisdom of the
Domestic Committee of the Board of Missions in their
generous appropriation to me of $500, and to the other
missionaries of $400 each, for special outfits when we
were going forth to our work. To speak again in defense of my stage-coach friends, they show that the large
amounts demanded of the United States government for
the carrying of the mails over the " Star Routes " may
not have been really exorbitant.

I arrived at Boise, Saturday afternoon, October 12th,
"with broken neck, bruised head, aching bones, sore
throat and disturbed temper." One of my letters says :
" Of all the uncomfortable routes I ever traveled over,
that from Salt Lake to Boise is the worst.

" The road is more of a solitude than any in Montana.
For hundreds of miles you see no vestige of civilized
man except the stations and the stock-tenders kept by
the Stage Company. We came in sight of Boise soon
after noon on Saturday. As the name implies, the river
on which this town is situated is wooded with willows
and cotton-wood. It is very pleasant to see these green
growths. The town has about fifteen hundred inhabitants.
A mile off is Fort Boise (now called Boise Barracks),
where at present there are about fifty United States
soldiers. As I rode up to Wells, Fargo & Co.'s office,
Miller met me. He is looking well and doing well. He
took me and my traps over to Mr. Redway's. Mr. R. is
a merchant here. I sleep in the room which Miller has
all along occupied. M. now sleeps in his own house, in
the parlor of which house I write this. We both board
at present at Mr. Redway's. M. is at present in the room

hanging his pictures, arranging his books, and manufacturing bookcases out of dry-goods boxes. He has
bought the furnishing of this house, such as it is, for
$250. He has some chickens, is manufacturing for him-
self a wardrobe, a cupboard, etc., and is doing right well
and royally I assure you. We cannot yet find out
whether Mary (Mrs. Miller) sailed the 1st of October or
not. Strange to say there is no Roman Catholic church
or priest in this town. Besides M. there is only a Methodist minister; he preaches in a Baptist meeting-house.
St. Michael's is quite church-like. The singing and responses are hearty and good. I was much pleased on
Sunday, I felt more as if I were in church than I had
done since I left Denver. At the morning service I
confirmed five."

"*Silver City, Idaho, Sunday, October 20, 1867.*
"I have just come in from visiting and catechizing the
Sunday-school. Mr. Vass, the superintendent, is a communicant of the Church of England. Mr. and Mrs.
Smith, teachers, are also communicants. Mrs. Webb,
teacher, I am to confirm to-night. So, although it is a
'Union School,' and all kinds of children, even Roman
Catholics, are in it, we may feel that it has a Church
leaning. This is one of the most forlorn spots I was ever
in. I look out of my window upon a rough, rocky, bar-
ren mountainside. The mountain is 'War Eagle,' rich in
gold quartz, but most forlorn looking. Silver has, I
think, a population of 1,000. No minister of any kind is
here, not even a Roman Catholic. The Sunday-school
is the only thing witnessing to Sunday. Three male and
six female communicants of the Church are all there are
here, so far as I can discover. Seven or eight quartz
mills are hereabout, and on these this camp depends for

life and business. Ruby City, three-fourths of a mile distant, has a meeting house, but R. is a desolate, deserted town, and it would be no good to have services there. We met for services this morning and are to meet to-night, in the ' Orofino Saloon,' an old deserted drinking place. I wrote you last from Boise on the 15th. In the evening I attended a vestry meeting of St. Michael's.

" I was pleased with the vestry and with M.'s way of dealing with them. He opened and closed the vestry meeting with prayer, and the members present earnestly discussed the plan of starting a school at once. They told me they thought they could raise $500 per annum, greenbacks, for a salary for Mr. M. I shall press them to make it $600, at least. They promise to pay it promptly and regularly, quarterly. I shall probably give them some help in building their schoolhouse. And if they buy (as they talk of doing) the house in which M. lives, for a rectory, I shall help them do that. I called also on Governor Ballard. He is a rough man. His wife is a Methodist. He, like Secretary Stanton, has been suspended by President Johnson. He has been a doctor, and though not regularly practicing, is the family physician of the *élite* of Boise. On Wednesday Mr. Chick who is to marry Miss Hyde, M.'s organist, called in at M.'s study. Presuming he was on delicate business I stepped out. Soon M. came into the work-shop, back, and said : ' Mr. C. wants you to marry him.' I marched back and explained to Mr. C. that I could not do it, that M. must do it, etc. I am going into the chancel, however, with M. Of course the only reason I was asked was on account of the *éclat* that would be given by having a bishop perform the ceremony. I explained this to M., so he understands and it's all amicably settled. A letter from George tells me the Mormons now refuse to sell land to him at any price. Probably they have got wind of our plans, and have received counsel from Brigham.

"Thursday at 3 A. M., M. and I were routed out by the night watchman to take the stage to Silver. I did hate to get up. In due time we got aboard the stage and were rolling off in the dark, early morning to Silver, sixty-five miles distant; stage fare, $13.37. Generally the country through which we passed was a monotonous, sage brush plain; towards the end of our journey, however, we began to wind in and out of the cañons of this Owyhee range. We came through a hostile Indian country, and again had loaded revolvers at our sides. In the driver's seat we saw three loaded rifles. But we had no trouble and we arrived safely here about 4 P. M. Friday night a fall of snow made all about us white, but M. and I had projected a tramp to the top of 'War Eagle' and we were not to be cheated out of it by the snow. After breakfast, yesterday, therefore, we started. We had a rough mountainside to walk upon, and 2,000 feet up to make, but we succeeded and found from the top just the immense, limitless, indescribable view that we get from every high peak of these Rocky Mountains.

"In general, Idaho does not seem to me to be as rich or as homelike as Montana. Less land is cultivated; the towns are smaller and poorer. Boise City, however, and Boise valley round about the town, are very pleasant places. They have snow, they say, for many months, six and eight feet deep. The great thing they complain of is, not the cold, but the vast amount and depth of the snow. At the court-house to-night a band of wandering minstrels gives a concert. One of the Sunday-school children, this afternoon, must have got things somewhat mixed when he asked M.: 'How much, sir, will I have to pay to come to the meeting to-night?'"

"*Boise City, Idaho, October 23, 1867.*

" Mr. M. has lighted a lamp and we both sit at his table in his cozy study, writing. It begins to get dark early now, and winter will soon be upon us. It must needs be somewhat long and dreary to us, but our kind and loving Father will help us to live and work, and love and hope, through it all.

" Monday evening, at my invitation, the people of Silver met me. Colonel Webb was much interested in securing a pastor, and so were others. They voted that ' Silver will raise $150 per month in greenbacks for a salary'; and appointed a committee of five to keep in communication with me. On the strength of that meeting I have to-day written to *your* Mr. Sam,[1] to ask him to come to Silver; salary, $2,800 a year. Do you think there is any chance of my getting him? Perhaps Mr. Smith and Mr. Vass will keep up lay services at Silver throughout the winter. If so I shall feel as if Church work were already begun there.

" At 5 A. M., Tuesday, we left Silver. When twenty miles out we took in two men who had the previous day escaped from Indians. One of them, a United States army sergeant, told this story: ' Sergeant Denoilles, his wife, and myself, started in an ambulance to come to Boise. When about nine miles from here' (where he got in), 'yesterday, about 11 A. M., as we were riding down a hill we heard a rifle shot. I was going to say to Sergeant D. " keep your lines steady. I'll watch the Indians if it be them," when he exclaimed, ". O God, I am shot!" and rolled off the seat. I clutched for the reins but

[1] Rev. Samuel Upjohn, D. D.

missed them. Then more shots came. The horses ran, ungoverned, down the hill. Soon one fell and blocked the way and stopped the ambulance. I jumped off, having my rifle. The woman jumped out and started up the hill. I tried to keep her back but could not. She rushed screaming right up among the twenty Indians who were hooting around the dead body of her husband. That's the last I saw of her. Shot at by the Indians, and shooting at them warily with my Henry rifle (a sixteen shooter) I retreated towards the rocks. Getting ensconced between two of them, and protected by them, I kept the Indians off till towards dark, when they went away. I afterwards crawled out stealthily over the hill to this station. They stole our four horses, burned the ambulance, and, alas! none know what they have done or are doing to the woman.' The other man, named Hardy, told this: ' About 2 P. M. I was riding along alone on my horse, when I spied a smoke ahead in an unwonted place' (this was of the burnt ambulance). ' While I was looking wonderingly a bullet whizzed near and struck my horse. Wounded as he was he carried me bravely some distance, then he tottered to his fall. I leaped off. Five Indians were after me and firing. I had no rifle, only two navy revolvers. I fired once or twice and the fire checked the Indians. Then I retreated towards the rocks, dodging behind little hills all I could and aiming my revolver every now and then to check the one Indian who seemed foremost and most courageous. Thankfully I got to the rocks and hid among them. Indians hate to chase white men among rocks, where the latter may have the advantage over them. Lying in the rocks I saw the Indians attack two other parties ; after night I crept from my hiding-place and came to the station.'

" So the Indians were murdering and scalping within

nine miles of us. We all grew grave. We felt specially sorrowful at the fate of that poor woman. We clutched our arms nervously when we went through a deep, rocky, dangerous, Indian infested cañon that lay on our route. M. and I had our pistols with us and six rifles besides were in the stage. Thank God, we came safely through. But the Indians about Silver City and on the route from here to Silver are bitterly hostile. I confess I'm glad I have not got to go over there again just yet. We arrived here safe, but dust-covered and alkali-begrimed, about 4 P. M. To-day, at 11 A. M., in St. Michael's, M. married Mr. Chick and Miss Hyde. Everything went off nicely, and guess what fee M. got. He brought it home unopened and I opened the parcel. Out rolled two double eagles and two half eagles — fifty dollars in gold. A good fee, eh ?

" A letter from Mr. Goddard informs me that he is to leave Helena for Claremont, New Hampshire, October 28th. I am very sorry for the work's sake, but cannot find it in my heart to blame him. Whom can I get for Helena now ? From his letter I fear that things are all at sixes and sevens in Virginia City. Dr. Cornell has been at Helena and seemed to have the blues over Church matters in Virginia City. I judge, by Mr. G.'s report of Dr. C.'s report, that lay services went down at V. after two Sundays, five or six only attending on those Sundays ; that the vestry can't agree on procuring a building ; and that they won't meet to call Mr. Roberts,[1] as I asked them to do. May God give me patience and courage and wisdom and strength to do cheerfully my single-handed work in Montana, against all the opposing forces this winter. Pray for me and

---

[1] Rev. Daniel C. Roberts, D. D.

for my work. I shall have to try to get over to Helena at least once through the snows of this winter. Mr. Goddard strongly advises me to leave Virginia and stay at Helena this winter, but I don't think it wise to do so. D. V. I shall stay at V. until they get some one to see to them."

"*Idaho City, Idaho, Sunday, October 27, 1867.*

"It's a queer place in which I write this. I am in the law office of Col. Samuel A. Merritt, a Virginian, who was a rebel officer in the late war. Through the thin partition on the right I hear the tramping and talking of men coming and going into and from the post-office, which is also a stationery and book store, and the depository of a circulating library. On the left two or three men are unloading wood, huge wagon-loads of which they have taken Sunday as a fit day for bringing in and selling. In a little room back of the office is Colonel M.'s bedroom, which he has hospitably given up to Mr. Miller and me during our stay. We left Boise at 7 A. M., Friday, and arrived here (distance forty miles) at 4:30 P. M. The road is one of the wildest and roughest I have been on. Fortunately it is free from Indians. Steep hills up and down, dug-ways along ravine sides, and narrow trails in cañons, barely wide enough for the stage to cross through, are constant features of it. I was pleased with the wild variety. Trees, many and large, fir and pine, quite line the road in many places. And the trip, with all its slow creeping up the hills and dangerous plunging down them, is far preferable to the monotonous one over the tiresome, dusty, sage-brush plains, through which much of the road to Owyhee (Silver) runs. By the way, the Owyhee country and range is named from *Hawaii* or *Owyhee* of the Sandwich Islands. There were some *Kanakas* (Sandwich Islanders are so called) among the early settlers of Oregon and Idaho. Our stage was crowded full, nine inside, three outside. Inside were five Chinamen. A Chinaman always rides if he can afford it. They are among the most constant customers of the stage lines. Chinamen in this town abound, there are 3,000 of them in and about here. They have here a joss house, or temple.

" I think there are in this town two male and three female communicants. We had service this morning in the court-house. This court-house was built for a ' church.' The first preacher in it (Kingsley, a Methodist) dabbled in merchandise, as well as preached. While he was in the pulpit on Sunday, his clerks were selling goods from his store. The same K. lives here now, a secularized preacher, a struggling tradesman. A Baptist preacher, also demoralized, is now a ' judge.' He has lately maltreated his wife and was yesterday going about the streets taking measures for a divorce. After Kingsley retired, other preachers, Methodist North and South, Baptist, etc., attempted to build up a congregation and complete and pay for the projected church. The last one here, a Methodist (Roberts, now of Boise), paid from his own pocket the debts resting on it ($1,500). The people not supporting him, however, at his departure he turned round and sold it to the county for a court-house, in order to secure his $1,500.

" Two Romish priests are here. One has gone down to Oregon to bring up three or four ' sisters ' who are going to open a school at once. The people of the town have subscribed $2,700 for starting such a school. This sum, all or nearly all, comes from Protestants.

" This is a disorderly town of, I should think, 2,500 white inhabitants. Many families are here, many clever men, many children, but there is no school of any kind. There again the Romanists are going to make a strike.

"In the circulating library I observed 'Buckle,' 'Renan,' 'Herbert Spencer,' 'John Stuart Mill,' prominent and much bethumbed. These clever men of intellect here are all tinctured with rationalism. Last night Miller and I had a long talk with Colonel Merritt and Major Foote (son of Senator Foote of Mississippi, also in the late rebel army) and we found in them clever, college-bred, gentlemanly rationalists. Here M. says, 'Give your wife my love, and tell her this is one of " Herbert's " Sundays.' As he says this with a twinkle, shouts come from the street, arising from the crowd, who are watching and betting on a horse race that is taking place just before our door. I can hardly think and write, for hundreds of men and boys are shouting their best in exultation over the winning horse coming in. The street is a fair specimen of pandemonium. My imagination must be laid under tribute for me to think it Sunday.

" Well, dear, however men shout and the world sins, I have still my prayers, my valued Church services, my thoughts of and writing to you. The Church provides sweet things for us. We use the same prayers, we hear the same lessons, we are conscious of the passing of the same portion of the Church year, as Sunday after Sunday comes and goes. With tearful eyes I say longingly, 'How I wish we could be and live and love together!' Then I brush away the tears and say, 'God be thanked for all His loving kindness to us both; God help us both to do the much needed work for Him put before us; God keep us both, mercifully, for each other and for Him;

God guide and help and bless our dear boy as he grows. All these things we humbly beg, poor sinners that we are, for the loving Saviour's sake!' I do not think it *hard* exactly to be so separated. That is not my feeling. I don't speak of the *hardness* of it. Only, I am often so full of longing for my own dear wife and child that it makes the present and the future seem lonely and deserted. But, I do assure you, that, on the whole, our dear, kind, loving heavenly Father does wonderfully help me to be patient and even cheery."

Idaho City had been known as West Bannack. The region round about was called Boise Basin. In this " Basin," besides Idaho City were the towns of Placerville, Centreville, Quartsburg, and Pioneer. The last named was, in the vernacular, " Hog'em." At first I went only to Idaho City. In after years I visited the other towns. Boise Basin had been rich in gold placer diggings, which had been discovered in 1861–2. At the time of my coming the yield of the mines was much diminished, yet gold dust was still the currency in the basin. In the offerings at church services several diminutive bags of the " dust " came to me. In other parts of Idaho, as on all the Pacific coast, gold coin was the standard. And for several years I remember that greenbacks in Idaho passed at a settled rate of seventy-five cents to the dollar.

Many violent and bloody deeds, characteristic of early mining days everywhere, were committed in the basin. But no such formidable, organized band of miscreants flourished there as in Montana. Chinese were working many of the diggings around Idaho City. White men if they could not make five or eight dollars a day would throw up their claims in disgust or sell them for a song. Chinamen making one or two dollars a day

could flourish. Still not a few white miners were busy
at this my first visit, and their unfailing concomitants,
hurdy-gurdy dance houses, faro banks, Sunday desecra-
tion, extravagant expenditure, and lavish generosity were
manifest on every side. Offerings at services in mining
camps were seldom less than twenty-five dollars, and
often were as much as seventy-five dollars.

On Sunday night I confirmed two women. Monday
morning I went to visit a sick and dying miner named
Hopkins. After prayer with him, I well remember his
earnest thanks to me and his long holding of my hand
and whispering " Sweet! Sweet! " referring to the prayers.
In the afternoon I baptized two children. At night I
met all interested in securing the services of a pastor.
Twenty-four persons came. They subscribed $1,400 a
year on the spot, and appointed a committee, or quasi
vestry, to represent them in communications with me.
It was not easy to find and secure suitable pastors from
the East for this frontier work. For some years Silver
and Idaho City, both, were cared for by an occasional
visit from Mr. Miller, and by my yearly visitation. Perhaps I, and the pastor if secured, would have found the
committee, or vestry, a frail staff to lean upon. Of the
five men appointed at Idaho City, the very head and
chief, the treasurer of the county, before long proved to
be a defaulter in a large amount. I think it was the very
next year, at the time of my visit, that he rode with me
from Idaho City to Boise and made himself most agreea-
ble as a stage companion in intelligent conversation
upon affairs of Church and state. That very day he
was making off with public funds in his pocket. The
next day he went on to California and he was never
seen in Idaho more. On Tuesday M. and I returned to
Boise City.

" *Boise City, Idaho, Sunday, November 3, 1867.*

" Mr. Miller sits near me, in dressing-gown and slippers, looking over the lessons. Service is to begin at 10:45. His advertised time is 10:30. I've been scolding him for the immorality of such proceeding. . . .

" Last Thursday evening the vestry had a meeting in Mr. Miller's room. All were present. They resolved to pay Miss G. $140 a month in gold ($186 in greenbacks), and seemed to enter with much interest into the prospects of the school. Before they left I sent M. out of the room and called their attention to these two facts : (1) That they had voted to pay Miss G. $186 a month (for which I was glad, as I want to see teachers well paid) ; (2) that they propose to pay M. only $500 a year. I then insisted they should do more for him, and suggested to them how to do more, which was by canvassing the whole town and getting everybody to give something. I let them off at last with these two understandings, (1) That Mr. M. shall not be called upon to pay any rent for this house ; (2) that they will give him $800 a year, payable quarterly. Yesterday I dined at Mr. Logan's with M. and Mr. Bishop. Have I told you about Mr. B. ? He is a Cumberland Presbyterian minister, but is now filling a territorial civil office, and comes steadily to church. Indeed he is lay reader for M. when the latter is absent, he helps us in singing, and he seems to grow every day more and more favorably disposed towards the church. I like him much, for he is a jolly, joking fellow ; but I fear that these very proclivities, with a dash of imprudent political radicalism manifest in him, detract from his good name and influence among the sober folk here."

" *Boise City, Idaho, 9:30 A. M., November 7, 1867.*

" I rejoice to say that our parish school opened last

Monday. We have now fifteen scholars. M. thinks he more and more likes Miss Gillespie; I really hope that she will prove to be the woman for us. If so I've no doubt our school will be a successful thing. We've both been eating apples since we came in. Yesterday Mr. Blossom, a merchant here, a Presbyterian, brought us a present of one or two dozen huge fall pippins, that we have found to be delicious. They come from Oregon. They tell me that in Oregon and Washington Territory, apples and pears, the largest and finest in the world, are grown. The price of them per pound is twenty cents, gold (twenty-six cents greenbacks).

"About 11 A. M., Tuesday, Governor Ballard and his wife called for M. and me to take a ride with them to the 'Warm Springs,' about five miles distant. There were two other carriages. The Hot Spring is so hot that you cannot bear your hand in it. It bubbles up out of the ground like boiling water. By the side of it were marks of the utilitarianism of the ranche people. There were hog bristles and hen feathers in abundance, showing that these people save fuel by bringing all animals, needing to be scalded and 'dressed,' up to this spring. There are several warm springs besides. Water from there, joined with one cold stream, is collected in a little pond fitted for swimmers. How I wanted to plunge in and have a swim. I said so aloud several times. But I had no bathing clothes.

"After wandering about we sat down at an improvised table and had our picnic dinner. The day was warm and pleasant and all the more pleasant for being cloudy. We took our dozen or two of eggs, tied them up in two handkerchiefs and put them in the Hot Spring. In a few minutes they were beautifully boiled. After the dinner, feeling in good spirits I foolishly said, ' Now, Mr. Bishop,

I'll run with you or jump, as you like.' He as foolishly replied, 'Well, I'll do it, where shall we run?' (Our foolishness was in undertaking such violent exercise immediately after eating.) 'Up to the top of that hill yonder,' I said. He agreed and stripped off his coat and hat. I took off mine, and Governor Ballard held them. Then Captain Porter beating 'one, two, three' on his old hat gave us the word. We started off; Mr. Bishop got ahead and kept the lead along the level till we struck the hill, but I saved myself for the hill. Consequently, in ascending I soon caught up with and passed him. Much to the amusement of the people below, we scrambled up the hill, till at last Mr. B. called out: 'Hold up, bishop, that's far enough; I give up beat!' Great merriment we all had over the affair. Mr. B. is a remarkably strong, athletic, active man; but while weighing as much as, or more than, I, he is shorter, and hence, when we came to that up-hill business I got the better of him.

"After our picnic we got into the carriages and went two miles further on to visit an Indian encampment. We found one or two hundred Indians in twenty or thirty lodges. A lodge is made by poles and brush stuck in the ground leaning against each other, thatched with straw or rudely covered with gunny bags and old pieces of canvas, a hole being left at the top for the smoke. The Indians seemed pleased to see us, and shook hands with us, saying, 'How?' One asked us for a shirt for his papoose, and also for tobacco. Poor things! All, old and young, male and female, were forlornly half-clad in blankets and dirty cloths. Many had no coverings for feet or legs, and some little ones were as naked as when born. The only pleasant things I saw were the wondrously bright eyes and white teeth of the papooses."

" Boise City, Idaho, Sunday, November 10, 1867.

" I wrote you last on Thursday morning. In the afternoon M. and I made four calls. As we were coming home from one house, situated a mile out of town, we heard strange noises down the road. Soon we saw some cavalry coming in the distance. We stopped and waited for the troops to pass. The noise continued. As the horsemen neared and passed us we found the explanation. First came a squad of soldiers mounted; then a squad of about fifty mounted Indians, clad in United States uniforms and furnished with United States muskets. After them came some hundreds of pack mules, laden with commissary and quartermaster stores. These were all coming into Fort Boise from General Crook's army, that is campaigning against the hostile Indians. The fifty Indians were United States scouts, friendly of course, and in their delight at getting near the fort they were singing. The words sounded something like this, ' Hoch-la, Hoch-la!' repeated in chorus up and down the gamut. They sang lustily and loud, with eyes bright and faces cheery, if dusky. Friday forenoon I spent in the parish school. On the whole I was pleased. Miss G. is sensible, orderly, firm, and neat, and the children seem to like her well. She seemed thorough, too, and, when I heard the classes, was quiet, and betrayed none of the nervousness lest they should miss, and the eager readiness to help and apologize for them, that careless, superficial teachers are wont to show. She has fifteen scholars. I think the school will grow. Unfortunately Miss G. does not sing a note. This is a drawback to our and her success in choir, parish, and day-school.

" In the evening we called on Mrs. Greer. We found in her a bright, cheery, dumpy young Mexican, very intelligent, speaking broken English with the utmost piquancy. While we were conversing, her mother, who cannot speak English, was busy, I saw, rolling up something. By and by she came towards us and with her bright eyes sparkling with hospitable feeling said something gracefully polite in Spanish about *cigaritas*. As she did so she held out one of said articles for each of us, which she had been making with tobacco and paper. Although no smoker, as you know, I could do no less than accept mine for politeness' sake, showing all my teeth in amends for my ignorance of Spanish. M. of course accepted both the *cigarita* and the match the old lady also extended to him, and forthwith began puffing away. She, returning to her seat, having provided us, made a *cigarita* for herself; this she lighted and smoked in company with M. Mrs. Greer and I laughed at them and chatted away by ourselves while they smoked. Mr. G. afterwards came in. He is the collector of internal revenue for the territory, a right sensible and valuable man, born in Ohio. In religion he is a Universalist, but he willingly helps us and our parish at present. Yesterday I wrote to Mr. Margary, clerk of the vestry, as follows : ' To the Vestry of St. Michael's, Boise; gentlemen : I go away, understanding that you on your part will try to do these two things : (1) To raise a salary of $800 (greenbacks) per annum for Mr. Miller, and pay quarterly ; (2) to see to it that Mr. M. have to pay no house rent. I go promising on my part : (1) to give you $100 (greenbacks) if you will purchase the house Mr. M. is in ; (2) to give you $100 (gold), at least, to help in building your schoolhouse.' To-morrow at 6 A. M. I take (D. V.) the Overland ' jerker ' for Virginia City."

Though I had run the gauntlet of danger from the Indians in crossing the plains in June, I had not seen any large number of them until I came to Idaho. In all my career as missionary bishop I did not do any missionary work among the Indians. I did not see how it was practicable to do so. Those whom I came across were wandering bands, here to-day, gone to a distant fishing stream to-morrow; the homeless rovers would be impervious to any evangelizing influence that I could bring to bear upon them. As to those who were in homes, gathered at agencies, Roman Catholic missionaries were already caring for the Cœur d' Alenes and Pen d' Oreilles in Northern Idaho, and the Flatheads in Western Montana; the Presbyterians had charge of the Nez Perces in Northern Idaho; and the Methodists, of the Blackfeet and Crows in Montana and the Bannacks at the Lemhi Agency in the Salmon Valley, Idaho. Among the Utes in Utah the Mormons had done work and had made a large number of proselytes. In all these cases except the last the division and distribution of the Indian missionary work among the different religious bodies were in pursuance of the policy adopted by General Grant's administration. Our Church had much work assigned to it in Minnesota and Dakota, but none in Idaho and Montana.

The explanation of the marked Roman Catholic success among the Indians seemed to me that the priests came and stayed and lived among the Indians. They did not come and go. They did not some go away and others come to fill their places, but, for the most part those who came settled down and lived with the Indians and learned their language and habits and ways, so becoming their trusted counselors and guides. A dozen priests were so serving among the Indians when I went to the field. Some of them, like my dear old friend and brother whom I highly esteemed, Father Ravalli, had come among them in the 40s and so had been among them for near thirty years. Father Ravalli was a physician as well as priest. In many a case of surgery he served the miners. We all esteemed and loved him, and when an old man beyond seventy he lay on his dying bed in the Bitter Root valley, I visited him and had prayers with him. For a generation he lived among the Indians. He never went away from them, he died among them. Educated, godly men working in this way must win success.

CHAPTER VIII

WINTER IN VIRGINIA CITY, 1867-8

I LOOK back upon the winter of 1867-8, spent in Virginia City, as an important era of my life. In outward things I did not accomplish much. But my experiences were such as to deepen and strengthen principles and habits, that have been of great value to me in after life. I left Boise City on Monday morning, November 11, 1867, and reached Virginia City at 11 : 30 A. M., Sunday, the 17th. Had the coach been on time I should have reached Virginia City for morning services, but various mishaps impeded us. Among other discomforts, I got no breakfast that Sunday morning, until noon. Such things have often happened me. More than once I have gone well into the afternoon of a day in staging without having had a morsel for breakfast. For such discomforts I am most happily constituted. Fastings of this sort I do not mind at all. I grow hungrier and hungrier, of course, but as for headaches or stomach disturbances, I never have a touch of them from such forced irregularities. Even my good humor has never been discomposed by them. On my arrival I went to the Planters' House and got breakfast, or dinner. Then I went out and told my friends there would be service in the evening in " Tootle, Leach & Co.'s " old deserted store. This we soon after fitted up with seats and named " Reception Hall." I was quartered in No. 6 in the Planters' House, a corner bedroom seven feet by nine, without any stove. For these accommodations and board I paid twenty-five

dollars a week. I felt very lonely, only the clear conviction of being in the line of duty sustained and cheered
me. As long as the novelty lasted of the new preacher
and the Episcopal robes and the Prayer-Book services,
large congregations came out, especially on Sunday evenings, the greater proportion of them being men. The
Romish services and our own were the only ones held in
the town. After being in Virginia City a week I wrote
my wife: " I had a very full congregation this morning,
and the singing and responses were good, and so the
service quite inspiring. But when I came to the sermon,
I tried to make it too impressive, I think. I was thinking
of myself too much, of God's truth and men's souls too
little, and I don't believe I preached as I ought. I was
cold and self-critical, and wanting to see the effect on the
audience. I know, if God will send me the grace to be
really humble, and faithfully prayerful, I can accomplish
more for Him and for souls than by all my highest flights
of eloquence. God help me! Don't you remember my
once telling you how sometimes I wished my life were all
over, lived faithfully unto Him, and I laid away to my
rest ? I said that the temptations and responsibilities in
going through life to death seemed so terrible to me that
I wished all were over. I sometimes find myself thinking the same thoughts and wishing the same wishes now,
—that my life here were all done and well done and I
simply at rest. This is chiefly because I feel my short-
comings in meeting with fidelity what God appoints and
sends me, not because I do not enjoy life. I do enjoy it,
and often from heart and mouth, when none but He
knows, thank Him for life and health and present happiness. It is because life in probation has so fearful a side
to it that I feel it would be sweet to know that all was
over. That I had laid my burdens down. That peace-

fully, restfully, not perplexedly, I could at last view things."

But I was uneasy over personal expenses. I had been a country parson on $1,000 a year and I did not feel it right to spend twenty-five dollars a week on my own living. Soon I found a log cabin to go into. It was empty and seemed abandoned, but I hunted up the person with whom the key had been left and I got the use of the cabin for nothing. I fitted it up and furnished it and went into it December 15th. During my month at the hotel Mr. and Mrs. Chapin were very kind to me, and Charlie, the Chinese chamberman, drawing his wages of sixty dollars a month in gold, was very attentive and helpful. During that month I met as fellow guests several of a class whom I have always found respectful and courteous, and towards whom my heart entertains most kindly feelings,—I mean actors and actresses. Mr. and Mrs. Langrishe, Geo. Paunceforth, Mr. C. W. Couldock and his daughter Eliza, were all in Virginia City that winter. Three years after at Salt Lake I baptized Miss Couldock, and on her dying bed administered to her the holy communion. She lies buried at Salt Lake. Mr. Couldock, far beyond threescore and ten, in his journeyings about presenting the part of the Old Miller in "Hazel Kirke" comes to visit me nowadays, whenever he is near. We were talking together lately of the old times and I asked him after Mr. Langrishe. "Why," he said, "Jack Langrishe is now a State Senator in Idaho." He deserves his post. "Jack" Langrishe was a hard working, upright, honorable man, known to all the old mountaineers, and with whom I have had many a cheery and helpful chat. I met Mr. and Mrs. Langrishe last in the Cœur d' Alene Mountains in 1885. It was eighteen years since we had first met and become friends; I was still preaching and they still playing. The deep wish of my heart is for a happy and honored old age to them both.

In cool figuring I find my change to the cabin did not save me much after all. My good friend, Mrs. Davis, in her home near by took me to board for fifteen dollars a week it is true. But I gave her servant a dollar a week to come in to make up my bed and tidy the room ; afterwards, I gave a colored man $2.50 to come three times a week and do the same. The other four days I did the best I could for myself. I made a poor hand at it, however, as I did also at replacing buttons or sewing up rents. I was never made for a celibate, and have always needed the care of a woman. To fit up and furnish the cabin cost me $244.75. I paid twenty-three dollars for a small sheet iron stove, thirty dollars for a pine bedstead ; twenty dollars for a hay mattress, and forty dollars for a wool mattress. The roof, moreover, was only pine poles covered with a foot or two of dirt. I soon found it leaking and was obliged to put boards over the dirt at a cost of ninety dollars. A little calculation will show that the winter's stay in the cabin was no saving over the hotel. The ladies, bless their hearts ! soon managed to find out that I was not very comfortably fixed ; so they went out and collected $200. Then they came, and ordering me out took down my little stove and put in a better one, laid a carpet on the floor, and added a lounge and an easy chair.

However the cabin was better for me every way. It was my own to retire to. It was a little bit homelike. I got a white cat, Dick, and his presence added to the homelikeness.

I couldn't always keep free from fits of dreary lonesomeness and Dick was then the greatest comfort to me.

He would welcome me home from my walks, with all the joy a cat can show, and in the cabin would crawl up on my shoulder when I was reading or writing. At night his place was on the buffalo robe at the side or the foot of my bed. Often, however, if it got right cold before morning, he would crawl in between the sheets and lie at my side. Dear, faithful, friendly old Dick! You were more of a help and a comfort to me that winter than ever your cat's brains could know, and to this day my heart warms to think of you!

I could write sermons, and I did too, and could read them aloud, according to my habit. Besides, I had a fit place for people to come to who desired private counsel, while Room No. 6 at the hotel would give away to the ears of the lodgers in other rooms any word uttered in it.

Next to the sense of loneliness, I was most oppressed with the sad conviction of the prayerlessness and godlessness of the people among whom I found myself. Of them, women, especially good women, were a very small minority. Men were kind personally, generous in giving money, respectful and courteous; but I was appalled to discover day by day how almost universally given up they were to vicious practices. I had served my ministry in an agricultural community, where good men, diffident spiritually, needed to be urged to come to confirmation. I had not been long at my new work before I learned that one or more who were greatly pleasing me by asking to be confirmed were in reality profane swearers of steady habit. Caution, begot of knowledge, so ruled that in eight months of uninterrupted work in Virginia City I did not find one single person to be confirmed. December 8th a Sunday-school was opened, with four teachers and twenty-seven scholars. It afterwards grew to nine teachers and fifty-three scholars. But the boys, when out at play from their day school, I would hear, alas, too often swearing. Among the best of my teachers were a Quaker, a Baptist, and two Methodists, while one " Churchman " of them was accustomed every now and then to get woefully drunk, and another was a habitué of the gaming table. These helped to read the responses vigorously in church worship, and I have little reason to think that they did not read, earnestly desiring forgiveness as poor sinners. But such cases made keen whiplashes for the pastor's shoulders. One energetic Methodist woman, whenever I called on her always belabored me with representations of the scandal of allowing such to be leaders in religion and conductors of the worship of Almighty God. There was nothing for me to do but meekly receive the punishment inflicted. Of the vestry of St. Paul's church which we got together, one vestryman, high in civil office, got into an altercation with a lawyer over some matters retailed by gossip, and would have shot him dead had not a friend near by struck up the pistol. One was a Unitarian. Another, the most godly of them all, and the one on whom I most leaned for Christian and churchly earnestness, became involved in a dispute, and missed, by the smallest margin, the fighting of a duel. Still another was an appallingly steady drinker, though he was never mastered by drink. Another, a kind, good-hearted man too, grew so mad from drink that one night his wife fled from him in terror. I was sent for and I stayed with him in his delirium and nursed him, saving him from self-destruction. On New Year's Day when all called most kindly at my cabin, it would have been irresistibly funny had it not been inexpressibly sad, to see the anxious efforts made to keep forms and eyes steady and tongues straight. My heart

was grieved and distressed at this, but I never hated the
people, they were too kind and good to me for that.
And God's Holy Spirit, in spite of my lonely living and
my single-handed fighting, sustained me in such patience,
perseverance, and cheerfulness, that I sometimes wondered at myself. Some quotations from my letters again
may give the state of my feelings.

"*11 P. M., Saturday, December 14, 1867.*

" I have just come in from the party, and am quite sick
at heart. In the room back were wines and whiskeys
and nearly all the men drank too freely. I joined in the
amusing plays with much pleasure, but was sad to think
what a drinking community there is all around me. Oh,
why cannot people take the blessings God gives them
thankfully and thoughtfully, with hearts thinking about
the Giver, and grateful to Him, using, not abusing, His
gifts. I shall pray for these people to-night, and I shall
ask God to keep me patient and persevering. The work
to be done here is, to judge humanly, preëminently difficult. God the Holy Ghost alone can change these
hearts of unbelief and excess.

" Sunday, 10 : 20 A. M. I have taken my walk and
read over my sermon. In my walk I could not shake
off the sadness remaining from last night's experience.
Up on the hill, in a nook between the rocks, I kneeled
down and tearfully asked God to send His Holy Spirit
to do His purifying work among this people and to
help me in spite of all difficulties to keep humble,
trustful, earnest, faithful, patient, persevering, and
cheerful. And I came home with a lighter step. What
a blessed comfort it is that here, where absolutely not
one old friend, or spiritually-minded friend, is, I can
always go to Him, as a friend, and near, just as near as

ever He was of old in dear Morris.   I can, indeed, say
with Keble to-day :

> " ' Blessed be God, whose grace
> Shows Him in every place
> To homeliest hearts of pilgrims pure and meek.' "

" *February 6, 1868.*

" Before I went to choir meeting Major Veale, my
only faithful churchman here, called.   He and I are
putting our heads together about the election of a new
vestry at Eastertide.   We mean to cut down the number
from nine to seven.   We mean to throw out at least
drunkards and violent swearers.   Aside from him the
other six, at the best, will have to be Unitarians, moderate drinkers, and decent world's men.

" Alas ! the longer I live here, the worse, the more
deeply bad, the more thoroughly soaked in irreligion,
do I find the entire community to be.   Looking earth-
wards, trusting in human agencies, the work of the
Church here is the most discouraging that can be conceived.   But God the Holy Spirit will take care of His
own.   His Kingdom will come.   *Magna,* ay, *maxima
est veritas divina et prævalebit.*   The Lord be thanked
that He appoints us only to sow the seed.   He gives
the increase.   Under Him that seed groweth up, *we
know not how.*   I am sure it is only His blessed Spirit,
comforting and helping, that keeps me cheerfully at work
in a community where absolutely no earnest spiritual life
is manifest in one out of a hundred of the inhabitants."

Advices from Salt Lake also now troubled me.   The
Mormons, supreme potentates there, would not allow us
to have any land for the stay of our feet.   Some of the
business men who were hand in glove with the Mormons
disliked the tone of our appeal to the East for help,

and said they would have nothing to do with us.
Finally, we found an apostate Mormon to sell us a lot.
The cost was $11,000, but how in the world to get
that much money I did not know. We must pay
$1,000 down, and, March 1st, must pay $4,000 more.
The other $6,000 could wait. Until March I was there-
fore very uneasy about the $4,000. On the day it was
needed, however, the Domestic Committee at No. 22
Bible House, New York, advanced it for our pressing
need, and before very long enough " specials " had come
in to pay back the advance. Then Rev. Mr. Foote fell
sick and was confined to the house for some time. I
was telegraphed to once or twice to come down to Salt
Lake, but it seemed so important to me to push steadily
my pastoral work in Virginia City that I would not
leave. Through letters and telegrams, however, I managed as best I could the necessary decisions for Salt
Lake. It was an anxious winter, it was a struggling
winter, it was a lonely winter, but I never lost heart or
hope. God indeed wonderfully upheld and blessed me.
And not a few outward and visible helps too He sent me.

In the first place my health was uninterruptedly firm,
and I found the climate for me magnificent. Montana
winters are not so cold as those who have never been
there would expect. The isothermal lines bend to the
north in that region. And even when the winter air
is cold, it is also dry, sunny, exhilarating. Every morning in my cabin before going to breakfast I read a
chapter in my Greek Testament. Every morning, soon
after my breakfast, I took a long walk of two or three
miles upon the mountainside. These daily walks were
to me a great delight. Eyes, lungs, legs, spirits,
thoughts, were wonderfully refreshed and invigorated.
A perfect reservoir of strength those steady long walks

of the winter laid in for me. Then I would go home and usually write, for I commonly wrote one sermon a week. I had few books, my Bible, Prayer-book, Greek Testament, and Horne's Introduction were about all. But the sermons I wrote in the lonely cabin are not the poorest in my barrel deposit. One lad, a nephew of Colonel Sanders, came to the cabin and recited Latin to me. It was a pleasure to me to teach him.

In spite of the wickedness of the people their personal kindnesses to me were unceasing and overwhelming. The legislature was in session that winter, and Virginia City was the capital. I was elected chaplain of the House of Representatives, and the members were always courteously respectful during the opening service of prayer. On my frankly telling the vestry and people that I did not think it right they should pay no salary, they voted me a salary as rector, of $2,500 a year, and they paid it too. When I found a poor, suffering, neglected, paralyzed man, and bringing him to an empty cabin near mine ministered to him and took care of him for many weeks, all the people helped me gladly. On two or three occasions, when by some entertainment, money for charity was raised, it was brought to me that I might act as almoner. Two men, hard drinkers, one day came to my cabin and brought me $106 for charity. The poor man whom I had been privileged to take out of his miserable, squalid surroundings and provide for in cleanliness and some degree of comfort, when I bade him good-bye and turned him over to the care of others, looked his thanks through his tears—and spoke with a faltering voice. Ah! of rewards that earth can give such thanks are among the most blessed.

When I saw my way to build a church the people gathered to my help with abounding generosity. The way the building of the church came about was this. We had held our first services in the council chamber, the hall over a saloon, in which one branch of the Legislature had held its sittings. Then we moved to " Reception Hall," which was the old deserted store of Tootle, Leach & Co. Then we occupied the deserted store of Erfort, Busch & Co. All the time I was thinking about a church building, but being determined not to move in any way that meant debt I did not see my way to move at all. Finally the Methodist minister, Rev. Mr. King, came among us, and with true Methodist enthusiasm and energy within a fortnight he set to work to build a church. I felt quite in the depths of meekness to see how in energy he was distancing me ; yet for the life of me I could not see how I could wisely do other than I was doing. The frame of Mr. King's building went up, but before it was shingled and weather-boarded, and ere the minister had been three months in Virginia City, he left, shaking the dust of our town from his feet. He never appeared again and mechanics' liens were soon clapped upon the church. One of the Methodist trustees came to me of his own accord and told me of them. In conference with him I suggested that perhaps I might take hold and finish the church for one of our own. He replied : " It is just the thing for you to do. Or else the Roman Catholics will buy it in when it is sold on these liens. Here are fifty dollars remaining in my hands that I will turn over to you to help you in the matter."

I therefore went to work to find out the amount of the liens. They were $1,286.74. I gave $500 myself and then prepared and passed a subscription book. I got such responses as justified me in pushing on, so I bought up the liens, at about their face value, and when the

sheriff's sale came on bought in the property. I afterwards finished the church at an entire cost of $3,409.08,
and on the Sunday after Ascension, May 24, 1868,
entered it as " St. Paul's Church." The day we entered
it I had the comfort of reporting to the congregation
that every bill had been fully paid, and that there were
sixteen dollars left, over and above in the building account.
This was a happy day for me. Prayers and tears and
thanksgivings of my own were built into that church as
into no other that I have ever had to do with. And my
own wicked people, whom I loved and prayed for, in
their generous kindness gave me the $3,000 for building.
The old church yet stands ; [1] has stood for near a generation, in use for the holy worship of Almighty God. It
stands (I say it with grateful memory and loving thanks)
the outward and visible sign of some work accomplished
by the humble earnestness I was able to throw into the
lonely pastorate of the winter of 1867.

Nor was I left entirely devoid of spiritual companionship. There was my faithful churchman and vestryman,
Major Veale. A poor, honest man, forty years old or
more, bred a Methodist, used to come to take counsel
with me on religious matters, and in such evident simplicity of spirit and earnestness of devotion that his visits
greatly cheered me. A year or two afterwards he was
confirmed by me. A youth in his teens came steadily
to Sunday-school and to service, and between services
often called for explanations and information concerning
the Church. Men called him a little " off " and " peculiar." But others besides Shakespeare's fools have a
wealth of heart and wit and wisdom under the motley
exterior. For shrewd insight into things theological,

[1] The new church, in memory of Mr. Henry Elling, was erected on the
same site in 1904.

Francis was head and shoulders above the average man. And principle and honor were his watchwords. He also, later, was confirmed by me, and in all my thirteen years' care of Montana, whenever I came within reach of Francis I found him ready for service and for Holy Communion, and with purse open (for he had become a thrifty miner) for any Church needs.

There was an old wood-sawyer in Virginia City, a German Lutheran, whose home life had been sadly wrecked. He too was in his lonely cabin. He came to church constantly; and as he visited me also in my cabin, I found him a cheerful, patient, prayerful, faithful Christian, abundantly conversant with Holy Scripture, and greatly interested in the question of prophecy and its fulfilment. Many lonely hours were comforted by his holy converse in my cabin. His plaintive voice in some sweet old German hymns often sang tender Christian love into my heart and tears into my eyes. And what cheery greetings we gave each other, as going round the streets I would see him working diligently at his saw-buck. Faithful old Mr. Shook! You were a source of sustaining strength to me in all our association together, and a silent rebuke to me if I became impatient or despondent. After that cabin winter I never saw you more, but I feel sure that if God through His mercy in Christ brings me to His Home, I shall surely see your faithful, cheerful, earnest, singing self again.

God gave me also a dear and helpful friend in Mr. James H. Gamble. He was an Irish Presbyterian, an earnest, godly man. He was in Virginia City to represent the interests of a brother-in-law, who had largely invested in quartz mining. (I am sorry to say, as it afterwards appeared, that he sustained large losses in such investment.) Actively, untiringly he stood by me, soul to soul, a Christian brother. Coming in from his mine, twenty miles off, he often stayed with me in the cabin and prayed with me and slept with me. Dick grew to be almost as fond of him as of me. One night when poor Dick had been for a day or two so sick that I feared his catship might die, after we rose from our silent prayers Mr. Gamble said : " Bishop, do you know whom I have been praying for? I have been praying for Dick that he might get well. I couldn't help it—I know what an almost needful companion he is to you." Dick did get well, and afterwards I left him in Mrs. Goddard's care when I gave up Virginia City to her husband. Mr. Gamble's presence was everything to me that winter. The strength and comfort which it ministered were measured by the despondency into which I fell when he left for the States on the morning of March 31, 1868. Up the street, in an unobserved nook, I said as best I could my inarticulate good-bye. Then I wrung his hands and hurried up the hillside on my morning walk. I would not go to the stage office to see him start and thus expose my feelings to the crowd. On the top of my hill alone I watched the stage as it wound down the gulch below carrying him away, then I could do nothing but throw myself on my knees on the ground and pray God to help me to be patient and cheerful, and to play the man. Some time before he went Mr. Gamble had told me he would be in the confirmation class whenever I should have one in Virginia City. In the autumn when I went East I confirmed him at one of my old home churches, St. James' the Less, Scarsdale, and soon after I married him. He and Mrs. Gamble now live in North Conway, N. H., and he is warden and lay leader in the parish. Within a few days of his leaving me and my cabin he gave me the deed of a house and lot for a

" St. Paul's rectory." The gift was worth $1,200. He also ordered unique and beautiful red cedar work for the altar and chancel-rail, and furniture for the church, at an added expense of $650. Mr. Gamble's association with me was, under God the Holy Spirit, the sustaining tonic of my spiritual life in that winter of 1867. Some few more quotations from letters may be pardoned.

" *Sunday, March 22, 1868.*

" I have been on the lounge playing with Dick since I came in. He gets lonely when I am away; and it is with evident delight that he pounces upon me for a frolic when I come in. It would make you laugh if you could wake up as I do o' mornings and see him in bed. He never goes to bed with me, but when I go is either stretched by the stove or lying on the buffalo robe. But by morning (generally at about midnight) he creeps in between the sheets, with his head invariably fixed in easy and digni- fied pose on the pillow. Evidently he takes after his master in dread of suffocation. His head he wants on the pillow and out in the ' open air.' I laugh almost every morning at the little rascal, he looks so funny snoozing at my side. Sometimes those formidable little paws of his are stretched towards me in his sleep; once or twice in his dreams, or in my dreams when I have been threatening to crush him, his claws have been let into me most unmercifully, bringing me with startling suddenness to the realization of where I was and who was my bedfellow. He is thoroughly well now, and his lean- ness is rapidly changing to fatness.

" Soon after I came back from my walk this morning, Mr. Shook came in, ' getting lonesome at sight of my cabin,' he said. He stayed till church time, so that I had a chance to read over my sermon only once. I preached a sermon this morning, written yesterday and day before, on the miracle in the day's gospel, but really on the subject, 'What think ye of Christ?' It was unsatisfactory to me, it was written in haste, and seemed wandering, or wanting in unity. Yet I cannot but think that the Holy Spirit took it up this morning and preached it home to the hearers as I could never do. There was a large congregation, and towards the last there was breathless attention, and I saw tears in the eyes of the strongest men. As this occurred in the delivery of a poor sermon, the Holy Spirit's work is manifest, and I have thanked Him from my knees since I came home, beseeching Him ever to help me, and to save souls, and to keep me humble while faithful. Ah, dear wife, my only spiritual hope and comfort for the future of this field is in Him."

"*Sunday, March 29, 1868.*

" I have entered on what is going to be a very trying week to me. God help me for Christ's sake! Not only must I write a lecture and a sermon this week, but I must also next Tuesday morning bid good-by to Mr. Gamble. I know it will be very hard for me to come back to this lonely cabin after I have seen him off in the coach.

"Four P. M. I've been resting and reading and thinking since I came from Sunday-school. I look into the future, and the look, though sad, is very peaceful. I look on and on and on, not troubling myself much about what I shall do or what shall be done to me here; not despairful even at the prospect, the sure prospect, of my going away from earth, leaving you, or you going away from earth leaving me,—on, to the rest after this world is certainly left and sin is dead and struggling is over. If all be well then, dear, through and with the Saviour, what matters the now? I think God is helping me to get rid in some little of my old shrinking fear of death. If this world, clouded by sin, is so beautiful, what must not the next world be in the excellence of beauty? I do honestly think that my main wish is humbly to try to do my duty, and in as inconspicuous a way as possible, earnestly to love my Saviour, so to leave everything, life, death, work, weariness, loneliness, affliction, success, in His hands, hoping at the last to go to be with Him and you and all my dear ones."

"*April 29, 1868.*

"I hear of one vestryman as having been in a gambling den all day long yesterday; and of another as drinking desperately. Ah, dear, do you not see and know that if I leaned on, or trusted in, this community, or in my large audiences, or in aught human here, I would now be plunged in the lowest deep of despair? It astounds me to think of and realize the breadth and depth of wickedness and vice in which this whole community is steeped. Nothing but God's Almighty power, with His loving, cheering grace, keeps me patient and courageous, or in fact restrains me from giving up in despair and fleeing Eastward across the mountains, scarcely daring to look behind me, any more than Lot upon the cities of the plain."

"*Sunday, May 3, 1868.*

"Friday was the anniversary day of my consecration as bishop. I rose early, read over the office of consecration, read Keble and Croswell on ordination, and kneeled down and with many tears thanked God for His love and mercy and help abundantly given to me in the year past. Then I prayed Him for the dear Saviour's sake to guide and help me in the year entered on. I was

particularly struck with two of the solemn promises which before God I have made; viz., the sixth, to exercise discipline; and the seventh, to be merciful to the poor and needy and 'strangers.' May God help me!   . . .
"It is terribly dull here. People are woefully blue. Yet God helps me to be persevering in the work of getting subscriptions for the church. And He ministers hope that on the day we enter St. Paul's we shall worship in a building on which not one cent of debt rests. At present not a cent of debt is on it."

"*Ascension Day, May 21, 1868.*

"I have just come home from service. We had full services, singing and all, but without the Holy Communion. I preached the sermon that I wrote yesterday and the day before. Five men and five women were present. The mud is deep and the air is cold. Yesterday three inches of snow fell, and we are likely to have more this afternoon. If it continue thus cold we will not be able to get into ' St. Paul's ' next Sunday, stoveless and windowless as it is. . . .

"I see by this morning's paper that Wells, Fargo & Co.'s fares are reduced. The fare from here to Omaha is now $250; from here to Salt Lake, $100; from here to Boise, $140; from Salt Lake to Omaha, $150; from Salt Lake to Boise, $100. This is a large reduction in the prices charged when we came here first. Then we paid $210 from Omaha to Salt Lake; and $120 from Salt Lake to Virginia or Boise."

"*Sunday, May 24, 1868.*

"Rejoice with me. Thank God for me. Not even the news of your last letter telling me that our boy seemed to be threatened with sickness can stop the full

beat of my thankfulness to-day. This morning we held
our first service in ' St. Paul's.' It rained, the mud was
very deep, it was chilly and we had no stove. Yet our
congregation was decidedly a good one. Our collection
was for ' Rector's Salary.' I told the people of my
thankfulness to God and them ; I reported that our expenses for St. Paul's amount to $3,409.08, and that not
one cent of debt is on the building. I gave notice for
Holy Communion next Sunday (Whitsunday). It was a
great comfort to worship in our chancel. We had a
most untoward time for moving yesterday in the rain
and mud, yet we did move. I worked hard all day, carrying benches, picking up old lumber, shoveling away
débris, etc., and I got so much exercise that I did not
sleep first-rate last night. I also got some troublesome
letters yesterday, and had to sit up till after midnight
with them. But I am right well to-day, cheery and
buoyant. In spite of all troubles my spirit says, ' The
Lord be praised for His abounding mercies and goodness
to me!' Yesterday, when everything had been moved
out of the ' old store' and I was there alone, I kneeled
down and tearfully thanked God for letting me preach
for Him in those four walls, begging Him to forgive all I
had said amiss, and praying Him that some little that
through the Holy Spirit I had spoken there, might be as
seed sown in good ground to spring up and bear fruit to
His glory. My thoughts of the old store where I have
labored and wept will ever be tender ; even while glad
and thankful thoughts spring up for the new church into
which we have entered."

" June 4, 1868.
" In the afternoon of last Monday (June 1) I received
this startling telegram : ' St. Louis, Mo., May 30, 1868.

You were unanimously elected Bishop of Missouri on first ballot. M. Schuyler, President Convention.' I kneeled down and prayed God to help me. Wifeless, friendless, at least counselorless, as I am here, it is hard for me to face the responsibility of decision of acceptance or declination. On Tuesday I wrote to Bishop Potter, pleading with him to help me to decide aright. I shall hardly decide fully till I get his answer. My inclination is to decline. My reasons are : I am too young to be over twenty-nine clergymen, all perhaps longer in the ministry than I; too immature and inexperienced to administer a diocese containing a city like St. Louis. Even if I could do it wisely, the strain and anxiety would ruin health, hope and good spirits. I ought not to leave this missionary field, I know about it, I am in condition to plan and act wisely for it. A successor could not be so fit as I, at once. Mormonism ought not to be dealt with by new men; and a succession of new men. Therefore I ought to stay in the field. So things look to me now. Of course I await the details of the mail which will probably reach me about the 15th."

Bishop Potter's letter did not reach me till July 7th, when I was at Bozeman. His views reënforced my own judgment that I ought to remain in the missionary field. Therefore, that very day I wrote the Rev. Dr. Schuyler my letter of declination as follows :

" *Bozeman, Montana Territory, July 7, 1868.*
" REV. AND DEAR BROTHER :
      " Your letter of the 15th of June has reached me this evening. It becomes now my duty and your right that I should immediately acquaint you with my decision in the matter of your call to me to become the successor of your late bishop. My dear and kind brother, I must decline your call; I cannot do otherwise. I do trust, and I beg to assure you of the confidence of this my

trust, that thoughtfully, conscientiously, prayerfully I have come to this conclusion. My youth warns me against assuming the responsibility of directing the work of the Church in a field so great and so ripe unto the harvest as yours in Missouri. The errors which my inexperience would commit, however unintended, would be in what is perhaps your critical transition period big with harm to the Church and the cause of her Lord.

" It is not long since the Church at large called me out of an obscure country parish and sent me here. I think she wants me to stay here ; and duty to my present field is loth to entertain any thought of my going from it. I beg therefore, my dear, kind brother in the Lord, that you will make known to the clergy and the laity of your late convention and to the official authorities of the diocese of Missouri my respectful declination of the call to be their bishop. For the high mark of esteem and confidence which the churchmen of Missouri have shown me, I am, believe me, deeply grateful. I would not dare to disobey their summons to come down and work by their side did I not think the Holy Spirit points me to the decision I am making. May God be with them and cheer and strengthen them in their work for Him. My heart's affections will henceforth be specially enlisted in the life and growth and work and triumph of the Church in Missouri. May our heavenly Father smile upon you, and may the Holy Spirit soon replace at your head a good and faithful and wise bishop, for the loving Saviour's sake, is the earnest prayer of

" Your grateful friend and brother
" DANIEL S. TUTTLE.
" To the REV. M. SCHUYLER, D. D.,
" President of the Diocesan Convention."

" *June 14, 1868.*

" My last Sunday's sermon on ' The Trinity,' pressing the point of the Church as older than the Bible has got for me the name of being ' dreadfully High Church,' and 'won for me a smiling congratulation from Father D'Aste,

the Jesuit, on this wise: 'Ah, beeshop, good-morning!'
'Good-morning, father!' (the two of us shaking hands
with mutual and smiling cordiality). 'Ah, beeshop, I
glad to hear dat you preached an excellent sermon last
Sunday morning.' 'Thank you!' 'You preached de
infallibility of de Church' (his eyes twinkling and his face
laughing all over). 'O no, father' (I smilingly answered),
'not quite the infallibility of the Church; but I urged the
point, too often forgotten, that the Church is older than
the Bible and is the witness and keeper and interpreter
of the truth.' I was quite amused at this congratulation.
From others I hear that Father D. says with much glee:
'De beeshop is seeking after de trut. He is an inquirer.
He will yet die in de bosom of de Catholic Church.' I
told my informant good humoredly, that I hoped that
prediction would certainly come true. 'I do hope to die
in the Catholic Church, but not in the Roman Catholic.'
Last Wednesday evening in the church, on the pulpit
lectern, I found a Testament, and in it this inscription:
'The bishop says we need not read this book. The
doctrine and law of the Church repose all responsibility
of reading the Scriptures with the clergy.' I said no such
thing in my sermon. I pressed only this, that on doubtful and disputed questions, and concerning the funda-
mental articles of the faith, like the doctrine of the
Trinity, the Church in her history, her creeds, and her
councils, and not private judgment, must be the judicial,
authoritative interpreter. But I am not sorry that I have
preached such sermons as on 'Hades,' and on the
'Trinity.' Popular as I am here it is most meet that I
should present the unpopular, or unusual Church doctrines
myself, and not leave to Mr. Goddard to incur any
added unpopularity of 'not being as liberal as was the
bishop.'"

"*Cabin, June 25, 1868.*

"It is the last time I shall write the caption above. I sit at the old table, in the midst of a room all confusion from my overhauling and sorting things, some for Mr. Goddard, the rest for myself. To-night I go to the hotel to sleep, so that I can put the bed and bedding in the rectory and have all things ship-shape for the arrival of Mr. and Mrs. G. to-morrow morning. Last night was my last sleeping here. I feel like parting with old friends to say good-bye to the cabin and to Dick. Poor Dick and I and it have become strangely attached to one another, lonely as we have been together. I gladly leave them to fly to you, dear; but so fond am I of old ways, so disinclined am I to give up old things, that it is not without pangs that I leave this spot and my cat. So it will be all my life, won't it? I shall have to move about, change constantly, leave places and things just as I have grown attached to them! Well, God help us, dear. There is a place, a Home, where change no more enters. May the loving Saviour fit us for it!"

"*St. Paul's Rectory, Saturday, June 27, 1868.*

"Here I sit by Mr. Goddard's side in the rectory. Mrs. G. is in the kitchen, putting things generally ' to rights.' They arrived safely yesterday morning in the rain, and I am having a delightful visit with them. It has done me great good to welcome them here. Everything is very cozy. I have brought dear little Dick down and he is quite domesticated already. He is now sleeping on the bed. But he came near scratching my eyes out when I brought him. When I had landed him safely in the room he bounced past me, like a panther, through the door, across the street, and up the hill to his old mountain cabin home."

Just after noon on Sunday, June 27th, I was obliged
to leave Virginia City for Mountain Home, in order
to catch the weekly mail-wagon that traversed the
Gallatin valley. On Sunday morning, therefore, I
preached my good-bye sermon, from which I venture
to quote :

" I have thought it not improper to lay before you to-
day an account of our work in this parish for the past
eleven months. My first celebration of divine service
with you was on Sunday, July 21, 1867. On every
Lord's day since, with, I believe, one exception, the services of the Church have been continued uninterruptedly
by either minister or lay reader. I have celebrated the office
for holy matrimony twice. I have baptized sixteen children, and celebrated the Holy Communion twice. There
are now on the parish register the names of ten communicants. I have read the office for the burial of the
dead over seven persons who have returned, ' dust to
dust.' On December 8th, I opened the Sunday-school
with four teachers and twenty-seven scholars. Now on
our books are nine teachers and sixty scholars. The con-
tributions have been as follows :

```
" For rector's salary .    .    .    .    . $1,470.35
Subscriptions for building the church  .  2,287.55
Collections for parish expenses  ·    .    .  188.05
Collection for the Sunday-school    .    .   24.75
Communion alms  .    .    .    .    .    .   12.60
                                          ──────────
     Total  .    .    .    .    .    .    . $3,983.30
```

" Besides this sum, money was generously given last
winter to furnish comfortably the cabin in which I have
lived. Our melodeon has been purchased and paid for,
and some lamps have been kindly donated, It gives me

great pleasure again to state to you, with a heart full of gratitude to God and to you my helpers, that this church building is out of debt, even to the uttermost cent."

I find myself thinking of the year I spent in Virginia City as perhaps the most valuable one of my missionary experience. It furnished me ground for full sympathy with the clergy of the border. I was the immediate pastor of a frontier community, and could readily afterwards put myself in the place of any other pastor in considering his pastoral work. I knew the excitement of preaching to hundreds massed. I knew the trial, when novelty and enthusiasm were gone, of preaching to ten and twelve. I realized in daily experience how hard and cold to spiritual things were the minds and thoughts of the men, and how hopeless it seemed to rouse or touch them by human effort. So it was easy for me to understand the confession of any downcast clergyman. "There is no one to be confirmed, there seems no spiritual growth"; and not to make his sadness deeper by any harsh judgment on my part.

It taught me loving forbearance towards wicked people. I did not compromise with their sin, I hope, but so good and kind were the people there to me personally, so true and loyal were they in their respect and helpfulness, that I could not help loving them, and my prayers for them were not perfunctory but heartfelt and warm. I wanted to be a friend to them, I tried to be a friend to them, I grew to be a friend to them, without, I hope, becoming in any way a partaker in their sins. I seemed to get a way of looking at wicked people, different from what I had had before, and much more tender. Perhaps Abraham, if the mythical story told of him contain truth, experienced some such change. As the patriarch sat by the door of his tent one evening, a wearied and dust-covered old man came near. He sorely needed food and rest. Abraham invited him in, gave him water to wash, and set food before him. But he noticed that the old man before eating did not ask God's blessing on his meat. He asked him why he did not. " I worship the fire," said the old man, " and I acknowledge no other God." The patriarch, in righteous indignation, turned him out of his house forthwith. Soon the Lord called unto Abraham and said, " Where is the old man, thy guest?" He answered, " Lord, I bade him begone from my house, for he would give Thee no honor in prayer and blessing." The reply came from the Lord, " I have suffered him these seventy years; and couldst thou not bear with him one hour?"

It gave me a useful lesson of patience under small gains and slow results. It was wholesome self-restraint to remain in the " old store " for six months and more because to build a church earlier seemed the sure way to plunge us into debt. It was the exercise of wise pastoral oversight, although very distasteful to my ambitious hopes, to have no confirmation at the end of my year's work. The one man prepared could not be present on my last Sunday. To corral and brand (using mountain phraseology) the unprepared were very unsuitable pastoral work indeed. It bred in me a habit of cheerful bearing up against discouragements, disappointments and overthrows. Many a lesson I had the opportunity of learning and practicing in not being able to have my own way. And many another one lesson I had, that to stand steady, not to give up, and never to bate heart or hope in a good cause, is the way blessed of God and admired by men. The experience of being outwardly beaten in your best efforts, while cheery faith and vigorous resolution do not falter within, is a discipline for life and conduct of immense value.

So count I my year of cabin life in Virginia City a blessing. It made me tenderer, broader, sturdier, and laid up in my heart a reservoir of sympathy and love.

CHAPTER IX

WINTER IN HELENA, 1868–9

ON Sunday afternoon, July 28, 1868, I bade good-by to Dick, the cabin, the new church, the log rectory, and to Mr. and Mrs. Goddard, of Virginia City. The Sunday succeeding I spent at Bozeman. A small building with dirt and sawdust for floor, and with slabs and planks for seats, served as both court-house and meeting-house for the community. There I held services in the morning; at the invitation of Major La Motte commanding, going to Fort Ellis, three miles distant, in the afternoon. At Bozeman I found only two communicants of the Church. The place as yet had only a weekly mail; I went in and out with the mail carrier, and was the guest for a week of Mr. Tom Cover, who had been one of the original discoverers of Alder Gulch, and who had now built at Bozeman a flour-mill. I quote from the letter I wrote from here to my wife:

" *Bozeman, July 6, 1868.*

" Saturday I crossed over the East Gallatin on an insecure pole, and, pistol-protected, took a long walk on the bluffs that are on the edge of the Indian country. The views obtained of the valley were most magnificent. I saw no Indians. But without doubt we are in the country of the hostile Crows. A few weeks ago a band of twenty or thirty stole the fort mules while they were feeding in a herd, and ran them off from under the very walls of the fort. By celerity and persistence most of the animals were recaptured. Mr. Cover has told me the story

of a late encounter of his with Indians. He and Mr.
Bozeman (after whom this town is named) started on
horseback for Fort C. F. Smith to see about some contract for furnishing supplies to the government. As they
were to go through the Indian country they supplied
themselves with the swiftest and best horses they could
find. Now I'll give Mr. Cover's words as nearly as I can,
for he told me the story in his room a night or two ago.

"'I told Bozeman that we could whip small parties of
the redskins, and run away from large parties. So we
started. When twenty miles or so out we met some men
coming in, whose outfit had been attacked by Indians and
whose stock had been stolen. I said, " Bozeman, these
Indians will be after us, we must look out." When we
were about fifty miles out we camped for dinner. The
place was not suitable for a camp, but Bozeman said his
horse was tired and he begged to stop. He seemed
despondent, and I have since learned that he told people
he would not get through this trip. When we had eaten
and before we had cleared up things five Indians hove in
sight. I drew my Henry rifle (a Henry has sixteen shots),
and said to Bozeman, " Let's let them have it now!"
One of the redskins, as I aimed, threw up his hands and
called out in Crow language, " We good Indians, don't
shoot, we want to talk." Bozeman called out, " Don't
shoot, Tom, I think I know that Indian." I, knowing
that Bozeman had lived much among the Indians, let
drop the muzzle of my gun. So the redskins came up
and stretched out hands to shake. But I shook my head.
I didn't like their looks. I feared that while two might
hold us by the hand, the others might shoot us. Three
of them were armed with rifles, two with bows and arrows. They then asked for something to eat. I pointed
with my gun to the remains of our dinner, and they sat

down and ate. I said to Bozeman, " What do you think
of these Indians ? Do you know them ? " " No," he said,
" and I guess we shall have trouble." " So do I," I replied,
" and my vote is that we shoot right now. We can kill
two and then we are enough for the remaining three."
" No, hold on," says Bozeman (he seemed to me to act
strangely and almost cowardly, though I knew him for
one of the bravest of men), " hold on ; perhaps we can
get off. You get up the horses and I'll watch them." So
I laid down my gun by him and with my pistol in my
hand went for the horses who were picketed near. When
I had got the bridle on one I looked towards the Indians
and saw one of them drawing out his rifle as if to show it
to Bozeman. I shouted, " Shoot, Bozeman, shoot ! " but
before he did so the Indian shot him and he fell forward
on his face. I began firing with my pistol at once.
Another Indian fired at me and hit me in the shoulder.
While firing my pistol I made for my gun. I got it and
fired at an Indian and he fell. But in getting the next
cartridge in place something stuck. I kept threatening
the four by pointing the muzzle at them, and at the same
time working the lever to get the cartridge into place.
Luckily it got right and I fired. The Indians had driven
me back some distance, but when I fired this second time
they began to give way. Their guns were empty, and
they only fired arrows at me. These went very wide for
they were excited and demoralized by my firing. But a
thicket of bushes being near I thought I would get out
of the way of their ugly arrows. When I had thrown
myself into it, my courage and strength and manliness
and presence of mind all left me. I was completely unnerved, and had they come on then, they could easily
have scalped me. But they did not come and I could
not see them. In five minutes my courage returned, and

looking carefully to the order of my gun I emerged, determined to kill more Indians if I could and to see what had become of Bozeman. Going to him I found him stone dead. I took his watch and then looked for the Indian whom I had shot. His comrades had taken him, and all were gone, with our two horses and pack horse and outfit. Accordingly, I gathered up a little of the food still remaining and started home afoot. It was fifty miles, and I very fatigued and weak from the blood flowing from my shoulder wound. As I walked on I put snow every now and then on the shoulder to keep it cool. I went eight miles off at right angles from where the fight occurred, that if the Indians should come back they might not find me, and then I struck my course home. I walked all night, weak, wearied, and worn, and finally came to the Yellow Stone River. This I had to swim, but the swim in the cold water refreshed me, and I plodded on. When twelve miles from here I overtook the same train we had met as we went out, and they brought me home, where I was laid up with my wound for some weeks.' He was a brave fellow, don't you think so? He says of Bozeman : ' It seemed to be his destiny to be killed as he was. Had we fired at the Crows when they first hove in sight, all would have been well. Or, had we killed them when eating before they had time to kill us we should have got along all right. But Bozeman seemed to have a presentiment that he was to die on our trip and it took all the nerve out of him.' "

My summer visitation of Montana this year included only seven points, Bozeman, Gallatin City, Radersburgh, Helena, Blackfoot, Deer Lodge and Bannack. In Radersburgh and Blackfoot I held no services. In both I stayed over night, sleeping on my blankets on the floor. For such " lodging " at Radersburgh I paid a dollar, and a dol-

lar and twenty-five cents each for my supper and breakfast. There was a ball at the hotel where I stayed, but
the noise and confusion, though my "bed" was in the
hallway off the bar-room, did not keep me awake. From
Radersburgh to Helena, fifty miles, I missed the time of
the regular coach and was obliged to hire a livery team
to take me. The expense was thirty-eight dollars. Gallatin City, known also as the Three Forks, is at the head
of the Missouri River. The confluence of the Jefferson,
the Madison, and the Gallatin Rivers, just there, forms
the Missouri. Gallatin City consisted of a store, a blacksmith shop, a flour-mill, and Major Campbell's hospitable log cabin, which served as the hotel of the place.
In the cabin I held a service and baptized one adult and
two children. This spot seemed the worst place for mosquitoes in all Montana. At Bannack, which was the
mother town of Montana, I found no minister or church
of any kind whatever. An old man, a baker, was faithfully trying to gather the children together, Sunday by
Sunday, for teaching. I baptized several of the little
ones. At Deer Lodge I secured a lot given me by the
town site company, and at a cost of one hundred dollars
I ordered it fenced. Of Helena I marked the growing
importance, and I made up my mind that it must be supplied with a pastor, even if after returning from the East
I should have to take up the work there myself. I quote
again from letters to Mrs. Tuttle :

"*Helena, Montana, Sunday, July 12, 1868.*
" I have dined with Mr. Tutt, and have returned to the
back room of the First National Bank, where I slept last
night. This bank is closed to-day, but nine out of the ten
stores are open. While I write the shouts of five or six
auctioneers are dinning in my ears. They are all selling

goods, and the streets are filled with hundreds, even thousands, of men. There are also scores of wagons, and hundreds of ox-teams, coming in from Benton. It is a perfect Babel here, and no Sunday at all. The town has grown greatly since I was here last September. I think it must have in it 5,000 or 6,000 inhabitants. I must secure some one to come here soon and begin efficient church work. I had a large congregation this morning, spite of the threatening rain. I wore my robes, putting them on in Mr. Thomas' house, where Mr. Goddard and I went last year. In fact the service at Gallatin City last Wednesday is the only one in which I have not worn my robes. The responses this morning were good, there being quite a large number of Prayer-Books in the congregation."

"*Blackfoot, Montana, July 16, 1868.*

"I am in the back room of a log store. In this room we are to sleep to-night. Mr. Tutt, who brought me over here from Helena in his buggy, is snoozing on the bed. Dr. Higgins, the genial but deaf proprietor of the store, is also taking a nap, and I sit down to write. I look out upon the houses of Blackfoot (all without exception being log cabins) and stores and saloons. The doctor tells me that there are only two ladies in the town. I shall not have services here. Mrs. Higgins, a devout Churchwoman, has returned to Lexington, Mo. Mr. Goddard once had services here (thirty miles from Helena), but I have met no one as yet who could tell me about him. Not a shade tree is in all this town, and hence, though it is cool in here this afternoon, it is very hot in the streets. The hills and mountains about are nicely wooded, however, and they look to me very beautiful. I wrote you last from Helena, on Sunday. In the evening I had a large congregation, and I am quite convinced that if I cannot find a suitable man to send to Helena you and I ought to go there in November and spend the winter and begin the needed work."

Mr. Goddard was at this time, as I had been, the only Protestant minister in Virginia City. Questions besetting him in that position he referred to me. Here, for instance, is an answer:

"*Boise City, Idaho, August 18, 1868.*
"My dear Mr. Goddard:

"On reaching here yesterday from Idaho City I found your two letters awaiting me. . . . With regard to the question of 'other denomination' communicants, the principles upon which I should act, and on which I would desire you to act, are these two:

"1. Within due bounds of fidelity to truth and honesty, to be painfully diligent to 'give no offense in anything, that the ministry be not blamed.'

"2. To be careful that we, who as priests of the Holy Catholic and Apostolic Church are set to dispense the precious sacraments freely, without money and without price, keep ourselves free from niggardliness and exclusiveness in the dispensing.

"On these principles, in the questions and cases before you, my unhesitating decision is that mercy, on your part, is better than sacrifice; that your leanings should be towards mercy, and all your doubts construed for mercy; and that your discretionary exercise of the power lodged in you as a priest of the 'One Church' throughout the world, on the side of mercy, may free you, under present circumstances, from minute and undiscriminating obedience to the letter of the rubric, which is a director for our own branch of that 'One Church.'

" Therefore, if you please, my *directions*, in the order
of answers to your questions, are these :

" 1. ' Do you desire or advise that such be explicitly
invited as such (*a*) publicly; or (*b*) privately ? '   Ans.
Publicly, give no invitation other than the regular church
service gives. Privately, act your own pleasure, use your
own discretion. Generally, I should think it better to
take care not to offend or repel, rather than actually to
invite.

" 2. ' If not to be explicitly invited are they to be
constantly received without question ? '

" Ans. ' Constantly received,' yes, if morally and
spiritually fit. ' Without question,' no, at least not without conscientious and persistent calling of their attention
to the law of our branch of the Church as contained in
the rubric after the confirmation office.

" 3. ' Of what force am I to regard the rubric at the
end of the confirmation office ?   And how to explain it
to those questioning me ? '

" Ans. Its force is that of law. The explanation of
your disobedience would be that, for mercy, from custom,
under guidance of your bishop, you willingly assume the
responsibility of holding its operation suspended in individual cases, or under such peculiar circumstances as surround you at ' St. Paul's.'

" Of course you understand that my desire would be
that you should not acquiesce in the coming of any one
to the Holy Communion statedly, repeatedly, and for a
long time, without asking such an one, and pleading with
such an one, to be confirmed. By waiting for ignorance
to get enlightened, and allowing a year's time for this enlightenment, both at Salt Lake and at Boise persons have
now been confirmed, who, from the sects, have long come
to the holy communion; but who, if we may judge

humanly, would not have taken this step (confirmation), had they been at first excluded or warned off, for discipline, from the Lord's table.

" I think you must be misinformed as to my having publicly invited ' other denomination ' persons to the holy communion in Virginia City. I never did so. Though on the day of the first celebration while the communicants were coming to the chancel I did nod my head to Mrs. F. and to Mrs. I. who seemed to be hesitating whether to come. And I told Mr. D. the night before to tell Mr. Shook that I should be most happy to have him (Mr. S.) come to partake of the blessed sacrament. And I did tell Mrs. C., an evening or two afterwards, that, ' We are not close-communion, as you call it. I shall be most happy to administer the holy communion to all who will come, who " truly and earnestly repent them of their sins, and are in love and charity with their neighbors, and intend to lead a new life, following the commandments of God, and walking from henceforth in His holy ways." ' Of course, at the fit opportunity of an approaching confirmation I should have pressed upon all the consideration of the rubric that is our law.

" You say, ' If you do not direct, my judgment would lead me to ask, etc.'

" Now what you say therein I heartily approve of, only begging you in your practical carrying out of this to explain, when asked, that members of ' other denominations ' ought not to come regularly, and that I should not advise them to come steadily for any length of time, unless they be really ready and willing to be confirmed. At the same time be extremely careful to instruct earnestly, rather than repel harshly, and keep free from rousing prejudices before you have given a year's time or more to honest

ignorance to learn by seeing, and hearing, and watching
the church's system of truth."

In after times I changed my own views and practice.
When administering the holy communion in towns where
perhaps my visit was almost the only religious service of
the year I did not hesitate to invite people publicly in
these words : " All Christians, by whatever name they
call themselves, who will come with us in faith and penitence and charity to partake of our blessed Lord's body
and blood in the holy communion this morning will be
cordially and lovingly welcomed." And I grew to in-
terpret the rubric after the confirmation office as applicable, in the strictness of its warning, only to the children of our own church homes and Sunday-schools, not
to devout Christians of other names, who, in the hunger
of their souls, might earnestly desire to be fed by us at
the Lord's table. Possessed of the only church building
other than the Roman Catholic in Virginia City, I advised and sanctioned the loaning of St. Paul's more than
once (once particularly) to the godly and learned Bishop
Marvin of the Methodist Church, South, when he was
visiting Montana. So, circumstances and experience
constrained a mellowing of my thoughts and an erasing
of some of the hard and fast, barbed lines, that as a strict
sort of churchman I had deemed it my duty to set up.
So much courtesy, brotherly kindness and Christian love
were shown me that I would have had less than the warm
heart of a man within me had I not gratefully recipro-
cated in every way that one in my position could reasonably and rightly.

In the summer of 1868 I visited also Salt Lake City,
Boise, Idaho City, and Silver City ; at Salt Lake confirming twenty, at Boise nine, and at Silver two.

At length, September 8, 1868, I started from Salt Lake

for the East, to go to Morris, where the wife and child
were, from whom for nearly sixteen months I had been
separated. I reached them on the 17th, and a joyful reunion we had. Through our long separation God had
preserved us all in health and strength. Mr. Rulison was
the rector of Morris, and I took sweet counsel with him.
I confirmed forty for Bishop Potter, including five at
Morris. Among those I confirmed were my own dear
brother, Lemuel, and the husband of my sister, at Windham; and my good friend Mr. Gamble, at Scarsdale. It
was the year of the General Convention, which was to be
held in New York City, and October 6th found my wife
and boy and myself guests of our dear friend Mrs.
Griffin, of Stuyvesant Square, who has made a home for
us for a score of years, whenever we are in New York.
Mrs. Griffin, and her sister, Mrs. Hamilton Fish, were
granddaughters of Gen. Jacob Morris, the early patriarch
of my country parish, so her loving heart was inclined
kindly to care for us from the first.

I entered the House of Bishops to find four members
my juniors, Bishops Young, Beckwith, Whittle, and
Bissell. My first speech in the House I made in the dis-
cussion upon the confirmation of the election of Rev.
C. F. Robertson to be Bishop of Missouri. I said of him
that he was my classmate at the General Seminary, and
that he was the best equipped man intellectually and
theologically of our class. I also said that it would be
a mistake to argue from his pale cast of countenance that
he was lacking in physical vigor; for I knew, as a fellow
student could know, that there was much of muscular
strength and endurance in him. I closed by saying that
I should vote against the confirmation for the simple
reason that I wished to do to others as I would have
others do to me. That to ask so young a man to take

up the hard work and anxious care involved in the
Episcopal oversight of so large a field as Missouri and so
important a city as St. Louis, was to impose upon his
unseasoned shoulders a cruel burden. My speech and
vote surprised, and I think displeased, my dear father,
Bishop Potter. But I spoke exactly what I felt; and I
was not thoughtful or experienced enough to consider
what a grave wrong my way of viewing and voting, if it
should prevail, would work both to the brother elected
and to the diocese of Missouri. The wisdom, energy,
devotion, and success that characterized Bishop Robertson's episcopate of over seventeen years afterwards showed
how completely wrong I was in the vote I cast.

In the main, in this session of the House I was very
quiet, as it well becomes all junior bishops to be. The
meetings were held in the Sunday-school room of Trinity
Chapel; while the House of Clerical and Lay Deputies
met in the Church of the Transfiguration, four short
squares distant. October 7th was the day of meeting of
the General Convention in Trinity Church, the bishop of
Delaware (Lee) preaching the sermon. On the 4th I
had confirmed my dear Presbyterian friend, Mr. Gamble,
at Scarsdale. On the 6th I had married him in the
Church of the Annunciation, New York. Introduced
into the House of Bishops at thirty-one years of age I
may be permitted, I trust, to recall some of my thoughts
and observations. Forty bishops were present. In voting,
in accordance with the old traditions, lines were drawn
between " High Church " and " Low Church." From
that General Convention of 1868, however, the strict
lines of demarcation began to fade, until now they seem
to have quite vanished. The evangelicals had resolute
and wise leaders in the Bishops of Ohio (McIlvaine), and
Delaware (Lee). And they had sturdy followers in

Johns, Eastburn, Lee of Iowa, Clark, Bedell, Stevens, Vail, Cummins, and Whittle. But the majority was evidently on the other side. And splendid leaders the other side had in the Bishops of Maryland (Whittingham), and Connecticut (Williams). I was amazed at the prodigious industry and untiring watchfulness of Bishop Whittingham. He jotted down the number and substance of every message that came from the House of Deputies. He kept his own record of the " Acta " of the House. And as for the " Agenda " none so well as he knew what they were and when they should be presented. Not only was he chief in depth and accuracy of theological and ecclesiastical learning, but his knowledge of parliamentary law, and his skill and power in urging any matter in hand before a deliberative assembly, were most remarkable. As the leader of the majority he, more than any other one man, was responsible for the legislation made by the House of Bishops. Wise and true, loyal and devoted was he in carrying the responsibility for the American Church. Personally modest and humble to the last degree, he was officially firm as a rock and a resolute claimant of all his rights.

I remember noticing from the first the different standpoints from which the Bishops of Maryland and of North Carolina (Atkinson), viewed Episcopal prerogative and right. To Bishop Whittingham Episcopal authority was inherent and dominant. Constitutions and canons of the church were regulative and restrictive. In all matters which were regulated and restricted by these, bishops must be loyally obedient. In other matters, each bishop in his own cure, and, *a fortiori*, the House of Bishops, could fall back upon inherent right and act by authority of it. To Bishop Atkinson, however, the bishops as legislative and executive officers of the American Church

were subject to her declared law, and their authority to
exercise Episcopal right for her must be clearly derived
from, and defined and determined by, her Prayer-Book,
her constitution, and her canons of General Convention.
I think the Bishop of Connecticut, as scholar and theologian, saw with Bishop Whittingham. But his natural
temperament would lead him to act with Bishop
Atkinson.

The Bishop of Kentucky (Smith), was the presiding
officer. He was then seventy-two years old and had
been thirty-five years a bishop. In presiding, Bishop
Smith was always careful of heart to aim for the right.
But he was not always so clear of head to execute the
right. Two accomplished parliamentarians were near
him in rank, to whom he often turned for counsel and
guidance. These were Bishops Whittingham and Lee.
At times he called one or other of them to occupy the
chair. The former, nervous and decisive, used the gavel
with vigor, and its quick blows warned every one of us to
be on the sharp lookout as to what we should do or say.
The latter was most patient and gentle in his ways, but
with no lack of clearness of comprehension of how the
business of the House should be directed, or of wisdom
in directing it. The Bishop of New Hampshire (Chase),
seventy-three years of age, was feeble, but stood faithful
to duty, as was his constant habit. Those of my seniors
who, with me, were for the first time in the House at a
session of the General Convention, were Clarkson,
Randall, Kerfoot, Wilmer (of Louisiana), Cummins,
Armitage, and Neely. Dr. Cummins in the House of
Deputies three years earlier had spoken nobly and worked
earnestly to secure consideration for the Church in the
states of the late Confederacy. Perhaps this attitude
paved the way for his being made the assistant Bishop

of Kentucky. I was with him in the House of Bishops in two General Conventions. The contrast between him and Bishop Whittle, both radical low Churchmen, was marked. The latter was always sturdy, honest, fearless ; the former, diplomatic, plausible, conceited. There is no need to declare to which the deep respect of the House always tended.

To me the Bishop of Massachusetts, Eastburn, was the most picturesque member of the House. He showed marked hauteur, was unbending in loyalty to his convictions, and yet was not without humor and kindness of spirit. He was plainly a low Churchman, and yet " *nullius addictus juvare in verba magistri*," and he was so independent in thought and action that his *confreres* found themselves not infrequently quite at sea in making calculations that might be dependent on his vote. A seeming arrogance in his lecturing of the House would be forgiven and forgotten in a burst of laughter over his recital of the woes besetting him in the music in some country parish, furnished on the occasion of his visitation.

October 13th one of the great missionary meetings which Dr. Twing used to exert himself to get up was held in the Academy of Music. I was appointed one of the speakers, but coming last on the list and the hour being late I cut my speech very short. Mrs. Tuttle wrote to Mr. Goddard of it :

" One of the delegates in the House of Deputies [1] is staying here with us, so from him and the bishop we get a very good digest of the business every day. The missionary meetings at night are very enthusiastic and interesting. I have enjoyed the different reports very much. The

[1] Rev. J. Mills Kendrick of Kansas, since missionary Bishop of New Mexico and Arizona.

meeting at the Academy of Music, the programme of which I enclose, was very interesting. The house was crowded, many having to go away for want of room. The collection amounted to $4,000, I believe. Dr. Paddock (B. H.) and Bishop Cummins made very interesting addresses. Dr. Carver was long and stupid. Our bishop spoke for just three minutes, and was greeted as he appeared on the stage with applause after applause. It was the most magnificent thing I have ever heard when the whole multitude there said the creed together ; and it was beautiful and touching when every head seemed to bow at the name of Jesus. Dr. Twing seems a great manager."

The meetings of the Board of Missions were held in the evenings at the Church of the Transfiguration. One evening in debate a member urged that the missionary bishops should be requested to remain at the East to visit different parishes and infuse into them missionary spirit and interest. At that time there were only four domestic missionary bishops, Lay, Clarkson, Randall and myself. I was sitting in the back part of the church and at once I rose in my pew and said: " I hope such duty will not be laid upon the missionary bishops. For one, I feel that the need of my mountain people of my personal attention and care is paramount. And I already have my plans made, with all details arranged, for hastening back to Montana in November." Miss Mary Coles of Philadelphia was present that night, and what I said seemed to meet her approval. Before then she had never seen me to know me, she said. Since that time for more than a score of years she has been to me and to the missionary work under my charge a thoughtful, untiring and most generous benefactor.

After the convention I visited and made addresses in

New Haven, Hartford, and Philadelphia. It was at this time in St. Mark's, Frankford, Philadelphia, that the classes of Miss Mary Welsh got themselves ready to be named, " Bishop Tuttle Boys," and " Bishop Tuttle Girls."

I went then to the home at Windham for a Sunday, and as I have said, in the home church had the great happiness of confirming my dear brother Lemuel, and the husband of my younger sister. From there I went to Big Flats, Chemung County, near Elmira, to visit my elder sister, and to pick up Mrs. Foote, my wife's mother, and our child George, who were to accompany us to Montana. We four left Big Flats, November 24th, and stopping for Thanksgiving Day at De Veaux College, where Mrs. Tuttle's youngest brother, Charles E. Foote, was at school, and for a Sunday at Omaha, and a Sunday at Salt Lake, and a Sunday at Virginia City, we arrived in Helena on Friday, December 18, 1868.

In the autumn of 1865 good gold diggings were discovered in " Last Chance " Gulch, and by the next spring a vigorous mining camp was growing. To it the name of Helena was given and miners and business men gathered to it from Virginia City and other parts of the territory. It was a hundred miles nearer Fort Benton than was Virginia City, and the cheapest route for transporting goods was by the Missouri River to Fort Benton, Helena being about a hundred and forty miles from Benton. It thus came about that when I reached the territory in July, 1867, Helena, though not yet two years old, was already contending with Virginia City for the palm of chieftaincy. For two or three years the contention was sharp and bitter, until Virginia City, recognizing the logic of events, gave up. Then the seat of government was removed from Virginia City to Helena. Ever since, Helena has remained the capital of the territory and of the state.

Mr. Goddard and I had held the first church services in Helena in August, 1867, and he remained there as resident pastor for three or four months. Then he departed for the East. I was unable to find any suitable minister to send, and so concluded to go to Helena myself and stay and start the work. It was by this time a town of about four thousand inhabitants. A Methodist Church (Rev. Mr. Hough, pastor), and a Methodist Church, South (Rev. Mr. Baxter, pastor), were here. So many Missouri people during the civil war, to get away from internecine conflicts, had jumped aboard boats and come to Fort Benton and Montana, that the two classes of Methodists, quite irreconcilable, were scattered over the territory. In push and vigor Mr. Hough's adherents were the stronger, but in numbers, Mr. Baxter's were the greater. Mr. Baxter himself was a ranchman (so in mountain language a farmer was always called) as well as preacher. Besides, a Mr. Campbell, a Christian (or Campbellite) preacher, was on the ground teaching a week-day school, preaching irregularly on Sundays, and jointly with Mr. Baxter conducting a Sunday-school. One or two Roman Catholic priests cared for a little church, and a zealous congregation attended it.

The first thing was to find a place for services. On Saturday I visited the three county commissioners, and secured their consent to our use of the court-house. Mrs. A. M. Holter loaned us a melodeon, Mrs. Tuttle and Mr. Gostling (who had formerly been a helper to me in Virginia City) taking turns as organists. Accordingly, on Sunday, December 20th, in the morning and in the evening I held services in the court-house. These I continued, morning and evening, every Sunday thereafter, uninterruptedly, until August, 1869.

I was happy to have one more stronghold of my field

occupied by the church.   Messrs. George W. and Henry
L. Foote, and Haskins were in Salt Lake; Mr. Goddard
in Virginia City; and Mr. Miller in Boise City.   I had
won my spurs as a missionary the year before in the log
cabin in Virginia City.   I had no fear of meeting whatever, under God's providence, was to be met in Helena.

Well, here we were at Helena, after a ride by stage-
coach of six hundred miles and more.   We had come on
the Union Pacific Railroad to its terminus in the Bitter
Creek region, and thence by stage, twenty-four hours,
to Salt Lake.   And now for a home, for we had had none
for nearly two years.   At first we went to the hotel, but
prices there for the four of us were $100 a week.   It was
evident that we could not stand that expense long, so
other forces than love for a home impelled us actively to
cast about for a house of our own.   We found it on
Jackson Street (by the miners known as Pig Alley).
Opposite us lived Mr. A. M. Holter, whose wife was a
Churchwoman; she kindly loaned us her parlor organ
for church services.   Next door to Mrs. Holter lived Mrs.
Maginnis, whose husband was afterwards, and for several
terms, the popular delegate to Congress from the territory.   Our house had two rooms above and two, besides
the pantry, below.   The parlor served us for sitting-room
and study; and the dining-room was kitchen also.   We
paid for rent $37.50 a month.   Afterwards the landlord
added a kitchen; then he raised the rent to fifty dollars,
afterwards still further increasing it to $62.50.   He said
he would sell the house for $2,200.   The absolute neces-
saries for house furnishing cost me $700.   We cut the
table service as short as possible, contenting ourselves
with six plates, six cups and saucers, etc., because crock-
ery was dreadfully expensive.   Table linen and sheets
and blankets we had brought with us in a trunk, but as

extra baggage it had cost us enormously. Sixty cents a pound from Salt Lake to Helena for all baggage over twenty-five pounds, for each passenger, was the charge. Our extra baggage cost us $195. Gold dust at eighteen dollars an ounce, was the substantial currency. Every business man had his scales for weighing it, and men usually carried it in buckskin pouches. Greenbacks also passed, but at eighty per cent. instead of par. When prices were given one was always obliged to add one fourth more to have the cost in greenbacks. My salary of $3,000 was worth there only $2,400. Things to eat frightened us by their cost. Sugar was nearly fifty cents a pound, eggs were a dollar a dozen, butter was any-where from fifty cents to a dollar a pound, apples were fifty cents apiece. For house-servants women could not be had. If, however, one could be found, fifty and sixty dollars wages a month must be paid. Chinamen charged the same. At the time of Mrs. Tuttle's confinement (our second boy was born in Helena), we esteemed ourselves fortunate in securing as nurse, a Mrs. Brown, at seventy-five dollars a month. She was loquacious and almost talked her patient to death, and she was rheumatic and could not bend her knees to sit on a low seat, but must sit high, so the poor baby had no lap to nestle in, but was in constant danger of rolling off on the floor. She was asthmatic and must smoke her pipe full of tobacco every afternoon ; she was democratic and socialistic, I fancy, for to her astonishment and distress, the sick mistress noted how her own brush and comb were put to use at the needs of the nurse's toilet. Washing was three dollars or four dollars a dozen pieces, so Mrs. Foote and I made a compact ; I bought a clothes wringer for twenty dollars, and fitted up a pounding barrel from an empty whiskey barrel (this was one of the few things which were cheap

—cheap from abundance—in the gulch). On Mondays she and I did the washing, she presiding at the wash-board and I at the pounder and wringer. For wood I paid nine dollars a cord, and for coal oil four dollars a gallon. I sawed and split my own wood, and Mrs. Tuttle was her own cook and chambermaid, so we kept expenses down and were never more cheerful and happy in. our lives than in those seven months of housekeeping in Helena.

We stayed only nine days in the hotel. When we got into our own house I fell at once into regular pastoral work. I wrote at and mostly wrote out one sermon a week. Normal domestic life was gradually asserting itself. In my pastorship of seven months I married four couples, and baptized eleven children. But funerals were very infrequent; in this time I had only two. The pioneers in the main were in vigorous young manhood.

January 31st, I opened a Sunday-school with four teachers and fourteen scholars. I visited all the people in their business places or their homes, convinced (and the experience of my life deepens the conviction) that pastoral visiting is a stronger force to win souls for Christ than is even the most eloquent preaching. The Presbyterians and Baptists, especially, I looked after, for they had no pastor of their own. Among my Sunday-school teachers of the winter two of the best were Presbyterians. I found fourteen communicants of the Church, and at the end of the seven months added twelve to them by confirmation. I insisted on the people's paying me a salary, and they cheerfully responded. The income I used to help the parish in Virginia City which was languishing, and for other church work. I knew that for my needs and as well for their good it was wisest and best for me to insist upon receiving a salary. In the seven months the people gave $2,370.25. Besides, my good friend Mr. Thomas E. Tutt, one of the earliest to welcome me to Montana, one of the sturdiest to stand by me in Montana, and in after years one of the first to welcome me to St. Louis, gave me $500 to help in furnishing my house. In the Cathedral in Salt Lake City will be found a handsome clock, which cost seventy-five dollars, and was also the gift of Mr. Tutt.

Mrs. Tuttle came direct from New York to Helena. She was not seasoned with mountain experience as I had been by my year in Virginia City. She looked for hardship and expected also primitive simplicity in frontier life, so her amazement was great to find the ladies who first called on her arrayed in silk and adorned with gold and jewels. She had yet to learn that the mountain people would have the best of everything, regardless of expense. She was surprised, also, that the number of calls upon her mounted into the sixties. Ladies did their own housework, largely, as she did, and there were some ladies of refinement, cultivation, and education in the three-years-old-town. They were, however, it must be confessed, comparatively few. Men here outnumbered women, seven or ten to one.

The men were from everywhere. Helena was, indeed, that far cosmopolitan. There were more from Missouri than from any other one state, and the next greatest number I think were from Iowa. Multitudes had come, also, directly from California and Nevada, and there were, besides, a few Englishmen and a good many Canadians. Among the miners were many Cornishmen and Irishmen. To crown all, a considerable squad of negroes, mostly from Missouri, had wandered over from the boats and landing of Fort Benton. John, a faithful colored servant, who had been assigned to serve me once or twice on my visits to Helena, had fallen very ill and was near death. My visits to his sick room and my prayers with him were blessings to me. And his tearful thanks were precious rewards.

Across the way from us, next to Mrs. Holter's, was a log cabin, in which five young men were living and keeping house. They did their own cooking, making their own bread and flapjacks. On Saturdays Mrs. Tuttle would bake a large pan of gingerbread, extra, and send over to them. So with pastoral work and sympathy we won our way to the regard and affection of the Helena people. On New Year's Day I received calls from twenty-six men. I was greatly pleased by their courtesy, for I had been only two weeks a resident. On Christmas Day seventy-five, on Ash Wednesday twenty-three, on Good Friday forty, and on Ascension Day seven, came to church.

During our stay in Helena two fires broke out; one on February 22d, and the other on April 28th. The latter was the great fire, as great for Helena as was that of 1871 for Chicago. The alarm was given soon after midnight, and I dressed hastily and ran to the scene, to offer any service possible. At one time the flames seemed sweeping down towards our own house and I ran home to warn Mrs. Tuttle and her mother to get themselves and the household goods ready to go out into the street at the shortest notice. Then I hurried back to fight the fire. There was no engine, no fire department, no organization; so the fire had every advantage. Besides, the buildings erected of pine and fir lumber, pitchy at that, were exceedingly inflammable. The utmost that could be done was to tear down some buildings in the track of the fire, haul off all the débris, and so, if possible, stop the progress of the flames. But the fire spread too rapidly for us, the wind speeding it. I was willing to work in any and every way I could, and was strong and enduring, and so was not a little conspicuous in the fire-fighting of that night. A year or two afterwards, also, in Deer Lodge I helped at a fire, carrying water and pouring it persistently and successfully upon a burning building, in the vaults of which much powder was stored. These efforts of mine, exaggerated and decorated by the reporter's imagination, were related in the papers, and at the time of my coming to Missouri were swollen into a sensational article, which recounted how the three heroes at the fire were a noted gambler, a leading, tough gulch miner, and myself. A little before daylight the flames caught the International Hotel, a three story wooden structure, and were consuming it with frightful rapidity. Directly across the street Parchen & Paynter had a drug store, with a very valuable assortment of goods. They had been hurrying all of them they could into the dug-out, dirt-covered room at the rear, which was fire-proof. But the big iron door of the room was not shut, and the scorching heat had driven every one away except Mr. Paynter himself. His strength was not sufficient to swing the door to and fasten it securely; so I went to his assistance. In the few seconds that the hissing flames held off without assaulting our persons we got the door closed tight and locked fast. Up to that night Mr. Paynter had been courteous to me, but cold and careless. After that, for all the future, I had no more helpful or devoted friend in Helena than was he. He was an earnest and faithful vestryman of St. Peter's, Helena, for many years. The fire was finally checked by coming up against two good buildings of brick, one on either side of the street. When I went home at eight or nine in the morning, Mrs. Tuttle made gallons of coffee to distribute to the men who had been fighting the conflagration. By noon she and I went down the street, where we took note of the wonderful pluck and grit and force of the mountain people. Here and there and everywhere were smoking ruins; and yet in two places draymen were hauling lumber and mechanics were clearing away débris and laying beams for the foundations of new buildings. In less than a week not a few buildings were up all along the street, and active business was going on inside them.

People were now more than ever kind to me. A lot one hundred and fifty feet square in "Storey's Addition," across the gulch, was given me for the church. But when the deed passed, the verbal understanding was that I was to build on it a church or a parsonage within twelve months. It did not, however, seem to me then a suitable location for a church, and I did not see my way prudently to expend money for a parsonage; so at the end of the year I re-deeded it to the giver. It would now be worth many thousands of dollars. It may be said, " You ought to have erected a small building upon it and so secured it." Well, for wise decisions any one knows that hindsight is ever so much better than foresight. I did what at the time I thought prudent and best. God's goodness was great in keeping me out of wild speculations in my youthful years on the frontier; often miners came and wished to give me feet in mining claims, which some day, they were sure, would yield rich results. These offers I invariably declined, saying I wanted them wisely and honestly to make the money, and a great deal of it, and then give a tenth to me for church purposes.

Major Hanna, an earnest Churchman, paymaster in the United States army, was stationed at Helena. In our day of small things his presence and help, morally and pecuniarily, were of inestimable value. One day in the early

summer, General Hancock, who was upon a tour of inspection in Montana, called at our house. Never do I
write or think of the men of the army without feelings of
the warmest gratitude swelling in my memory and my
heart. In my association with them on the frontier, in
garrison and camp, they were always true, kind, helpful
friends to me and mine. General Hancock seemed to me
a strikingly handsome man; I greatly enjoyed, as did
Mrs. Tuttle, his visit.

Early in my stay in Helena I bought the lot on which
St. Peter's church now (1893) stands, paying for it $1,200.
The lot was a lumber yard. I had only $400 to pay down,
but the $800 I borrowed. The lender let me have it free
of interest for one month, after that I paid three per cent.
a month. Subsequently, generous friends in the East
sent me funds, and holding some in trust for future and
not immediate use, I in turn became a lender. I loaned
$3,300 to a merchant for a year at twenty-five per cent.
interest. His store burned, but the insurance policy having been assigned to me, the lot and the insurance money
made me whole.

In February triplets were born to a good woman in her
home on Rodney Street. I went more than once to visit
the mother and the three vigorous little ones. The family,
however, ere long moved away from Helena and I have
no knowledge of their after history.

On the morning of May 22d, while we were at breakfast, there came a rumbling sound as of a heavy wagon
dragged rapidly across a bridge. With it came a shaking of the house which threw down some pieces of furniture and some dishes in the pantry. The ladies said,
" Some great piece of furniture has fallen somewhere." I
thought one of the large freight wagons in the street
which ran close by our front door had by the awkward-

ness of the driver collided with the corner of our house and shaken it, but going to the door I saw no wagon. Looking up-stairs and down I could find no large piece of furniture that had fallen anywhere. While finishing our breakfast we could only discuss the matter and wonder about it. Soon after, I went down Main Street and discovered that the same disturbance had been noted everywhere. We were therefore sure the town had been visited by an earthquake. About midnight the same day, another shock came. A sudden violent rocking of the rooms and beds was felt by all who were awake. No damage, however, or only very trifling damage, was caused, either at morning or at night.

Memory goes very pleasantly back to the winter I spent in Helena. In health I was entirely well and strong. The cutting and splitting of the fire-wood, with the " chores " attendant upon housekeeping, took the place, as exercise, of my usual long walks. The pastoral work among the people was very congenial and very interesting. To have a home again, with my loved ones around me, was inexpressible happiness. I wrote sermons, and though I found it hard to do so, was happy in the work. I made the acquaintance of almost everybody. I learned to appreciate the force of their pioneer language.[1] Persons and property were safe there. It

---

[1] I subjoin some of the expressions that occur to my memory—" Cinch." To "cinch " a man is to catch him at a disadvantage, and to press and corner him with the disadvantage. The word is taken from the act of the packer in drawing tight the band securing the burden upon his pack-mule, as also the saddle upon his horse. With knee against the animal's ribs he draws the strap with all his might, so tightly, indeed, that it seems as if it must squeeze all the mule's breath out.

"Grub," a meal, food. " Outfit," like Mr. Doe and Mr. Roe of legal phraseology, does duty for all kinds of purposes. It is one's horse and wagon, one's ranch, one's clothes, one's belongings of any sort, even one's

was four years since the Vigilantes had hung their score or more of murderous desperadoes and had established law and order for the territory. The secret of the membership of the Vigilantes has never been told, but nobody doubts that such men as Colonel Sanders, Mr. S. F. Hauser, afterwards governor of Montana, J. X. Beidler and Neil Howie were leading members. To these and

wife. " Lay-out," provision, preparation. One has a good " lay-out "— when one is well provided against an impending need, or for an enterprise to be undertaken. " Played out," exhausted, ended, come to naught. " A man for breakfast," a homicide has been committed in the mining camp during the night. " Petered out," quite the same as " played out," though used specially of the vein or lode of ore when it fails in richness or worth. " On the hurricane deck of a mule " or " a cayuse," on horseback. " Heeled," armed. " Dead broke," and " Strapped," without money or resources. " Down to bed rock," at the last end of something, or back to foundation principles. " I'm not here for my health," and " I'm on the make," were ways in which the pioneers expressed their determination to look out to get money. They all expected, when it was got, to go home to use and enjoy it. " God's country," the States, the boyhood's home. " Nobody is holding you," a challenge to a braggart to do something and not to threaten. His kind of talking too goes as " Shooting off the mouth." " Dying in his boots," killed in a quarrel, or hung. " Road agent," highway robber. " Got the drop on him," first to get pistol or gun cocked and aimed, and so get the advantage of another. " Buck the tiger," gamble at faro. " Straight," does much duty for the men of the mountains and proclaims their abhorrence of weak dilutions and diplomatic mixtures. It is not only " whiskey straight," and " coffee straight," but " politics straight," and " religion straight." " A soft thing," an easy berth, an advantageous position. " A prairie schooner," a freight-wagon or emigrant wagon. " A bull whacker," a driver of oxen for the freight-wagon. " Wagon," for stage-coach. You would never hear a stage-driver or an experienced mountaineer using the word " stage " or " coach " or " stage-coach," but " wagon " or " the wagon." " To go for " one, is the expression for a vigorous assault upon one. " You git! " is the sententious mode of ordering one away from one's presence. " You bet your life! " is a strong affirmation. Concentrated strength and lucid meaning are in the words placed under a wood-cut illustrating the fact that a miner has found a suspicious character in his cabin. He points his pistol. The intruder starts hurriedly away. Four monosyllables only are men like them Montana owes an everlasting debt of gratitude. I was proud to meet and know them and call them friends. Of Colonel Sanders I have already spoken, in giving an account of the trial and execution of George Ives. J. X. Beidler was known as X. all over Montana. With a frame of iron, with nerves and muscles of almost electric quickness of play, absolutely fearless, of sunny temperament, unflinchingly devoted to upholding law and justice, he was an eminent tower of strength to good order during the troubled times. The winter I was in Helena he was about thirty-five years old. He died in 1890, in Helena, probably the best-known man of all Montana, and carrying to his grave a precious load of gratitude from all, except outlaws, who knew him. The history of his life of twenty-seven years in Montana would· fill a large volume with thrilling incidents and adventures. I may stop to recount one. Two cutthroats had been sentenced to death by the Miners' law, a little before the organization of the Vigilantes was effected. Their graves were dug, the gallows was erected. When brought to it a parley arose. That was step first, time gained. Then some friend of the doomed men mounted a barrel and asked to read the letter one of them had just written to be sent to his mother. Step the second gained, softer emotions aroused and pity engendered. Then a

uttered. The first two by the owner, the other two quickly, without an intervening breath, by the hatless suspect : "You git!" "You bet!" Sometimes "you git" is enlarged into "gr· up and dust." "Tenderfoot" and "pilgrim," a newly arrived immigrant from the States. To "whoop up," to arouse, to rally. To "round up," to gather a concourse. "Corral," an enclosure. To corral any one is to corner him, to secure and shut him up to your control. To "make a bad break," to make an unwise or disastrous move. To "turn loose," to make a sudden and vigorous onslaught. "Making their pile," securing the riches that they have come to the mountains for and that they intend to go back home to enjoy.

voice suddenly shouted: "Let those in favor of releasing the prisoners walk down the hill!" The mass of the gathered crowd stepped together downward. X. and a few resolute ones alone were left up at the summit. It was a verdict under appeal, in line with their imperfect law, and X. and his sympathizers were disgusted at seeing the two culprits pushed on the back of one horse, galloping away to freedom. A few days afterwards the two came upon X. standing in the doorway of a saloon. They rushed at him from behind, and one drawing his pistol and presenting it close to his face said: "So you dug my grave, did you? Now I'm going to blow the top of your head off!" "Bah," said X. coolly, "not with that thing, it ain't cocked." The outlaw was taken aback for an instant and dropped his hand sufficiently to look. Quick as a flash X. drew his pistol and covered his assailant, then marching both men off as his prisoners.

Mr. S. T. Hauser was, in my Helena sojourn, the president of the First National Bank of Helena. He was one of the earliest of the incomers into Bannack in the finding of gold there in 1862. Not only in the activities of the Vigilantes, but in Indian troubles also, his were stirring experiences. In the year 1874 Mr. John H. Rogers, a personal and political friend of Mr. Hauser, was thrown from a wagon in returning from a political meeting, and killed. I was at Helena in the course of my annual visitation. Mr. Hauser asked me to conduct the funeral services of Mr. Rogers, to be held at Deer Lodge. "When?" I asked. "To-morrow," he replied. "But," I said, "at 6 P. M. to-day I am to baptize a child of Mr. Kleinschmidt, and at 8 P. M. to-morrow I have an appointment for services at Unionville (a mining camp two or three miles from Helena), I do not see how it is possible for me to serve you." He rejoined, "If you

say you will go and hold the services at 10 A. M. to-
morrow at Deer Lodge, I will see that you get there and
get back." I replied, " Thank you, certainly it will give
me pleasure to be of service to you, if only I am not
obliged to fail in engagements made by me with the
public." " All right! " he said. Deer Lodge was fifty-
five miles from Helena. After the Kleinschmidt baptism
a team called for me, and in company with several of Mr.
Rogers' friends, at 7 P. M. I hurried off, reaching Deer
Lodge at 4 A. M. I then threw myself into a bed and
slept for four hours. At ten I conducted the funeral
services, and afterwards took the long march to the grave
for the committal service. All was not over till 12:30.
After a hasty dinner, at 1 P. M. I was in a buggy by
the side of Mr. Hauser, for the return trip. He had
come over before me and arranged for strong, fast teams
and relays, that he might get me back to my Unionville
appointment. And he accomplished the task. We
made the sixty miles to Unionville, and I arrived there
at a quarter before eight o'clock, to hold services and
preach. This was the kind of pioneering work to commend
a " gospel sharp " (mountain name for a minister) to the
miners. On that afternoon's flying trip from Deer Lodge
Mr. Hauser told me much of his early years in Montana, giving me, especially, the story of the expedition
into the Yellow Stone region of the Crow Indian
country, undertaken by fourteen men including himself,
under the leadership of James Stuart, in the spring and
summer of 1863.

In passing I beg to record my well-deserved meed of
praise for the brothers Stuart, James and Granville (of
Deer Lodge), whom I knew quite well. James died in
1873. Granville is still (1893) living. They were born
in the state of Virginia, but reared in Iowa and Califor-

nia; they came to Montana in 1857. They married Indian wives, and though white immigration poured in and settled around them when gold was found, they remained always true to their wives and children. This, as every mountaineer well understands, required the height of moral courage. James had had a medical training. Granville has scientific attainments and was for a long time correspondent of the Smithsonian Institute, Washington. Brave, true, pure, wise, upright, generous-hearted, whole-souled men they were. I count it no little honor to have known them.

Here are some extracts from letters I wrote at this period to Mr. Goddard.

" Helena, February 5, 1862.

"I've been busily shut up all the week on my lecture (on Charles I, and English constitutional history). Have almost finished it to-day. It is spiritless and long and I am vexed at it. Yet I have put hard and honest work into it, and my conscience, if not my taste, is satisfied. Clagett's lecture on Wednesday night was admirable— most eloquent and instructive. His idea evolved was that the ' Alkali ' of the plains is in no distant future to furnish the mineral fertilizing material for exhausted cereal soils. Last night I married Chadwick to Miss Ewing."

" Helena, February 13, 1869.

"I am in negotiation for a lot, ninety by one hundred and twenty, streets on three sides (viz., Breckenridge, Warren and Grand), just on the hill above me, and in front of the court-house; price, $1,200. It is now a lumber yard. For continuing to occupy it for this purpose until June 1st, the owners will leave the lot well fenced. The deed was to have been made out to-day, but I have not yet been called on to pay up. I have to borrow $800 of McCormick, but I deemed it my duty to step in and buy this lot. It is the only large piece of unoccupied ground, at all central, to be found. On the 6th I baptized Holter's little one; on the 10th I married Colonel Woolfolk and Miss Swallow. The latter is a Presbyterian. The next day I baptized Kleinschmidt's little one, and in the evening delivered my lecture to a moderately good audience. People were attentive and did, I think, like it better than I. Yesterday I visited one of the four schools here. I'm going to take them all in order. This morning I baptized the sick child of L. W. Stickney, and in the P. M. visited our famous triplets."

" Helena, March 2, 1869.

" ' Blue ' letters were the order of the day to-night. George (Foote) says Haskins is sick,—school suffering; coal out,—burning pine wood at twenty-five dollars per cord. In two weeks three stoves had burned eighty dollars up.

" Mrs. Webb writes from Silver City (Idaho) that many have left, and more are leaving, for White Pine (Nevada). Those staying behind are blue. Her stated facts are such that I now give up the idea of planting a man at present at Silver and shall be content, so far as Idaho is concerned, with trying to double force at Boise."

" Helena, April 6, 1869.

" Last night I got a most important mail. 1. A letter from Rev. W. F. Lloyd, of Portage, Wisconsin, saying that he accepts the call to Helena and will leave for here about July 1st. He brings his wife, his wife's sister, his daughter, and a young man to keep a parish school. I am much pleased with this letter. Things begin to shape themselves thus: (*a*) Henry (Foote) to go to Boise; (*b*) I to go to Salt Lake in August or September; (*c*) George to stay in Salt Lake; (*d*) to get one good man, layman or cleric, to devote his whole time to Salt Lake school, and George and Haskins and I to take classes.

"2. I received a letter from Haskins notifying me of candidates for confirmation at Camp Douglas, and of his desire to be ordered priest at my next visitation. In view of this, I take it, I must appoint a standing committee. I intend to do so. Suppose Mr. Lloyd were to be here August 1st, and I were to spend August in Montana, September in Utah, October in Idaho, and return to Utah in November. What think you of the supposition? It is rumored that Mr. Comfort is to leave here; that another Methodist minister is to come. I wish now that I could very soon secure a rectory here. I ought to do it."

" *Helena, May 1, 1869.*

"Please take notice, herewith, that I appoint for a standing committee for the missionary district of Montana, Idaho and Utah, according to Canon 13, Section 7, Paragraph 6, Title I of the Digest, the following named presbyters and laymen, to serve as such for the year from May 1, 1869, to May 1, 1870, viz.:

"Rev. Edward N. Goddard, Rev. George W. Foote, Moses Veale, and George Thexton.

"I do not think there is need,—and yet that you may know my mind, I will speak of it,—to suggest to you that although we are on the rude frontiers we are a part of the great 'Church Catholic,' and I hope you and I will feel it incumbent on ourselves to comply minutely with all canon laws, as we would were we in New York.

"I trust to you to exact rigidly, and in faithfulness to your office in the committee, all the requirements of papers, etc., demanded by the canon, in those applying to you to be recommended to orders.

"Last Saturday I read burial service for the first time here. Last Sunday P. M. I baptized four children, Tuesday evening I married a couple, and Wednesday we had our great fire. I have written a communion sermon this week. Rev. Mr. Comfort is very sick with mountain fever. I went to-day to see him, but the physician forbids visits."

"*Helena, June 15, 1869.*

"We're not much behind you. Know all men (or one woman, which is perhaps equivalent), by these presents that at 1:30 A. M. yesterday, son No. 2 arrived unto us. He's a bouncing boy. All aver his weight to be ten pounds, though I haven't tried the steel-yard yet. Georgie takes the nose-breaking quite cheerfully, and kisses, and smiles over, and talks about his ' brudder,' the ' ittie baby.' We have a nurse and get on pretty well with her, though she is an inveterate tobacco smoker. I am to pay her seventy-five dollars for four weeks."

I have alluded to the wondrous powers of correspondents of newspapers in amplifying and decorating their accounts of plain and simple facts. I may be allowed to adduce two examples in the following extracts :

"Well, the great lecturer has come and gone. He may or he may not be the greatest ecclesiastical orator of his day, but as a lecturer he stands alone, not even in the front rank. He is the fore of any rank. No matter who gets second money in this lecturing contest, the first must go to Mr. Beecher. When I sat and listened to his heavy and sonorous, voice, and reflected that thirty-five years had passed since I last heard him, the man seemed to me like a sturdy mountain oak. How his stalwart figure and wonderful voice have defied the spoliative fingers of time.

" At the same time, he is not altogether my ideal of a preacher, because he is a little too fond of keeping himself before the people. One cannot help admiring his elegant English, which even the harshness of an occasional Yankee accent cannot mar ; and as for his ideas, he is the embodiment of liberalism in religion. He is as far ahead of other minds in this century as was Galileo in the sixteenth, but he is not my idea of an ecclesiast. My man was here about four months ago, and if there was anybody who heard him and was not charmed with his unpretentious manner and his earnest utterances, I have yet to hear it. He is just as full of earnest piety, just as muscular in his advocacy of the right, just as fervent in his love of manhood, as is Mr. Beecher. And he is not the least bit sensational.

" I shall never forget the only time I ever met him. It was more than two years ago that I reached Baker City, bound for Boise, at two o'clock in the morning, being the only inside passenger. The night was chilly, and I sought out a place where pigs' feet were retailed with coffee and tea to those iniquitous men who sit up late at night and play at games of chance. When I got back to the stage office another passenger had got inside. He was sitting on the back seat of the little Concord wagon, so I took the front one and faced him. The coach lamps shed their lurid glare over the deserted streets as we rolled out of the little mining town and began the ascent of the long, steep hill that overhung the roofless timbers of the old Rockafellow mill. After a few moments of silence the newcomer asked:

"'Have I not deprived you of your seat? I am told you have come through from Pendleton.'

"'You have done nothing of the kind,' I replied. 'We are going up a hill now, but we shall soon have a long descent by the Express ranch, and then you will wish you had taken the front seat.' From this we got into a conversation, and as I found out we were in for a ride of one hundred and fifty miles together, it became necessary to introduce myself.

"'I am Bishop Tuttle of Utah,' he said, quietly, in reply.

"I never was so tired in my life as I was that night, for I had not closed my eyes since I left Pendleton. All along the road I had met old friends and had been exhilarated in consequence, until the reaction came in the shape of severe bodily fatigue. But sleep I could not. The man had fascinated me with his conversation before I had the slightest idea who he could possibly be. All that I could see of him through the pitchy blackness of the night, was that he had a burly figure and wore full beard. Had I been a pilot steering a deeply laden steamer down stream in dead low water that dark night, I could not have waited more patiently for daylight to come. Curiosity kept me awake in spite of all my fatigue, but at last there came a lull in the conversation. My head lolled wearily for a moment or two and then sagged into a corner of the stage with a drowsy nod. Somnus was master of the situation. For twelve or thirteen miles of that lonely route down the cañon of Burnt River the four gallant steeds galloped without my knowledge of the danger that overhung us as they rounded the steep grades and short curves on their course. All at once I was awakened by the sound of the mellow horn. Dave Cissley, the driver, was signaling the station, two miles ahead, to get the next relay of horses out.

"With a wide-spread yawn I awoke. The gray dawn was stealing down over the Weiser hills and a light veil of fog overhung Snake River, the boundary between Oregon and Idaho. And then for the first time I caught a sight of my traveling companion as he sat dozing in the opposite corner of the stage. He looked like a well-to-do cattle man, and was dressed in a suit of brown cotton duck, such as we use for shooting and fishing suits, with heavy boots and a slouched felt hat. It was warm weather, and he had not even as much as the professional white choker, but wore his shirt collar turned down in a decidedly *negligee* style. After the change of horses had been made at Miller's station (now called Huntington), I got outside to take the seat vacated by a man and his wife who had come from the North Powder. The new driver, George Ingman, was an old California acquaintance, and we soon got into conversation, which turned upon the bishop who was inside.

"'The boys all love him,' said George; 'he's just as quiet and modest as he is learned and scholarly. He can have my overcoat any night the snow flies. You hear me.'

"The good bishop simply dressed according to his vocation, which entailed upon him journeys of great length through a hot country, over rough roads full of alkali dust. And he preferred tan colored canvas clothing to seedy broadcloth or dusty cassimere. Peg one for the gospel of common sense. But there are those who will recall his massive figure and stately presence as he stood in the chancel of Trinity, last May, and closed his discourse with that touching peroration:

" ' Busy, busied here and there! It sums up almost
our earthly life! And throughout it the Master comes
along and puts not a few trusts into our hands. God help
us to hold them all firm and fast! May we never let slip
what has been given us to keep, until this struggling,
puzzling life be gone; and that other life which we believe will end the struggles and clear the puzzles, has
come with its reckonings, recompenses and rewards.' "
(*The Portland Oregonian*, of October, 1883.)

STIRRING STORY OF THE MONTANA OF TWENTY YEARS AGO

" About a score of years ago, before the railroad had
crossed the Rocky Mountains, Bishop Tuttle was sent as
a missionary to the Northwestern territories. The good
bishop might well have been appalled at the first view of
his diocese. It was an empire in extent, but it barely
afforded him a single congregation. Afterwards, when
he had planted the Church in a few of the chief centres
of population, he had congregations 1,000 miles apart,
requiring weeks of painful and dangerous travel to reach
them, for the hostile savages held sway on the plains,
while bandits, more daring than the savages, and no less
blood-thirsty, infested every mountain pass through which
the lines of travel led.

" But never was a man better fitted by nature and grace
for his high mission. Of heroic stature, in every physical
sense a man among men, he had a heart for every fate
and a courage and resolution equal to any demand. His
hand, strong as a giant's, was soft and white as a woman's,
and more than once he had made some insolent and sac-
rilegious brute feel its might, but far oftener it had
wrought sweet charity and tenderly nursed the sick and
brought comfort to the dying, to rough men in lonely
cabins in the wild mountain gorges, bereft of woman's

care. He entered into the lives of the people and made their troubles his own, and when the rude mountaineers, as they presently did, came to know this strong, brave and gentle man, his fame went through the mountains and he became the beloved bishop.

"The city of Helena, if it can be called a city, with its rabble of house, huts, tent and hovels, crowding a gulch between two high shoulders of a giant peak, and climbing up the steep slopes to perch on rocky ledges and platforms, was the metropolis of the northern mountains. One winter morning, soon after midnight, fire broke out among some shanties in the upper end of the gulch. The mountains were white with snow; a small rivulet which meandered among the rocks was locked in ice, while a biting blast blew down from the mountains, and, sweeping through the gorge, soon fanned the fire into a conflagration. Men rushed to the scene with buckets and blankets. There was no fire brigade and no other apparatus for fighting the flames. Everything was confusion, and the raving of the gale, the roar of the flames and the shoutings of men supplemented the frantic exertions of the people to save their property, and in many cases, to escape with their lives from the fiery furnace into which the narrow cañon that held the fated town had been converted.

"Finally, when many residences, hotels and shops of all sorts had been swept away, and the fire had invaded that quarter where were situated the large warehouses in which were stored the chief stock of provisions and necessaries, the bulk, indeed, of the supply for the whole territory, the situation seemed desperate enough. The people realized that here was the last rally of deliverance to be made. A thousand miles of plain and mountain, buried deep in the snow, lay between the people and the burning town and any other source whence the necessaries of life could be drawn.   In one moment these people were confronted with the present horrors of conflagration, to be inevitably succeeded by starvation, amid the rigors of a Northern winter.

" When it had been realized that to save the town was impossible, every energy was bent to the work of saving the magazines of provisions, and a few brave spirits had organized a defense and had gathered the populace for a last struggle.   The plan of operations was simple enough. It was to cover the precious houses with blankets and keep them wet.   A few daring men were to maintain themselves on the house-tops, while the others were to pass up unceasingly water in buckets, masses of ice cut from the streams, and huge balls of snow.   The men on the roof must brave fire, smoke and the freezing wind. To falter was defeat ; to retreat was ruin.   There was no faltering in the desperate struggle, and finally the battle was won.

" Morning had come, and with it the sun, which, as it rose over a shoulder of the mountain, gilded the forms of three men, who stood high on the parapet of the building where the fire had been stopped.   They were the chiefs, self-chosen, to lead in the conflict, but acknowledged and obeyed by the populace, who instinctively recognized their supremacy.   These three men, with their visages begrimed and black with smoke, their hair and beards singed, their hands torn and bloody, their hats torn away by the wind, and their clothing ragged and awry, and with the fire of battle in their eyes, and grim and stern lines of resolution on their faces, were terrible, almost ferocious.   They looked at the smoking ruins, then at the houseless people below ; then they turned and saluted each other, the two at the extremes regard-

ing their companion in the centre as if in some sort he
was their superior.   It was at this moment that the rising
sun shone upon the trio, gilding and glorifying them,
while the multitude below gave a great shout, recognizing, as it were, their deliverers.

" Who were these men ?   They were well known in the
mountains if not immediately recognized in the disfigure-
ment of battle.   The one on the right was Bitter Root
Bill, otherwise William Bunkerly, a noted desperado,
who got his cognomen from a daring adventure with the
Indians in the Bitter Root Mountains.   The man on the
left was Gentle Joe, a leading gambler.   His real name
was Joseph Floweree, said to be from an aristocratic Virginia family.   He was a handsome fellow of thirty, well
educated and so well known for his courteous deportment
that the public appreciation had crystallized into a title.
The figure in the centre, taller, more erect and heroic
looking than the others who had greeted him as their
chief, was no less than Dan Tuttle, Bishop of Montana
and the Northwest.   In the desperate turmoil these three
men had gravitated to each other and had risen to the
leadership.

" The good bishop was soon at the height of popularity.
The mountaineers had tested his manhood and they were
ready to love and trust him for the friend and counselor
he proved to be, and the popular verdict was solemnly
announced by Mr. William Bunkerly when he declared :

" ' He's full jeweled and eighteen karats fine.   He's a
better man than Joe Floweree ; he's the biggest and best
bishop that ever wore a black gown, and the whitest man
in these mountains.   He's a fire fighter from away back,
and whenever he chooses to go a brimstone raid among
the sinners in this gulch he can do it, and I'll back him
with my pile.   He is the best bishop, and you hear me

howl.' " (Correspondent in *St. Louis Globe Democrat,* September, 1886.)

The plans for a rectory at Helena miscarried. " Hard times " was a universal cry. My committee discouraged my making any attempt. Mr. Tutt said: " I should rather have gone out any other year to collect $2,000, than this year to collect $200." So I had nothing to do but to submit to their judgment. As soon, therefore, as Mr. Lloyd came, I arranged for my own family to go to Virginia City and stay there, while I made the visitation of Montana. We gave up the house we were in to Mr. Lloyd. The Helena people were to pay him a salary of $2,700. He assisted me in the services of Sunday, July 25th, baptizing our little boy, Herbert Edward. On Monday we took stage for Virginia City. My happy pastorate among the Helena people thus ended, though for nearly twelve years more I continued my bishop's care of them.

CHAPTER X

FIRST YEAR IN SALT LAKE CITY, 1869–70

With Mr. Lloyd at Helena and Mr. Goddard at Virginia, I was now at liberty to decide where to make my home. Everything seemed to point to Salt Lake City. It was the largest town, containing 20,000 inhabitants, while Helena had only 4,000, and Virginia or Boise only 1,500 or 2,000. The stage routes all started from Salt Lake. After one day's journey north, the Montana stage and the Idaho stage branched off at Bear River. The work in Utah was naturally beset with more anxieties and perplexities than that in either Montana or Idaho, and could so lay claim to my personal presence. Besides, Mr. Foote and Mr. Haskins all through the winter had been begging me to make Salt Lake my headquarters. When we left Helena, therefore, on the morning of Monday, July 26, 1869, our faces were set towards Salt Lake. We had resolved to make that our home. Mrs. Tuttle and the family would go over to Virginia and stop under Mr. Goddard's care while I should make the summer visitation of Montana. Then, in the fall, we would all go to Salt Lake.

Our great fire had not left houses or rooms plentiful in Helena, so the house which had been our home for the winter must be given up to Mr. Lloyd and his family. We left Helena at 9 A. M. Monday and reached Virginia (a distance of one hundred and twenty miles) early in the morning of Tuesday. Here for six weeks my family of four remained under the care of Mr. and Mrs. Goddard, while I met the eleven appointments for towns in Mon-

238

tana, which I had made and published. At Deer Lodge
I secured a lot for a church, it costing me seventy-two
dollars to perfect the title. I arranged to have it fenced,
Mr. Granville Stuart kindly taking charge of this work for
me. At Bozeman, also, I chose, and took measures for
securing, a lot. The *Spirit of Missions* had asked me to
write something for its columns. I answered from Deer
Lodge in part as follows :

" *August 21, 1869.*

" I cannot just now send what you wish. I am on my
tour of visitation. I preach in log cabins. I sleep on
blankets, sheets being unknown things. I am the guest
of bachelors in their dirt-roofed mansions. I travel by
stage, on horseback, afoot. I am moving about almost
constantly, and it would be hard for me to get my wits
to work on a condensed article for you now. I have gone
about five hundred miles, and have twelve hundred more
immediately before me. By and by, when I can get
time to gather my thoughts, and when I have a table on
which to write them, and convenient pen and paper and
ink wherewith to write, I mean to forward the *Spirit* an
article.

" In this little town of five hundred inhabitants with a
promising future there is only a Roman Catholic priest
at work. He has his church. I have a large lot donated,
secured and fenced. I trust by next year, if Boise and
Virginia City will give up some of their stipend money,
to place a man here.

" At present there are only three Church people (one
communicant) in the town. With a minister efficient
and persevering placed here, however, the whole population, under God's blessing, so far as it is religious and
Protestant, would be in the Church. As yet, most of the

religious people are Campbellites. I expect to hold
service here in the court-house morning and evening,
to-morrow, and to baptize an infant. I shall be back
(D. V.) at Virginia City, where my family is, on the 2d
of September. On the 6th, we all expect to leave for
Salt Lake City. The Roman Catholic priest has shut up
his church and gone from Virginia, so Mr. Goddard is
the only cleric of any name left in county or town."

At Bannack, the pioneer mining camp, large congregations assembled. The building in which I held service
was of logs, two stories high, with a saloon underneath
and a hall above. The people's generous offering was
$82.55. In one of the services there were not as many
present at the end as at the beginning. I told about it
in a letter at the time, as follows :

" In Bannack scarcely any other religious services are
ever held than my yearly ones. The Sunday I was there,
the inhabitants thoughtfully suspended for once their customary weekly sports of horse-running, foot-racing, and
cock-fighting, and came to the services. In the evening
the floor gave way in the upper room while we were singing the hymn before sermon. It sank four inches. We
all expected it to go utterly down. I am a great admirer
of bravery, coolness, presence of mind, unselfishness ;
methinks I have pointed some rhetorical periods in commendation of these virtues. But the humiliating fact to
be told is that when the floor gave forth that awful crack-
ing, I was the first to spring out of the door near by,
at the back, and down the stairs, in wildly-streaming
robes. When my own feet were on *terra firma* I was
full of valuable courage and valuable forethought and I
shouted to the surging congregation : ' Don't rush, don't
push, you'll break the stairs ; you'll crush the children.'
That kind and way of being courageous provokes a smile,

doesn't it? A carpenter went below and examined. An important under-prop had given way. We might come back and be safe, he said, if we would remain near the sides of the building, leaving the centre unburdened. So, a little ashamed of myself, I went back. Many of the people, also, though not all, came back, and we finished our usual services and sermon. It was of God's merciful goodness that the floor of that huge building, whose roof and sides were logs, did not go down and crush scores to death. Between my last year's visit and this, no religious service has been held in Bannack. Would that we could supply some one to look after the wandering souls of its inhabitants, and especially its children.

" In Bozeman I saw three hundred of the Bannack Indians, passing through to join the Crows. Should these bands be induced to join the hostile Sioux, we would indeed see bad times in Montana.

" I made out my annual report yesterday. The tone of it was not desponding. Nay, the Lord has always helped me to keep cheerful in this work.

" But there are discouragements, perplexities, embarrassments, ' fears and tremblings ' manifold. It is best. Pride and self-trust shoot up and thrive from unchecked success ; and pride and self-trust are not gospel virtues, neither pleasing to God in the present, nor to be of much good to us in the future, when we shall be called to give an account of our stewardship."

Having finished the Montana visitation we left Virginia City and the hospitality of Mr. and Mrs. Goddard for our ride of four hundred miles to Salt Lake, on Tuesday, September 7. The baby, Herbert, was not quite twelve weeks old. Unfortunately we struck the jerker line instead of the Concord coach line for our journey. The rough riding quite used the grandmother up ; but catching such rest and refreshment as she could at our meal stoppings, she courageously held out. George was then nearly three years old and he and I rode outside nearly all the way. The latter part of the route we found changed. We were to run into Corinne, a new town sixty-five miles north of Salt Lake. As we came through Marsh Valley an excited messenger hailed us with : " Dan Robbins has just been shot by some robbers of the express box, whom he was hunting. He lies wounded in the brush near by. We want you to drive as fast as possible to Corinne and hurry a surgeon to him!" Robbins was one of the division agents of the stage line, whom I knew well and who had been a good friend to me in my journeys. For the last seventy-five miles of our trip, therefore, we passengers had our work laid out for us. That was to keep our seats and hold on to the children. We were pushed forward at breakneck speed. I was relieved that the ladies could endure it. I myself exulted in it, because I was thinking constantly of poor Robbins' wound, and how necessary it was that a surgeon should reach him without delay. I am happy to say that Robbins recovered. He afterwards married and lived a neighbor of mine, in Salt Lake. He was a true, brave man, as modest as brave, as unselfish as true, and he is one of those men of the mountains whom I learned to love as a brother.

We reached Corinne at 6 A. M., Friday. It was a town of tents, and in one of them we spent the day and night. A new order of things had set in. The Transcontinental Railroad had been completed. The first rail on the Union Pacific out from Omaha was laid in July, 1865. Four years only were consumed in building 2,026 miles of railroad from Omaha to San Francisco. It was a wonderful feat. The Union Pacific track builders from the East, and the Central Pacific track builders from the West met at Promontory, May 10, 1869, and there the last spike was driven. Subsequently, the two companies agreed upon Ogden as their meeting point and common terminus. Corinne, in Utah, a little east from Promontory, and near the mouth of Bear River, where it flows into the Great Salt Lake, was a town three or four months old when we reached it. It was started exclusively by the non-Mormons or " Gentiles." The Montana and Idaho stage lines and freighting companies made it their starting place. A belief prevailed that it would become the commercial centre and the great town of Utah. Gentile merchants and apostate Mormon merchants of Salt Lake were already putting stocks of goods there, and getting ready to move there entirely, if events should make it wise. Our Rev. Mr. Foote, ever on the alert, had secured a lot there and was already putting up a modest church building. He raised about one thousand dollars on the spot, and Mrs. Minturn's gift of $1,500 helped him complete the " Church of the Good Samaritan."

Saturday morning very early we took cars for Uintah, thirty miles, and from there took a stage-coach to Salt Lake, reaching the latter city at 11 A. M. Brigham Young, we discovered, knew all about Corinne and the new expectations concerning it. Wide awake, he had organized a company to build a railroad from Ogden to Salt Lake City, and half of the track was already laid. He himself drove the last spike of this, the Utah Central Railroad, January 10, 1870. Every blow on the head of that spike meant death to the commercial supremacy of Corinne.

We had now reached Salt Lake, to make it our home. It remained our home for seventeen years. Four children were born to us there, the bodies of two of whom lie buried in " Mt. Olivet," on the hillside overlooking the town. I came to be the direct head of our church work in the Mormon land. I did not feel either elated or despondent at thought of crossing swords with the Mormons. Mr. Foote and Mr. Haskins had been on the ground for two years. They had met the first onset; they had fought out the first conflict, and so well had they guided the campaign and done their duty in it, that the way for my coming and ruling was made quite easy and plain.

During my two years of residence in Montana I had been constantly advised of what they were doing, and I helped them by correspondence as best I could in their straitnesses, perplexities and discouragements. Services had been kept up in Independence Hall unintermittedly. And during the last year the school had been housed there too. We paid sixty dollars a month rent. For the last year Rev. H. L. Foote and wife had been teachers. In July, however, they had moved to Idaho. Mr. Haskins had married, and had been appointed a chaplain of the United States army to serve at Camp Douglas. We had bought for $11,000 an original lot, ten rods by twenty, in the city, and had built upon it a house, in which Mr. and Mrs. Haskins were living, Mr. and Mrs. Foote boarding with them. General Gibbon, commanding Camp Douglas, had given Mr. Haskins leave to occupy quarters outside.

For the next year then, three places must be provided for occupation : (I) For church services. For this purpose we retained Independence Hall. Independence Hall, an adobe structure seating two hundred or more, on a lot six rods by ten, on Third South Street, near Main, was built in the following way. In November, 1864, the Gentiles of Salt Lake organized a society called the "Young Men's Literary Association." For its literary and social meetings it rented Daft's Hall, the second story of Daft's store on Main Street, at $100 a month. Subsequently they bought the lot on Third South Street, for $2,500, and built Independence Hall at a cost of about $5,000. They raised $4,000 in Salt Lake, and Rev. Mr. McLeod, chaplain at Camp Douglas, secured for them $2,200 from California. The title of the property was vested in " Trustees of the First Church of Jesus Christ (Congregational) of the first Christian Society connected with that Church." Mr. McLeod held religious services in it during the latter part of 1865 and the early part of 1866, beginning November 26, 1865. For four years, and until we went into the basement of St. Mark's Cathedral, May 21, 1871, we used Independence Hall for our services.

(II) For our school. For the first year we were in the old bowling alley which was situated where the Walker House now stands. For the second year we occupied Independence Hall. Now, for this coming third year, we rented Groesbeck's old store on Main Street, for $40 a month. Here, overflowing into two other old stores contiguous, St. Mark's school was housed, until we had built the new schoolhouse, opposite the City Hall, in 1872. The school had opened with one hundred and eighteen scholars. Miss Davenport, an experienced teacher in the public schools, from Brooklyn, was to be the caretaker. After making my Idaho visitation I was myself to assume direct personal charge.

(III) For a residence for myself and family. At first Mr. Haskins took us in for food and shelter. But in two or three weeks I rented from Walker Brothers an adobe house on the corner of Main Street and Third South for sixty dollars a month. It was originally built, I

feel sure, for a polygamist for there were three front
doors. The lot was twenty rods on Main Street, by ten
on Third South. The Walker Brothers said I could have
it in purchase for $6,000. If I had had means for pur-
chasing I could have multiplied my money manifold by
sales in after years. In this house I remained nearly
two years, till the spring of 1871. Then we removed
to the house we owned, as Mr. Haskins had moved out.
This house, which we called St. Mark's rectory, we
occupied as our home during our remaining fifteen
years in Salt Lake.

In Independence Hall, on Sunday September 19, 1869,
after having been bishop for more than two years, I
held my first ordination service, advancing Rev. T. W.
Haskins to the priesthood. Mr. Goddard had come down
from Montana to be with Mr. Foote as attendant presbyter. On Tuesday Mr. Goddard and I went to Idaho.
There, in St. Michael's, Boise City, on Sunday, September 26th, assisted by Rev. Messrs. Miller and Goddard, I advanced Rev. H. L. Foote to the priesthood.
Mr. Goddard then returned home, and I made my visitation of the towns of Silver City and Idaho City, Mr.
Foote accompanying me to the former, and Mr. Miller
to the latter. Mr. Foote was now stationed at Boise,
helping in St. Michael's parish school and assisting Mr.
Miller, so that Idaho City and Silver City, though respectively forty and sixty-five miles distant from Boise, could
have regular monthly services. Mr. Foote's wife, who
had been for a long time a great sufferer from rheumatism, died suddenly in St. Michael's rectory, Boise, on
the day after her husband had been ordered priest. I
returned to Salt Lake, October 23d. The journey from
Boise thither was one of about four days.

I now settled into a new home and new sort of work

for the winter. I entered St. Mark's school as head master and business manager. I opened it every morning, and taught from 9 A. M. to twelve, every day. Mr. Haskins taught for two hours in the afternoon. Mr. Foote was freed from school cares to give himself to the pastorate. Late in November, however, he went East and spent the winter spreading information and making appeals for funds for building a church. He was most diligent in his work, and very effective in his way of presenting his cause. He gathered over $17,000. Once more, then, I became a pastor, as well as school-teacher and bishop. Mr. Haskins had his duties at camp to attend to, and could be with me on Sundays only, in the evening, to read service. My pastoral duties were a pleasure; they have always been that to me. Absolutely all the non-Mormons or Gentiles were my flock. And the Jews were " Gentiles." Many dissatisfied and apostate Mormons, also, came for counsel and guidance.

One of the last named class, a sturdy Scotchman, would have no one but me with him when his wife died. A skilled worker in wood, he made the coffin himself, disdaining to call upon the only undertaker of the city, a Mormon. He and I alone, with the weeping children, took the sacred body to the cemetery, and after I had read the committal service, lowered it into its resting-place. Then and there a bond of lasting friendship was cemented between us. Through all my years in Utah I was a frequent visitor in his house; his sturdy character, shrewd good sense, honest independence, and faithfulness to duty filled me with admiration, and my own development was bettered and strengthened by contact with him. A nephew, from his home, is now a clergyman of the Church. By this time we had a Sunday-school of one hundred and sixty scholars; this I superintended myself.

Mr. Hussey faithfully taught the class of larger boys, and
Mr. A. W. Street, who had become our postmaster, also
helped us most efficiently in the Sunday-school. Mr.
Street belonged to a family of note. Two of his brothers
were in Bozeman, Montana, one of them being a judge
there. A brother-in-law was a pioneer merchant at Fort
Benton, Montana, and a brother was the agent of Wells,
Fargo & Co., at North Platte, in 1867, the year I came
over the plains. Mr. Street himself was a Methodist, an
earnest, godly man, but there was no Methodist pastor
yet in Salt Lake. In fact, there was no non-Mormon
minister of any sort, except ourselves. As the time for
confirmation drew near, Mr. Street said, " Bishop, I highly
approve of the work you are doing in this place, I want
to help you all I can, I would like to be closely identified
with you. But I am a Methodist, out from my father's
home, and I do not desire to be other than a Methodist.
Now, if, understanding this, and understanding that when
I go away from here I must resume my Methodist membership, you are willing to admit me to confirmation I
shall be glad to be confirmed so as to be fully united with
you in your blessed work here."

I answered : " Mr. Street, it is neither my duty nor my
desire to lay restrictions on you, or to require pledges
touching your future, when you shall have left Utah.
Here you are an earnest Christian man and are helping
us most efficiently in our Christian work. Indeed I shall
be rejoiced to admit you to confirmation." The sequel
may be told; after his incumbency of the Federal office
closed, Mr. Street departed eastward. A few months
afterwards I received from him a letter from Council
Bluffs, Iowa, in which he said : " When I arrived and
settled here I resumed my traditional relations and attended the Methodist Church; but something seemed

wanting, nor did weeks of faithful attendance relieve the want. The services of public worship were too bare and bald compared with what I had become accustomed to in use of the Prayer-Book. I found it would not be wholesome or edifying to me to continue a Methodist, so I concluded I must go to the Episcopal Church. I am now a member and a vestryman of St. Paul's Church, of this city." It may be added that Mr. Street is now (1894) living in Orlando, Florida, and is the senior warden of the Church there.

In our church services, this winter, Mrs. Tuttle presided at the organ, and led in the singing, too. In this and in manifold other ways, as in visiting, in matters of hospitality, in correspondence, in care of business details, in counsel, I pause here to say that she has been the very heart of influence and the very right hand of good work for and with me during all the years of close companionship with her with which a merciful God has blessed me. If the duties laid upon me have been at all successfully discharged, it has been her wise judgment and rare efficiency and unwearied activity that have made the success possible. Justice, at the expense of delicacy, demands this rendering of honor to whom honor is due.

Our organist at the first and from the first for the Salt Lake services had been Mrs. F. B. Hamilton. But she had now gone to California to sojourn for a year or two. At her departure Mrs. Foote took charge. This winter, however, the latter was at the East visiting. Mrs. Hamilton's long service deserves special mention ; she presided at the melodeon for the first services held by Mr. Foote and Mr. Haskins, on May 5, 1867; since then, almost constantly, for the twenty-six years, she has occupied the organist's stool of St. Mark's parish. She and Mrs. Tuttle planned and carried through the work of procur-

ing a handsome pipe organ, costing $8,000. The noble
instrument has been to her as her child. Playing upon
it, to her, has been touching heart-strings; under her
sympathetic touch it has continually produced grateful
strains of loving melody, which have risen like songs of
angels to the throne of God.

My school-teaching I much enjoyed. Mathematics it
has always been a pleasure to me to teach. In the cabin
in Virginia City I had conned Cæsar nightly with young
Upson, and now, for three hours every day in school, I
was teaching arithmetic, algebra, geometry, Latin and
Greek. A young lad, Samuel Unsworth, took with avid-
ity to the drill in the Greek verb. He is now an earnest
and useful clergyman in the Church, and known to be
one of the best Greek scholars among our clergy.

Yet the bishop could not be forgotten or laid aside in
the pastor and the schoolmaster. Mr. Goddard must be
upheld and encouraged, for Virginia was in its decadence,
Helena being now the capital of Montana and drawing
all the strength of population and commerce its way.
At Helena Mr. Lloyd stayed only till January. His
health was not good and he was incapable of the exercise
of that wisdom and patience that were necessary for dealing successfully with the Montana people. The Helena
people cried aloud to me for another pastor, offering to
pay one $2,500 a year. Mr. Miller and Mr. H. L. Foote
were looking after all of Idaho and in frequent letters
asked for active guidance. Mr. G. W. Foote was in the
East, assiduously visiting rectors and congregations, and
successfully gathering large sums for us for building.
Therefore, a lot for a church must be secured. Through
Mr. Hussey I got hold of such a lot, eighty feet front by
one hundred and sixty-five deep, for $2,200. On this
lot, when Mr. Foote came home with his plans, furnished

by the elder Upjohn, we began the work of building
St. Mark's.

The winter sped swiftly by.   I was busied to the full
every waking hour.   I was quietly learning from the
neighbors about me, and from the people among whom I
had come to dwell.   They treated me with neighborly
kindness.   As bishop and missionary I asked no favors
of the Mormon hierarchy, and gave none.   As neighbor
and friend I strove to be neighborly and friendly.   And
there does not dwell in my memory to-day the recollec-
tion of one unkind personal action from them to me or
from me to them.

This winter of 1869-70 was an epoch in Utah affairs.
In January the Utah Central Railway, from Ogden to
Salt Lake was completed, and now, for the first time,
ingress and egress for the outside world was made easy.
At the same time, some within the Mormon ranks grew
uneasy.   The Godbe-ite schism arose.   Some Mormons
of a literary turn, among whom were W. S. Godbe,
W. H. Shearman, and E. L. T. Harrison, started a
monthly periodical called the *Utah Magazine*.   As
mines and mining in the territory were attracting attention as never before, this magazine discussed them.   It
advised that the Mormon people should bear an active
hand in developing the mineral resources round about
them, and get from them what profit they might.   Just
this sort of enterprise, however, Brigham Young had
always discouraged his people from undertaking ; and it
must be confessed that they had reaped much benefit by
obeying his counsel.   From flour, potatoes, and peaches,
which they shipped and sold in the mines of Nevada,
Idaho, and Montana, the Mormons had gathered rich
income.   So now Brigham Young disapproved the teach-
ings of the *Utah Magazine* and peremptorily forbade his

people to take a hand in mining ventures. Then the
magazine writers gradually drifted into an unwonted realm
of argument, and even of resistance to authority. At last
they took the open ground that " The prophet, seer, and
revelator of the Lord had power and rightful authority to
direct and dictate in spiritual matters. But in business matters it was not competent for him so to direct and to dictate,
and that in these things the people had a right to judge
and act for themselves." It was not long, therefore, before the writers and their abettors were cut off from " the
Church." These were the Godbe-ite schismatics. Their
leaders were Godbe, Shearman, Harrison, John Chislett,
Henry Lawrence, and E. B. Kelsey. They had all been
earnest Mormons, many of them were polygamists. For
integrity of character, nobility of life and soundness of
judgment, Henry Lawrence was eminent. He was only
a lad when he came to Utah, and from his childhood he
had known for religion only Mormonism. To uphold
this religion he had earnestly devoted his energies and
prayers. He was one of the Mormon Church's most
trusted and valued young men, and he was a polygamist.
When " counsel " and " authority " pressed too hard on
him, however, his manhood revolted. In religious matters he had learned to obey ; he wanted to obey, but in
practical things he did not account himself a child. He
recognized powers of self-direction set within himself for
use, and he would not be a slave. Rebellious against the
tyranny that claimed to dictate in business matters he
drew back. Such drawing back gradually gave him an
outside standpoint from which to view Mormonism and
he soon saw that as a religion, in its spiritual aspect indeed, it was tyrannical, untrustworthy, and absurd. All
I have said about him was true, likewise, of John Chislett. The independence of the Godbe-ites would not

submit itself; they held on to the magazine and they held out in it. That magazine developed into the daily paper, *The Salt Lake Tribune*, which now for nearly a quarter of a century has been the vigorous anti-Mormon paper of Utah.

The day had gone by for open deeds of violence. Rebels and apostates from the Mormon Church could no · longer be slaughtered, so the Godbe-ites associated themselves together, and erected for themselves an adobe building, called the " Liberal Institute," in which to hold their meetings. Hundreds of the disaffected gathered to them. But the cohering force in the schism was wanting. Mormonism was a fierce and fanatical affirmation ; Godbe-iteism was only a sturdy negation. As a positive force developing growth and organizing its followers into unity and permanence, the schism was a failure. As a disintegrating force, preying upon the vitals of Mormonism, however, it was of great value, and it contributed mightily to the disenthralment towards which Utah was now reaching out.

March 29, 1870, a telegram from my father came, saying : " Lemuel cannot live long, he would like to see you." Alas, the school was on my hands, with all its business and no little of its teaching. The parish, too, was in an excited condition, and needed constant watchful care. I was obliged therefore to telegraph back the reply : " I cannot come. God help us all. Give Lem my undying love." It cost my heart a keen pang to refuse to go. In recounting earlier years I have mentioned how kind and good my brother was to me in my needs, during my student career. In 1868, also, as I have mentioned, I had confirmed him in Windham, where he was now lying sick. I longed to go to him to tell once more my gratitude for his goodness and to mingle my tears

and prayers with his, but duty seemed to forbid, and two
thousand miles away I could only in prayer commend
him to the heavenly Father and speak to my beating
heart the hope of reunion in the future home. Dear
brother! He died April 23d. He was thirteen years
older than I, he was as helpful as a father and as tenderly
loving as a brother to me, always. Upright, unselfish,
pure, true, generous soul! It was in no coldness of heart
that I refused to come to thee. God knows it all. He
will mercifully, through Christ, give us another home together by and by.

March 13, 1870, Rev. Mr. Haskins held the first church
service in Ogden. April 3d, I followed, with a second.
In the East, Mr. Foote had fallen in with a student at
Berkley Divinity School, at Middletown, Conn., named
J. L. Gillogly, and had interested him in our Utah work.
After his graduation in June Mr. Gillogly married, and
by the middle of July he and wife were in Ogden ready
for work. The faithful services of the Rev. Mr. Gillogly
and his devoted wife fill a bright page in my grateful
memory. He died in Ogden, February 14, 1881, after an
active pastorship of nearly eleven years. Ogden was his
one and only parish. His body lies buried on the hillside overlooking the town. The influence of his patient
and sturdy devotion to duty still widely and deeply en-
dures. The freight car, the passenger waiting-room, and
the old saloon, were the early scenes of his missionary
life and labors. But his sagacious eye soon discerned a
spacious lot in a not unfit locality, upon which was a
tannery structure, now disused, which he determined, if
possible, to secure for his future church. He told me of
his wish, and said that the property could be secured for
fifteen hundred dollars. I wrote at once to John D.
Wolfe of our plans and wishes. His reply came back

with an accompanying check for three thousand dollars, half of which he bade me use for the needs of the Salt Lake City Mission. Such were Mr. Wolfe's ways of giving, in the discharge of what he considered his duties of stewardship. I subjoin one of his earlier letters written to me:

> "*13 Madison Avenue, New York City,*
> "*December 18, 1869.*
> " Rt. Rev. D. S. Tuttle, D. D.,
>   " DEAR SIR:
>   " You will please find enclosed check to your order for one thousand dollars with my best wishes for your success.
>   " I notice with much pleasure the progress you are making and trust it may continue, and that the Church may keep you well supplied with funds. By the kindness of Rev. A. T. Twing, secretary and general agent, I have seen the advance sheets of the *Spirit of Missions* containing your highly gratifying report.
>   " With much respect,
>   " Truly yours,
>   " JOHN DAVID WOLFE."

The old tannery was bought and changed into a school-house, and there, also, church services were held. It was opened for the first service, May 28, 1871.

Mr. Gillogly was one of the most straightforward and fearless of men. Ogden was an eminently Mormon town. I had passed through it often in 1867, '68, and '69, on my stage journeys to Montana and Idaho, and many a dinner of excellent chicken, cooked by one of his polygamous wives, have I and my fellow passengers eaten at Bishop West's hotel. Not until 1869 were there any non-Mormons in the city, and then there were only a few railroad employees. Mr. Gillogly from the first assumed an attitude of strong and square opposition to

Mormonism. Though an uncompromising opponent, however, he was just and fair. His Mormon neighbors knew him for a foe, but they accorded him hearty respect. Consequently, he lived his eleven years among them uninjured. His fearlessness was a marked characteristic. Soon after opening the " old tannery," some hoodlum Mormons gathered at the services one Sunday evening, bent on making a disturbance. At first Mr. Gillogly contented himself with looking sternly at them when they were noisy. On the continuance of the disorder, however, he stopped in the services and said : " We are glad to welcome one and all here, but we expect respectful and reverent behavior from those who come. Young men in yonder corner, unless you are respectful and quiet, I shall take off my surplice and come down and put you out of here." He was a square-set, sturdily built man, and the youths deemed it wise to be quiet.

On another occasion a gentleman remarked to him, " Mr. A. says that you said thus and so." " Does Mr. A. say that ? " answered Mr. Gillogly. Then, seizing his stout cane, he added, " Come, put on your hat, and let us go at once to see Mr. A. If he asserts that I said that I shall be obliged to give him a caning."

In 1873, Mr. John W. Hamersley and his family, of New York City, promised me four thousand dollars for the erection at Ogden of a church in memory of Mrs. Livingston, a daughter of Mr. Hamersley, lately deceased. But the architect's estimate of four thousand dollars, under the lowest bid of contractors, grew to six thousand dollars. When the " Memorial Church of the Good Shepherd " was finished, it had cost, alas, eleven thousand dollars. And the Hamersleys generously paid all the cost. I am sure, however, that their opinion of my judgment and wisdom as a builder of churches, sank low indeed. But in spite of the perplexities it caused me and the disesteem it fastened on me, the beautiful stone church has been an untold blessing to the Ogden parish. It was consecrated February 6, 1875.

Subsequently, when land was bought and a new brick schoolhouse for the " School of the Good Shepherd " was built, Mr. Gillogly gave of his own money two thousand dollars towards the expenditure. He had saved a little money and placed it in town lots, upon which he had realized considerable profit. A goodly portion of that gain, with characteristic simplicity and with no slightest touch of ostentation, he gave back to the Lord in this gift of two thousand dollars.

The Utah Central Railroad, from Ogden to Salt Lake, forty miles, was completed January 10, 1870. Writing to Mr. Goddard, January 25th, I say :

" The 10th I gave the school a holiday and went to hear speeches and see Brigham Young drive the last spike of the Utah Central Railroad. It is to run one train a day (7 A. M.) to Ogden. Fare two dollars. My fare from here to Philadelphia now is $122.35." This railroad was built entirely by the Mormons, and was at first operated by them. Afterwards it was extended two hundred and forty miles south, from Salt Lake to Frisco, Utah ; then it became a portion of the great Union Pacific system.

The winter proved to be an exceedingly busy one for both Mrs. Tuttle and myself. School, church, parish, choir, home, correspondence pressed urgently their various duties. In the home we had hitherto got on by ourselves without any servant, but I now felt that Mrs. Tuttle must have some help. Living expenses, however, left but a small sum over to pay out as wages. Ellen Poxon, a young English girl in her teens, came to us with the understanding that we would send her to our school, and when school was not in session, that we would pay her wages.   When ten or eleven years old she had come over with a small company of Mormon immigrants under the leadership of Mr. Kay, father of Mrs. (Dr.) Robinson.   The cattle hauling their train over the plains at last gave out and died and many of the poor immigrants were thus set afoot.   Ellen herself walked nearly all the thousand miles from the Missouri River to Salt Lake.   She was in Mrs. Kay's family, and the latter was unwilling to give her up, but Ellen wanted to come to us and to go to school.   Mrs. Kay and I had the warmest kind of a contention over the matter, but I won.   I feared she would never forgive me, for our antagonism was sharp and determined.   She did forgive me, however, and in after years became one of my nearest and dearest friends.

As for Ellen she was a model of faithfulness in our home and at last came to be to us as a loved daughter. She improved so well her opportunities at school that in time she became one of our regular teachers.   She helped to rear our children, and her name is a household word in our family.   Eventually she married a miner and ranchman, settled in Baker City, Oregon, and became the mother of happy children.   She is the stay and comfort of the clergyman of the parish.   Sweet patience and unflinching fidelity were her characteristics.   It is a great pleasure to look back upon the clear shining path of such a life of faithful duty as hers has been.   One says in one's grateful heart, " God bless her ! " ere one looks away.

At Easter-tide of 1870 there came to Salt Lake a missionary delegation on the way to California.   There were twenty persons in the delegation and they had their own chartered car. I fancy that some of them were merchants combining business with the missionary feature of their trip. Two of them were Presbyterians ; the other eighteen were the Rev. Drs. Twing, A. H. Vinton, B. H. Paddock, M. A., de W. Howe, Leeds, and Cross; the Rev. Messrs. W. H. Hare and G. L. Locke ; and Messrs. Robert H. Ives, and Crocker of Rhode Island, Benj. Reed of Boston, C. C. Trowbridge and W. N. Carpenter of Detroit, Lloyd W. Wells, and Dickinson of New York, Sanger of Brooklyn, and Judge Forsyth of Troy, besides Mrs. Howe, the wife of Dr. Howe. The party spent two days in Salt Lake, including one Sunday, and insisted on my going on with them to California, and Mrs. Tuttle, too, as their guests. On Sunday morning, in Independence Hall, Dr. Vinton preached. In the evening we had a missionary meeting with addresses from Drs. Twing, Leeds, Howe, and Paddock. It was the rarest sort of treat to us of Salt Lake ; it came as a wave of cheering and uplifting helpfulness.

Mr. Haskins kindly offering to look after the school and parish, I resolved to accept the generous invitation, and Mrs. Tuttle and I went with the delegation to California, being absent two Sundays. Between Salt Lake and San Francisco we were two days in our car, assembling for prayers each morning and evening. Dr. Paddock was chaplain. The first evening out, before he began, I rose and spoke of my brother Lem. I told of what he had been to me, and how he was then lying on his bed of extreme sickness three thousand miles away, and I asked for prayers for him. This was on April 25th. I did not know that he had died on the morning of the 23d, for it took four or five days for mails to reach us. This request of mine is alluded to in the following letter from Bishop Potter :

" *New York, June 23, 1870.*
" MY DEAR BISHOP TUTTLE :
" I have the pleasure of enclosing my check for
one hundred dollars, the gift of Geo. D. Morgan of Irv-
ington for your work. I met him in a train a week or
two ago, and happened to repeat to him a story I heard
from Dr. Twing of a scene in the cars, just after you all
left Salt Lake City for San Francisco ; and he said at
once he would like to send you some money, and he intimated that I might forward it, and say how he came to
send it just at this time. So this will be only another
way in which your good brother has helped you. Mrs.
P. and myself were much interested in what you
wrote to her, as she may have told you. Of course we
are always the same in our affectionate interest in you
and yours, and in your work ; and will be always very
glad to hear from you. No doubt your faith and patience
are often sorely tried ; but I cannot help thinking that
with a blessing from above the fruits of your work will
one day appear to the devout admiration of all. God
bless you.
" Affectionately yours,
" H. POTTER."

A poor woman who had been inveigled into the delusion of Mormonism and polygamy went along with us
in the day car. Mr. Foote had known of her oppression
and her unhappiness for some time ; so the gentlemen of
the delegation made up a purse for her and she and her
two children were quietly taken with us to California,
where she had some friends.

We had a group of photographs taken while in California, a copy of which hangs now (1894) in my hall. I
bethink myself of the changes which the twenty-four
years have wrought. The two ladies of the party, Mrs.
Howe and Mrs. Tuttle, are still living. Queenly honor
was shown them and they have often spoken of the great
happiness they experienced on that trip. Three of the

presbyters afterwards became bishops, Howe, Hare, and Paddock. The first is now, in his eighty-sixth year, the Nestor of the House of Bishops, the oldest man among us. The second, sensitive and refined, and eminently fitted to do best work in the centres of civilization, has unmurmuringly stood steady to faithful duty among the Indians and frontiersmen of his difficult field, and his works of godliness are of the kind that are wide and deep in reach of influence. The Episcopate of Bishop Paddock in Massachusetts was one unsurpassed in American annals for well-ordered industry and discreet zeal. Dr. Vinton—he was then rector of St. Mark's-in-the-Bowery, New York—preached for us in Salt Lake and also in San Francisco. Strength, virile strength, was the characteristic of his utterances, as his very face and form and mien betokened. Dr. Twing was in his element ; his heart was always burning with missionary ardor, and this was his first visit to the Pacific coast. In Salt Lake, on the Sunday evening, he held a missionary meeting, calling Drs. Howe and Paddock and Leeds to his help in addressing the people. Dr. Leeds, distinguished for gentleness of manner and kindness of spirit, won our hearts completely. Dr. Cross had lately come into the Church from the Methodists, and I think was taking occasion to visit the western coast in search of a sphere of usefulness. Mr. Locke remains, as he was then, the faithful rector of St. Michael's, Bristol, Rhode Island.

Of the laymen who were with us, all, or nearly all, are dead. I do not know about the two Presbyterians and about Mr. Dickinson, but certainly all the others are dead. Mr. Reed left, as his magnificent gift to the Church, the Cambridge Divinity School. Mr. Ives, in the peaceful quietness of advanced age, much enjoyed the trip he was taking. Now and then, coming upon him in the train, one found him reading his pocket Bible, which he always carried with him. Messrs. Trowbridge and Carpenter, associated in Christ church, Detroit, were like an older and younger brother. Of old they had been under the pastorship of Dr. Paddock, as Mr. Sanger was now under his pastorship in Grace church, Brooklyn Heights. Mr. Trowbridge was one of my best friends and helpers throughout my missionary career; through him I became acquainted with one of the dearest of my friends, Rev. Canon Jacob, afterwards vicar of Portsea, Portsmouth, England, and later, Bishop of Newcastle, and of St. Albans. Through Mr. Trowbridge and Mr. Jacob, supplementing the efforts of Bishop McIlvaine, many of the English bishops became interested in the mission among the Mormons, and sent us help. The Society for Promoting Christian Knowledge also made us a grant of a hundred pounds, which enabled us to make the last payment on our church structure in Salt Lake. Mr. Wells was the clear headed, sagacious business man and the refined Christian gentleman, combined. Subsequently he served for several years as the treasurer of our Domestic and Foreign Missionary Society.

Dear old friends, most of them are now in Paradise. They installed Mrs. Tuttle and myself as their guests in the " Occidental" during our stay in San Francisco, and then came every morning for prayers together, making our parlor the chapel. Love was deepened, zeal was quickened, courage was strengthened, and patience added largely to her store of resources, under the influence of that visit to California with the delegation of 1870.

At the " Occidental " in San Francisco there had been entered on the hotel register : " Bishop Tuttle and Wife, Salt Lake City." Some wag turning over the pages took on himself to make " wife " into " wives," and suspicious curiosity was accordingly directed towards me. This was not the only occasion on which hailing from Salt Lake drew upon us watchful eyes. Once, in after years, Rev. Mr. Foote and wife and Mrs. Tuttle and myself visited the Hotel del Monte, at Monterey, and entered ourselves on the register as from Salt Lake. We were at once eyed askance by our fellow guests, and were quite avoided as being Mormons, until some one happened on the scene who knew our true position and corrected the mistake.

On another occasion I was in New York City. A forenoon of leisure came to me; a rare experience in my busy lifetime. I said to myself, " I'll go down-town, along the paths I used to tread in getting to old Columbia College in Park Place, and into the old book shops, where I was wont to loiter." There was a special second hand book store of one Bradburn, on the corner of Fulton and Nassau Streets, which formerly I much frequented. So I leisurely sauntered down Fulton near Nassau, marking the houses and reading the signs, in deep revery over the changes from the old times to the new. Soon there came an adventure which my readers will laugh at. It smacks of a scene in the " Vicar of Wakefield," with Moses, perhaps, as the actor. Up stepped a man and stopped me on the sidewalk, promptly rousing me from my revery. He was dressed in quite gentlemanly fashion and was polite in demeanor. " Good-morning, Mr. Thomson," he said, " I am glad to meet you." " No," said I, " there is some mistake." " Are you not Mr. Charles W. Thomson, of (naming some place in the West)?" " No," I said; then coming out of my dreamy revery into the present, I added,—he hesitating and inviting the statement: "I am Bishop Tuttle, of Salt Lake City." Uttering well expressed apologies for his mistake and lifting his hat respectfully he withdrew. I relapsed into my revery, especially as just then I came to the Nassau corner, the location of J. Bradburn's shop so well known in days of old. I was not noticing the jostling crowd, but was ready to stop and dream awhile. Again I was roused, and this time by a cheerful, ruddy faced youth in his twenties. He hailed me, and shaking hands vigorously, exclaimed: "Why, Bishop Tuttle, how are you? I'm mighty glad to see you. When did you come over the Union Pacific? I got here only yesterday. When have you seen my uncle up near Virginia City, Montana? Did he tell you anything of me? What news do you bring of him? Well, indeed I am glad to see you."

On and on he went, in glib fashion, like him who met Horace in the *Via Sacra*. I was pulling my wits back from the past to the present, and then gathering them together as best I could to recall to memory this youth or his uncle. He stopped not for any answers to his questions. I felt half conscious of blameworthiness at not remembering him or his kinsman, for in those days I did have friendly acquaintance with almost all the dwellers in the mountains. Finally he added: "The conductor, as I came over the plains, gave me this ticket and told me it would be worth my while to call at the office named on it and present it. That office is right here on Nassau Street. Have you got time? If yes, come along with me; let's go and see what it means." Like a simpleton I went with him, meek as poor Horace was, cudgeling my brains to discover who he was, and who his uncle was. On Nassau, a few doors from Fulton, he led me up two flights of stairs and into a room, at the door of which stood on guard a burly negro. My "nephew of his uncle" threw down the ticket upon a counter, back of which seemed to be only one man. The man took the ticket, and turned rapidly over several huge ledgers that were lying about, and then came back with his report to the youth. Whereupon the latter seized my hand and said: " Congratulate me, bishop, that ticket has won me two hundred and fifty dollars." Then the man behind the counter brought out some revolving wheel of fortune and asked me if I did not " want to take a chance." My youth also added his solicitations. By this time I knew where I was. At last I was wide awake. Promptly I began backing out of that room. Reaching the door I turned on the negro and sternly bade him let me go by. He did so, and I hurried down the stairs and into the open air, realizing the situation, thankful that no worse had come of it, laughing at myself, and, to use a boy's language, ready to kick myself for a fool.

I had read about this " Confidence game " in the newspapers, but reading about a thing is nothing like experiencing a thing, to give one a sure sense of it, I can vouch for that. If I, with an average share of intelligence, having been a resident of New York City for eight years, could be so taken in, is it any wonder that similar tricks are played constantly and successfully upon people, in spite of warnings issued by newspapers and the police?

When I had got over consideration of the absurd figure I had cut and the danger I had escaped, two thoughts supervened. First, what a bright young fellow that " nephew of his uncle " was, to make up and pour forth such a volley of pertinent questions in the two minutes allowed him after the " Thomson " confederate had reported. Second, why those confederates should think it worth while to inveigle a bishop into their den. They might know him to be impecunious. It might be supposed he would not be the one to make ventures upon the chances and bettings of a wheel of fortune. Turning it over in my mind I came to the conclusion that

" Thomson " and the " nephew " took me for a Mormon
bishop. Twenty " bishops " were in Salt Lake. Several
of them were among the leading merchants and business
men of the city and often came East for goods. The
two bright fellows, who evidently knew heaps of things,
doubtless knew these facts, and esteemed the game worth
the candle.

We came back to Salt Lake from California, May 11,
1870, and on the 13th Mr. Foote returned from the East
where he had succeeded in gathering $18,000 from gen-
erous givers to help build a church. He began upon
measures for building. I had already secured a lot of
eighty feet front and ten rods deep for $2,200. The
elder Upjohn, the builder of Trinity church, New York,
was our architect. I think our Salt Lake building was
the last church he erected. We laid the corner-stone on
Saturday, July 30, 1870. The Rev. Mr. Pidsley, father
of Mrs. Foote, had come from the East to be a helper to
Mr. Foote. Besides Messrs. Foote, Haskins, and Pidsley,
Mr. Gillogly from Ogden, and Rev. Morelle Fowler, late
of Batavia, N. Y., and on his way to serve Helena, Montana, for a time, were with us at the laying of the corner-
stone. We had also Rev. S. T. Nevill, of the Church of
England, who was on his way to New Zealand. This
clergyman, the year after, became the Bishop of Dunedin.

The autumn and winter, however, were filled with
troubles for me, the story of some of which will be told
later in the chapter on St. Mark's Cathedral, and in connection with Rev. Mr. Foote's removal from Salt Lake.
Mr. Foote's departure from Salt Lake, early in 1871, was
a sad loss to me and to the work. He went to San Jose,
California, was rector there for many years, was afterwards at Trinity church, Portland, Oregon, and then, by
reason of an affection of the eyes, was obliged to with-

draw from active service in the ministry. In my annual
report to the Board of Missions of 1871, I say:

"The Rev. Geo. W. Foote, the wise organizer of our
work among the Mormons, and that, too, in peculiarly
perplexing times, has resigned and gone to California. I
must be allowed to make record of my conviction that
the most of the success it has pleased God to bestow
upon us in Salt Lake that is due to any one man, is due
to Mr. Foote. Placed from the first where I would know
all his plans and acts, I vouch that his was a rare and
wonderful ability in planning and organizing, a most
prompt and earnest activity in doing. He has borne
away with him from Salt Lake the grateful remembrance of us all who know and appreciate the great and
good foundation work for the Church which he did here."

The Rev. Mr. Pidsley remained to help me for several
months after Mr. Foote's departure; then he also went to
San Jose. Rev. Morelle Fowler was to come to be the
Salt Lake pastor. On the night of Monday, February 6,
1871, he and his wife and three children stepped on
board the train of the Hudson River Railroad, en route
to us. Within a short hour or two all five were dead.
At or near Hamburgh there was a collision with a coal
oil train, I think upon a bridge; and a large number of
passengers met death by burning and drowning. In a
letter to Mr. Goddard I wrote:

"*Salt Lake City, Utah, February 11, 1871.*
"MY DEAR MR. GODDARD:
"Perhaps you have gathered from the public tele-
grams what a sad disaster has befallen me. The Rev.
Mr. Fowler and family left New York City, en route for
Utah, last Monday. They were to be here next week.
In that frightful accident on the Hudson River Railroad
all were killed; father, mother, and three sweet children.

"Alas! I am much cast down. I loved Mr. Fowler
as a brother and counted much on the helpful Christian
communion that I was to have with him. But, the Lord's
will be done, and, with His help, cheerily done!

"I know not now what I shall do. Plans are forming
in my mind to place a minister resident at Corinne and
to get on here in Salt Lake with Kirby alone.

"Sorrowfully and affectionately,

"DAN'L S. TUTTLE.

"P. S.—Haskins is still better, but I am obliged yet to
take all his teaching duties."

Mr. Fowler had been one of most earnest and successful pastors known to the American Church in his parish
at Batavia, N. Y. But his health failed. For a few
months he served faithfully at Helena, Montana. His
sound practical sense, his burning zeal, and his godly
devotion made him a great power for good everywhere.
The chancel window, costing eleven hundred dollars, was
placed in the Salt Lake church for a memorial of him;
and his old parish of St. James, Batavia, furnishing one
thousand dollars, St. James church, Deer Lodge, Montana, was built as another memorial of him.

Rev. Mr. Kirby came to my side just after Easter, on
April 23, 1871. Active, industrious and resolute, he
soon made it evident that we could get on without an
additional clergyman in the parish. He served in Salt
Lake nearly eleven years; and his name is held in the
greatest respect and his works in the most grateful memory throughout the length and breadth of Utah.

In February, 1871, also Rev. Ballard S. Dunn came
from California to Corinne. He was active and resolute,
but from the first was busied with the idea and plans of
"striking it rich" in some gold or silver mine round-
about. Almost from Monday morning to Saturday night,

with a pack on his shoulders and a pick in his hand, he was in the mountains " exploring," and " prospecting " for silver and gold.   When satisfied about the facts I said to him, " I am not opposed to the mining of the rich metals.   I recognize that we all in this country largely depend on it for sustentation.   But I do not think spiritual work can be well done by a pastor absorbed in mining pursuits.   My request is that you resign your charge here at Corinne ; and I may add, that while you are giving yourself enthusiastically to mining, I inhibit you from serving as a clergyman in my field."   He answered, " You have no right to do that. You cannot inhibit me."   I said warmly, " I have the right, and mark you, I do inhibit you."

After the warmth of the conflict was over, I looked at the canons ; then I wrote Bishops Atkinson and Williams for counsel, and discovered that Mr. Dunn was right and I was wrong.   A bishop may not inhibit his own clergyman from exercising the functions of his ministry.   If the bishop thinks the clergyman unfit to officiate, he may take steps for his trial upon charges made against him, and on his conviction upon the charges the clergyman may be suspended or deposed by the bishop.   But up to that time of sentence of conviction, his rights to exercise the offices of his ministry in the diocese or missionary district to which he belongs may not be abrogated by any autocratic order of the bishop.   Accordingly, the next time I met Mr. Dunn, I said : " You were right and I was wrong, I cannot inhibit you from officiating.   But I withdraw your nomination as missionary of Corinne ; and in Salt Lake, where I am rector, you will not be asked to officiate while you are so busied with secular interests."   He was angry and said he would sue me in the civil courts for " damage to his pecuniary interests, and for defamation of character." I said, " Very well, sue away !" I placed my case at once in the hands of a lawyer, but Mr. Dunn never entered his suit. He lived in Salt Lake for some time afterwards, pursuing the *ignis fatuus* of mining " prospects." Once at a convocation of the missionary district, I invited him to preach the sermon. He hardly returned courtesy for courtesy, however, for in the course of the sermon he uttered not a few abusive things.

I may be permitted to confess that twice I have been summoned as a party in a suit at law. In both cases I was defendant. In Salt Lake one autumn a lady whom I had well known in Montana came to our city with her daughter, and desired to fit up a house for taking boarders. I knew her to be a good housekeeper, and when she told me she had no funds, I went with her to a furniture store and told the proprietor to let her have the goods she needed, and said that I would be good for the bill if she was not. Six or eight months afterwards the proprietor brought me a bill to pay of one or two hundred dollars. In scrutinizing the bill, however, I saw that the goods sold were of date half a year after the day on which I called with the lady. I said: " I will pay for what may have been bought that day, or within a day or two afterwards, but I am not going to pay for this purchase of six months later." He answered: " Then I shall be obliged to sue you for this pay." " Very well," I said. The suit came before a justice of the peace and I was beaten. I learned that " being security" is a serious business ; and that as I could not on the witness stand affirm that I had set a limitation of time within which purchases might be made, " continuing security" meant serious things for me. I wanted then to pay, but my lawyer, Hamilton Gamble,

Esq., insisted on an appeal. In the higher court the decision was favorable to me. " ——— plainly owed the debt, but Tuttle was not to be held."

But mark the outcome. In making the appeal I was obliged to give bond. My senior warden in Salt Lake, George M. Scott, Esq., went on my bond. But somehow the bond was suffered to be for " ——— and Tuttle, appeal," and not limited to " Tuttle." Therefore, the decision being against ———, it was not long before an attorney called on Mr. Scott for payment of the debt. That of course I could not allow. So my technical triumph in the court was no practical gain. I satisfied the judgment myself and became a wiser and more thoughtful man.

The other instance happened in connection with a school to which I had fallen heir but which I had not managed. Examining my inheritance I found it sadly crippled by debt. Appeals to generous friends brought enough to pay half the debt in cash. The other half was put into notes secured by a second mortgage on the school property. The question then came who should sign the notes? I declined to do so, until in each of them was placed the clause " The holder of this note hereby agrees to look to the property for his pay and not to the signer of the note." Then I signed, " Daniel S. Tuttle, Bishop." The second mortgage proved worthless, and I was sued for payment of the notes. The suing party hoped, I think, in some way to hold the diocese responsible, but when the case came up in court and the lawyers on each side had spoken, before a witness was called, the judge, saying that the paper itself relieved the signer from responsibility, ordered the jury to bring in a verdict for the defendant.

In our complex, civilized life I recognize that suits in

courts must be; and I have the highest respect for judges, and for lawyers too as members of a most useful and honorable profession. But I prefer, if I may be allowed, to decline to be a suitor at their hands.

With Mr. Foote gone, Mr. Haskins sick, Mr. Fowler dead, and Mr. Kirby not yet come, another of the " busy times," of which my life has been full, came upon me in the spring of 1871. Of one good helper at this period, I want to recall the memory and record the worth. Miss Emily Pearsall, cousin of my junion warden in early days at Morris, had come in 1870, from Bainbridge, Chenango County, N. Y., to help us as " Sister " or " Woman Missionary." Mormonism aimed its fiercest shafts at womanhood. And in helping such sufferers in Utah a woman could accomplish much more than could any man. In my report of 1871 I speak of Miss Pearsall:

" Call her ' Sister ' if you like, or call her ' Deaconess,' or name her as you wish, the fact is that her help in our pastoral work, especially among the sick and the poor and the children and the ignorant and the strangers, is simply invaluable. She penetrates homes that we cannot so well enter. She reaches hearts that would close up against us. She hears confessions that would not be made to us. My decision is that she must remain with us to do her good and true ' woman's ' work in our parish. I hope year by year to secure part of her support from the parish and part from givers in the East who appreciate how the efficiency of the pastoral work of a clergyman can be more than doubled by the aid of a trained and devoted Christian woman of intelligence and refinement."

Miss Pearsall gave her work to us and her life for us. She died in 1872. When she was buried in " Mount Olivet," overlooking Salt Lake City, hundreds and hundreds of those whom she had loved and served, and who loved her and wept for the loss of her, followed her sacred body to the grave. The poor with their pennies gathered the eighty dollars which went to provide a decent head stone for her resting-place. Few go down to the grave more loved and regretted than did she.

My summer visitation of Montana in 1870 was made in June and July. Perhaps some letters to Mrs. Tuttle will best tell of it.

"In Mr. Goddard's Study, Virginia City, M. T.,
"June 12, 1870.

" . . . Pleasant Valley we reached Friday morning at eight o'clock. Mrs. Hall gave us, as she always does, a right good breakfast. Then my Nevada mining friend and myself started afoot up the hill. We sat on the crest and wondered that the stage came not on. By and by a man came up the hill on a galloping horse, and riding up to me said: ' Bishop, will you come back to the station? There is a little job needing you.' ' How so?' I said, ' anybody to be married?' 'Yes,' he replied. So we all went back and I married Mrs. Hall to Mr. David Allerdice, the driver that had brought us into Pleasant Valley that morning. David gave me twenty dollars (said twenty dollars I'll send you by check when I'm not writing on Sunday), and at ten o'clock we came along. I reached here yesterday at 5 P. M.

" To-night I am going to ask the congregation to stay awhile, that I may see what they want to do about raising a salary for Mr. Goddard.

" Dickens is dead. It is a calamity to the world, is it not? Do you not think, dear, that next winter we can revive our good old habit of evening readings aloud from Dickens or some other author?"

" Bozeman, M. T., Sunday morning,
"June 19, 1870.

" I've got all ready for church, and improve a little of the time before I must go, in beginning my letter to you. Mr. Goddard is at my side. We are in the sitting-room of ' Guy's Hotel.' An hour or two ago the man and the team that brought us from Virginia City left us to return. I had to pay sixty-one dollars for said man and team, besides paying all their road expenses. Thus far no one has charged me bills, but I shall have to pay at this hotel. Yet, however expensive it is, I am glad I have not adopted Mr. Goddard's suggestion that he and I should go about the country alone. Let me tell you of what happened to us.

" Thursday last, at 11 A. M., when we were forty miles from Virginia City and twelve miles from Sterling, we came to Willow Creek. This Willow Creek had grown very angry from melting snows, so the bridge had gone, with the exception of one stringer which still kept its struggling place across the stream and dammed up a few of the floating logs, keeping them from going down the current. Well, what was to be done? We got out and reconnoitred. We were all strangers to the place, and no one was in sight to inquire of. Finally our driver said: ' I think I can ford there,' pointing to a widened spot some distance above the bridge. I said: ' I shall try that stringer.' Then, getting a long pole to help me, I started on my uneasily balanced way across. I succeeded in getting to the opposite side with only one foot a little wet. I looked around. The driver and Mr. Goddard in the wagon were just pushing into the creek. At first they went in up to the horses' bellies; then they struck a shallow place in the centre, where the water was

less than two feet deep; from here they struck out for the
opposite shore. Soon I saw the water over the horses'
backs and knew that they had to swim. I rushed to the
edge of the bank and seized their heads, but the bank
was too steep altogether for them to come up. All I
could do was to hold their noses out of the water.
Knowing that Mr. Goddard could not swim a stroke I
shouted to him, 'Stick to the wagon!' He did so right
bravely, he also seized hold of my valise that was floating
off and saved it, though by this time he himself was up
to his waist in water and the rapid, whirling stream, six
feet deep or more, was threatening to carry him to instant
death. I shouted again: ' If you have to go, try to keep
your head out of the water to the bridge and I'll rush
there to save you.' The driver now jumped and swam
ashore, leaving Mr. G. in the wagon, the hind wheels of
the latter half out of the water in the shallow place, the
forward wheels and the forepart of the wagon and the
backs of the horses all submerged. Mr. Goddard was up
to his middle in the water, persistently hanging to our
baggage, especially my valise, and awaiting my directions.
Fortunately our two bags were in the hinder part of the
wagon and were not yet submerged. When the driver
got ashore I had him hold the horses' heads, that I might
rescue Mr. G.; then rushing to the bridge I brought up
two logs and put them from the shore to the wagon.
Mr. G. walked them ashore, but not until he had handed
over them to me the valise and bags; then he came
ashore. Immediately the wagon upset, and the driver,
exclaiming ' There they go, the team will be drowned!'
was forced to relinquish his hold of the horses' heads.
The poor animals rolled back into the water; in turning
over, however, they broke the pole, and extricating them-

selves managed to reach the other side. The driver crossing the stringer went after them; the wagon drifted to the bridge and stopped.

" Then I sent up thanks from mouth and heart to God our Father, for our safety, and that things were no worse. At one time I expected nothing but to see Mr. Goddard drowned. Thank God! thank God! we said, and addressed ourselves to the subject of repairs. Mr. Goddard sat on the ground, took off his boots, and wrung his stockings. I crossed on the stringer and held the horses, after the driver caught them, that he might go back on the road to get some miners to help us out with the wagon. When they came, I gave my key to Mr. Goddard to have him inspect my things in the valise, while I should help to get out the wagon. Mr. G. opened the valise and spread out the contents. My clothes were all soaked and he went to wringing them. Fortunately sermons and books were only half soaked. How we laughed as we saw our sermons spread out on the grass to dry; and our clothes wrung out as through a machine. Such destruction of starch! And my black suit, what a condition it was in! As Mr. G. got all the contents out and poured the water from the valise, we laughed and said we must make the best of it. Mr. G., who was wet to the neck, I kept in a working condition. I made him step round lively and take some of my brandy to keep from catching cold. Meantime, driver and miners crossed the horses, after their harness was taken off, at a ford down the creek, and strapped together pole and wagon. Mr. Goddard and I then walked along behind, pushing and pulling back, as was needed, till we all got to a ranch, two miles off. Here the owner, Mr. Paul, gave us dinner and kindly helped patch us up. At 2 P. M. we were on our way to Major Campbell's, Gallatin City, twenty-two miles off. We arrived in time to hold services there. I took out our wet things and hung them all round on Mrs. Campbell's clothes-bars to dry. But, oh, what destruction to starch! Whither had gone all your beautiful collars and cuffs? I often said: ' How I wish Mrs. Tuttle could be here to see this display.' Next morning many things were not dry, and I hung shirts and stockings out on the logs of the fence in the sun.

" Well, this trip does seem a chapter of accidents with me. Last week some Summit miners sent to me to come to S. (eight miles from Virginia City) to preach to them. I went. Half a mile out of Virginia City, going down a little pitch, the driver and I were turned over in our buggy, as completely as you please. Without premonition I found myself on the ground, my ' Mission Services ' scattered in every direction, I on top of driver, and buggy on top of me. Fortunately our mules stood stock still. We clambered up, found nothing broken, righted the wagon, and went on. Had the mules run we should have been badly hurt. Again, more than one earnest, " Thank God!" escaped my lips. At Summit I held service in a log cabin, and stayed all night. I returned to Virginia City on Wednesday, at 8 A. M., and the same day at eleven, we started for Sterling, twenty-six miles away. In the evening we held service there.

" I go to-morrow morning, at six o'clock, to see if I can secure a church lot here in Bozeman. At seven we leave for Helena. We had a full congregation to-night (I am finishing this letter after evening service), with organ and chants. Offerings $27.75. Have I told you how nicely I succeeded in getting pledges for Mr. Goddard's salary? I told the people on Sunday evening the facts of the case, and on Monday and Tuesday started out to get the $1,000 a year pledged for Mr. Goddard. To my happy disappointment, I succeeded readily in getting $102 a month, so now Mr. Goddard is fixed in Virginia City. If Mrs. G. wants to go, he will let her go for a visit of some months to Portlandville, but he will stay in Virginia City."

" *Missoula, M. T., Saturday, July 9, 1870.*

" Here I sit in the room of the ' Missoula Hotel,' which seems to be both general parlor and special room for us to occupy to-night. Now, while it is half daylight and growing dark, and while I am waiting for the ' Singers ' to come, I seem to have time to begin my letter to you. Mr. Goddard has come along with me from Deer Lodge, and on the whole is none the worse for it, for which I am very grateful. He has not been well lately, but I wanted him to come on, though I did fear that the journey of the ninety miles between Deer Lodge and this town would do him harm.

" Ours has been a valley ride of ninety miles, with some going over hills and mountains, where precipitous cañons forbade our following the stream. Five miles below Deer Lodge City the little Black Foot River empties into the Deer Lodge River. After the junction, the Deer Lodge River is called the Hellgate River, and for eighty-five miles we have ridden along it. Five miles below this town of Missoula, the Bitter Root empties into the Hellgate ; after that the Hellgate is called the Missoula River. A hundred miles or so down, the Flathead, running from Pen d'Oreille Lake, empties into the Missoula ; then the Missoula is called the Pen d'Oreille River. This Pen d'Oreille, as it flows on, becomes the Clark's Fork of the Columbia.

" Sunday morning.—Last night no singers came before ten o'clock ; then an old man, sheriff of the county, came with a bass viol, and another, a German brewer, with a violin. After them came two others, young men. The German brewer is going to be leader to-day, and with bass viol and violin accompaniment we are going to try to sing ' Balerma,' ' Old-Hundred,' ' St. Thomas,' and ' Greenland's Icy Mountains.'

" They tell us that this is the first Protestant service ever held in this town. I feel quite sure that the town is destined to be permanent, so to-morrow I'm going to see what I can do towards securing a church lot."

A very busy year indeed was this first one of our home life in Salt Lake City. The close of it, August and September, I spent in Idaho. I will speak of my sojourn there in the next chapter. October 16th, Sunday, came my first experience of absence from my post of duty because of illness. A strange abscess in the forehead, over my left eye, pained me dreadfully and quite incapacitated me for work. On the Sunday above mentioned by my physician's orders I was in bed. For the eighteen years of my ministry I had never missed a service or failed in an appointment, from sickness. God has been good to me and under His blessing my health and strength have been wonderfully preserved. As I write (1894) I have been more than thirty-two years in orders, and of my seventeen hundred Sundays of service I have been incapacitated only three. One was the Sunday I have just mentioned, one was the 12th of January, 1879, when I was laid up in Salt Lake with a violent attack of lumbago, and one was November 26, 1893, when I was sick in St. Louis with a severe cold. From accidents and sickness God's merciful goodness has spared me in a remarkable degree.

CHAPTER XI

A SUMMER IN BOISE CITY, 1870

In the work which God's Providence has assigned me in the Church Militant, the world will never know what a faithful and helpful fellow-soldier I have had in the Rev. G. D. B. Miller. As has been said, he was minister of the parish next to mine in Otsego County, N. Y., and he married a younger sister of Mrs. Tuttle. Now (1896) he has been associated with me almost constantly for twenty-nine years, save for three years he spent as a foreign missionary in China and Japan (from 1872 to 1875). As I have tried to discharge the important duties devolving upon me, he has been for all those years a veritable *fidus Achates*. Never has he swerved a hair's breadth from the line of loyal and loving and unselfish devotion. To him and his dear wife I owe a debt of gratitude, the depth of which I would seek to indicate by penning these few words.

Mr. Miller, it will be remembered, came with me to Salt Lake City in July, 1867, but he remained there only a week. He accepted my appointment of him to be missionary at Boise City, and several days before Mr. Goddard and I pushed on to Montana, left Salt Lake for his stage ride of four hundred miles to his post. Arrived in Boise City he found ready for his use the only church building existing in my entire field. And he alone, of all our missionary force in Montana, Idaho and Utah, had the steps of a predecessor to look for and walk in.

Rev. St. Michael Fackler, originally from Missouri, had gone to Oregon as a missionary. His pioneering zeal

brought him to Boise City in 1864, and he held the first
service there on Sunday, August 7th.   He remained in
Boise two years, holding services in such places as rooms
in private houses and vacant cabins, and wherever he
could. He officiated in as many as seven preaching
places of this kind. Finally the people, led, as is not
unusual, by three or four earnest and persistent women,
determined to build a church.   They raised two thousand
dollars and erected a plain building of wood, the first
service in which was held on Sunday, September 2, 1866.
Soon after, Mr. Fackler started for the East, dying en
route. He was greatly beloved by all who knew him,
and his memory is much revered.

Bishop Scott of Oregon was the only other minister of
our church who held services in any portion of the field
to which I was appointed.

Idaho City and the mining camps around were known
as " Boise Basin," and also as " West Bannack." Thousands had poured into Idaho City in search of the glit-
tering dust, and the town was busy and populous. Mr.
Fackler knew this fact, yet with rare foresight he passed
the affluent mining camp by and began his missionary
labors and built his church in Boise City, a hamlet with
few inhabitants and with a straggling street or two of log
cabins. How the vaulting ambition and unbounded
hopefulness of our Western folk is indicated in their use
of the term " City." A blacksmith shop, a store for the
sale of pins and matches, and three houses with a post-
office, have been in scores of cases material sufficient
with them to justify the appellation. When population
and energy build up the real thing the appendage "city"
at the behest of dignity is dropped.

Mr. Fackler showed wisdom in going to Boise. The
two years old Idaho City was rich and lustily thriving,

the two years old Boise City was poor and in swathing
bands. To-day, however, Boise is the beautiful and permanent capital of a prosperous commonwealth, while
Idaho is a semi-deserted mining camp with few to do reverence to her forsaken streets and her dismantled homes.

Mr. Fackler saw that Boise was situated in a fertile
valley. To the gold miner, the loom of mother earth
might seem the dirt of worthlessness, cumbering and hiding the dust of wealth, but to the missionary who had
been a farmer, it was the prolific soil ready to furnish
perennially abundance of food for the use of men. So
he chose Boise for his sphere of work, and the Church
has long since accorded him all grateful honor for his
happy choice.

In another matter, however, in my opinion, Mr. Fackler was not so wise, he served Boise City for two years
" without money and without price."

The Boise people were not mean. Yet because of the
wrong beginning, as I esteem it, made by Mr. Fackler in
his two years of free service, much patience and per-
sistency on my part of reasoning, urging, and admoni-
tion, for many years, became necessary to bring them up
to the standard of wholesome, manly self-help, and generous support of local Church expenses.

There is indication in the following letter that the
Boise people were at first not disinclined to go on in their
way of being served " without money and without price."
I saw to it, however, in my yearly visits to Boise, that the
missionary allowance should be steadily diminished, and
it was not long before the parish, by appeals to its reason
and its honor, was brought to the point of generously
providing for all its own expenses. When this letter was
written, Mr. Miller had been about six weeks in his
field.

" *Virginia City, Montana, August 20, 1867.*

" Yours of the 13th was yesterday received, giving me a report of matters in Idaho; I am much obliged to you for it. Don't you think Mary will dread the ocean trip as much as the ' Plains'? And aren't you as much afraid of ' Panama Fever' as of the Indians? For my part, the Union Pacific Railroad being now completed almost to the longitude of Denver, I don't feel that the danger from Indians on the stage route is very great. I know the papers are full of reports. But see how in succeeding issues such reports are branded as sensational and foundationless. My letters, especially from Hatty, come with unfailing regularity. As far as the mails are concerned, then, there can't be much detention on the plains.

" It seems strange to me that your people do and say nothing about a salary for your support. This thing shall be looked thoroughly into when I come on, rest assured.

" Without knowing yet all the facts, it appears to me now, guessing as I do, that your better way is to confine yourself to Boise, and not to divide yourself between Boise and Idaho.

" About the rectory, or the building proposed to be secured for the rectory, you ask, ' Can you secure for us a loan for $1,000 or $1,333?'

" I don't know whether I can or not, but I confess I had rather not try. I do not approve of going into debt. You say ' General Cartee is in favor of dividing burdens with future generations.' This theory may be well in the state; I question it not. The state has but to take care of itself. But the theory will not do in the Church, and in parishes. The Church has got more to do than simply to take care of herself. She is to do aggressive work in all the world. A parish has more to do than merely to take care of itself. It ought to help on the missionary work and the missionary agencies of all the Church. Therefore the present generation in a parish should not throw its burden on the next. The next generation shall have its own burden to carry. If the parish at home in that next generation is strong, it shall help the great work abroad. If the parish in this generation is helped by the missionary committee, let the parish of the next generation take the whole burden of its support upon itself. Let the next, and the next, generation in the parish make generous provision for their pastor; keep repaying the debt they owe the whole Church; keep helping in the good work for all the world; but let them not be cumbered by a home debt made by their fathers in the parish, dragging down their energies, and narrowing their views to selfishness ever afterwards.

"You will see, then, why I decline to borrow. I do not, let me say again, approve of going into debt. But I do approve of your securing a rectory at once; and I think the plan of buying rather than building a good one. This, then, is what I will do to encourage this buying, which I think to be wise. I will pay for part of the rectory. Let your people start a subscription, see what they will pay towards purchasing the house you are thinking of, and you can count on me to help you out.

DAN'L S. TUTTLE."

Five weeks in October and November of 1867 I spent in Idaho with Mr. Miller. He had bought, for six hundred dollars, his "rectory." Of this sum I gave one hundred and twenty-five dollars. It was a small frame structure, having in fact only three rooms and like most houses of the time it was not plastered. Cotton cloth was tacked over the inside, and wall paper was pasted upon that. There was no chimney; a pipe projecting through the roof carried off the smoke. Mr. Miller and I took up our sleeping quarters in it, going for our meals to some of the parishioners. In November, a week or two after I had returned to Montana, Mrs. Miller appeared upon the scene. She was only twenty years old, and she had come alone from New York by steamship and across the Isthmus to San Francisco. Then she had traveled some distance by the Central Pacific Railroad, and at last had come by a stage-coach ride of six days and five nights, from the terminus to Boise. Plucky little woman she! She had her trials and her frights, but she got safely through.

It is no reflection upon the courage or competency of Mr. Miller to say that the coming of his wife greatly strengthened his hands and promoted his efficiency. They lived in their box of a rectory for three years, cold as it was in the winters, and contracted as was it all the time. "Steady," is the adjective eminently applicable to their work. At times, I know, Mr. Miller felt discouraged, but he never succumbed to the feeling. According to the following letter he did once, when his father was growing old and was begging him to come back to New York, consult me about throwing up his work.

"*Salt Lake City, January 26, 1870.*
" My dear Mr. Miller:

" I wrote you yesterday, but I received yours of the 21st this morning, and I hasten to reply. My unhesitating decision is that it is your duty to remain the pastor of Boise City.

" Were your father suffering for aid, pecuniary or medical, or did he need nursing, the case would be different. But, now, as you present the case to me, it is the sad case of your aged father's desire for you to be with him, and your very natural desire to accede to his request.

" In this case of desire, versus the duty of remaining at your post and doing your important work, there is no question in my mind which must go to the wall.

" Go to your father ere he die; cheer him; pray with him; comfort him; tell him of your work; speak to him of the only abiding home, that one to come, which through the dear Saviour we are seeking; then, like a faithful soldier, return, though it be sad and hard to do so, to your duty.

" There is no room for question in my mind that, as between the two courses which you present to me, this is your certain duty.

" Permit me also to say that only on condition of your returning to Boise City after three months' vacation would I be justified in giving up my time to Boise for you next summer, leaving your salary to go quietly on.

" My dear brother, I do think that with God's blessing you have done and are doing a most important and blessed work where you are. Yours is a bright spot in my field. Desert not your post. Enjoy the leave of absence granted you, but return,—in love to your people, in kindness to me, in faithfulness to the Great Head of the Church."

In my first visit to Idaho in 1867 I secured a piece of ground in Boise City. It was a city block. Thus far the only bit of property owned by the Church in all my three territories was St. Michael's church and lot in Boise. In those early days land was free and open to be taken up as a " homestead " farm, or as a " claim " in any town-site area. In the latter case the cost to the claimant was simply the fence to enclose it and the payment of after taxes accruing. So I chose a block in Boise City, fencing it in at a cost of $325.88. On the block St. Margaret's School for girls now stands.

Here let me recount some of the experience of my early mountain life touching the different kinds of money used. As a general rule books were kept and accounts rendered in government currency. From 1867 this currency was slowly changing in value and in the line of appreciation. It sufficed to the miners and those with whom they traded to give a fixed value to their gold dust. This was eighteen dollars an ounce, though some " dust " was of low grade or too much accompanied with black sand and was rated at sixteen dollars.   Every merchant and business man had his scales.   In the camps gold dust, kept in buckskin purses or carefully tied up in pieces of paper, was the medium of exchange at the rate above mentioned.   In the alms-basins, in our church collections, the pinches of " dust " in their paper or skin wrappings were constantly found.

Two towns, however, Silver City and Boise City, were each a law unto itself. Silver City followed California, with which it was intimately connected in a business way, dealing as it did exclusively in gold and silver.   No greenbacks at all showed themselves there, people would not handle them.   Double eagles, eagles, half eagles, quarter eagles, silver half dollars and quarter dollars, were the currency.   I do not remember ever seeing silver dollars, and there was nothing in use smaller than a quarter dollar.   Dimes and half dimes, and of course pennies, were unknown.   At Silver City alms-basins were generously loaded with half dollars and quarter dollars, nor were gold pieces unfrequent.   The same remark about lack of any coins smaller than a quarter dollar applies to all my three territories ; a shoe-string, a paper of pins, an apple, a copy of a daily newspaper, was twenty-five cents.   If in making change you came within twenty-five cents of the sum required, it was all right.   Silver City never deviated from its gold and silver standard, until, with California, it found its currency and the United States currency at one again by the national resumption of specie payments.

Boise City made a curious law for itself, which it kept to for several years, disregarding changes in the standards of the world outside itself. It fixed greenbacks at a discount of twenty-five per cent. Books and accounts it kept on this basis, adding one-third to every transaction paid for in greenbacks. I paid for the fence in Boise $244.41, but I paid it from Montana in a draft on San Francisco. So, on the books, the cost of the fence was $325.88. The sixty dollars given me as a collection at Silver City when brought over to Boise brought me at the bank eighty dollars. Banks we had in those days, two in Salt Lake City, two in Virginia City, three in Helena, one in Boise City, and, I think, one at Lewiston.

In 1870 Mr. Miller, having been at Boise for three years, wanted to go for a trip East. I thought he deserved a generous leave of absence; therefore, Mr. Foote having returned to Salt Lake from his tour of solicitation, I arranged to spend August, September, and part of October, in Boise, in order that he be at liberty to go. Besides, he wanted to gather funds in the East for two improvements, (1) To enlarge the contracted quarters of his rectory. For this he needed $600. (2) To enlarge the vestry room of St. Michael's into a wing which he might use for the accommodation of his parish school of fifty-five scholars, the school for two years having been inconveniently gathered in the church. For this he needed $2,000. In a sober and sensible way, while on his visit, he told his needs, the consequence being that he brought back $1,700, mostly given by Western New York and Central New York. I was able to give $500. With this help and with the gifts of his own people he succeeded in accomplishing the two things desired. The schoolroom by folding doors could be made a part of the church on Sundays if crowded congregations demanded it, and the rectory became a pleasant six-roomed home, with a chimney.

To Boise City, then, in August, 1870, I went to serve for a while as pastor again.   Boise was eight years old, having first been settled in 1862.   More than twenty years before that time the Hudson's Bay Company had established old Fort Boise as a trading post, near the junction of the Boise River with the Snake.   The new Fort Boise, or rather " Boise Barracks," a United States army post, a mile from Boise City and fifty miles up the river from old Fort Boise, was established July 5, 1863. Some old time French explorer, or army officer who liked to think and speak in French, had named the river Boise (wooded), doubtless because of the groves of cottonwood lining its course, while all the rest of the valley, the plateau, the foot-hills, and indeed nearly all the mountains were treeless.

Boise City had a population of about 1,500 ; outside of Mormondom its population was more a settled one than that of any other place in my field, and it was more a town of homes.   So I really enjoyed my summer stay in it.   It was not old enough yet to have orchards and fruit, though these were to be abundant in later years.   Apples brought from Oregon still cost twenty-five cents or more, each.   But the people had homes and yards and gardens, and children, and I enjoyed its atmosphere of Christian civilization.

St. Michael's vestry were good and true men and loyal to Mr. Miller ; but I have noted above how and why they seemed slow and selfish in coming to his support.   Once a rumor came that an army chaplain was to be ordered to Boise Barracks.   Then " my occupation's gone," said Mr. Miller.   " I exacting a salary, and Mr. K. being in a

position to come from the barracks and serve St.
Michael's without a salary,—why, affectionate good-bys
will be pressed upon me without delay!" He opened
his grief to me and I wrote him as follows:

"*Virginia, Montana, August 31, 1867.*
"I am sorry you are anxious and troubled. But hold
on for the present. Stay where you are till I come, or
till things turn out decidedly otherwise. Yes, I well understand, my dear brother, your desire to settle and have
a home. And you shall have one, too, if in any way I
can help you to one. But I don't want you to flee just
because brother K. comes. I may want you both there.
Besides, a chaplain is under other orders than mine, and
one can never count on his staying at any one point. If
the Church is to be built up in Idaho and Boise, another
than a chaplain must be depended upon for the work.
You have your troubles, my dear brother, and we have
ours. My material here (*entre nous*) is of the hardest
kind, though our people are generous."

I may remark that the chaplain never came. The
only chaplain ever stationed at Boise Barracks was a
Roman Catholic priest, and he stayed only for a little
while.

I reached Boise for my summer stay, early in August,
1870, Mr. Miller having gone for his Eastern visit in
July. But Rev. H. L. Foote (younger brother of our Salt
Lake pastor) was in residence. He with his wife had
come to assist Mr. Miller in his work, and especially in
his parish school, in July, 1869. Not long after his
arrival his wife died suddenly of heart trouble connected
with rheumatism. This coming year I was prepared to
arrange for Mr. Foote (whom I had advanced to the
priesthood in St. Michael's in September, 1869) to visit

Idaho City two Sundays a month, and Silver City, one, while living at Boise and still helping in the school. He and I roomed at the rectory, a parishioner, Mrs. Alvord, daughter of the chief justice of the territory, giving us meals at reasonable cost. Mr. Foote was a good gardener and had raised a plentiful crop of muskmelons in the rectory garden, and on these we luxuriated. But alas! the rectory inside lost its wonted neatness and dignity. How we do deteriorate when deprived of the sweet and blessed services of womankind! Witness the following confession in my letter to Mrs. Tuttle:

" *St. Michael's Rectory, Boise City, I. T.,*
" *August 7, 1870.*
" Again I must resort to pen and paper if I would chat with you. It is a trial that we have to be so much separated; but it is God's will and we do both try, I trust and believe, to do His will cheerfully.

" I sit in the dining-room of St. Michael's rectory, at Mr. Miller's desk (Henry being at the other desk), writing. It would drive Mary (Mrs. Miller) crazy to see the house. In Henry's room, broken glasses, deserted bed, littered papers, dirty floor. (He calls that his store room now,—I say, lumber room.) In the kitchen, all things disordered,—blacking brush and blacking on the table, oil can beside it, wash-basin in place of honor, water-pail in place of dishonor. In this room, carpet removed, dirty floor, on which is spread out H.'s old shawl, and on that two pillows; canes, clubs, letters, papers; with boots and shoes in inextricable confusion all over the house. H. laughs when I ask: ' What would Mary say?' and replies: ' Ha, ha! Mollie isn't here now. I am luxuriating in my thoroughly enjoyable sense of littering independence.'"

But, a little bit of exculpation for the disorder may be offered. The rectory was to be enlarged. We had made up our minds to that. Carpenters and masons must be allowed to come in and we must make it as good a sort of lodging-place for ourselves as we could, under their incursions. Mrs. Miller had insisted that she must have a cellar, which she had not hitherto had. A great part of that cellar I dug myself with pick and shovel, mostly while left alone by Mr. Foote's absence in Idaho and Silver. I was glad to labor in so good a cause. I consider a rectory an excellent sort of endowment for a parish.

Sunday, August 14, 1870, I went over with Mr. Foote to Silver. In the afternoon I wrote to Mrs. Tuttle: " Henry and I left Boise at 5 P. M., Friday, so there are no services in St. Michael's to-day. We rode all night and reached here at 7 A. M. Saturday. We room at this hotel, and take our meals at Mrs. Grayson's. After breakfast, Saturday, we both lay down on the floor in our room and took a three hours' snooze ; then in the afternoon and evening we made eleven calls, besides meeting the singers for practice. We have services in the Masonic Hall. This morning Henry baptized an infant during service ; to-night, after service, he is to marry a couple. The groom came to me yesterday to ask me to officiate. But alas for your fee, my dear ! I had to take him apart and tell him that the proper thing for him to do was to apply to Henry. So Henry is to officiate to-night, I to be present, to read the exhortation and pronounce the benediction."

Mr. Foote was in pastoral charge of Silver City and Idaho City. It has been a rule of my bishop's life scrupulously to respect the pastoral rights of my clergy. Marriages, baptisms, burials among their own flocks, belong to them. In exceptional cases only, and at the earnest request of all parties concerned, may the bishop intervene. As missionary bishop, of course there was opportunity for me often to officiate where there was no settled pastor, so at the date when I write (1896), my marriages have been 194, baptisms 1,348, and burials 198. Wedding fees among the mountain frontiersmen, much to Mrs. Tuttle's delight, were generous. They were often one hundred dollars each, or fifty dollars; seldom were they less than twenty dollars. A double eagle fell into Mr. Foote's purse that evening at Silver City.

Sunday, August 28, Mr. Foote and I spent in Idaho City. I wrote to Mrs. Tuttle:

"*Idaho City, Sunday, 9 A. M., August 28, 1870.*

"I sit in the bar-room and office combined of the 'Luna House' to write this letter. And I sit by a fire, for our nights and mornings are now decidedly cold. Henry, since breakfast, has gone out for a walk 'to warm himself up,' he said.

"It is going to be a busy day for us. Service this morning (in the court-house) at eleven; Sunday-school at two; service and confirmation at the jail at three; dining out at five; service this evening at 7:30. Also, baptism to-morrow at 3 P. M. Then, perhaps to-morrow I shall have to take the 'Subscription Book' and see what I can secure here to pay Henry or Mr. Miller for services for next year. The town is exceedingly dull and very few families mean to live here through this winter; so I fear I shall not be able to secure much financial help towards the support of our services."

Evidently I got on with the "Subscription Book" better than I had expected. This is indicated in my next letter to Mrs. Tuttle:

" Boise City, Idaho, August 31, 1870.

" I wrote you last, on Sunday morning, from Idaho City. That proved a busy day. Besides morning services, at 1 P. M., I baptized two children ; at two, visited the Sunday-school ; at three, held service and confirmed one convict in the prison ; at five, dined out ; and at 7:30 P. M., held evening services. Offerings were $28.15.

" Monday I was busy as a bee. I took a subscription book and got $600 subscribed for services twice a month this next year. I collected $135, cash in hand, for the first quarter, and gave it to Henry. H. and Mr. Miller are going to be very busy this year, with Silver and Idaho to look after."

This preparing subscription books for ministers' salaries, solicitation of names, and often, collecting payments, formed a frequent and important part of my missionary work. It was not a pleasant work, yet the unpleasantness never hurt much, because the people were full of considerate kindness, and in the main had a generous desire to help. The experience I have had as solicitor and collector has made higher rather than lower my esteem for average human nature. Men are kinder and more unselfish than they are thought to be. One will be gratified, I think, more than grieved, by surprises, when he sets himself to ask an average American public for help to any work of Church or charity. I would not willingly give up the proof which lies nestling in the deep of my heart, that my fellow men all around are kind, considerate, responsive, appreciative, sympathizing, helpful, generous.

In doing this sort of duty, experience developed for me some simple rules. Under or alongside of these I learned to try to keep myself. They are such as these : (1) Keep your temper, you are in no fit place for indulging bitter criticism, or swelling indignation, or aching to give " that man a piece of your mind." (2) Don't take other men's estimates of your fellows. Mistakes are made, use your own judgment. Go to every one to whom you have the right to apply. Get at first hand their own answers to you. Frequently others have said to me, " Don't go to Mr. A., you will certainly get nothing from him. It's no use in the world for you to go." I have always declined that sort of advice. Resolved with God's help not to lose my temper, I have gone to scores of A.'s, and in not a few instances have met with compliances and helps instead of refusals. (3) Go to men, not to women, with your subscription book, save in the cases where women have their separate fortunes and incomes. If the wife be a churchwoman and the husband an infidel, go to him first. If he refuse you help, even then do not go to the wife unless with his permission asked for and obtained. (4) When you have soliciting business in hand to do, do it ; don't play with it. When you have found the man to whom you are to apply, and it is your right, in turn, to have an interview with him, don't beat about the bush, don't try to construct pleasant bridges of approach, don't talk about the weather or the crops or the dulness of trade or the pleasantness of the last social party or the measles of the children or the doctrines of religion or church history and church growth, but in a straightforward way tell him what you have come for and ask him if he will allow you to show him your book for securing his name. If he and you have ʌny time for pleasant conversation, let the chat come after, and not before, your business. (5) Don't " nag " or " bore." State plainly to the man what you want his help for ; put your appeal as concisely and strongly as you courteously can. Then, as a general thing accept his decision and withdraw. Only in rare cases follow up with argumentation. Your book having pages allotted to larger and smaller amounts, of course it is all right for you to call up for brief use your powers of persuasion to try to induce him to place his name on the former. (6) Don't make your estimate of what other people ought to give into a fixed, governing law. Too many data are unknown to you for you to indulge in such lawmaking. Some of them are: the real income, the multiplicity of other calls, the proportionate value in the esteem of the giver of the cause you plead for, the uncertainties impending over the provision he has made for home and business. (7) Be cheery and hopeful. If you meet with a refusal where you looked for a compliance, don't lose heart; say with a smile that you hope when you come next time that the good man will be able to help you. If one gives much less than you think he ought to give, don't scold or fret, but return good-natured thanks. Remember that you are not to make yourself judge in this matter. If you can make your thanks cheery and hearty over the small gift, the best kind of a lesson in the joy of giving will be afforded to that man. Growth in the grace of giving will thus not unlikely ensue, and when next you come to ask that man he will probably give more than he did before and enjoy the giving, too, as he never did before. His heart once warmed over a little giving will win him to the ways of generosity more than would a ship-load of logical arguments. Criticism of his illiberality and reproaches for his penuriousness will do no good to him nor win any gain for you; they will only steel his mind and heart to a yet greater degree of hardness. (8) Don't exhaust all your tact in getting names on your book; employ a portion of it in keeping some names off your book. In every community there are some people quick to promise and slow to perform, enthusiastic and generous to subscribe, but found utterly lacking when pay day is to be met. Either leave such folk entirely off of your book, for they belong to a class whose feelings are not easily injured; or, if civility require that you ask them for help, kindly persuade them to put their names on the pages of lower amounts.

September 5th, St. Michael's parish school, Boise, opened for its fourth year. Miss Leonard was the teacher, and there were from forty to sixty scholars. Mr. Foote and I, however, also taught, he taking the forenoon and I the afternoon. On Mondays, when Mr. Foote was returning from Idaho or Silver, I taught all day. For three years St. Michael's had done the steady pastoral work for the Boise community. A Baptist church building had been erected some years before, but its minister had got so interested in the care of bees and the profits from honey that he had thrown up preaching. The building was now irregularly occupied by the Methodists. We were so much the acknowledged religious leaders in Boise that the " *noblesse oblige*" was felt to rest upon us.

Once, in 1869, when on my visit in Boise, I saw one day on the " Overland Hotel" register the name, " Bishop Weaver, of the United Brethren." I said to Mr. Miller, this must be a bishop of the Moravian Church. I hear he is to stop here over Sunday, en route as he is to Oregon. I think we ought to show him some courtesy. So we called on him with an invitation to dinner on Sunday, also asking him to preach in St. Michael's in the afternoon. We told him the church was his for him to use for his own service, our own regular services being in the morning and at night.

At dinner I thought the expected refinement and spirituality of a Moravian saint were not conspicuous. And during the services in church afterwards the illogical ramblings and violent denunciation of the sermon obliged us to conclude that somehow we had made a mistake, that the preacher could be no Moravian. We said good-by as courteously as possible to the "bishop" and found on inquiry afterwards that "United Brethren" is the appellation of some emotional and unscholarly religionists who have a little strength in Indiana and the middle West, and that our "bishop" was one of these, on his way to do some missionary work in Oregon.

The following is a letter to Mrs. Tuttle:

"*Boise, Idaho, Sunday, September 11, 1870.*

"I am alone in the rectory and have been so since yesterday at 6 A. M. Henry has gone to Idaho City and will not be back until to-morrow night.

"I have been thinking that to-morrow will be our wedding anniversary. We have been one, five years. And now, as I count it up, we have lived together three of those five years, and apart, two. I suppose we may regard this as a fair average for our life through. We may live together three-fifths of the time, we must be content to live separate two-fifths. God help us to be submissive, content, and thankful. Five years ago to-morrow morning we went up the aisle of Zion, Morris; you with George, I with mother; while many, very many friendly and loving hearts were all around us in the congregation. We walked down the aisle together, satisfied with each other, proud of each other, I know, but not yet doing the impossible thing of loving each other so honestly and fervently as we do now."

The courage and content breathed in the letter were in the face of constant troubles. Rev. Geo. Foote, writing from Salt Lake, was anxious and despondent about funds for continuing the building of his church. Through col-

lectors, Mr. Johnson at Virginia City, and Mr. Pope at
Helena, I was care-taker for the monthly payments of
salary to be made to the Rev. Messrs. Goddard and
Fowler, the latter of whom had come to Helena for a
few months. Worriments, as indicated by the following
sentences in a letter to Mrs. Tuttle, were not infrequent:

" Boise City, Idaho, September 14, 1870.
" Monday I was in school all day, Henry not getting
home till 3 P. M. One of our 'Committee' in Idaho
City, husband of one of our most prominent churchwomen, lately county treasurer, has proved a defaulter for
$20,000, and has run away to the East. His name is
P. E. Edmundson; we trusted in and consulted with him
in church matters more than with any one else. Isn't it
sad?

" Another man here, husband of one of our communicants, shot a man in a quarrel day before yesterday, and
is now in jail. The man shot was yesterday reported
dead; but he is not dead this morning, and there is some
hope of his recovery."

My Boise sojourn was drawing to its close. Kind and
loving the people were to me. God bless them ever!
But from first to last I was not unthoughtful of efforts to
lead them in the way of sturdy self-help, they having
been started wrong in that respect, as I conceived, by Mr.
Fackler. Before I came for the sojourn I wrote to Mr.
Miller:

" Salt Lake, February 22, 1870.
" Please let me say here while I think of it and that
you may prepare your people for it in the best way you
choose, that when I come to Boise next summer to take
your place I shall expect my living expenses to be met.

I have only my salary to live on, and it no more than suffices for running this house in Salt Lake; indeed it barely does that. Therefore, I cannot pay extra expenses at Boise. If you leave it to me to arrange, I shall simply ask the vestry to provide for me. If they do not, I shall take up collections to meet necessary outgoes,—board, rooms, lights, washing. I mention this thus early, not to give you trouble, but that there may be no room for misunderstanding in money matters hereafter."

My reports of two vestry meetings are in letters to Mrs. Tuttle:

" *Boise City, Idaho, August 25, 1870.*

" Monday evening I met the vestry here, and with God's help I think I succeeded well in putting things before them, and drawing decisions from them as I wish. They found themselves in debt to Mr. Miller, one hundred and thirty-five dollars (since then, fifty-five dollars have been paid, so they now owe him eighty dollars); and for parish expenses, ninety-two dollars. The vestry heretofore have been opposed to offerings in church, on the plea that they keep people away. So for a year they have had no offering, except at the communion. Last Monday night, however, they frankly said they had been mistaken, that they agreed with Mr. Miller and Henry and me that it was best to have offerings at every service in church. In this way, therefore, they propose to pay off this ninety-two dollars. With this decision I was pleased. Then I told them that for 1871 I must diminish Mr. Miller's missionary stipend to $600, and I asked them to raise $1,200. I did not force the decision, but will have another meeting the latter part of September, when I think they will yield to my wishes. Last, I asked to be allowed to enter all the church property here in my name and to be allowed to hold the deeds. This they cheerfully gave me permission to do, I to pay the expenses of transfer. On the whole I was much pleased with this meeting, and the results have lifted burdens from my mind; I now think that I shall be able to secure Mr. Miller's and Henry's salaries for another year, and get $200 away from their missionary stipends besides. By the way, at the meeting the account of the bell fund was brought in. It showed a debt of forty-six dollars with only fifteen dollars subscribed wherewith to pay. So I said, ' I want a part in this bell. I wish to give personally twenty-five dollars.' I gave it on the spot and the vestry made up the six dollars (Henry giving one dollar). Accordingly the bell fund is now entirely square."

" Boise City, September 30, 1870.

" I am pressed with the duties of winding up everything here preparatory to leaving next Monday morning, and with helping Henry to line these rooms with cloth. Mary's wall paper came day before yesterday and Henry and I are going to try to put it on to-morrow. As soon as I get up from writing this I am going at some of it alone, while H. is at school. Tuesday evening we had a vestry meeting. The vestry would not quite engage to secure $1,200 for Mr. Miller next year; so I frankly told them that I would retain, against contingencies, $200 of the $500 I had promised to St. Michael's church. Henry is not going to be able to get the cellar in perfect shape, nor to get the house entirely in order for Mary. He can't hire any more, because the pump will use up all that is left of the $650 to which he is restricted; and after I leave him he will have a hard and busy time in school all day. Therefore I must get to work, tacking the lining. Good-by; I hope to see you in four or five days."

I am happy to say that the vestry did raise the $1,200 for the rector's salary. My experience with the Boise vestry was that they were always wisely slow in promising, but that they grew to be even more wisely just and generous in meeting all reasonable expectations made of them.

At Kelton, where the stage line struck the railroad I arrived, en route to Salt Lake, about 9 P. M. Mr. and Mrs. Miller, from the East en route to Boise, arrived about 11 P. M. and were to take the stage at 3 A. M. So we sat up together for the four hours and chatted. It was a cheery chat, the East had been kind to Mr. Miller, Boise had been kind to me.

Idaho is now (1896) a state. For more than nineteen years, when it was a territory, I was its bishop. In fifty towns and hamlets in it I held services. On the map it is shaped like a boot. In the south, or the foot part, the Mormons overflowing from Utah settled; in the north, or the top of the boot leg, at Lewiston and the mines round about, were the first white settlements, other than Mormons. Yet I did not visit the Lewiston region until 1881. This was because between the floods of spring and the snows of autumn there were not days enough for me to get all over Montana and Idaho. When Montana was set apart in 1880 and Bishop Brewer took charge, I visited Lewiston and the Cœur d'Alene country; after that I went there yearly. Previously, Bishop Morris and the Rev. Dr. Nevius of Oregon had kindly looked after Church work for me in Northern Idaho. Lewiston, being at the head waters of the Lewis Fork of the Columbia, was naturally closely connected with Oregon. Idaho is rich in minerals, farms, and lumber. She alone greeted me with some Church work done when I went to the mountains. All the nineteen years of my association with her I found her and her people kind and loyal and helpful. On her soil, at Soda Springs, on the afternoon of August 9, 1886, by official reception of the notice of the consents of majorities of the House of Bishops and of the Standing Committees, I ceased to be her bishop and became the Bishop of Missouri.

With the letter in my hand I hung my head as if I were a deserter, and tears accompanied the good-by I whispered within. I love her still. I wish to her and her people now and alway, health, wealth and happiness.

CHAPTER XII

THE MORMONS

THE " Latter Day Saints," as they desire to be called, for they regard the name " Mormons " as a nickname, give their organization the title of the " Church of Jesus Christ of Latter Day Saints." I must be excused from writing a detailed narrative of the history of Mormonism, or a theological disquisition upon its doctrines and polity. Any encyclopedia will furnish the history of it, and little good would result from an attempted analysis of whatever scientific theology it professes to have. I lived in the midst of it, however, for seventeen years and it may not be amiss for me to record my impressions of it.

I first entered Salt Lake City, July 2, 1867; I left it September 1, 1886. In November, 1869, I moved my family there and made it my home. When I came, the town was twenty years old. July 24, 1847, the Mormon pioneers entering the valley fixed the site of the city about fifteen miles from the lake. They chose a spot on City Creek, just at the mouth of the cañon, whence its refreshing waters poured themselves from the mountains. Though sick with mountain fever, Brigham Young was at their head. April 7th, they had left Winter Quarters, Iowa (now Florence, a few miles northwest of Council Bluffs). The date of the organization of their church of six members, under Joseph Smith, in Fayette, Seneca County, New York, was April 6, 1830. April 6th has therefore ever since been the date of their " Annual Con- ference." They also have a semiannual conference every October 6th. April 6, 1847, Brigham unfolded his plan

of emigration westward to the saints assembled at Winter
Quarters. Next day, under his leadership the pioneer
body set out. It comprised one hundred and forty-four
men, three women, and two children. To be more exact,
there were one hundred and forty-four men, three women,
two children, ninety-three horses, fifty-two mules, sixty-
six oxen, nineteen cows, seventeen dogs, and some chickens. For three months and a half, and for 1,300 miles
of distance, the wagons and mother earth were their beds
and the sky their shelter. Brigham divided them into
companies, introduced military rule, and kept sharp guard
against the hostile and thieving Indians. They met immense herds of buffaloes, but he forbade them to slaughter
any more than were needed for fresh meat for their subsistence. Some of the pioneers were left behind, *en route*,
to make preparation for the immigration of the next year.
Some members from the Mormon battalion that had
gone to the Mexican war also joined them on the plains.
Accordingly about 143 entered the valley on July 24th.
Not one of the original 149 had died *en route*.

Brigham Young was born in Vermont, in 1801, joined
the Mormon Church at Kirtland, Ohio, where he first
met Joseph Smith, in 1832, was made one of the Twelve
Apostles in 1835, and not long afterwards was sent
among the first of the missionaries to England. In 1841
he became president of the twelve, and June 27, 1844,
soon after the murder of Joseph Smith in Carthage prison,
succeeded to the leadership of the band. When the
murder took place, Brigham was in the Eastern states,
but hearing of it he hastened to Nauvoo. Being president of the twelve, with the vigor and determination
which characterized him he resolved to make good his
claim to the leadership. The person to dispute the claim
with him was Sidney Rigdon, an able and eloquent man,

who had been co-laborer with Joseph Smith and perhaps brains for him. Rigdon was one of Smith's two counselors, the three thus making the First Presidency of the Church. At once Brigham took an aggressive stand; he denounced Sidney as ambitious and a self-seeker, and as moreover secretly unfaithful to the customs and laws of the church. By his boldness he soon won a speedy victory, thus becoming the acknowledged Mormon chief. He managed wisely to settle the troubles of the Mormons with the Illinois people, to whom they had become obnoxious; he advised and accomplished the evacuation of Nauvoo, and he led the saints westward to Winter Quarters in 1846.

For the three years subsequent to the death of Smith, Brigham with active brain had been planning for the westward migration of the saints. He had heard of the Great Salt Lake in the interior basin of the Rocky Mountains; the pioneer, Jim Bridger, had seen the lake in 1824 and had fully described it. Brigham had determined that he and his people would get off somewhere by themselves. They had tried living among others in four states, New York, Ohio, Missouri, and Illinois, and everywhere suspicion, jealousy, hate were engendered against them, so that their lives were in constant turmoil. The thought came to him: " Let us go where we will not be interfered with." And he waxed resolute to carry it out. None can deny the energy and courage of his action. In the autumn of 1847 he went back to Winter Quarters; in 1848 he superintended the migration of two or three thousand of the saints to Salt Lake. In the Jubilee Celebration in Salt Lake City, of July 24, 1897, it appeared that there were still about 650 survivors of those first immigrations of 1847 and 1848.

The question is often asked, wherein does the power

of Mormonism over people lie, and what constitutes the strength of its coherence and continuance? I answer— a good many things. Suffer me to allude to them as they come into view. Scrutiny of the personnel of the one hundred and forty-four men of the pioneer band may help towards the answer. Out of them there were eight apostles, fifteen high priests, seventy-eight seventies, four bishops, and eight elders,—one hundred and thirteen in all. That left only forty-one to be of the rank and file. One hundred and thirteen officers and forty-one privates! This is typical of the Mormon organization.

Besides the president of the church, " the prophet, seer and revelator of the Lord," (Joseph Smith, the first, Brigham Young, the second, John Taylor the third, Wilford Woodruff [1898] the fourth and present) and his two counselors, there are the apostles, the patriarch, the high priests, the priests (both of the Melchisedek priesthood and of the Aaronic priesthood), the seventies, the bishops, the elders, the deacons, and the teachers. And every high officer is provided with two counselors. Much satisfaction is thus given to the self-assertion, ambition, and desire for leadership, natural to man. There is strength in this. Furthermore, may it not be said, and might not bishops and rectors of our own Church be profited by taking heed to the saying, that the intelligent interest and loyalty and devotion of disciples are sure to be promoted by according to them some authority and devolving upon them responsibility.

I pause to remark that if some strength accrues to Mormonism from its adjustment to the nature of man, some unsuspected strength also is won to it by its appeal to the nature of woman. The self-sacrifice in woman, the appeal is made to that. One knows not much of human life if he is ignorant that one of the dominating characteristics of woman is the power of self-sacrifice. If self-sacrifice in woman is continually in evidence in mothers, in wives of worthless husbands, in sisters in religious communities, and in women giving up all in devotion to love or duty or religion, who wonders that the appeal to it, as in the matter of polygamy, strange as it seems, must be accounted an element of strength to Mormonism. As matter of fact, there were no more strenuous and determined upholders of polygamy than most of the Mormon women who were personally sufferers by it. To their nature it was a calamity and hateful. To their spirit it was religious duty and a call for self-sacrifice. Therefore they were loyal to it, determined to live in it, and if need be, to die for it. Spirit, roused and active, evermore predominates over nature.

In the popular belief, polygamy is the distinguishing tenet of Mormonism; as can be shown in several ways, however, this conclusion is a mistake. In the first place, the Mormon Church was not founded in polygamy, and it lived for thirteen years without anything being said about polygamy in the Book of Mormon.[1] In the second

---

[1] The Book of Mormon is the alleged translation by Joseph Smith of the writings, in " Reformed Egyptian " characters, on the golden plates which he claimed to have dug up, under angelic direction, near Palmyra, New York, in 1827. The Book recounts under fourteen headings or " Books " the stories of two migrations to America—of Jared and his kin from the Tower of Babel, who were supposed to have disembarked on the coast of Southern California; and of Nephi and his kin, at the time of King Zedekiah of Jerusalem and the taking of the city by Nebuchadnezzar— landing on the coast of Chili. The historic portions are not remarkable for lucidness. Moral and spiritual exhortations, commandments and doctrines are freely interspersed. Prophecies, more or less obscure, are included. For style of diction and for text matter the old and New Testaments are freely drawn upon. The Saviour is represented as descending in America after His ascension from Palestine, and commissioning twelve American apostles. So the Church of Jesus Christ of the Early Saints was

place, a very considerable number of Mormons, with their
descendants and adherents, who did not go to Utah under the leadership of Brigham Young, but who still reside
and flourish in the older states, especially in Missouri,
Illinois, and Iowa, never did adopt polygamy. They are
under the leadership of Joseph's son, Joseph Smith, Jr.,

constituted. The Nephites were for the most part loyal and devoted to it.
But some of them waxed unfaithful, and their defection swelled the ranks
of the Lamanites who were open enemies and infidels. The Lamanites
were the ancestors of our North American Indians. About the year 400
A. D. there came a pitched battle between the opposing forces. The
Lamanites were victorious. Moroni had been forewarned by Mormon the
prophet, his father, that the battle was imminent and that the Nephites
would be exterminated. Mormon therefore gave to his son to preserve
the sacred records and revelations. These constituted the records of the
golden plates. Moroni hid them up in the hill Cumorah, overlooking the
plain on which the great battle was fought. There they remained in
safety for nearly 1,500 years, when the angel directed Joseph Smith to
bring them forth for the enlightenment, guidance, and salvation of mankind. Subsequently John the Baptist appeared to Joseph Smith and
Oliver Cowdery, and admitted them to the Aaronic priesthood. There-
upon, Joseph baptized Oliver by immersion, and Oliver then baptized
Joseph. Still later, Peter and James and John appeared to Joseph Smith
and Oliver Cowdery and admitted them to the Melchisedek priesthood.
Joseph then ordained Oliver an elder, and Oliver ordained Joseph.
Furnished with the new and hitherto unknown revelation, extending from
the time of the Tower of Babel to A. D. 384, and equipped with the
highest authority of priesthood, at the hands of saints and prophets and
apostles who had come down from heaven to commission them, Joseph
Smith and the country schoolmaster, Oliver Cowdery, were now ready to
take in hand the establishment, or the reëstablishment, in the Latter Days,
of the Church of Saints of Jesus Christ. This establishment, in conjunc-
tion with four other persons, they made in Fayette, Seneca County, N. Y.,
April 6, 1830.

This is the belief of the faithful touching the Book of Mormon and the
reëstablishment in the Latter Days of the Church of Christ. The strong
probability is that the Book of Mormon is in substance a religious
romance written by Rev. Solomon Spaulding of Conneaut, Ohio, an in-
valid Congregational minister, to while away a time of enforced retire-
ment, and to embody his conviction that the original inhabitants of the

who was born at Kirtland, Ohio, in 1832. His followers
are called Josephites. They call themselves the " Reor-
ganized Church of Jesus Christ of Latter Day Saints."
They repudiate Brigham's authority and sharply condemn
the practice of polygamy. They maintain that the
prophet Joseph never taught or countenanced it. Yet in
the Book of Doctrine and Covenants,[1] Section 132 looks

Western Continent are descendants of the lost tribes of Israel. Joseph
Smith and Sidney Rigdon probably got hold of this manuscript and appropriated it to their use; Sidney, who had been a capable and eloquent
" Christian " or " Campbellite " preacher in Ohio, adding to it most of the
prophetic, hortatory, and doctrinal ecclesiasticism needed. There is not
one word approving the practice of polygamy. On the contrary there is
this express prohibition of it (Book of Jacob, Chapter II, v. 27), " Where:
fore, my brethren, hear me and hearken to the word of the Lord; for
there shall not any man among you have save it be one wife; and concu-
bines he shall have none."

[1] The Book of Doctrine and Covenants is the compendium of the various
revelations made to and through Joseph Smith, with one only added, given
through Brigham Young. The high claim of divine guidance made by
the Mormon Church may be noted. It has five sources of revelation:
(1) the Old Testament, (2) the New Testament, (3) the Book of Mormon,
(4) the Book of Doctrine and Covenants, (5) the Revelations oral, made
from time to time to and through the president of the Church, who is the
" prophet, seer, and revelator of the Lord." To the faithful Mormon all
these five sources are divinely inspired. When he is arguing with the ordinary Christian he fully grants the Divine inspiration and authority of all
the Holy Bible. But he claims, also, that he enjoys the privilege of access to three other sources of Divine guidance and revelation, to which he
will be only too happy to conduct his Christian brother, if he be willing to
come. A Mormon logician never argues against the Holy Bible of the
Old and New Testaments. He professes entire adhesion and loyalty to it.
The winged shafts of many of his opponents, therefore, to their astonish-
ment, can never be made to hit him. He will agree with them; then
after they have taught him all they know, he will invite them to come
with him that they may win and use the further divine knowledge with
which he is blessed. Many arguers and arguments against Mormonism
have fallen to confusion and nothingness, because of the false assumption
that the Mormons consider themselves to have superseded the Bible.

much like a sanctioning of polygamy. It comprises a revelation given through Joseph Smith at Nauvoo, July 12, 1843, a little less than a year before he was murdered. In the Brighamite edition the section is headed (I do not know what the Josephite heading is) : " Revelation on the Eternity of the Marriage Covenant, including Plurality of Wives." Verses sixty-one and sixty-two read as follows : " And again as pertaining to the Law of the Priesthood ; If any man espouse a virgin, and desire to espouse another, and the first give her consent; and if he espouse the second, and they are virgins, and have vowed to no other man, then is he justified ; he cannot commit adultery, for they are given unto him ; for he cannot commit adultery with that that belongeth unto him and to no one else; and if he have ten virgins given unto him by this law, he cannot commit adultery, for they belong to him, and they are given unto him, therefore is he justified."

Open sanction and formal promulgation of the right of polygamy there was not, until it was made by Brigham Young in the Tabernacle in Salt Lake City, in 1852. It is said that when the bold avowal was made known in England, where for fifteen years Mormon missionary work had been done, the consternation among the " Saints " was great, and scores and hundreds drew back from a church which unblushingly corrupted itself by such a heathenish practice. Always in foreign missionary work, polygamy has been adverted to as an esoteric doctrine, and never urged as a general practice.

In the third place, by manifesto of the Church authori-

Theoretically, logically,—whatever may be the case practically,—they accept the Bible as God's truth and their guide. They claim to supplement it, not to supersede it, by their Book of Mormon, Book of Doctrine and Covenants, and living Revelations.

ties, September 24, 1890, the further practice of polygamy was forbidden. Yet Mormonism still (1898) thrives
in its missions, in increase by immigration, and in its
organic life. Polygamy, therefore, is not a corner-stone
of Mormonism, or even one of its necessary doctrines.
That it is a doctrine of the church and a divine ordinance is, I dare say, still taught by men and women
among the " Saints "; but the practice, save in sporadic
and sly cases, is given up in deference to the government
and in obedience to the laws, and I may add, in compliance with the demands of the nature of the young
women, and the will of the young men.

Polygamy in Utah was lifted to the plane of religious
duty, consequently it did not work the awful corruption
in society one would have expected. That women's lives
were clouded and their hearts embittered by it is true,
but not seldom the glory of the sacrifice hallowed the
agony of suffering. It is God's will; it is the church's
law; it is my duty; were the injunctions women repeated
to themselves, while they bore their sorrow and were
silent. Sometimes, however, nature would cry out its
bitter resentment. I recall to memory two polygamous
widows of Salt Lake City, one of them an Irish woman,
the other from the Isle of Man. The husband was an
Irishman; he had been bred to the law, was most intelligent, and had been a leader among the people. I may
pause here to say that it is unusual to find Irishmen
among the Mormons; you can almost count on your ten
fingers all the Irish converts, men and women, to be
found among them. These two women were as good,
true, faithful, pure women as I ever knew. They had
refined and ladylike natures, and they were exceedingly
kind to me and my family in times of sickness. My
heart warms in tender gratitude as I recall all they were

to us. They lived in different suites of apartments in the same house, and each had several children. The love of the two for each other, and the harmony and affection existing among all the children, were remarkable. Mrs. Tuttle once asked the older one: " How is it, Mrs. F., that you two can, under the circumstances, so forgive and forget and be so fond of each other?" " Ah, dear Mrs. Tuttle," she answered, " it is because we have so suffered together that we love each other."

Polygamy was practiced by the men of means and the men of official leadership. Questions of cost rather confined it to the former class, although, Mormon women being all workers, an added wife was not seldom a saving in wages for hired help. There was shrewd policy in insisting that all the latter class must be polygamists. Whatever might be their positive bonds of brotherhood, strong negative bonds, also, of defiance to Christian law and civilization, and of ostracism from Christian society, bound them together. Bishops were all polygamists. In my day Salt Lake was divided into twenty-one wards; it now has twenty-four. Each ward had its bishop and its meeting-house; I think Utah had, in all, about one hundred and fifty bishops. It so happened that my residence .was almost next door to the twelfth ward meeting-house. One semiannual conference in September, when multitudes from the country were assembled in town, a person came to our door and inquired: " Is the bishop in?" " No," was the answer. " Is the bishop's wife in?" " No." " Is any one of his other wives in?" My proximity to the meeting-house, I suppose, gave ground for the inference that I was its bishop. It will be noted that the saint inquiring accorded a precedency to the " wife " above the other wives. A sort of precedency the first wife had. She must be asked for consent before any added wife could be taken, yet her refusal of consent need by no means be sacredly respected.

The bishops were officers in temporal things as well as spiritual. The bishop looked after the poor of his ward, and, if necessary, gave orders for their subsistence from the tithing fund. The bishop and his two counselors, as a court, adjudicated matters in dispute between inhabitants of his ward. If settlement was not reached, there was an appeal to a higher court of the high priesthood. The bishop was the one particularly responsible for the peace and health and all-around welfare of the people in his bailiwick. In the early years of my residence in Salt Lake there was a vast deal of destitution and poverty among its inhabitants. In eking out our slender communion alms in rendering assistance I more than once went to the ward bishops for help. They did not refuse me. Bishop Wooley of the thirteenth ward was quite a favorite with the Gentiles. He was good-natured, kind-hearted, but not very refined. He held also the office of county recorder. Having taken a deed to him for record, when I called to get it and asked the cost, he replied, trying as well as his shortness of stature would allow to rest his hand upon my shoulder : " O nothing, nothing ; we bishops, you know, must try to favor each other."

Much has been written about the " Endowment House." A plain two-story building of adobe, it stood, in my day, near the Tabernacle, and not far from the Temple, which was in process of building. No one not a saint could enter it. In it the mysterious rites were unfolded and enacted. Also, generally, polygamous marriages were sanctioned therein. In the completed Temple, rooms take the place of the old Endowment House. *Omne ignotum pro horrifico*, and it therefore has been supposed that the walls of the Endowment House, could they speak, might tell of words and deeds, foul and dire, which they had witnessed. It has always been felt that the secrets, oaths, obligations, and sanctionings, centering there, were the very heart of the strength and shame of Mormonism. The Endowment name, never to be other than whispered ; the Endowment robe, to be buried with the dead body, enshrouding it, and to clothe the rising body in glory ; the Endowment adjurations, promisings and privileges,—these invested Mormonism with a mysterious and perhaps unholy importance, sharpening the interest and piquing the curiosity of the Gentiles to a tantalizing degree. I wanted to secure, to put into this chapter, a plain statement from some honest and intelligent person who had passed through the " Endowments," and I wrote and asked a lady to furnish me with the information I wanted. Her father had stood high with the Mormons before he apostatized, but he was never a polygamist. Her mother was a devout, spiritual minded " Saint," a refined lady, and of the loveliest personal character. My correspondent was confirmed by me in 1877, and still lives in Utah. For both her honesty and her intelligence I desire to vouch unqualifiedly. The following is her reply from her home :

" December 6, 1893.

" I hope you will not think me tardy in replying to yours of August 19th. Last evening I was thinking you might be ready for the information you ask ; and the fear of delaying you is the impetus which prompts me to write this morning.

" I have no prickings of conscience about telling you what I remember of the Endowment House, because I consider that an oath forced upon a girl of fourteen has no binding quality.

"I well remember how my brother J. and myself grumbled together, under the sweet scent of the peach blossoms, against going; but the children of the aristocrats, the Kimballs and Youngs, were to be initiated on that special day, and papa's children had been included as a special mark of esteem to him; so we were made to go. Ever since, to me, the peach blossom and its odor have been associated with something awful and religious and disagreeable.

"Early in the morning, exhilarated by the balmy freshness of the pure air and surrounded by the glorious beauty of the grand mountains, carrying the clothes we were to wear during our incarceration, we sought the sacred square, wherein was situated the 'Holy of Holies.' The dress for a girl was of white, with linen moccasins, with hose, white linen 'garments' (so called, just like the combination suit now worn), white linen underdress, and a white linen robe. This robe contains the whole width of very wide linen; it is long enough to cross the shoulder and touch the ground behind and before; without seam it was fastened with loops on the shoulder —which shoulder I do not remember—was crossed over to the waist on the opposite side, and was tied there with a long, wide sash, used as a belt. Over all this was worn a small apron of green silk, either outlined with brown silk thread, in palm leaf shape, or having the silk itself cut in that shape. The 'cap' was of white 'swiss,' round in the back, gathered with a small ruffle underneath the hair, and falling over the head and face down to the apron belt in a long, full, pointed veil, tied under the chin to keep it securely on the head. I forgot to state that the 'garment' had cuts, worked around in button-hole stitch, a right angle on the right breast, a heart on the left breast, a straight line at the navel, and a straight line at the right knee. The significance of these symbols I do not remember. The man's dress, I think, differs only in having the 'cap,' which is identical with that worn by plasterers.

"We entered a large apartment informally, men and women together, for morning salutations, and mutual congratulations on the rareness of the 'privilege' now about to be granted unto the 'faithful.' I remember thinking that herein there was 'much ado about nothing.' From this room the men were conducted into one part of the building by men, and we were taken into another compartment by women, where we received our 'Washings and Anointings.' This 'Washing' is simply a comfortable but ordinary bath in tepid water, the bather wearing a chemise. Eliza Snow performed for me the offices of a maid, and Mrs. Newell Whitney did the same for another novitiate in the same room. The 'Anointing' consists in using olive oil ('Consecrated Oil' is its technical term, it having been 'blessed by the laying on of the hands of the priesthood' while it was yet in the bottle) on the hair, and so on downward to the feet, each organ being specially anointed and its use indicated, the holy office of maternity being emphasized as the sacred duty and glorious 'privilege' of the mothers in Israel for the purpose of reproducing the 'Kingdom of God upon earth.' While the anointing was going on, the names which we were to bear in eternity were given us. We were then taken into another room and favored with an extempore lecture by Eliza Snow. Not one word of this, however, do I remember, so amused was I by the appearance of the women in their strange costumes, and so interested in trying to discover 'who was who.' I have learned since that the lecture was a sort of physiological and psychical succotash, intended to impress the feminine mind with the absolute necessity of maternity to secure ' Salvation and Exaltation.'

" The next three rooms were devoted to the dramatization of the Creation, following the story as given in the Bible, except that the devil instead of being a serpent was represented by a man. I remember that this man was the ugliest mortal I ever beheld, and that his name was Phelps. I remember, also, that the fruit on the tree was a cluster of raisins. Eve (Eliza Snow) was arrayed in a black velvet dress covered with red leaves, and Phelps in a black suit. Of ' Jehovah ' I have no remembrance. My husband tells me he was represented by a very handsome man named McCalister, dressed in the Endowment Robes, and let down ' into our midst' from some trap-door arrangement above. My husband also tells me that in each of these rooms lectures were delivered by the highest priests in the Church,—Young, Kimball, Grant, etc.,—explaining and enlarging, according to their own thought, the scene represented. I remember the altars in each room, because my brother and myself were called upon to kneel at them and illustrate the oath which was common to all.

" These oaths were of the direst nature ; they included decapitation and disembowelment as threatened penalties for the divulging of the secrets of the Endowment. Then followed a room wherein the history of the Mormon Church was given. Its superior doctrines were set forth in an argument between two supposed antagonists, a Latter Day Saint elder and a minister of an orthodox sect ; in this argument the latter was beaten at every turn, until he was utterly demolished. Here were taken the oaths of vengeance against the ' murderers ' of the 'martyrs, Joseph and Hyrum,' and all others who had persecuted or might persecute the Mormon Church. With these oaths were given grips, which are said to have been taken from Free Masonry, whereby a Mormon could tell a Mormon in daylight, dark, or moonshine, in Pekin, London or the Antipodes, without language and instantly.

"Afterwards we were taken into a smaller room before 'passing through the veil,' and seated silently until our turn came. I remember thinking contemptuously of the veil, which was nothing more than a partition of unbleached factory cloth, with a sort of window through which we whispered the name we had received when anointed and by which we were to be called in eternity. This name was given to some loved one; mine, to my father. The sweetest sight I had seen that day was my mother, waiting there to receive me. It reconciled me to all the wearying inanities that had preceded. I remember telling her, as I hung on her arm going home shortly afterwards, hungry in body and soul, weary and ill-tempered: 'If that is religion, I want none of it.' Nor did she reprove me for the reflection.

"That day I did not see the 'Sealing Room,' but since, I have been in it twice with friends who have been married there. The room is full of sunlight, being nearly all glass, and is brilliant in white and gold. The altar is of scarlet velvet, with kneeling stools all round it covered in the same color. Brigham Young sat on an elevated seat at one end; the couple (or couples) to be sealed kneel around, and the witnesses stand behind. The ceremony I saw was between a young man and his first wife, and it in no way differed from the ordinary ceremony, except in its claim of lasting for eternity as well as for time. I have had an account of a plural marriage (the parties

being no other than our mutual good friend, Mrs. ———,
her husband, and a woman who was to be second wife).
When the persons interested were properly placed, first
Mr. ———, then Mrs. ———, then the woman; Brigham Young turned to Mrs. ——— and asked: 'Are you
willing that this man shall take this woman to be his law-
ful wife?' The customary answer is 'Yes'; the ceremony goes smoothly on to a near conclusion, when hell
begins for three; but on this occasion the answer came
clear and cold, 'No!' A long pause followed. Every
one, Brigham Young the prophet of the Lord included,
was in consternation. When Young had collected the
shattered remnants of his outraged authority he sternly
demanded: 'What then are you here for?' The woman
answered: 'To do the will of my husband.' The ceremony was then completed, whereby the man sacrificed
the love of his youth.

"Such is a brief and fragmentary sketch of a crude and
cruel institution, the outgrowth of the vilest in man's
nature.

"I am glad in justice to my Mormon friends to state
that, aside from 'vengeance' on their 'persecutors,' and
the solemnization of plural marriage, nothing unrighteous,
immoral, indecent or indecorous, is carried on within the
walls of their 'Holy of Holies,' called the 'Endowment
House,' or in the 'Temples,' which have now superseded
the Endowment House. This is true, so far as I know,
and according to my best belief.

"We believe that the entering into this plural arrangement is now abandoned, however we may doubt the conduct of those thus married. Whether or not this 'vengeance' is still taught, we have no means of knowing and
would not venture a conjecture. But publicly it is no
more heard in the pulpits even of their strongholds.

What statehood might bring back of the darkness of twenty five years ago is in the dim future. I for one most fervently do not wish statehood for Utah."

Polygamy, without question, was the most odious feature of Mormonism. But it must be remembered that it was not openly promulgated as a doctrine and enjoined as a practice until August, 1852, when Brigham Young enjoined it in the Tabernacle in Salt Lake City. Even then, as practiced in Utah, it was not opposed to statute law. To Christian custom and to Christian civilization, and, I suppose, to common law, it was opposed. But in America the different states and territories provide their own statutes about marriage. It was not until 1862 that the United States Congress passed any law on the subject. Then a provision was adopted to prohibit polygamy which was known to have been a practice in Utah for ten years. But the statute was a dead letter; the penalties affixed to disobedience could not be enforced, as conviction on the charged offense of polygamy must be procured by a jury. Public opinion in Utah and the consciences of all the jurymen who could be summoned upheld the divine right and duty of polygamy. How then could the statute enacted by Congress be enforced in Utah? It was not until the passing of more stringent laws by Congress concerning the competency of jurymen in Utah, not until the coming in of a considerable population that would be free from fanatical belief in the divine right of polygamy, not, indeed, until the careful provisions of the "Edmunds Bill" of 1882 had been enacted, that arrested polygamists could be convicted and punished. It was, also, not until the passage of the Edmunds Bill that any law existed in Utah concerning the officiant at a marriage ceremony, or concerning providing for witnesses, or enjoining the deposit with the civil authority of a certificate of the act. I have before me the volume of the "Acts, Resolutions and Memorials, passed by the First Annual, and Special, Sessions of the Legislative Assembly of the Territory of Utah, begun and held at Great Salt Lake City, on the 22d day of September, A. D. 1851," and not a line can be found in it regulating the ceremony of marriage.

This silence indicates that the "Revelation" through Joseph Smith at Nauvoo on plural marriage was having its effect, even though the promulgation of the right and duty of polygamy had not yet been made. In all my earlier years in Utah there was no territorial statute whatever to guide me or other ministers in the performance of the marriage ceremony. It is easy to understand this. In the first years of the history of Utah as a territory, all its legislators, and in the later years, almost all, were Mormons. Privileged as a people to practice the divine right of polygamy, there was no call for them to follow in humdrum fashion along the beaten paths of modern legislation concerning marriage. And so long as it was a territory I think no laws whatever concerning the ceremony of marriage were enacted by Utah's Legislature.

August 29, 1852, through the voice of Brigham Young, "the prophet, seer, and revelator of the Lord" in Salt Lake City, polygamy was sanctioned and adopted as a divine precept by the Mormon Church. September 24, 1890, through the voice of Wilford Woodruff, "the prophet, seer and revelator of the Lord," the Mormon Church prohibited the further practice of polygamy by the saints, in conformity to the law of the land.

The facts about polygamy then are these:—That, from 1830 to 1852 the Mormon Church did not promulgate it as a divine precept; from 1852 to 1862 it enjoined its practice as a divine right and duty, in defiance of Christian custom, but not in disobedience to statute law ; from 1862 to 1890 it enjoined and continued the practice in defiance of statute law ; and from 1890 onwards, while doubtless still believing polygamy to be a divine precept, it has forbidden the faithful to practice it because the practice would be in violation of the law of the land.

When the Mormons reached the Salt Lake valley in 1847 the region belonged to Mexico. Subsequently, by treaty at the close of the Mexican War, it became a portion of the area of the United States. In 1849 the Mormons organized themselves into the " State of Deseret," but in 1850 Congress, taking no notice of what they had done, organized Utah as one of the territories of the United States, its population being 11,354. In 1862 the Mormons, reverting to their " State of Deseret " organization, applied to Congress for Utah to be admitted to statehood. For thirty-four years, however, Congress gave no ear to the plea. It was not till January 4, 1896, that statehood for it was secured. On that day Utah became the forty-fifth state of the Union, with a population (1890) of 207,905.

When Utah was admitted as a territory in 1850, Brigham Young was appointed governor by the President of the United States. Young served four years, when Colonel Steptoe of the United States army was appointed to succeed him. When in August, 1854, however, the appointee reached Salt Lake he found Brigham Young unwilling to turn over the office. In a sermon the latter said : " *I am and will be governor, and no power can hinder it until the Lord Almighty says : 'Brigham, you need not be governor any longer!'* " The Mormons seemed so belligerent that Colonel Steptoe, having only a small escort, esteemed it wise to pass on to California.

For three years the Mormons, isolated as they were,

carried on affairs in their own high-handed way. In 1857 Amos Cumming was appointed governor by President Buchanan, and Col. Albert Sidney Johnston, with 2,500 United States troops, was sent to Utah to protect the appointee and enforce the laws. Excitement ran high. The shedding of blood seemed imminent. But in the end Brigham yielded. With all his unquestioned firmness of character he knew when and how to yield wisely.

In September of this same year, 1857, the " Mountain Meadows Massacre " was perpetrated. A hundred and more emigrants from northern Arkansas and Missouri were crossing the plains to California. They were not hospitably received at Salt Lake, they were not proffered the supplies in food and forage that they were in need of and wanted to purchase. So they pressed on their weary way, southward and westward, from Salt Lake. In a little valley called " Mountain Meadows " they were set upon and massacred, men and women perishing, every one. Only seventeen little children were spared, who were afterwards sent back to Arkansas.

This brutal massacre, and the execrable murder of Dr. Robinson in Salt Lake City, are two stains upon the Mormons, deep and ineradicable. They claim that the massacre was by Indians. But, without doubt, Mormons aided and abetted it. Twenty-one years afterwards, in 1878, Bishop John D. Lee was convicted as one of the murderers and was shot to death. He was taken to the very place, Mountain Meadows, to be executed. In 1857 the Mormons were particularly vainglorious and arrogant. Their " prophet, seer and revelator " governor had held his own against everybody. He had ordered that bodies of men should not be allowed to enter or pass through Utah without being under surveillance. Perhaps the resentment of the Mormons against their old Missouri enemies thus took occasion to kindle itself into vengeance. Perhaps the Indians, and the baser sort among the Mormons, were greedy for the plunder promised. Perhaps some Mormon leaders, swollen with pride, were ready by a brutal blow to strike terror into intruding outsiders. Perhaps the emigrants themselves, stung by the inhospitality shown them, had given way to some sharp retaliation. Anyway, the dreadful massacre took place; and the Mormons cannot clear themselves from the charge that they did it. This cruel butchery of over a hundred, and the dastardly killing of Dr. Robinson, give pith and point to the assertions popularly made that the Mormons had a " Danite band" of destroyers to put enemies out of the way, and that they practiced constantly " Blood Atonement,"—the doing to death of the offending body, for the securing of eternal salvation to the indwelling soul.

In looking for the causes of the strength of Mormonism, there needs no piercing eye to see one of them in the death of Joseph Smith. " The blood of the martyrs is the seed of the Church." Smith was not thirty-nine years old when he died, and so he was in the prime of his strength, physical and mental. He had given himself up to the officers of the law, and had peaceably submitted himself and his older Brother Hyrum to be incarcerated. He had received the pledge of safe conduct, while waiting for his trial, from the governor of Illinois. While thus a voluntary captive he was set upon by a mob and he and Hyrum were shot to death in Carthage jail, June 27, 1844. John Taylor, an apostle, afterwards the president of the church, was wounded. Willard Richards, another apostle, escaped unhurt. The martyrdom of the prophet consecrated his memory in the hearts of the faithful for all time to come. An exaltation of his character upon the pedestal of dignity and sacred worth at once took place. And the admirable behavior of Taylor, Richards and the other leaders tended to promote the apotheosizing process. Richards hurried the following message to Nauvoo: "Twelve o'clock at night, 27th June, Carthage, Hamilton's Tavern. To Mrs. Emma Smith, and Major-General Dunham, etc. The governor has just arrived—says all things shall be inquired into, and all right measures taken.

"I say to all the citizens at Nauvoo, My brethren, be still and know that *God reigns. Don't rush out of the city*—don't rush to Carthage. Stay at home, and be prepared for an attack from Missouri mobbers. The governor will render every assistance possible—has sent out orders for troops. Joseph and Hyrum are dead, but not by the Carthage people. The guards were there as I believe. We will prepare to move the bodies as soon as possible.

"The people of the country are greatly excited, and fear the Mormons will come out and take vengeance. I have pledged my word the Mormons will stay at home, as soon as they can be informed, and that there will be no violence on their part; I say to my brethren, in Nauvoo, in the name of the Lord,—Be still, be patient; only let such friends as choose come here to see the bodies. Mr. Taylor's wounds are dressed, and not serious. I am sound.

"WILLARD RICHARDS."

The Mormons in Nauvoo, accustomed to obey instructions, gave heed to the above pleadings, and feelings of exasperation were not allowed to pass into deeds of violence. With much dignity and in remarkable calmness

they appealed to the courts of heavenly justice with the
earnest utterance, "Vengeance is Mine, I will repay, saith
the Lord." And for all the years onward from that day
they have continued their appeal to God's justice rather
than to man's arm for vindication. This remarkable self-
control on their part added to the consecrating influences
that seemed to attend the martyrdom of their prophet.
So his tragic death shed a halo of almost divine glory
around him.

On the other hand, one may contemplate what would
have been likely to happen if he had lived on, say fourteen years more in addition to the fourteen years he had
already spent in the genesis and nurture of his " Church."
Nobility of character did not pertain to him, either by
inheritance or by acquisition. The dignity of education
was not his. Even with all the care that Sidney Rigdon,
who was somewhat of a scholar, gave as co-worker with
Joseph, I find in the Book of Mormon such sentences
as :—" They done all these things "; " The people did
raise up in rebellion "; " Ye had aught to search
these things "; " Cometh on all they that have the
law "; " Hath set down on the right hand of God."
And the translation of Genesis, and I think of other books
of the Bible, which Joseph alleged to have put forth by
inspiration, was so full of gross blunders that shame and
ridicule worked the suppression of the volume. Smith
was up more than once, when a youth, before justices of
the peace in Central New York for getting money under
false pretenses, by looking with his *peep* stone. After
organizing his " Church " he and his family got into
trouble in New York and so removed to Kirtland, Ohio.
They got into trouble at Kirtland, and moved to Jackson County, Missouri. They got into trouble there, and
moved over into Clay and Caldwell Counties. They got

into trouble there, and moved to Nauvoo, Ill. Nor were they freed from trouble in Nauvoo. The arrogant claims of the Mormons were probably one cause of trouble. " The earth is the Lord's," they said; and they added, or acted as if they added, " and belongs to His saints, and we are His saints." Also, they sank the state in the church. " Revelation" was for direction of things both temporal and spiritual. Political fealty would cut no figure with them. They were ready to throw their votes unitedly in whatever direction would best serve their Church. This practice made them a disturbing element at elections. There was no forecasting which way they would vote. And American voters round about them grew exasperated with their possession of the balance of power and with their use of it in so irritating a fashion.

It came to be well known that there would be Mormon disturbances on the eve of, or immediately after, important or contested elections. This was one great reason why the people in Missouri and Illinois were unwilling to tolerate the stay of the Mormons among them. In addition to such external antagonisms, disintegration, a more dangerous thing, was engendering within. Orson Pratt, one of the most honest and able of the apostles, had in high councils more than once spoken and voted in opposition to the prophet. Others had done the same. Dissonance and apostasy had reared their heads at Nauvoo, and had set up a rival paper, the *Nauvoo Expositor*, against the orthodox *Times and Seasons*. The arrest of Joseph and Hyrum and their summons to Carthage, the county seat, grew out of the violent destruction of the office and material of the *Expositor*. Malcontents not a few were on the corners of the streets of Nauvoo, and whisperings were growing louder about immoralities practiced and sanctioned by the prophet.

Puffed up by vanity, intoxicated with success, arrogant from power, sore at opposition, self-absolved from restrictions imposed on ordinary mortals, self-indulgent to passions and ambitions forcibly besetting him, the prophet would not be able long to hold things well in hand, or to check the downflow of deterioration and disintegration setting in. In the assumed twenty-eight years,—or one generation,—we may well conclude that Mormonism would have run out its life into feebleness, or quite corrupted itself unto death. But the martyrdom of the prophet did check the downflow. His weaknesses were forgotten. His memory was sacredly enshrined in the hearts of the faithful. Dignity and heroism were won for his character. Loyalty and devotion among his followers were intensified. A new and strong impetus was given to the strange religion; and so the death of Joseph contributed to make the 350,000 of the faithful of our day, where probably his prolonged life would have smitten and scattered the 35,000 of his day.

Over-weening arrogance, usually going before destruction, was conspicuously displayed by the prophet in his correspondence with Henry Clay and John C. Calhoun in the fall of 1843, in view of the approaching presidential election of 1844. On the same day he addressed the following letter to each of these distinguished men:

" *Nauvoo, Ill., November 4, 1843.*
" DEAR SIR:
" As we understand you are a candidate for the presidency at the next election; and as the Latter Day Saints (sometimes called Mormons), who now constitute a numerous class in the school politic of this vast republic, have been robbed of an immense amount of property,

and endured nameless sufferings by the state of Missouri, and from her borders have been driven by force of arms, contrary to our national covenants ; and as in vain we have sought redress by all constitutional, legal and honorable means, in her courts, her executive councils, and her legislative halls ; and as we have petitioned Congress to take cognizance of our sufferings without effect, we have judged it wisdom to address to you this communication, and solicit an immediate, specific and candid reply to '*What will be your rule of action, relative to us as a people*, should fortune favor your succession to the chief magistracy ? '

" Most respectfully, sir, your friend, and the friend of peace, good order and constitutional rights.

" JOSEPH SMITH,
" In behalf of the Church of Jesus Christ
of Latter Day Saints."

Mr. Calhoun replied that he should endeavor to administer the government in accordance with the Constitution and the laws ; but candor, he said, compelled him to add that he did not think the Missouri expulsion came within the jurisdiction of the federal government, which is one of limited and specific powers. Mr. Clay replied that he could make no pledges or promises to any particular portion of the people of the United States. He held that all were entitled to the security and protection of the Constitution and the laws.

Neither reply was satisfactory to Smith. In a long letter he hurled satirical abuse at Mr. Calhoun. He thus drew out a second letter from Mr. Clay, which was even less satisfactory. In his final reply to Mr. Clay, Smith reveled in angry vilification. Here is an extract : " The renowned secretary of state, the ignoble duelist, the gambling senator and Whig candidate for the presidency, Henry Clay, the wise Kentucky lawyer, advises the Latter Day Saints to go to Oregon to obtain justice and to set up a government of their own." Over and above this correspondence, he suffered the consciousness of his personal importance to manifest itself by allowing his devotees to put him in nomination for the presidency of the United States.

If Joseph's death brought strength to Mormonism, Brigham's life continued, guided, and promoted that strength. He reigned undisputed master of the Church for thirty-three years, dying August 29, 1877, at the age of seventy-six. Shrewd, practical, industrious, energetic, temperate to the degree of abstemiousness, he was conscious of fitness to rule, and others unhesitatingly accorded him leadership. Persistent of aim and firm in will he was, and yet he knew how and when wisely to bend or yield. This last characteristic of Brigham was statesmanlike, and it was one of the two great things that saved Utah from the shedding of blood in the settlement of the question of Mormon disobedience to the laws. The other thing was the wise combination of patience and firmness on the part of the United States Government in dealing with the question. Heroic methods of excision and suppression would have roused the fierce fanaticism of the Utah religionists, and blood would have flowed like water. Fortunately, the American spirit, the according of the largest freedom to the rights of conscience in religious views, kept president after president, and Congress after Congress, to the ways of considerateness, forbearance, and kindness, while perfecting legislative and executive operations to the compelling of obedience. It is to the credit of American wisdom and patience that the perplexing Utah problem was settled without the stings of burning hate or the explosions of bloody violence.

Brigham's shrewdness and practical sense were in many

ways conspicuous. This was shown primarily, in his leading the saints off into the wilderness by themselves, where unvexed they might have room enough for the operation of their peculiar tenets and practices. Two years after they reached Salt Lake, in 1849, gold was discovered in California and the wild fever for getting it set in. Then followed the opening of silver mines in Nevada; the Pike's Peak excitement over gold in Colorado of 1859; and the Florence and Bannack discoveries of gold in Idaho and Montana in 1861 and 1862. In all the fever, Brigham exhorted his people to have nothing to do with mining. "Leave it alone," he said, "and stick to your farms and crops." This was good advice. Following it kept the Mormons compact and consolidated; and money flowed in to them in the high prices they obtained for the flour, potatoes, and peaches they furnished to the miners of Nevada and Colorado and Idaho and Montana; and from the oats and forage they sold to the "Overland Mail," the "Pony Express,"[1] and the quartermaster's department of the United States army.

In 1869–70 arose in Salt Lake the "Godbe-ite" schism, so called from Mr. W. S. Godbe, one of its leaders.

Young knew well the value to his people of their isolation in the "Zion" of their Mountain Valley, so he hindered, rather than helped, the building of the Union Pacific Railroad. When, however, in 1869 it was com-

[1] The Overland Mail was established, I think, daily, and by the Santa Fé route, in 1859. The Pony Express was established in 1860. The latter passed through Salt Lake; so fleet were the beasts and so expert the riders that they made the course from St Joseph, Mo., to Salt Lake (about 1,200 miles) in 124 hours; and from St. Joseph to San Francisco (about 2,000 miles) in 240 hours. The stage-coaches of a daily mail were put on the route not long after, making the time from St. Joseph to San Francisco in about twenty-eight days. Telegraphic communication first reached Salt Lake City, October 18, 1866.

pleted and came through the valley at Ogden, about forty miles north of Salt Lake City, he accepted the situation and at once set to work to build for himself the Utah Central Railroad, connecting Salt Lake with Ogden. With his one will directing the energies of a multitude he was in excellent position to reap for his church the benefits of combination and coöperation. From the first settling of the valley much attention was given to irrigation. Water rights, water ditches, water masters were, through the church organization, managed with less friction, both for the city and the farms, than in any other community. It was not long before Brigham had central telegraphic headquarters in his own office, with wires stretching all over the territory, so that the click of the instrument served him as finger on the pulse and orders through the bugle, to all the people.

In October, 1849, Young founded the " Perpetual Emigration Fund." This fund is raised by donations and subscriptions from the faithful, its purpose being to help the poor saints, especially of Europe, to come to Utah. Grants from it are loans, not gifts ; its beneficiaries after reaching Utah are to consider their obligations to the fund as the first lien upon their industry and income. In almost all cases these loans have been repaid, the amount in the fund has increased, and the money has been turned over and over again in doing its work. With the proceeds of this fund kept for working capital, and with other supplies laid by, it is said that Brigham was the second or third largest depositor in the Bank of England.

In settling the valleys of Utah, and in establishing colonies wherever there was water enough to supply the needs of irrigation, Brigham's practical wisdom was conspicuous. He would select the locality, and then in April

or October, in their General Conference, would designate
the young men who were appointed to go forth to enter
and settle it. With this designation he would couple the
counsel that they must marry before they go. So, year
by year, settlements were pushed into every nook and
corner of Utah.

Brigham's practical sound sense was manifested in his
abstention from issuing " revelations." The multiplicity
of those pronounced by Joseph Smith were an evidence
of weakness; had Smith lived their continuance would
have been much more of an embarrassment than a help
to him. In all his career, Brigham allowed himself to
promulgate only one revelation, and that one at Winter
Quarters, in January, 1847, before he set out for Salt
Lake. In a sermon in General Conference, in 1850, he
shrewdly expressed his opinion in the matter as follows:
" Do you know the word of the Lord when you hear it?
It is the will of the Lord that He wants His people to
do. As for revelation, some say it has ceased; it has no
such thing. I could give you revelation as fast as a man
could run; I am in the midst of revelation. Do you want
more revelation written ? Wait till you obey what is already written.

" The last two years of Joseph's life, Joseph laid out as
much work as we can do for twenty years. I have no
disposition to seek for more until I see these we have
obeyed."

The opportune death of Joseph Smith and the energetic life of Brigham Young both contributed to the promotion of Mormonism. But its greatest strength lies in
fractions of truth embraced in its system, and in the fanatical, religious zeal of its disciples. I may call attention to
some of the fractions of truth:

(*a*) *The Truth of Divine Revelation.* Every Mormon believer holds to it firmly, though by unauthorized exageration of its existence and frequency he weakens its wholesome influence.

(*b*) *The Duty of Prayer.* Prayer in public worship, prayer in the family, prayer in the blessing at meals, and even prayer before social dances, was enjoined. In this last case may it not be admitted that the Mormons managed the matter of amusements most wisely ? In the theatre which they erected soon after settling at Salt Lake the actors and actresses were their own people, encouraged and applauded by their parents and friends. Some of Brigham's daughters were among them. In the dances, held in their meeting-houses, the benches being pushed back against the walls, fathers and mothers and children, married and single, apostles and elders and people, all participated, and wholesome, innocent enjoyment had no chance to run into the rioting of injurious excess. In his own life Brigham gathered together his wives and children for family prayer every evening. Most of them lived in the one " Lion House " though in different suites of apartments. When gathered they must have made quite a congregation.[1]

When Brigham had been a member of the church for nine years, and was a leading missionary in England, he wrote to the Mormon official paper, the *Millennial Star*, published in Manchester, the following letter on family prayer :

[1] If I may judge from the text of Brigham's will, he left fifteen surviving wives. Three had died before him. One, Ann Eliza, had been divorced or separated from him. Besides these, three " spiritual " wives, to whom he was sealed, are mentioned in the will. He left forty-six living children. Some had died before him.

" Liverpool, March 10, 1841.

" DEAR BROTHER :

" I have felt anxious to address a few lines to you on the subject of family prayer (and shall feel obliged by your inserting the same in your next *Star*), for the purpose of imparting instruction to the brethren in general. Having traveled through many branches of the Church in England, I have found it to be a general custom among the brethren I visited, that when any of the traveling elders are present, they wait for the elder to go forward in family prayer instead of attending to that duty themselves ; that is not right, and I would say to them that it would be better for them to understand their duty on this subject.

" My dear brethren, remember that the Lord holds all of us responsible for our conduct here. He held our father Adam responsible for his conduct ; but no more than He does us, in proportion to the station we hold. The kings of the earth will have to give an account to God for their conduct in a kingly capacity. Kings are heads of nations, governors are heads of provinces, so are fathers or husbands governors of their own houses, and should act accordingly. Heads of families should always take the charge of family worship, and call their family together at a seasonable hour, and not wait for every person to get through with all they have to say or do. If it were my prerogative to adopt a plan for family prayer it would be the following : Call your family or household together every morning and evening previous to coming to the table and bow before the Lord to offer up your thanksgivings for His mercies and providential care of you. Let the head of the family dictate, I mean the man, not the woman. If an elder should happen to be present, the head of the house can call upon him if he chooses to do so, and not wait for a stranger to take the lead at such times,—by so doing we shall obtain the favor of our heavenly Father, and it will have a tendency of teaching our children to walk in the way they should go,—which may God grant for Christ's sake. Amen.

"B. YOUNG."

(c) *Sacramental Grace.* Baptism, with them, is for the remission of sin. This is so unqualifiedly true that if one has fallen into disobedience or apostasy, upon his repentance and reformation there is no hesitancy in rebaptizing him. Baptism is by immersion, and children are not competent to receive it until eight years old. Infants, however, may be taken in the arms of elders and blessed. The form of baptism promulgated by Joseph Smith is this: "The person who is called of God and has authority from Jesus Christ to baptize, shall go down into the water with the person who has presented him or herself for baptism, and shall say, calling him or her by name, 'Having been commissioned of Jesus Christ, I baptize you in the name of the Father, and of the Son, and of the Holy Ghost. Amen.' Then shall he immerse him or her in the water, and come forth again out of the water."

In the first years of our own work in Utah we ignored Mormon baptism. Any one and every one coming to us from them we baptized. We assumed that Mormonism was so gross a heresy as to vitiate the validity of the sacrament. But later a lady presented herself for confirmation, an estimable married lady in whose excellence of character we had full confidence. Her parents were earnest, faithful Mormons, and under them she had been baptized in her girlhood. She declined to be confirmed unless we would recognize her baptism. She was unwilling to cast any stigma upon the religion of her parents, whom she still loved. I asked for a month in which to consider the question. I studied it and wrote to older bishops and theologians for their opinions and their advice. Then I came to the conclusion that as Christian baptism is the Saviour's appointed sacrament, so He may be in a certain sense regarded as the real baptizer (St.

Augustine somewhere puts it this way), and that the
sacrament is valid where there are these three things
present : (1) Water applied to the person of the re-
cipient. (2) The scriptural formula recited. (3) Seriousness of intent to obey a divine ordinance. Thereafter we
recognized Mormon baptism, though hypothetically baptizing any convert if he or she desired. The lady spoken
of was confirmed.

The laying on of hands upon those baptized, for imparting the Holy Ghost, is also one of the Mormon practices. They do not often call it confirmation. They
keep, as they claim, as in the taking of infants in the
arms of the elder to bless them, to scriptural practices
and scriptural terms of designation.

The Sacrament of the Lord's Supper is insisted on. In
the Book of Moroni, the last of the productions em-
bodied in the Book of Mormon, is recounted the way of
administering the sacrament among the early American
saints. Joseph Smith, by a revelation given out at the
founding of the Church in 1830, provides the same law
for the Latter Day Saints. It is as follows :

" It is expedient that the church meet together often to
partake of bread and wine in remembrance of the Lord
Jesus, and the elder or priest shall administer it—he shall
kneel with the church, and call upon the Father in solemn
prayer, saying, ' O God, the Eternal Father, we ask Thee
in the name of Thy Son, Jesus Christ, to bless and
sanctify this bread to the souls of all those who partake
of it, that they may eat in remembrance of the body of
Thy Son, and always remember Him and keep His commandments which He has given them, that they may
always have His spirit to be with them. Amen.'

" The manner of administering the wine. He shall
take the cup also, and say, ' O God, the Eternal Father

we ask Thee in the name of Thy Son, Jesus Christ, to
bless and sanctify this wine to the souls of all those who
drink of it, that they may do it in remembrance of the
blood of Thy Son which was shed for them ; that they
may witness unto Thee, O God, the Eternal Father, that
they do always remember Him, that they may have His
spirit to be with them. Amen.' "

In Salt Lake it is their habit to administer this sacrament every Sunday, at the afternoon service in the Tabernacle. I cannot find any written authority for their dispensing with wine and using water instead,[1] but in Salt
Lake I know they use water and not wine. I have been
told that in their early settling in the valley they said,
" When we can raise our grapes and make our own wine,
then we will use wine. Until then water will suffice."
The power of immediate and oral revelation, always ready
at hand to order and regulate matters, sufficed to make
this change, and suffices also, I suppose, to continue the
use of water, though they have long since raised grapes
and made wine in Utah. After the blessing of the bread
and water, a score of young men, officially, perhaps
" elders," perhaps deacons or teachers, carry the elements
around to the people who, sitting in their seats, all of
them who are over eight years old, partake. Meanwhile
the preacher has chosen his theme and is vigorously
preaching his sermon. Scant reverence is shown this

[1] Though perhaps the following, in a revelation through Joseph Smith in
1830, may be their sufficient warrant:

" For behold I say unto you, that it mattereth not what ye shall eat or
what ye shall drink, when ye partake of the sacrament, if it be so that ye
do it with an eye single to My glory : remembering unto the Father My
body which was laid down for you, and My blood which was shed for the
remission of your sins; therefore, a commandment I give unto you, that
you shall not purchase wine, neither strong drink of your enemies ; where-
fore you shall partake of none, except it is made new among you."

sacrament. The doctrine concerning it is bold Zwing-
lianism. The prayers do indeed ask that the eating and
drinking of the elements may be to the sanctifying of the
souls; but there is no assertion of the conveying of
spiritual grace, as there is in the sacrament of baptism.

(d) *Tithing.* There is high scriptural authority for
the Mormon practice of tithing. It has conduced greatly
to the practical prosperity of their church. By this means
their meeting-houses, tabernacles, and temples have been
built. Their poor have been succored and kept from utter destitution. Certain necessary expenses entailed by
organization have been met. The officials of the church
receive no salaries. The apostles, bishops, etc., have their
own worldly businesses, as farmers, tradesmen, merchants,
artisans, and pay their own way. There is never such a
thing as a collection taken up at any Mormon meeting.

The Salt Lake Temple, begun in 1853 and finished in
1893, cost almost ten millions of dollars. Temples, less
expensive, yet large and costly, have been built at Logan,
Manti, St. George and other towns. Tabernacles also,
for large general assemblings, have been built in many
places, and hundreds and hundreds of "schoolhouses" or
meeting-houses, besides. The proceeds of tithing have
provided all these expenses, the faithful Mormon willingly
paying it. If he is a poor man, working three hundred
days in a year, he gives thirty days of labor; if a farmer,
he brings in a tenth of his annual increase of cattle or of his
harvested crops. A church farm is procured and stocked
from the tithing; the "church herd" grows rapidly by
accretion, and from sales of course much money is raised.
Much of the tithing goes into the hands of the bishops
for the care of the poor, the erection of meeting-houses,
and for certain necessary expenses; the surplus is put in
the general tithing fund. The president of the church is

the trustee-in-trust to have charge of that. Brigham, at his death, left about $3,000,000. About half of it his executors turned over as church funds to the next trustee-in-trust, John Taylor; the other half yielded $20,000 apiece to his wives and children.

The Mormon Church as a corporation, or the trustee-in-trust for it, was holding millions of property. A general law of the United States Congress forbade any corporation in the territories to be the owner of more than a limited amount, a few thousands, I think. Accordingly the Mormon property escheated to the United States government and some time in the 80s was seized by it. Pending the carrying out of the order for its forfeiture it was placed in a receiver's hands. The fact that the " property " had been given for religious and charitable purposes, however, and the force of American public opinion, which is that every kind of religion should have fair play, brought about in the end the return of the property to the Mormons.

(*e*) *Missionary Zeal.* The missionary activity of the Mormons in the way of propagandism is most remarkable. In 1835, when the church was only five years old, they sent their preachers to England, and ever since, year by year, generally twice a year, on April 6th, and October 6th, missionaries have been diligently sent from Salt Lake to England, Wales, Scotland, Denmark, Sweden, Norway, Switzerland, Australia, and the Sandwich Islands; and to various states of the American Union. In later years particularly to some of the Southern States. All sorts of advantages have accrued from this. Thousands of immigrants have been pointed to Utah, and with the help of the Perpetual Emigration Fund have reached it. Bright men, in whose breasts the shrewd leaders can see some germs of disaffection engendering, are appointed upon a mission, and in most cases flagging loyalty and dying zeal are forthwith reinvigorated. But besides these, earnest and faithful disciples are appointed for missionaries, men well calculated to deepen and strengthen the fire of religious devotion, and fitted by knowledge of the Bible to make its tale tell on their side. These missionaries go forth at their own expense, but without purse or scrip; and they get their food and other necessary supplies from the foreign saints among whom they sojourn. Their families in Utah in the meantime industriously provide for themselves. Such acts of self-sacrifice promote loving loyalty to the cause for which the sacrifice is made. And the fresh converts, constantly coming with the glow and fervor of their religious devotion, dispel the chill that would otherwise creep over the old inhabitants of Utah. In every way the missionary work of the church is the vital force of its present prosperity. Its leaders have all of them at one time or another been missionaries. The protecting body-guard of its most sacred interests are the missionaries. In discomfort, danger, hardship, and even persecution, their unflinching courage and fidelity are worthy of a nobler cause.

If one considers the religious earnestness that belief in revelation begets, an earnestness nourished and perpetuated by prayer and by attendance on divine ordinances, and made deep and strong by self-sacrifice in the giving of means in tithes, and of time and strength in missionary work, one will not be surprised to find in Mormonism an amazing vigor, even though for forty-four years it crucified the nature of woman, for thirty-four years defiantly flouted the laws of the land, and for all its existence has seemed little more than a laughing-stock to the intelligence of mankind.

In the following letter written by me to Mrs. Tuttle

from Boise City, Idaho, October 15, 1867, I give some of my first impressions and experiences about Mormonism. I had made two short sojourns in Salt Lake, one in July, and one in September and October.

"Do you know that my last visit at Salt Lake has made a great change in my views of Mormonism? I think it now a desperately, hideously, growingly strong institution; and have more fear (humanly speaking) that it will swallow us up than that we will cause much weakness in it. In numbers, by immigration and polygamy, the Mormons are multiplying astonishingly. They hold all the soil. Their children are carefully trained and see and know nothing else, as to religion and social life, but Mormonism and polygamy. Their organization is perfect. Their autocrat is terribly crafty and wise. Their tithing system heaps up riches for power.

"Monday, the 7th, I attended the Mormon 'Conference' morning and afternoon. It was held in the 'New Tabernacle.' This is a wonderful building; a huge tortoise shell roof supported by complicated, tied, arched small timbers on prodigiously strong side walls of stone. All along the side walls at intervals are fourteen doors (double), five feet wide each, so that in an instant, by the simple shoving of fourteen bolts, a space one hundred and forty feet in width for egress, may be opened. Over the doors, all round, are the windows. Entering, one is in the largest audience-room I ever saw. It is 250 feet by 150, elliptical, plastered, and is capable of seating 10,000 people, and of holding 12,000. At one end is one of the largest organs in America (they say that only the Boston organ and H. W. Beecher's, are larger), though it is not yet fully completed. In front of it is the 'President's' throne, in front of this the pulpit, in front of this again the seats for the twelve apostles; and alongside of the 'throne' and 'pulpit' and 'seats' are places for the choir, and gallery seats, like ours. All these are on a raised portion of the room. The congregation, generally, are in the vast region below. I heard the speakers distinctly, but I am assured that the acoustic properties of the tabernacle are not first rate, that the echoes prevent good hearing. The organ I thought to be a good one, and Nelly and Mr. Haskins agreed with me.

"In the morning I went alone. It rained, but in spite of this drawback ten thousand men and women were assembled. As I went in, a fine looking, stout man, with a very intelligent forehead, a long flowing white beard, and a pleasant and well-managed voice, was speaking. He spoke fluently and well. His ideas were absurd and his theology wild, but rhetorically, oratorically, grammatically, he did admirably well. Let me give a sentence or two : ' Brethren, we know not the height and breadth and depth of the glory awaiting the saints. We are to be clad in immortality and with eternal happiness. We are to be gods. Ay, we are to be God. Do you ask how this is ? Why, even the ordinary Christian world will tell you of the Trinity of Persons in the one God. Now in one sense all three are one God. In another, each of the Three is God. So, brethren, will we all be, one day, in one sense, one God ; and in another sense we will be, each of us, millions of us, gods ; just as truly gods as is our God the Eternal Father, now inhabiting yonder heaven.' His sermon, it seems, had been on these two subjects : (1) The Atonement. (2) The personality of Deity. As he closed he made some apologetic remarks on this wise : ' Perhaps in my writings and in my preaching for the last twenty years, in treating of these subjects, I may have used language that may have misled some. It has been intimated to me that such is the case.

It has been said to me that I have seemed to advance the idea that an attribute can exist without a person for it to be tabernacled in. I have not meant to teach such doctrine. If I am wrong in my language used, and have unintentionally conveyed wrong ideas to my hearers or readers, I hope the authorities of the church will correct me, and that you will forgive me.'

" He sat down. I said to a man at my side : ' Who is that ? ' ' Orson Pratt,' he replied. Then Brigham arose. He stood in conscious ease and strength ; he spoke without effort, and yet so clear was his tone, so well enunciated were his words, and so rapt was the people's attention, that he was easily heard by every one. He had his favorite white vest on, and looked the keen, firm, vigorous, strong willed man he is. He speaks, not deliberately, but readily, almost rapidly, and in a businesslike, almost nonchalant way. He said : ' I approve in the main of what Brother Pratt has preached to you. There are one or two exceptions. I take the liberty to point them out. Brother Pratt keeps telling you what the Latter Day Saints believe ; that they believe this and they believe that. Now he has no business to preach anything like this. He may get up here and tell us what he believes ; but to tell us what the saints believe is another thing. I can tell—what I believe. I know I can tell the saints what they should believe ; but what they do believe is another thing. Brother Pratt speculates too much. Brother Pratt philosophizes too much ; and I appeal to any or all the elders of Israel here if, when they read what he writes or hear what he speaks, they do not find themselves in the swamp, in the fog, not knowing the way out of it. Speculations are ruinous. I have had to warn three of our apostles on this point. One of the three we shall cut off from the quorum forever and ever, and that is Brother Lyman. And I tell Brother Pratt if he goes on with his vain, befogging speculations, there's not a saint in heaven nor a saint on earth nor a saint anywhere else who will follow. And I warn him not to get up to talk more unless he knows what he talks about, and can tell people what he knows and believes, and not enswamp us with speculations about what would have been if Christ had not died, and what would have been if Eve had not eaten, and what would have been if man had not fallen, and what would have been if Joseph Smith had not been killed, and what would have been if it hadn't have been, and what would have been if it had have been. If Brother Pratt will stick to the truth and come out of the swamp, I will be thoroughly satisfied with him.'

"Then Brigham adjourned the conference to 2 P. M., and the choir sang an anthem with the organ accompanying. They did it well. The large body of bassos seemed particularly fine.

"At 2 P. M., Nelly, Mr. Haskins and I went up again. We kept Nelly by us and insisted on seating her between us, an arrangement which greatly astonished the on-lookers, for the Mormon women were all seated by themselves in the middle seats, the men filling the side seats along the walls. Heber Kimball called to order, 'Apostle' Benson offered up a Methodistical prayer, and then Brigham rose with a paper in his hand. 'Ah,' whispered a young Mormon in front of us, ' now some one is going to catch it!' But this guess was wrong. Brigham said : ' I have some texts here which I want to lay down as subjects to be preached upon by those who shall speak to you this afternoon. (I) The Perpetual Emigration Fund. I want a subscription to be opened at this conference to provide means for bringing immigrants here next year. Especially I call you to notice the fact that there are 1,200 young women waiting now in the old country to come here. Now let each man say how many of these he will bring over. Let one man say, I will bring ten, and another man four, and so on. (2) The education of the young. Brethren in Israel, we must give more attention to this matter. Heretofore we have had to work hard to get the wherewith to eat and wear. Now we are forehanded and we must give more heed to the education of our children. I want our boys taught in the arts and sciences, that they may be as other boys. I want our girls taught that they may be in all mental acquirements the equals of the women of the world whom they may meet.' (I couldn't help suspecting that our school may have had something to do in stirring up Brigham to the promulgation of this text.) '(3) I want the young women to learn business. I want them to be our telegraphers and clerks. Why, go into a store now for a yard of ribbon, and a great lazy, lubberly fellow comes rolling up like a hogshead of molasses' (and he illustrated in actor-like style the whole lubberliness and rolling-ness of the thing), 'and cuts off the ribbon for you. Now that fellow we want out in the fields, up in the cañon, at work, and we want his and his fellows' places supplied by the young women. (4) I want seventy-five young men to go to the south of the territory to establish a new settlement. The names of those sent on this mission will soon be announced. It is expected that these young men will take with them at least one wife a-piece.' (Here, and wherever else wives and polygamy were alluded to, I noticed that all would smirk and smile and giggle and laugh outright, showing conclusively to me that polygamy is

no sober, serious, earnest part of their fanatical creed.)
' (5) I want five hundred wagons to come here to draw
three loads each of stone for building the Temple. I
want you to come within a week or two. Camp where
you like ; only bring your own provisions for yourselves
and teams. (6) I want the young to marry. I don't set
any age. Some girls are as old at fifteen as others are
at twenty ; some men at sixteen as others at twenty-two.
But so soon as you are old enough I want you young men
and young women to marry and be fulfilling the first
commandment of the Lord your God. There are too
many bachelors. And I now want every man to feel that,
if he is twenty-five years old and one month after this day
is unmarried, he owes $200 in gold to the Perpetual Emi-
gration Fund. The best immigration we can have is from
the spirit world by the production of children. But in
lieu of this the next best will be to compel every bachelor to pay his assessment to the fund. (7) I want this
people to learn better the laws of life, and to take care
of their health. (8) I want them to lay up wheat
against a time of want coming.' "

Wednesday morning at 6:30 before I had half swal-
lowed my breakfast the stage came for me. My fare to
Boise (393 miles) was $120. I was much outside with
the driver. The first driver lives mostly at Ogden, forty
miles from Salt Lake. Ogden is quite a large town. I
asked, " Are there any Gentiles there ? " " Not half a
dozen in the whole town," said the driver. " Do you
have any society ? " (The driver was a fairly educated
and quite gentlemanly Californian.) " No," he said, " I'm
never invited anywhere to call or to take tea or to spend
an evening. Even to the public dances I cannot go
without a special written permit from the Mormon bishop.

This same want of sociability prevails also among the people themselves. Their young men never call upon, or spend an evening with, or visit the young women. When they go to and from meeting the young men go by themselves and the young women by themselves. Even at the balls the men sit on one side of the room, the women on the other. When the quadrille is over you take your lady to her side and come away to your own side. They don't seem to have the least idea of sociability." "What do you think," I said, "of the young women who have been brought up here in Ogden and know absolutely no other social system than polygamy? Do they like it or are they willing to fall in with it?" "They fall in with it," he said, "for they can't help themselves. They've nothing else to turn to. Should they renounce it, the church would cut them off, no one would have anything to do with them or employ them, and they would starve. But as for liking it, they don't. I am acquainted with several, and they tell me freely they don't like it, and if they could in any way flee from it they would do so. Did you notice that good-looking, intelligent, forty-five year old man at Ogden, the landlord, where we got dinner?" "Yes," I said. "Well," he replied, "that was Bishop West. He has eight wives and has just taken a ninth."

In the earlier part of his career Brigham Young seems to have been a sincere fanatic. Later, doubtless the exigencies of his position relegated religious earnestness to the rear and brought to the front eager aims and plans of selfish scheming. In this I think he was like Oliver Cromwell.

While I have been writing this chapter (September 2, 1898), Wilford Woodruff, the president of the church, has died, aged ninety-one and a half years, having retained his powers and exercised the duties of rulership to the very last.

In the Mormon theology spirits, innumerably created by the hand of the Almighty, are existent in their own world, waiting and yearning for the provision of human bodies into which they may enter for their career upon the arena of earthly life. So the birth of children not only supplies citizens and soldiers to the state, and disciples and workers to the militant church, but also promotes the divine plan in setting free, so to speak, spirits from their imprisonment.

Mormon theology is densely, grossly anthropomorphic. A magnified Adam is its God. It holds firmly the Christian doctrine of the resurrection of the body, and yet the Mormons do not give that sacred, reverent care to the dead body that we might expect. Their cemeteries are the most forlorn of all forlorn places. The one in Salt Lake was so forbidding a place, without trees or grass or care, that we all shrank from burying our dead therein. In 1877, through recommendation of the secretary of war, and by special act of Congress, our junior warden, George E. Whitney, Esq., succeeded in getting a grant of twenty acres from the United States reservation at Camp Douglas for a Gentile cemetery. We named it " Mount Olivet," and bringing water to it planted trees through it and beautified it. Our example shamed the Mormons into taking better care of their own ground.

Perhaps they would claim that their seeming neglect was due to their poverty. It is more likely that it was a part of their lack of all that is refining, tender, beautiful or reverent, bred by their low spiritual and social standards, and by their arrogant and despotic organization.

Mormon theology not only has revelation at hand to

guide and illuminate the present and the future, but it also reaches back to condone and rectify the past. By their doctrine of " baptism for the dead," living ones, submitting themselves to the sacrament for their dead friends and relations, can secure salvation to those that have perished in ignorance and unbelief.

Mormon shrewdness crops out in many directions: it appears in their seemingly free voting. In every annual conference the president, his counselors, the apostles, etc., are voted for by show of hands in open meeting. " It is moved to sustain ———— or ————, for such, or such an office," is the form, " all those in favor of the motion will signify it by raising their right hands; all opposed, by the same sign." When I have been present I have never seen an opposing hand raised, I think one never is raised. I say, therefore, that it is " seemingly " free voting. But the list is entirely settled beforehand. The " sustaining " by a show of hands is a delusion.

It appears in their management of the Indians round about them. They preach to the " Lamanites " the Mormon gospel. They baptize and direct them. If they behave themselves, the Mormons are just and kind to them. But if they give way to thievery or violence the Mormons go after them vigorously and administer sound thrashings. Indian depredations are rare occurrences in Utah.

It is seen in their management of woman suffrage. The Mormon Legislature of Utah in 1870 extended the franchise to women, and the Gentile governor, though having the right to an absolute veto, signed the statute. He thought the persecuted women would in righteous rebellion vote against their persecutors. The Mormons more shrewdly thought the women would stand by their religion, bitter as it made their life. And the Mormons proved to be in the right. Woman suffrage was abolished by the amended Edmunds Bill of 1887; but it was restored in the State Constitution of 1896, and is the practice in Utah now. Once, in Salt Lake, when we wanted to swell the anti-Mormon vote in the election of a delegate to Congress, I was a committee of one to see to the getting out of all the opposition vote on our block. One lady, a member of our own Church, a Southern woman, I could not prevail upon to come to the polls. She shrank from such an act with womanly horror. All the others I prevailed upon to come. I took Mrs. Tuttle and her mother and they both voted. When the grandmother told my boys, on her return home, how she had had to swear that she was eighteen years old and had never lived in polygamy, they indulged in hilarious shouting. I need hardly add that we of the opposition did not carry the day. We polled only fifteen hundred votes out of about eight or ten thousand.

It is seen in their methods of trading. Soon after the Union Pacific Railroad came through in 1869, the Mormons established their " Zion's Mercantile Coöperative Institution," placing Z. M. C. I. stores in all the towns. By their combination of capital, industry, and skill, made easy through their perfect church organization, this huge stock-company concern, getting low prices both in purchasing and in transportation, has been able to control the whole, and absorb almost the whole, of the mercantile trade of Utah.

Mormonism has little in it for prompting a genial laugh. Fanaticism usually is too stern and uncompromising a thing to have room for the play of the lighter affections. Yet there is a touch of humor in the story told of the method the saints pursued at Nauvoo in ridding their town of idlers. Whenever one of this unpromising fraternity was spied and located, forthwith three or four elders with their jack-knives came and seated themselves beside him on the bench where he would be lazily disporting himself. They did not talk. They would not ask or answer questions, but they whittled and whittled, in trio or quatrain, for hours; then they silently took their departure. Next day they repeated the visit and the whittling. It would not be long before nervousness would assert itself in the system of the laziest idler and in uncomfortable irritation he would hie himself out of the town. In the main the Mormons are industrious. It is accounted an honor to work. Drones and tramps are not tolerated among them.

Mormon faith is of the strong kind. It preserves the sea-gulls unharmed around the Great Salt Lake to-day. Never a shotgun is aimed at them. In the summer of 1848, when the pioneers were raising their first crop in the valley, innumerable swarms of black crickets came and attacked the growths. Before them the fields were green and glad and promising; behind them was dearth and desolation, not a blade or a leaf being left. Men, women and children turned out to fight these strange hosts of the enemy, but without avail. The saints were in despair. Starvation faced them if their crops were all to be destroyed. So they gave themselves to prayer. Then, Mormon faith believes, by divine interposition the gulls came in vast droves and pounced upon the crickets and devoured them. Since that time the Utah gull is a sacred bird; every man is its defender.

The February after the summer of the happy deliverance by the gulls, the thermometer in Salt Lake sank to thirty degrees below zero; a lower point than was ever known in all the years I lived there. Had the crops of the saints been destroyed in 1848, what extreme suffer-

ing would have been theirs in the cold winter afterwards.

Two or three years put them in condition to raise
abundant supplies, not only for themselves, but for sale
to emigrants and miners. A Salt Lake farmer raised
eighty bushels of wheat from an acre; and harvests of
sixty bushels an acre were not infrequent.

Mormon faith held such a man as Orson Pratt true to
the service of the church all his life through, although
many snubbings, and oppositions, and mortifications were
visited upon him. He was a mathematician, a surveyor,
an astronomer, a Greek and Hebrew linguist, and a very
learned man. His wife, whom he truly loved and who
dearly loved him, and who was a superior woman, re-
nounced him when he took up polygamy. Then she
rebelled against the church and brought up her children
in rebellion. I knew her well and esteemed her and her
children. In pathetic bursts of outraged affection she
would sometimes speak of the personal goodness and
kindness of her husband.

Mormon faith impels their preachers constantly to
assert: " I *know* this doctrine (or this principle) is true."
Not simply to say: " I believe it," or "can prove it," but
" I *know* it is true, the Lord has assured me." This persistent iteration and reiteration of " I know!" and " I
know!" while not very satisfying to the judgment of a
reasoning man undoubtedly has a tendency to strengthen
confidence and assure conviction with the multitude.

With polygamy abjured, the great evil working to-day
in and through Mormonism is priestly domination. A
priesthood, not only commissioned from heaven but receiving constantly thence messages of guidance and
direction and commandment, touching all human affairs,
must be acknowledged to be a power with tremendous

and terrible possibilities enwrapped in it. The infallibility of the priesthood and the domination of the priesthood cause the state to die of inanity, or of absorption into the church. Every thoughtful mind must be convinced that God has given three Divine institutions for the help and guidance of mankind, the Family, the State, the church. Whenever an ecclesiastical organization sets itself up as supreme, swallowing either or both of the other coördinate powers, then it becomes a despotism to be resisted and a danger to be resolutely fought.

Mormon priestly domination is un-American and anti-American. By all Americans it should be firmly opposed. But let the instruments and weapons of opposition be reason, argument, education, enlightenment, influence, persuasive truth. In my years of contention with the Mormons I did not feel at liberty to use any other weapons. On the morning of the day when I was sadly saying good-by to my Salt Lake home of many years, as I was riding down the street a high official of the Mormon Church halted me. He apologized, and then said, " But I felt that I must speak to you. Bishop Tuttle, we are sorry that you are going away. We know you, and we know where to find you, and we have always found you true. It is with real regret that we see you withdrawing from our midst. But if you must go, I am glad you are going to Missouri. You know some day we are all to gather there and in Jackson County for a centre and a home. Good-by!"

I may be pardoned also, for reprinting here the editorial in the next day's issue of the *Daily Evening News*, the Mormon official paper of Salt Lake City:

SPEAK OF A MAN AS YOU FIND HIM

" A gentleman who has become identified with the

history of Utah is about to leave the territory to make his home in Missouri. His face is familiar to the people of Montana and Idaho as well as the denizens of the country near the shores of the Saline Sea. Bishop Tuttle of the Episcopal Church, who was some time ago elected to the bishopric of Missouri, will leave a favorable impression upon all who have become acquainted with him during his sojourn in the region of the Rocky Mountains. Kind, courteous and urbane, yet dignified and firm in his demeanor, he has made friends among people of various shades of opinion.

" Although very pronounced in his opposition to the ' Mormon' faith, he has not acted as an enemy to the ' Mormon ' people. So far as we are aware he has not, like many of his cloth, used his ecclesiastical influence towards the oppression and spoliation of the Latter Day Saints, but has on many occasions borne testimony to their good qualities, in public and in private. We respect a consistent antagonist. We accord to every man the right to oppose that which we believe, if he conscientiously differs from us. We claim no more for ourselves in this respect than we are willing that others should enjoy. We admire the courage of conviction in any man, no matter how much we may consider him mistaken in his opinions.

" Bishop Tuttle is not only frank enough to express freely his dissent from the doctrines of the ' Mormons ' while among them, but brave enough to speak in defense of that unpopular people when in the midst of their enemies. There are few prominent men who dare do this. Many declare themselves averse to the unfair course pursued towards the ' Mormons ' and avow the conviction that they are the worst maligned people on the globe. But public sentiment is so strong against them, that those who express these views in private are afraid to utter them openly for fear of being accused of being ' influenced by the Mormons.' Bishop Tuttle, by his consistent course, has gained the esteem of the ' Mormon ' people without losing the respect of his own class and denomination.

" We bid the gentleman farewell, with the best wishes for his welfare. We do not agree with him in religious belief, but we are in accord with that spirit which in any society promotes fairness, friendship and good will among men, which encourages morality and right conduct, and which breathes charity and peace. We hope to hear that Bishop Tuttle and his partner in life are enjoying prosperity and contentment and the cordial feelings of a host of friends in his new field of labor in old Missouri."

CHAPTER XIII

OUR SCHOOLS

I HAVE had to do with schools all my life. I began early and have kept it up late. In 1852, when fifteen years old, I was a pupil teacher in the academy at Delhi, N. Y., under its most excellent principal, Merritt G. McKoon. While studying Horace and Homer and trigonometry I taught classes regularly in Cæsar and Anabasis and algebra. In 1853 I was assistant to the Rev. Mr. Olssen in his Parochial and Classical School at Scarsdale, N. Y. One of the two years elapsing between my graduation at Columbia College in 1857 and my entrance into the General Theological Seminary in 1859 I passed as an assistant teacher in the Columbia College Grammar School on 4th Avenue, near 23d Street, New York City. The other year I was busy to the full as private tutor to numerous pupils.

In referring to my teaching in the Columbia College Grammar School I may be forgiven an extract from a book " From School to Battle Field," written by General Charles King, United States army, who was one of my pupils at that time :

" There were three more school-days that week, and they were the quietest of the year. On the principle that it was an ill wind that blew nobody good, there was one instructor to whom such unusual decorum was welcome, and that was poor Meeker, who noted the gloom in the eyes of most of the First Latin, and responsively lengthened his face, yet at bottom was conscious of something akin to rejoicing. His had been a hapless lot. He had

entered upon his duties the first week in September, and
the class had taken his measure the first day. A better-
meaning fellow than Meeker probably never lived, but he
was handicapped by a soft, appealing manner and a
theory that to get the most out of boys he must have
their good-will, and to get their good-will he must load
them with what the class promptly derided as ' blarney.'
He was poor and struggling, was graduated high in his
class at college, was eager to prepare himself for the
ministry, and took to teaching in the meantime to provide
the necessary means. The First Latin would have it
that Pop didn't want him at all, but that Meeker gave
him no rest until promised employment, for Meeker had
well known that there was to be a vacancy, and was first
to apply for it. But what made it more than a luckless
move for him was that he had applied for the position
vacated by a man Pop's boys adored, ' a man from the
ground up,' as they expressed it, a splendid, deep-voiced,
deep-chested, long-limbed athlete, with a soul as big as
his massive frame and an energy as boundless as the skies.
He, too, had worked his way to the priesthood, teaching
long hours at Pop's each day, tutoring college weaklings
or would-be freshmen in the evenings, studying when and
where he could, but wasting never a minute. Never was
there a tutor who preached less or practiced more. His
life was a lesson of self-denial, of study, of purpose.
Work hard, play hard, pray hard, might have been his
motto, for whatsoever that hand of his found to do that
did he with all his might. Truth, manliness, magnetism,
were in every glance of his clear eyes, every tone of his
deep voice. Boys shrank from boys' subterfuges and
turned in unaccustomed disgust from schoolboy lies before they had been a month in Tuttle's presence; he
seemed to feel such infinite pity for a coward. Never

using a harsh word, never an unjust one, never losing
faith or temper, his was yet so commanding a nature that
by sheer force of his personality and example his pupils
followed unquestioning.   With the strength of a Hercules,
he could not harm an inferior creature.   With the
courage of a lion, he had only sorrow for the faint-
hearted. With a gift and faculty for leadership that
would have made him a general-in-chief, he was humble
as a child in the sight of his Maker, and in all the long
years of his great, brave life, only once, that his boys
ever heard of, did he use that rugged strength to discipline
or punish a human being, and that only when courtesy
and persuasion had failed to stop a ruffian tongue in its
foul abuse of that Maker's name.   It was a solemn day
for the school, a glad one for the Church Militant, when
he took leave of the one to take his vows in the other.
There wasn't a boy among all his pupils that would have
been surprised at his becoming a bishop inside of five
years,—as, indeed, he did inside of ten,—and the class
had not ceased mourning their loss when Meeker
came to take his place. ' Fill Tut's shoes!' said Snipe,
with fine derision. ' Why, he'll rattle around in 'em
like shot in a drum.'   No wonder Meeker failed to fill
the bill."

Even in my pastorate at Morris I had taught some
young men and women in Latin, and Greek, and mathematics, among others my dear young friend Mahlon N.
Gilbert.   In three schools I have been interested since I
have been in Missouri, and in one of them, " Bishop
Robertson Hall," I am teaching church history now.
Forty-eight years of experience may justify me in giving
expression to my views about church schools.

(1) Church schools are excellent instrumentalities for
training the young to become intelligent churchmen and

churchwomen. The Christian Church from the very earliest has enlisted learning to be the handmaid of religion. Education to be complete cannot ignore any one of the constituent elements of the tripartite man. It is not enough that the body shall be exercised and the mind trained, but the soul also is to be enlightened, guided, and disciplined. And in such spiritual enlightenment, guidance, and discipline, the potent forces of the will, the conscience and the habits are involved. Out from the threefold training in church schools may emerge in most wholesome manner and degree, faith that is not afraid to reason and reason that is not ashamed to adore.

(2) Bishops and other clergymen, however, may well go slow and be careful in launching their schools. If it were a question of launching only, warning might not be called for. But the responsibility entailed is no small matter. Not seldom it grows to be a sore and grievous burden. It is not easy to select, secure, and retain the right principal and efficient teachers. It is no more easy to make and keep parents and guardians judicious, reasonable, and just. If rates of tuition are placed low, the income will not suffice for engaging a good supply of well-qualified teachers. If rates are high, the constituency of patrons will be disastrously diminished. Loss may be counted on, from pupils who have promised to come, failing to do so; from pupils withdrawing before the end of the school year, and disregarding the school rule that payment in any case must be made to the end; from pupils who cannot pay, from others who will not pay until they are forced to; and from sickness, and panics resulting therefrom. The competition of Roman Catholic schools and the public schools, graded and high, is strenuous and unceasing. Save in the case of endowed schools and a few highly favored ones of conspicuous repu-

tation, a deficiency of income to meet current expenses may be counted upon as a thing to be faced at the end of each school year.   If the bishop or clergyman be the promoter of the school, back upon him comes the burden of such deficiency.   The antagonisms engendered, the perplexities evoked, the worries developed in the management of a school are no small tax upon the time and temper and nervous energy of a clergyman.   I question if the good done by his school would not be done more and better were he to devote the time and temper and energy he spends on it to preaching the gospel and feeding the flock, to reproving, rebuking, and exhorting, with all long-suffering and doctrine.

(3)   To declaim against the public schools of America as being secularized, godless, profane, I hold to be unfair and unwise.   True, we may not rightfully read the Bible in them if the unbelieving tax-payer objects outright, or if the Roman Catholic objects to our common English version.   This does look like godlessness, and it seems a handicapping of religion in the very field where its best victories are to be won, that is, in the hearts and lives of the young.   But it should not be forgotten that living examples influence the young far more than any books, though they be the best.   Now, most of the teachers in our public schools, I feel safe in asserting, are Christian believers.   Their Christian faith embodies itself and implicitly manifests itself in their acts, words, looks, and lives.   Faith cannot do anything else than just that. And teaching is made up of those four things, the acts, words, looks, and lives, of the teachers.   It is, therefore, unfair to say that our public schools are infidel.   It is unwise, too, to declaim against them, especially for the Christian clergyman.   They are a power in America. Americans take a great and just pride in them.   Such

declamation is inept speaking out of time, dissonant singing out of tune. Would it not be a better thing for him to visit the school or schools in his bailiwick every now and then, to the encouragement of the teacher and the joy of the scholars, and so put himself in kindly touch with the forces which, next to homes, do most towards moulding and determining the character of life of American communities?

It may be easily gathered that when I became a bishop I had no dread of schools as of untried things. On my reaching Salt Lake City for the first in 1867 I stayed only ten days. These ten days, however, sufficed to enable me to discover and to approve heartily the wisdom of Messrs. Foote and Haskins in deciding that a day-school would be a most efficient instrumentality in doing good missionary work. They acted promptly upon their decision and two days before I reached the city had opened the school. In Utah, especially, schools were the backbone of our missionary work. Adults were fanatics, and so beyond the reach of our influence; or else were apostates, and so, grossly deceived once, were unwilling to listen again to any claims of the supernatural. But the plastic minds and wills of the young we could hope to win to better views and mould in nobler ways.

Our greatest school was St. Mark's, of Salt Lake City. In recounting the story of its beginning let me use the pen of one of its two founders, who was also its first principal, even though it dwell also on the entire history of the opening of the Salt Lake City mission. In 1891, when Rev. Mr. Haskins was a pastor in Los Angeles, California, Mrs. (Dr.) Hamilton of Salt Lake wrote to ask him to put on record for her an account of the early days of the " Episcopal Mission in Salt Lake City." The following was his answer:

" Los Angeles, Cal., December 10, 1891.
" DEAR MRS. HAMILTON :

"I very gladly comply with your request to jot down reminiscences of the Church in Salt Lake City. Those days of ' Auld Lang Syne' are very dear to memory, upon which they are graven in characters deep and plain.

"It should be known that the presence of the Episcopal Church in Salt Lake City, as the first Christian body to stay and work, is due mainly to the Rev. Horace B. Hitchings, then of Denver, and Mr. Warren Hussey, then of the banking house of Hussey, Dahler & Co. Mr. Hussey had become a member of the Church in Colorado under Mr. Hitchings. Mr. Hussey removing to Salt Lake City, together they influenced the missionary authorities of the Church to establish a mission there. The Rev. Daniel S. Tuttle, rector of Zion church, Morris, N. Y., had, in October, 1866, been chosen Bishop of Montana, with jurisdiction in Idaho and Utah.

"Messrs. E. N. Goddard, G. D. B. Miller and Geo. W. Foote were all young clergymen stationed near Mr. Tuttle, who volunteered to accompany the bishop elect to Utah. The following March Mr. Foote, who was a deacon, went to New York to be ordained to the priesthood. While there he picked up a young man in the seminary, Mr. Thos. W. Haskins (your humble servant), who also volunteered for this then distant field.

"I was ordained to the diaconate, and together on the 4th of April, 1867, we started from New York for Salt Lake City. This place we reached just a month later, encountering delays and difficulties from floods, Indians, swollen streams and snowdrifts, which were common in those days, but which travelers in Pullman cars now know nothing about.

" Between Denver and Salt Lake we overtook the coach which had left Denver a day ahead of us, but which had been detained at North Fork by a sand blizzard. Mr. Foote obtained permission to go on immediately, in the advance coach, by which it happened that he reached Salt Lake City on Friday, May 3d, I arriving on the following day. We stopped at the Revere House, kept by Mr. Jenks. The first service was held in Independence Hall on Sunday, May 5th, being the second Sunday after Easter. The Rev. Mr. Foote preached both morning and evening, but I have no record of the texts or subject.

" Those who know Salt Lake City to-day, with its churches, schools, railways, and its increasingly powerful Gentile and Christian element, should know also that one of the redeeming features in the transformation of the community was this Christian mission which was then so modestly undertaken by the Episcopal Church. Little did we realize the importance of the work then begun in Independence Hall, or into what it would grow. The then secretary of state, Mr. William H. Seward, however, said eighteen months later that ' the church and schools undertaken by the Episcopal Church in Salt Lake City would do more to solve the Mormon problem than the army and Congress of the United States combined.'

" The services begun on that memorable day have been continued uninterruptedly ever since. No Sunday has passed without its morning and evening worship, and the day-school which was opened on the first day of the following July with sixteen pupils has continued its beneficent work now for over twenty-four years.

" At that time everything was intensely and defiantly Mormon. Composing the entire population of the territory and city—except perhaps four or five hundred Gentiles and apostate Mormons in Salt Lake—the Mormons controlled absolutely everything they wished to control, —the government, the schools, the religion, the trade, the domestic economy, the morals, the amusements, and even, should any venture to express his mind contrary to the controlling will, the opinions of the people. No Mormon's property or life was safe if he opposed 'counsel.' Isolated from all communication with the outside world, except by Wells, Fargo & Co.'s overland stages, they were restrained from coercing or expelling the little company of Gentiles only by the wholesome influence of Camp Douglas, which had been located on the bench overlooking the city, by General Connor, a few years before. The moral influence of this strong arm of the government protected the Gentiles in the city, as well as furnished a refuge for such apostate Mormons as succeeded in fleeing to the military post.

"The little company of the Gentiles were as practically ostracized as if they had been in the heart of Africa. Every effort thus far made to establish religious services had failed. A Roman Catholic priest, Father Kelley, had visited the city, and through the efforts of the Gentiles had secured a lot of land, but he had then prudently retired.

"The Rev. Norman McLeod, a Congregationalist, who came to Salt Lake City with the troops as chaplain, went farther, and with the assistance of the Walker Brothers and others, not only secured the land, but put up a building and began services—or rather, the delivering of lectures. Though this property was held by trustees for 'The First Church of Jesus Christ, Congregational, in Salt Lake City,' yet it was built and maintained by the united efforts of all the Gentile population of every creed and no creed, for the definite purpose of antagonizing the

Mormon power. The name given to the building, ' Independence Hall,' expressed the spirit of the enterprise, while Mr. McLeod devoted himself chiefly to lecturing against polygamy.

" Associated with Mr. McLeod in this enterprise was Dr. J. King Robinson, who had been an army surgeon but who had married a most estimable young woman of a distinguished Mormon family, Miss Nellie Kay (now Mrs. Longmaid), and had also acquired property in the city. While Mr. McLeod was in the East in the interest of this missionary effort among the Mormons, Dr. Robinson was basely assassinated in the very month that the House of Bishops elected Mr. Tuttle as the missionary Bishop of Utah.

" After the excitement attending the assassination of Dr. Robinson had subsided and Mr. McLeod had been advised to stay away, those interested in this effort to antagonize the Mormon power looked about for a leader. Just at this juncture, learning of the election of Bishop Tuttle they turned to the Episcopal Church, as they would have turned to any Christian body, to advocate the cause of the gospel and morality. Mr. Hussey and two or three members of the church stated the case to the bishop-elect, which information inspired the zeal of the Rev. Mr. Foote to seek an associate and hasten to the field at the earliest possible moment.

" Reaching Salt Lake City as stated, two months in advance of Bishop Tuttle and the rest of the missionary party, they found a small " Union Sunday-school " in charge of Major Chas. H. Hempstead, the United States district attorney, meeting in Independence Hall. The hall and this nucleus of Christian work were at once turned over to these Episcopal ministers. The intelligence was speedily communicated on Saturday, through the only Gentile paper, the *Salt Lake Vidette*, to the few Gentiles in the city and to the officers of the post, that two clergymen had arrived and service would be held on the following day. On Saturday night a rehearsal of music was held in the room of Mr. Hussey. [It is worthy of note that the rehearsal was conducted by one of the only two communicants of the church then in the city— both women,—Mrs. (Dr.) Hamilton, who, if I mistake not, still presides over the music in St. Mark's Cathedral.]

" The service was conducted without break or omission, as quietly and orderly as it would have been in New York or any other city. It is likely that many went away disappointed that there was no red flag of war thrown out to excite the vengeance of the Gentiles or the hatred of the Mormons. No allusion whatever was made to the place, or to the religion of the dominant power. Notice was published of a meeting to be held in the bank on the following evening, to organize the mission ; it was announced that the clergy had come to stay, and that services would be regularly held.

" This opening service gave the key-note to the position and policy of the Church, which, I believe, has ever since been uninterruptedly maintained by the Church in Salt Lake City. It was, not to antagonize evil by direct assault, but to plant and maintain a positive good. It sought to win the judgment, the conscience, the affection, the respect and the allegiance of men, whether Gentiles, apostate Mormon, or Mormon, by putting into competition with Mormon doctrine and practices the faith and practice of the Church, saying not a single word against the Mormons. For years, neither in the school nor in the services was any public mention made of the Mormons, of their peculiar tenets or their horrible crimes, any more than if they had never existed. While at first this caused some disappointment, to many seeming nothing less than cowardice, its wisdom was demonstrated as time went on. The Mormon authorities could get no handle to make war on the Church. All they could say publicly was that ' these people's faith is all very well as far as it goes, but it does not go far enough.' Their bitter and malignant efforts to blacken the character of the missionaries and of the women connected with the school received their completest answer in the public teaching and private lives of all connected with the mission.

" To return to the inception of the mission. Early in the week after the first service to which I have alluded, a meeting was held in the banking house of Hussey, Dahler & Co., and the mission organized. On the committee then appointed were a Roman Catholic, a Methodist, and an apostate Mormon (Mr. Thomas D. Brown). Among the first contributors and regular attendants at the services were members of the Jewish faith. The intensity and sincerity of the anti-Mormon feeling drew all together in the common effort to sustain any reasonable faith and practice which would plant the seed of a better civilization. Pupils flocked to the Sunday-school and every Sunday brought new and regular attendants at the services. All listened with good attention to the simple statement of the old gospel and often the whole congregation waited to see the administration of the Lord's Supper. Instruction classes were formed for nearly every evening in the week, in the Bible, in history, in music, and in studies preparatory to baptism. These classes many young people attended, and the seeds of present growth were then abundantly sown.

" Perhaps even more potent than the church services was the educational work inaugurated by St. Mark's schools. The Episcopal Church considers education as the chief handmaid of religion. In this work she was single-handed and alone for two years in Salt Lake City. Other Christian bodies have since carried to a great degree of success that which the Episcopal Church will ever have the honor of first successfully planting in Mormon soil.

" Within two or three days after their arrival the missionaries were earnestly solicited to open a school, and were promised the patronage of all the Gentile and apostate Mormon elements. But the field did not seem inviting nor the time propitious. Summer was coming on, few were able to pay tuition adequate to the necessarily (in those early days) great expense, a room with proper facilities was hard to find, and the expense of fitting it up was enormous. Two or three private, semi-Mormon or commercial schools were dragging out a precarious, starving existence, with an irregular attendance, sometimes of not half the number on the rolls.

" On the other hand, there was no public school system in Utah ; the Mormon policy had been inimical to education, the Mormon leaders knowing that intelligence would expose the fraud upon which their claim to revelation was based. The need was the attraction, so the missionaries resolved to open a little day-school. Its conduct was entrusted to me. Some difficulty was found in securing a suitable room, as all the places large enough, except Independence Hall, where services were held, were controlled by the Mormons. Not to leave any stone unturned, however, Mr. Foote and I called on Brigham Young, to whom we had letters of introduction, and made our desires known. Mr. Young received us cordially and treated us with much apparent courtesy. He expressed his pleasure that we had come among his people, promised us every facility in planting the church, said he would secure us the Social Hall on First East Street, near the theatre, for the school, and invited us to preach in the Tabernacle on the following Sunday. He spoke frankly of the Episcopal Church and of his knowledge of its ministry and its members. This seemingly cordial reception almost threw us off our guard, but we had determined to accept no courtesy from the Mormons, so we declined his invitations. We expressed ourselves willing, however, to enter into a business contract to rent Social Hall. As we withdrew he followed us to the door; in parting with us he said to Mr. Foote: 'What a pity we Christians cannot see eye to eye!' In this he overdid the thing; we saw the fang of the serpent in the leer of his eye and in his sensuous mouth as he watched the effect of his words.

" We subsequently discovered that his promises of assistance were hollow and hypocritical; we learned that the Social Hall could not be had, nor could any other place controlled by a Mormon. After discovering that we could secure no place under Mormon control we found through Mrs. Kay, the mother-in-law of Dr. J. King Robinson, the half ruined adobe bowling alley on Main Street, between Second and Third South Streets, where the Walker House now stands. This place had been gutted by the Mormons shortly after the assassination of Dr. Robinson, under the pretense that it was an immoral resort. The securing of this building, the raising of necessary funds, and the expeditious conversion of the place into a very fair school building were due to the energy, faith and good judgment of the Rev. Geo. W. Foote, who saw the opportunity and was not slow to seize it. Two single unpainted board partitions were thrown across the alley near the centre, leaving the centre for entrance and hallway, and each end for a schoolroom, one room to be for the primary, and the other for the grammar department. A few plain pine desks, such as were used a hundred years ago, were ordered. For this work, slight and simple as it was, if memory serves me correctly, about one thousand dollars was required, so enormous was the cost of labor and material in those days. For this sum Mr. Foote assumed the responsibility, and he was nobly sustained by his friends and the friends of the Church at the East. A day after the successful inauguration of the school, on July 2, 1867, Bishop Tuttle arrived in the coach from the east.

"During Bishop Tuttle's stay in Salt Lake City the policy and the work of the mission were marked out in a conference between him and the other clergy. The bishop's residence was to be in Montana, whither he went in a few days with Mr. Goddard, Mr. Miller going to Boise City, Idaho. Shortly after he left, through the aid of United States Judge Drake we purchased the Fox property on First South Street. This was to be the headquarters of the mission; it has also, since the year after Bishop Tuttle's removal to Salt Lake City in 1869, been the bishop's residence.

"When the bishop arrived, yourself and Mrs. Durant, you remember, were absolutely the only communicants of the Church. Mrs. Theodore F. Tracy was added to the number a few days or weeks later, on her arrival from San Francisco. During the bishop's visit, eleven were confirmed, including Mr. and Mrs. Hussey and other residents of the city.

"THOS. W. HASKINS."

Our schools in Utah were four—at Salt Lake, Ogden, Logan, and Plain City; we had also one in Idaho, at Boise City. Besides, for short periods we also did some school work in Corinne, Utah, in Silver City, Idaho, and in Virginia City, Helena, and Bozeman, Montana. In Salt Lake we had really three schools : (1) St. Mark's grammar school, a day-school for boys and girls ; (2) St. Mark's school for girls, also a day-school ; (3) Rowland Hall, a boarding and day-school for girls. The grammar school had four houses, first, the old bowling alley on Main Street, second, two old stores opposite the alley on Main Street, third, Independence Hall, fourth, its own building opposite City Hall, erected at a cost of $22,000 (of which $4,000 were given by Salt Lake people), and first occupied in 1873.

The day-school for girls was housed in the Sunday-school room of St. Mark's Cathedral. This was entirely a self-supporting school. Some small boys were allowed in it. Throughout its history Miss Charlotte E. Hayden was for the most part the admirable teacher and manager of it. Eventually it became merged in Rowland Hall, as its primary department. The lot and building for Rowland Hall were given in memory of Benjamin Rowland of Philadelphia, by his wife and daughter ; the boarding-school was opened in 1881.

As Americans and as churchmen we did the right thing to take hold of school work in Utah. There were no public schools in the American sense among the Mormons. It is true that they called their churches " schoolhouses," and day-schools were kept in them. But these were under the control entirely of the " Church " authorities, and payment of tuition was exacted. Besides they were very elementary affairs. Apostate Mormons hailed with delight the opening of our schools and gladly sent us their children, willingly paying for their instruction if they were able to do so. Even some of the orthodox Mormons sent their children. They said they wanted their children to get a good education, and they declared that our schools were the best places in the territory for them to get this education. They said furthermore: We can look after our children in the home and on Sundays, and can see to it that they do not embrace the heresies of the mission schools. Therefore we have no hesitation in sending them to you for the good mental training they will get from you.

Our schools are to be reckoned, I am quite sure, among the redeeming, regenerating, and disenthralling influences which have changed the fanatical, oligarchic community of 1867 into the American Utah of to-day (1900), it being now the forty-fifth of the sovereign states of the Union.

To provide for extending the blessing of our schools into homes too poor to make payment, our scheme of scholarships of forty dollars a year, devised by the Rev. Mr. Foote, stood us in good stead. In my service of nearly twenty-one years, five hundred scholarships were provided. One of these was continued for twenty years, four of them were given for nineteen years. A good many of them lasted for only one year; others of them were given for longer or shorter times between the extremes. Sunday-schools furnished *two hundred and twenty-one* of them; churches, *eighty-seven;* individual women, *one hundred and forty-five;* men, *forty-seven.*

It touches my heart to note how women, especially, helped in doing good work for women in Utah; and further to record how many thousands of children, who are now men and women, have borne a more important part than they ever knew, in the regenerating influences set in motion in the Mormon land. I cannot too often put on record my grateful acknowledgment of the generous way in which churchmen, churchwomen, church children everywhere stood by the missionary work of my earlier years. It humbles me now to remember how steadily they poured in their supplies of succor. It cheered me and warmed me and strengthened me at the time. I did not, however, appreciate how many were the helpers. Had my eyes been opened, like Elisha's young man I could have seen hosts and hosts of them on every side. Ah! the grace of the Holy Spirit and the help of these thousands of generous friends carried me sturdily and cheerily through those early days.

Our school work was plainly Church work. Every morning at the opening of the school, shortened Prayer-book services were held. The heads and managers of the schools were all clergymen. Large numbers of the pupils came into our confirmation classes. Eight of the pupils and three teachers became clergymen in the Church. One teacher to whom I refer is Mr. Chas. G. Davis, now rector of St. Stephen's, Ferguson, Mo. He was our most efficient teacher, first in Logan, then in Ogden. I confirmed him and ordered him both deacon and priest. Another of our teachers was Alexander Mann, now a distinguished clergyman of Grace church, Orange, New Jersey. Still another of our teachers was Mahlon N. Gilbert. A few months ago (I am writing in 1900), I buried his sacred body at St. Paul. In 1862 he was my Sunday-school scholar in Morris; in 1863 I presented him to Bishop Horatio Potter for confirmation. I also taught and guided him in his preparation for Hobart College. Failing health compelled him to abandon his college career when he was a sophomore. A sojourn in Florida checked the progress of his disease; then, October 15, 1870, he came to Ogden, Utah. We soon rented an abandoned saloon, put some benches into it, and installed him as teacher of a parish school therein. His earnest, genial, kindly, sympathetic ways gave the school the best sort of start. But he was deeply desirous to become a clergyman, so in 1871, under my guidance, he went to Seabury Divinity School, Minnesota, for a three years' course. In 1874 he came back to serve at Deer Lodge, Montana, during his diaconate. There, in 1875, I ordered him priest. He built and paid for the stone church at Deer Lodge; the church still stands as a monument of his wisdom, his industry, and his popularity. He told me once of the severe straits he was in for the need of two thousand dollars, during his work of building. That sum he knew he must have. Accordingly, he went into the bank and said to Mr. Larabie, the cashier, " Mr. Larabie, I need and must have $2,000. I want it on my note. I'll pay you as soon as I can. I have no security to offer, and I do not want to ask any one to go on my note. How much interest will you charge me?" Mr. Larabie looked at him a bit and laughingly answered: "Mr. Gilbert, a man who has the cheek to come in and ask a bank cashier for a loan without offering security or endorsers deserves to have it, I think, without any interest at all. You can have it." Not long after, he had the satisfaction of paying the loan; the ladies, by means of a fair, had secured $1,800 for him. While busied with Deer Lodge he founded also the parish at Butte. He was warm with missionary zeal, and he abounded in missionary successes here, and there, and everywhere. In General Gibbon's battle of the Big Hole with the Indians he mounted his horse and rode scores of miles to give his help to the wounded. In 1878 he became rector of Helena. In 1880, when I gave up Montana, he accepted the rectorship of Christ church, St. Paul. In 1886, when I became Bishop of Missouri, he was elected Bishop Coadjutor of Minnesota. Side by side our earthly lives coursed steadily for thirty-eight years. At first he was to me a loved and loving son, then he gave me great help as an energetic and successful teacher, missionary,, and pastor ; lastly in the House of Bishops and out, he proved himself an unusually wise, faithful, and efficient brother and over-shepherd of Christ's flock in His Church Militant. Much of help and cheer went out of my life when he died, but it is a comfort to remember his friendship and love, and to feel that, while he was markedly humble of heart, and unassuming to almost utter self-effacement, his earthly life was glorious in its great usefulness to the Master and His Church.

In the Ogden and Logan and Plain City schools we must have trained as many as a thousand pupils. The Ogden School of the Good Shepherd was opened, as we have seen, in 1870, the other two were opened in 1873. In Logan and Plain City all the scholars were of Mormon birth, there being no Gentile population whatever in either town. All three of the schools mentioned were possible because of " scholarship " sustentation.

Rev. Mr. Gillogly was the founder and manager of the Ogden and Plain City schools. At one time he gave $2,000 out of his own pocket for the Ogden school. Strong in character, wise in judgment, energetic in action, he was a most helpful adjutant. He died during my prolonged visit at the East, after the General Convention of 1880.

Rev. Mr. Unsworth succeeded Mr. Gillogly. He was one of our own St. Mark's schoolboys. I taught him Greek and Latin, and now he is one of the best Greek and Latin scholars of all our American clergy ; in these accomplishments he has far outdistanced his old teacher.

The Rev. Mr. Stoy started St. John's school, Logan, in 1873, one of his assistant teachers being the lady who furnished me with the account of the Mormon Endowment House for this book. Logan is in Cache Valley, a picturesque and beautiful part of Utah. It used to be a delight to me to visit there, although only Mormons inhabit the whole length and breadth of the valley, with its dozen villages and towns. When Mr. Stoy went to Northern California in 1878, Mr. Gillogly kept an eye upon the Logan school; he was assisted in teaching by Rev. Mr. Bleecker and Rev. Mr. Davis.

Rev. Mr. Miller opened St. Michael's school, Boise City, Idaho, in November, 1867. He had trouble at the very start. His imported teacher from San Francisco, whose expenses of transportation he had paid, was within a few months taken for a wife by one of his vestrymen. The laughter of all the world quite drowned Mr. Miller's grim chagrin over the fact that the happy vestryman had been the rector's agent to select, when on a business trip to San Francisco, and bring to Boise the new schoolmistress. Experience taught us in the passing years to take care to have a way to reimburse ourselves in case a contract of marriage should (as in the nature of the case it certainly would) get the better of our business contract. Under the circumstances I think we would be called wise and prudent, and not sordid and mean; for (except in Utah) women were *aves raræ in terra*, and traveling expenses for teachers imported were from $100 to $400 each. The Rev. H. L. Foote, brother of the Rev. Geo. W. Foote, assisted in St. Mark's school, Salt Lake, between 1868 and 1869, and in the school and missionary work of St. Michael's, Boise, in 1869, '70 and '71.

Mr. Miller stayed in Boise five years. In 1872 he and Mrs. Miller went as missionaries to Japan and China, staying in the Orient for three years. In 1875 Mr.

Miller came back to me and became the principal of St. Mark's school, Salt Lake City, where he remained fourteen years.

The heads of St. Mark's school of my day were three: (1) Rev. T. W. Haskins, from the opening in 1867 till 1873; (2) Rev. J. M. Turner, for two years. Mr. Turner was the son of the Professor Turner of the theological seminary who had treated me at first so gruffly, and afterwards so kindly, when I was a theological student. In the father's "kindly" time this son had been my pupil in Greek. (3) Rev. G. D. B. Miller.

For five years Mr. Miller was head of St. Michael's school and pastor of St. Michael's parish, Boise, Idaho. For fourteen years, from 1875 to 1889, he was head of St. Mark's school, Salt Lake. Since 1889 he has been bishop's secretary and editor of the *Church News*, our diocesan paper, in St. Louis, Mo. He served me as chaplain in the Lambeth Conference in London in 1888. Wise counsel and industrious coöperation, unswerving loyalty and unstinted affection, has he always given me. God's blessings be on thee, my faithful brother, for all thou hast been to me and done for me during these thirty-five years of our closely interwoven lives!

In connection with this notice of Mr. Miller's service as a missionary in Japan and China, I may add that Frederick R. Graves became a candidate for Holy Orders under me during his seminary course. When near the time of graduation he wrote me that he felt impelled to respond to the urgent call for missionaries for China, and asked me if I would release him that he might go. I told him I needed him greatly in Utah; that his earnestness and activity would have there much room for exercise; that I would be grieved indeed to lose him; but that I could not stand in the way if he felt called to such an important work as that in China. So he bade me good-by and entered on that course of duty which has resulted in making him the loved and honored and successful missionary Bishop of China.

The schools of my day certainly did definite and far-reaching good. My connection with them was very intimate. Not only had I to look out for their finances, but in St. Michael's, Boise, I taught for some months. In St. Mark's, Salt Lake, I taught for over a year, day in and day out. All of these schools I visited for inspection and examination. In the course of my inspection I had to do with more than a hundred teachers and more than four thousand scholars. No unimportant part was that of my missionary life.

CHAPTER XIV

ST. MARK'S CATHEDRAL

THE American cathedral is in the process of evolution. As yet we have no perfected type. In Salt Lake City I had to do with a cathedral for sixteen years; in St. Louis I have had to do with another for twelve years. In neither case did I set out to have a cathedral, and yet in neither did I feel warranted in refusing to adopt the system when it was urged upon me.

An American cathedral must be, I take it, a bishop's church; a church in which the bishop is immediate as well as ultimate controller and rector. Out of that principle the cathedral is to be developed along lines adapted to American ideas and adjusted to American habits. We cannot import any ready-made article for our service. Even the noble foundations of our mother Church of England must be object lessons for us to study, rather than patterns for us to imitate. Their ancient endowments are not ours, and a great difference in methods is called for by this fact. For the English, centuries of prerogative, traditions, usages have fixed cathedral law and moulded cathedral life. For us, no such centuries exist. Further, Americans are markedly different from the English, in spirit and in habits, and it is not surprising if an institution well suited to the one people is entirely unsuited to the other. I count it an error, therefore, to copy with painstaking carefulness the nomenclature, method of organization, mode of worship, and rules of management, of English cathedrals. Let us observe and study them with diligent attention. As venerable institutions they deserve our respect and reverence. Not infrequently the observation and study may afford us wise ground for deciding how to change and where to differ from them.

And it is not alone theorizing and study that are set to solve the problem for us. Experiment and practice are, also, lending their aid. In the seventy-six dioceses and missionary districts of the American Church there are thirty-nine cathedrals. If more than half of our dioceses have adopted the cathedral as an institution helpful to their diocesan life, the fact is evidence that there is something in the cathedral useful and valuable, towards which Church folk naturally outreach. Yet these thirty-nine cathedrals, in organization and character, are of all sorts and kinds. There is no fixed type yet of the American cathedral. Some of them are simply parish churches, with the usual complement of rector, church wardens, and vestrymen, in which privileges are accorded and stipulated to the bishop touching his use of them for ordinations and special services. Some are adopted as cathedrals for a term of years, the progress of the experiment to determine whether the plan is to be continued or abandoned. Some of them have their wardens and vestrymen elected the same as in other churches, with the provision that the bishop is to be the rector, with more or less of authority in his nomination or appointment of the assistant clergy. Some have a chapter instead of a vestry, said chapter made up of the bishop and specified ones of the assistant clergy, some lay-members chosen by the congregation, and others appointed by the bishop or the diocesan convention, or members because officials of the diocese. Some, with throne and chapter and dean and canons and precentor and chancellor and treasurer and code, have with elaborate care ranged themselves along the line of the English system. It is a happy circumstance to have such richness and fulness of experimentation : and we may well await in hopeful patience the outcome in fixing a fit and perfect type for the American Cathedral.

There seem to be reasons why it is well for a bishop to have his own cathedral. Some of them are these: (1) He does not wish that the pastor element of his nature should be left to perish of atrophy. True he is *pastor pastorum,* but that oversight is found to have really more of the administrative and the executive than the pastoral in it. He has been a pastor before he was a bishop, close to the hearts and lives and souls and love of people; it is a joy to him that in the cathedral congregation there is room enough for him to have gracious exercise of this longing of his heart. (2) It is not seemly that he and his family should be merely parishioners in some parish church, in which church his right and authority are no greater than in any other church of his diocese, and where, if he wish to preach, or to confer orders, or to celebrate the Holy Communion, it is necessary for him to ask permission of the rector. For a bishop to be a suppliant for such privileges is hardly in keeping with the proprieties. (3) One of the important duties of a bishop is to look out for young men ; to win them for entrance into the ministry, and to watch over them when the entrance is won. The work of the cathedral and the assistantships in the clerical staff thereof afford excellent opportunity for the influence and training which he desires to give them. (4) In the " uses " and " directories " of public worship as he moves around his diocese, the bishop cannot be a martinet;

he cannot insist that the services shall be minutely and exactly as he prefers they should be. Yet in the rubrical and canonical and historical and doctrinal proprieties of public worship and ceremonial his very office sets him to be an example and guide. In the cathedral, he can so regulate the services that they can stand forth, not by a hard and fast law, but by way of steady example, as the norm for the diocese.

On the other hand I feel bound to say that the cathedral, like many another good thing, brings with it inconvenience and care. Does the bishop wish to indulge his pastoral propensity, to his own pleasure and to the comfort and edification of the cathedral congregation? He needs to take great care in the exercise of this indulgence. He must have a dean; the dean wants to be, and ought to be, the real pastor. The bishop cannot stay at home enough and cannot find time enough to be pastor. If the bishop interfere in baptizing and marrying, and in the diligent exercise of other pastoral functions amongst the cathedral flock, the inevitable result will be that he cannot get a clergyman, or keep him long, who will be sufficient in calibre or strength of character to be the care-taker which a dean ought to be. The bishop will find brethren politely declining his urgent invitations to them to come to his side, and will be obliged to put up with young deacons, or with men negative and spiritless, for his assistants. And the same result is likely to be precipitated if the bishop be too minute and exacting in his directions of the order of public worship or of the general movement of the cathedral work. The bishop's dream of a church of his own, therefore, becomes much modified in actual experience; in the management of it, so much of prudent self-restraint and such constant exercise of considerate cour-

tesy are demanded, that he finds his hand and will
very much less free things than he thought they would
be.

Again, in establishing cathedrals in large cities where
parishes claim vested rights, troubles thick as blackber-
ries are likely to intervene. Rectors are jealous, vestries
are jealous, and specially bitter and relentless will the
jealousy be if it is attempted to locate the cathedral fabric
amidst the well-to-do parishioners of these parishes.
Such a cathedral will incur Ishmaelitish condemnation.
The rectors and vestries will say that its hand is against
every man; and they will claim that every man's hand
ought to be against it. "The bishop belongs to us all
equally," cry they, and, "What right has he to establish
his cathedral church in our midst to lure away and ap-
propriate for it our parishioners?" By the time the
bishop has discovered how difficult is the question of
choice of locality where he may venture to plant his
church, and how painstakingly watchful he must be not
to infringe on the prerogative of his dean, he will conclude that to have a cathedral is not so deliciously satisfying an experience as perhaps it promised to be.

In theorizing many excellent uses for the cathedral
may be predicated: It may be a centre of diocesan unity.
True, it may be, and I trust it will be, after the evolutionary process now in operation has produced for us "The
American Cathedral." But it may be, as has been suggested above, a very storm-centre of disunity and dis-
harmony.

It may be eminently God's house in its richness of
beauty and in its freedom of privilege. The rich and the
poor may meet in it together without conditions of entrance or lines of separation. No exactions of taxation
shall set their mark upon seats here and there, designating

these as mine, and those as thine. That is true, if adequate endowments be in hand. If not, then in the region of hard fact it may be asked, how are the beauty of appointments and the richness of accessories to be obtained and perpetuated, save by some plan like pew rents, for securing steady income?

It may be the heart unto which shall gather and in which shall be stored the forces which beget and nourish the missionary and educational and eleemosynary beneficence of the diocese. Yes, but only if such jealousies, as have heretofore been adverted to, be allayed, if suspicions be removed, and if hearty coöperation of all the parishes be secured.

In my own mind I am quite convinced that very much yet remains to be wrought out by the evolutionary process going on, before the American cathedral can be commended as a perfected institution, to be adopted by the thirty-six dioceses which up to the present do not have it.

Growth according to circumstances, and not the carrying out of any preconceived plan, was the history of our work in Salt Lake. For over three years things went on without any local organization. Rev. Mr. Foote superintended the pastoral work, Rev. Mr. Haskins, in the main, the school work, Mr. Hussey took the laboring oar in securing local supplies. From the very first Salt Lake supported its own pastor, paying $2,000 or $2,500 a year. I, most of the time in Montana, was ultimate reference. In the autumn of 1869 I came to Salt Lake to make my home and Mr. Foote went East, for nearly six months, in the interest of our mission, visiting parishes and individuals and soliciting funds, specially for building a church. His spirited appeals were eminently successful and he returned about the middle of May, 1870, having secured something like fifteen thousand dollars. The winter preceding his return I changed from an ultimate referee into an active combatant. In Mr. Foote's absence I was the pastor. Mr. Haskins had accepted the chaplaincy at Camp Douglas, though he continued some duties of teaching in the school. I was, however, manager of the school and spent all the forenoons in it in active teaching.

In the autumn of 1870 the people of Salt Lake wished to organize a parish. To this I could not reasonably object, as they had always been self-supporting in the matter of the pastor's salary. So November 12th, I issued notice convening the congregation for the 15th for the purpose of organization. On the latter day they met and constituted " St. Mark's Parish " by the election of two wardens and five vestrymen. The vestry met on the 18th and elected me as rector. Promptly on the 19th Rev. Mr. Foote resigned as missionary, his resignation to take effect January 1, 1871.

Not a word had been said about a cathedral. Yet in the above rapid sketch of events it is not difficult to see such a thing incipiently emerging, and to note in the emerging some of the friction and perplexity to which we have already referred. Mr. Foote was the father and founder of the work in Salt Lake, and had been the faithful pastor of the people for more than three years. Naturally it would be a sore grief to him not to be chosen rector. Why did not the bishop tell the people, it may be said, that they must so elect him? Ah! American bishops need take care how they use the emphatic *must*. As a general thing not much good comes from that sort of thing. Quotations from a letter I wrote Mr. Goddard at the time may show what I tried to do, without succeeding.

" *Salt Lake City, Utah, November 29, 1870.*

" . . . Our Herbert is quite sick; lies now under a decided fever, with our fears that there may ensue cerebral trouble. If it be the Lord's blessed will, may He spare the dear little one to us! I am almost unmanned with the combination of troubles that are falling upon me. Pray for me, dear friend.

" George (Mr. Foote) has resigned here, his resignation to take effect January 1, 1871. This has been brought on by the friction incident to the formation of a parish, and the call of myself as rector. Hussey and Taggart are wardens; Tracy, White, Humphreys, Nowele, Moulton, vestrymen.

" Hussey does not like George and has engineered for his withdrawal. I foresaw the storm; advised George to nominate me rector, and then, after my unanimous election, said I would appoint him assistant. He thought best, however, to allow the voting to go on, and I was chosen rector by five to two. He thinks me wrong in allowing them to organize here; but I saw no way in equity or wisdom that I could present objection if the people demanded organization. So troubles interior here are precipitated upon me. I am sorry to lose George and must take the church building matter entirely upon myself until the vestry can get into shape to assume care.

" Mr. and Mrs. White and mother are indignantly aroused for George; and so family unpleasantnesses, even, arise. Dear friend, were it the Lord's will, how much happier would I be at Morris.

" But praying to Him I am doing the best I can, leaving results in His hands. I shall strive to acquit myself conscientiously of the trust the church has given me, without shirking responsibility and trouble when they will come."

Here is another letter :

" Salt Lake City, Utah, December 8, 1870.
" MY DEAR MR. MILLER :

" I preached Thanksgiving Day the same sermon of last year with appendix. Mr. Pidsley was with me ; George, feeling sore over the on-going troubles here, was not. Herbert has been dangerously ill. We all (doctor included) feared that we would have to say good-by to the dear little fellow ; but since yesterday, I am happy to be able to state, a decided change for the better has set in. *Laus Deo !*

" I do hope you will get through church building without debt. To finish ours we must have, I fear, $15,000. We are $4,500 in debt to-day, and the roof not yet on. When completed our church will have cost, I fear, $40,000. Alas ! Alas ! this debt is a great pain and grief to me. I came near deciding to have no Christmas tree for the school here. But the lady teachers took the matter up with vigor and brought me $160, and so a tree we are to have.

" I have made three conditions before accepting the rectorship here : (1) That primarily I belong to the field, only secondarily can give attention to the parish ; (2) that not less than $2,000 a year of salary shall be paid to me, quarterly ; the interest being chargeable at one per cent. per month on all remaining unpaid each quarter day ; (3) that an assistant clergyman be chosen by the vestry only on my nomination. These conditions have not yet been accepted.

" The vestry are taking hold of the matter of completing the church. They are trying to see if they cannot borrow $10,000 at one per cent. per month and so go immediately on with the work. Of course I shall have to give a mortgage on the church for security; but while they make preparations for paying the interest, leaving me only to secure the principal in my visit East next fall, I shall not object.

"Mahlon spent last Sunday with us. By the upheaving changes of railroad matters, he is losing all his pay scholars; and almost all of his thirty-five or forty in attendance will soon be the children of poor non-paying Mormons. So, though it is just the work that we are in Utah to do, there in Ogden I have another school upon my hands."

The reasons are obvious why it was best for me, as bishop and as the brother-in-law of Mr. Foote, to keep out of the contentions surrounding the settlement of the rectorship. I talked with no one except Mr. Foote in giving advice as I have stated. I did not attend the meeting of the congregation to organize a parish, nor the meeting of the vestry to elect a rector.

Yet, when my three conditions were accepted I in turn accepted the rectorship. Mr. Foote remained in Salt Lake until February 7, 1871; then he removed to San Jose, California, having accepted the rectorship of the parish there.

For nearly four years the plans for founding and developing the "Salt Lake Mission" were those of the Rev. Mr. Foote. And I am convinced they were wiser plans than I would have made. His faith and enthusiasm were better things in their day than would have been my prudence and carefulness. Sagacious foresight, prompt assumption of responsibility, unhesitating grasp of opportunity, and wide hopefulness were all his. These characteristics of the leader conduced to make the foundations of our Utah work broad and deep and strong. There were some sad and sore things attendant upon Mr. Foote's withdrawal from Utah, but the good results of our work there, now witnessed for a whole generation, are largely due to the courses which his wise energy planned and the lines which his zealous fidelity laid down for the currents of our missionary activity to flow in. Let the name of the Rev. George W. Foote never be forgotten as the organizer and founder of a great regenerating force in that strange part of our American land.

No elaborate system or ceremonies attended the establishment of our cathedral in Salt Lake. It was evolved out of the circumstances which have been recounted. I had said not a word about a cathedral, I had not planned for a cathedral. Yet one of the three conditions upon which I accepted the rectorship of St. Mark's parish squinted in a cathedral direction. It was that the nomination of all assistant clergymen of the parish should be lodged in the rector alone, that is, the bishop. Not long after, a vote of the vestry was placed on record that the building in course of erection should be called St. Mark's Cathedral and that the bishop of that region or district of which Salt Lake City should form a part, should always be, *ex-officio*, the rector of the cathedral parish. These two propositions adopted and recorded, first—that the bishop is always, by virtue of his office, the rector; and second, that in the rector alone is lodged the initiative of nomination of assistant parochial clergymen, constituted the sum total of anything like formulated cathedral organization. We made no talk of a dean or of canons or of a chapter. The Rev. R. M. Kirby was in charge of the congregation for nearly eleven years and we called him the pastor; the Rev. N. F. Putnam for nearly four years, and we gave him the same appellation. I suppose the understanding that the cathedral parish should be in metes and bounds coëxtensive with the limits of Salt Lake City was a corollary of our incipient organization. Therefore, in 1880, when St. Paul's was built, we did not organize any new parish but called the building St. Paul's Chapel, providing also that one or two of the members of its congregation should be in the vestry of the Cathedral parish.

Since my withdrawal from Salt Lake the name dean has, very properly I think, been put into use; and the congregation of St. Paul's, growing restless under the leading strings of the cathedral, have been allowed to organize themselves into an independent parish. These are instances of the adaptations and changes which experience and development will constantly force upon cathedral experimentation wherever made.

St. Mark's Cathedral was one of the last buildings of which R. Upjohn, the elder, was the architect. The corner stone was laid by me July 30, 1870. On May 21, 1871, we changed our services from old Independence Hall which had given us shelter for over four years to the basement of our new building. We stayed in the basement until September 3, 1871. Then we entered the church proper.

To complete the church we had been obliged to borrow $15,000. This Mr. Hussey furnished to us as a loan. In 1873 came the world-wide hard times, following upon the failure of the great firm of Baring Brothers. Mr. Hussey was in danger of submergement, and in November, at his request, I hurried on to the East to try to place his loan there for his relief. I went about diligently among friends, Mr. Gerry, Mr. Cisco, Mr. Aspinwall, Dr. Twing, Dr. Dix, and Dr. Dyer, but nothing could be done. Discouraged and very heart-sick, preparing to return home I went down to the office of my old pupil and friend, Cortlandt De Peyster Field, to say good-by. Making some kindly enquiries of me, he elicited facts touching my failure to get help and my depressed state of mind on account of my failure; then, after turning to take counsel with his father, Benjamin H. Field, who was in the office, he said, " I think we can fix you up!" And he did. He took the loan. Nor only so. But in the very midst of those hard times he went out with me and we collected two thousand dollars in gifts, so reducing the obligation to $13,000. Tears of gratitude were my tribute for this timely succor. Among loving and loved and helpful friends to me in my earthly career no one has been nearer and dearer than Mr. Field.

The obligation for $13,000 I placed upon the school property, but it was paid off in a few years by the kindness of generous helpers. So we were in condition to get ready for the consecration of the church.

This consecration took place May 14, 1874. Afterwards, before I left Salt Lake, one transept was added and an organ put in. Nearly all the money for these improvements was given by Salt Lake itself. Mrs. Tuttle and Mrs. Hamilton, by diligent effort extending over three years, raised the amount needed for the beautiful organ. Prayers and tears and hopes and fears and sacred memories, as well as altar and walls and gifts and memorials, were consecrated in that noble building in the mountains, to which my heart turns even now in the deepest tenderness.

CHAPTER XV

ST. MARK'S HOSPITAL

" I was sick and ye visited Me " are words of precious
commendation from our blessed Lord. In all ages and
all countries the Christian Church in loyalty to Him has
given much thought and care to hospitals. Salt Lake
City was a town twenty years old when we entered it.
But such a thing as a hospital had never been thought of.
In fact, with the healthy and hardy lives of the pioneers
in the mountains, with their strong feeling of interde-
pendent brotherhood, with the homely skill and treasured
experiences of the women in nursing the sick, and with
the Mormon belief that prayer and the laying on of the
elders' hands avail for cure, there was little call for expert
medical science and no sense of loss in the lack of a hospital. I think there were only three physicians, all told,
for the fifteen thousand and more of Mormons in and
around Salt Lake City. By the Mormon plan, the poor
in each ward, and so the sick poor, were looked after by
the bishop of that ward. For ourselves, Mrs. Geo. W.
Foote, from the time she came was faithful in visiting and
caring for any sick ones brought to her notice. In the
winter of 1869, when in the absence of Mr. Foote in the
East I had charge of the parish, I joined with Bishop
Wooley and Colonel Morrow in extending the same care.
Bishop Wooley was the Mormon bishop of the thirteenth
ward in which I then lived. Colonel Morrow, the com-
mandant at Camp Douglas, was allowed to use from the
army commissariat certain supplies for private relief. I

remember gratefully the kindly and helpful coöperation of both of these gentlemen.

When, however, with the completion of the Overland Railway in 1869, and of the Salt Lake City branch a little later, mining operations were opened up or enlarged, entailing more frequent accidents demanding surgical care, the need of a hospital became urgent. Major Wilkes, the manager of a mine in the vicinity of Salt Lake and a vestryman of St. Mark's, felt the pressure of such need. Dr. John F. Hamilton, who for a time had been in the service of the United States army at Camp Douglas, was practicing medicine in Salt Lake City. His wife was our organist and one of the three communicants whom we found in Utah on our arrival. Dr. Hamilton was noted for his skill and his success as a surgeon. At last Rev. Mr. Kirby, Major Wilkes, and Dr. Hamilton, got together and, aided by Mr. Hussey, April 30, 1872, launched the hospital. The following statement, which appeared in the *Spirit of Missions* at the time, describes accurately our work.

ST. MARK'S HOSPITAL, SALT LAKE CITY

" To persons who have felt an interest in Bishop Tuttle's work and mission in Salt Lake City, and in his account from time to time of St. Mark's church and St. Mark's schools, a little history of the origin and present workings of St. Mark's hospital may also be of interest, as showing what may be accomplished even with little means, when the heart is in the enterprise, and the work is carried on perseveringly and with wise, judicious management.

" To Mr. Wilkes, one of the vestrymen of St. Mark's church, is due the credit of having first presented to his friends and others the urgent need of a hospital, where the sick and maimed might be cared for; and of showing the feasibility of the plan for getting funds for its maintenance, which, with slight modifications, has since been successfully carried out.   Miss Pearsall (since deceased), lady-assistant and parish worker, and Mr. Kirby, assistant minister of St. Mark's church, were also deeply interested in it, and to the credit of some of our most prominent business men be it said, that they too entered into the scheme most heartily, and have given it, from the first, their cordial support; but Messrs. Wilkes, Hussey, and Kirby were the gentlemen who really started the hospital. They rented the house and grounds, which are still occupied, and took steps towards securing the necessary funds for carrying it on.

"There are many large mining companies in the territory, employing a great number of hands.   These companies—most of them—give a liberal monthly subscription, while the men in their employ give each one dollar per month, which entitles them to a bed and care in the hospital when sick.

"During a portion of the month of March, and all of April, 1872, Mr. Kirby was busy getting the house ready for the reception of patients.   Of course the necessary alterations and repairs, the purchase of furniture, etc., etc., made the expenditures large.   The assured income was subscriptions from the Emma and Miller mining companies, and a monthly fee of one dollar each from the men in their employ, together with a monthly subscription from a number of business men of the city.

"To meet the indebtedness which arose, Bishop Tuttle from time to time advanced money from his trust funds, and Messrs. Hussey and Wilkes loaned each $250 without interest.   Owing to the fact that many demands were made upon the citizens for church and school purposes, it was not thought advisable or wise to press upon them the needs of the hospital.

" The Board of Trustees appointed at the first meeting (May 13, 1872), asked no donations to start the work, but trusted entirely to the monthly income to meet all expenses. At that meeting the Board effected an organization, and the hospital was put into their hands by the original promoters. It is also placed under the auspices of St. Mark's Episcopal church, and this church is responsible for its proper management. The Rev. Mr. Kirby was elected superintendent, Dr. Hamilton, physician and surgeon, and an executive committee of three gentlemen appointed.

" I cannot half so well give an account of the successful workings of the hospital as by quoting from the superintendent's first report for six months from April to November 22, 1872.

" ' The income for the month of April amounted to $239, while that for the month of October amounted to $501.15, being a little less than the present monthly average. The regular current expenses for the first six months amounted to $2,788. Expenses for building and furniture to $2,328. The monthly income has been sufficient not only to meet all current expenses, but has also paid $1,198 of the permanent expenditures. The result of our efforts is surely gratifying and encouraging.

" ' Patients were first admitted to the hospital on April 30, 1872, and during May we received twenty-one. Each succeeding month has brought a larger number to us than the one preceding. Up to November 1st, 116 patients have received treatment at our hands. As our patients come from *all* the different mining camps, you will at once perceive that the benefits of our institution are experienced very generally by the miners throughout the territory. I have always been particular to inquire the religious connection of the patients, and have, when practicable, invited their pastors to visit them. I have also invited the clergy of the city to visit the hospital at their pleasure. We have, on an average, taken care of from two to three charity patients every month, and have never refused admittance to any one while there has been a bed at our disposal.

"'Our first matron, Mrs. Belknap, entered upon her duties May 1st. From her experience at the East she was able to put everything relating to the internal arrangements of the house into proper working order. Much of the present efficiency of the hospital is due to her efforts. She resigned her position in August, 1872.

"'The thanks of the Board are due to Mrs. Foote, who kindly took charge of the hospital after Mrs. Belknap's resignation, and remained one and a half months, managing the household with great efficiency. When Mrs. Foote was obliged to give up this care, Miss Pearsall, though far from well, took her place. The last work of her life was given to the hospital. I can only say that she managed everything *well*, and won the respect and love of all in the house, as was abundantly evidenced by the honest tears shed for her by rough men, when tidings of her death reached them.

"'On November 1st we secured the services of Mrs. Bray as matron. She is efficient in her management, and kind and attentive in her treatment of the patients. As chaplain I have had daily prayers at the hospital, and a service on Sunday afternoons. I gladly bear witness to the respectful, and I trust, devout attention of the patients to these religious services. I doubt not at all that much good has been done, by affording a Christian home with

Christian influences to those who have been under our care.

" 'And here I would express my thanks for the help I have ever received from Dr. Hamilton (who has given his services gratuitously) and can honestly and sincerely assure you, that it is owing to his faithful and skilful services, as much as any one thing, that our work commands the respect and confidence of the community to the degree it does. The receipts for the first six months were $5,422.03, including loans.'

" The printed report for the past year shows that the receipts were $9,133.27. Balance on hand, $11.68.

" The thanks of the Board have more than once been tendered to Mr. Kirby for having managed the affairs of the hospital with so much wisdom and efficiency. As he states in his last report, the necessity for a suitable building of their own, is being felt very much. The friends of the institution are particularly anxious that a *ward for women*, with suitable attendants, should be a feature of the new building, should they succeed in procuring funds for the same. But the difficulty lies in meeting the necessary expenses of such a ward.

" Will not some kind friends, who have means and to spare, remember our ' Woman's ward,' if ever our new hospital building is completed, and endow a bed or a number of beds ?

" There have but a few boxes reached us from the East, *especially* for St. Mark's hospital, though some articles, in almost all the boxes sent for the poor, have been specified as for it. These were comfortables, blankets, bed linen, shirts, and a few dressing gowns.

" *Two* boxes have been sent to us especially for the hospital. The first was from Central City, Colorado. The last, received within the past month, was from Grace church, Medford, Mass., and contained old linen, a large number of sheets and pillow cases, also shirts, towels, dressing gowns, etc., etc. All of which articles were much needed, and were most thankfully received.

" During Miss Pearsall's residence here, before taking charge of the hospital, she visited the wards regularly once a week, talking and reading to the men; and her influence for good was undoubted. Since her death, there has been no regular lady visitor. A few ladies interested in the institution have paid to it occasional visits, and attended the Sunday afternoon services held there. Several of the young ladies of the Church attend these services regularly, one of them playing the organ, while the others sing, and thus render the service more pleasant than it could be otherwise.

" During the past week, the Rev. Mr. Prout, recently missionary in Virginia City, Montana, has been elected assistant superintendent and chaplain of the hospital, and his wife, who is soon to arrive from the East, will take charge as matron. Mr. and Mrs. Prout are to reside in the hospital, and it is hoped by the bishop that they may soon be able to establish a good missionary work among the poor people of the neighborhood."

The first hospital was a rented structure, a small adobe dwelling house, on the corner of Fourth South and Fifth East Streets.

I gave up Utah in 1886, but was for fourteen years one of the Board of Trustees of St. Mark's hospital. Substantial citizens served upon the Board, perhaps Mr. R. C. Chambers being the most interested and efficient member. Dr. Hamilton was chief medical director, and throughout, the matrons of my experience were Mrs. Belknap, Mrs. Bray, Mrs. Foote, Miss Pearsall, and Mrs. Prout. Dear Mrs. Foote, my mother, went in for several

weeks to meet an emergency, as by my side she had met
laundry emergencies in Montana. Miss Pearsall's was also
emergency service. Mrs. Prout, coming in 1874, was
matron during my last twelve years. Her husband died
May, 1879, and is buried in Mt. Olivet, but she went on
with wisdom and vigor in her ministering care. For four
years we remained in the humble quarters first entered.
Then we removed one block north, to the corner of
Third South and Fifth East Streets.

In the report of 1879 I write: " St. Mark's hospital,
Salt Lake City, planned by the Church, begun and fos-
tered by the Church, and essentially a Church institution, the Rev. Mr. Kirby has succeeded this year in
placing in most substantial position. He has bought
the property (a large lot and a good structure of brick),
which the hospital of late has occupied, for $4,500, and
has paid already $2,700 of the purchase money. This
amount was given him in Salt Lake. In seven years
2,308 patients have been cared for in it. Its receipts
have been $63,873.07 and of the entire amount less than
$1,500 have been called for from abroad. Its expendi-
tures have been $64,870.98. Current debt $997.91. Mr.
Kirby may well be proud of such excellent management.
So thoroughly has the hospital won the confidence of
the citizens of Salt Lake, of all kinds and shades of
belief, that they have willingly entrusted these sixty-two
thousand dollars to Mr. Kirby to use for the Master's
service and the Church's work in caring for the sick and
suffering."

Rev. Mr. Kirby remained for over nine years, until
November, 1881, superintendent and treasurer of the
hospital. Then, for the remaining five years of my
trusteeship, Rev. C. M. Armstrong, pastor of St. Paul's
chapel, Salt Lake City, filled the place. In my last

report of 1886, my reference to the hospital is as
follows :

"St. Mark's hospital goes on in its beneficent work as
usual, under the wise care of the Rev. Mr. Armstrong.
In it 409 men have been cared for this year, besides 516
out patients, at an expense of $12,414.55, all met by our-
selves here at home."

In recounting the history of our St. Mark's hospital
it is worth while, I think, to dwell upon two things.
First, the fact of the self-helpfulness shown throughout
its history. I mean local self-helpfulness. By 1886 the
expenses had been $143,178.25, but of this large sum less
than $1,500 had been given from the East. Of this
$1,500, Mr. John D. Wolfe, without any solicitation, sent
$500. Not infrequently the West has been chided for
its selfishness, its seeming mean-spiritedness in accepting,
and even demanding, large gifts from the East for its
missionary and benevolent work. I am free to confess
that at times the chiding is deserved. It should be remembered, however, that in the nature of things new
western communities have in their possession little unused
capital and few stored-up sources of income. Anyway,
an honest pride tells out the fact that St. Mark's hospital
used the kindly eastern nursing-bottle to a very small
extent indeed. There were givers among our business
men, there were supporters among our mining companies, there were dues from the miners themselves.
And once every year there was the "Hospital Ball,"
bringing in one or two thousand dollars. In the mountains, dancing has never had in the public estimation any
stain of moral reproach. With houses too contracted
for large social functions, with domestic service a thing
among the almost impossible, with the exactions of
steady and strenuous labor pressing on both men and

women, and with the irrepressible outcry of healthy
natures for occasional recreation and amusement, it was
most natural and most reasonable that dancing parties
should be given for old and young, rich and poor, married
and single. In Mormondom the meeting-houses of prayer
were also the halls for dancing, and the Mormon religious
chiefs, apostles, prophets, bishops, and elders, were leaders
of both functions. In Montana and Idaho, fathers and
mothers from earnest Christian homes, people honored
in social or in business life came to the dance and participated cheerily in it. It may not seem strange, then, that
the dear mother, Mrs. Foote, who stood by me in so
many other things, led off once in a while, with her son-
in-law and bishop, in the grand march of the Hospital
Ball.

Secondly, I would call attention to the fact that when
the Church takes the lead in beneficent activities for
human welfare, sneering at or captious criticism of her,
is never heard. St. Mark's hospital commended itself to
all the people, whatever their beliefs or doubts or denials
in dogmatic theology and doctrinal religion. The county
authorities, all of them Mormon, asked leave to send
their sick poor and paid for them out of the county
revenues. After a time Holy Cross hospital (Roman
Catholic) and Deseret hospital (Mormon) followed where
we had led. The kindliest feelings, the most generous
helpfulness, were shown us by all sorts and conditions of
people. One leading business man sent for me more
than once, giving me large gifts and asking me to be his
almoner for the sick and poor; with the annexed caution, however, that I was not to use the money for the
Church, in which he did not believe and which he did
not wish to help. In buying tickets for the " Ball " and
in many ways, people of all the different churches and

of no church, as well as unbelievers, and saloon-keepers, marched in the line of loyal and generous help.

The willingness of men to stand by me for help, whether they agreed or utterly disagreed with me in belief, was so striking and cheerful a part of my missionary life that I ask leave to dwell upon it. Is not the Church at liberty to welcome all impulses to the good in men, and to gather up and utilize the help that may spring therefrom? I learned to think so and to believe it right to welcome any and all coöperation in the campaign for the good and against the bad. It seemed a part of my bishop's duty to circulate in person subscription books for securing the salaries of the pastors. I count up seventeen towns in which, year by year, it was my business to do this thing. In doing it, one of my early experiences was receiving this message from a saloon-keeper: " Bishop Tuttle has not called on me. I am ready to help him." I did not hesitate to make my decision. I went straight to his saloon and received his subscription. So I did in not a few such places. Often the keepers had children in our Sunday-schools, and often, too, wives on our list of communicants. And never in all my experience was there anything but respectfulness and generosity in their way of giving. Memories of their own childhood, loyalty to their own homes, responsiveness to the good, not yet utterly expelled from their hearts by their wretched business, led them to proffer the help they gave. What was I that I should turn my back and refuse, when they were so uniformly respectful, so personally kind, and when they so evidently wanted to do what they did? Might not their giving be a little seed of God's grace to help one or another of them into a better business and a better life by and by? In some instances I know the result was directly along that line.

A Roman Catholic, Mr. Callihan, a hardware merchant, was one of our first committee (or vestry) in Salt Lake City. A Roman Catholic, Phil Shenon of Bannack, called me into his arastra (or quartz mill) and gave me an ounce or more of gold (twenty dollars) to put into a seal ring. Later John Henry Hopkins, Jr., the son of Bishop Hopkins and the celebrated editor of the *Church Journal*, took the gold and superintended the making of my ring, furnishing the design. This was, the dove above, the cross below, and the beehive (arms of Utah) between. The surrounding device: " *Sigil. D. S. Tuttle, d. g. Episcopi miss.*" Of course this was short for *Episcopi missionarii.* In later years, when I came to Missouri no one offered me a new ring, and I did not think I could afford one, so my reading of the inscription became: " *Episcopi missouriensis.*"

It was a Roman Catholic, Jo Brown, in whose bachelor cabin at Argenta, neat and most inviting, I was hospitably entertained.

In the following letter there happens to be much that illustrates how the Church in an all-around way may reach people, and win people, and help people, and be helped by people. The man who came with the " American horses to pull us out" was my same Roman Catholic friend, Mr. Brown, who had moved from Argenta and become the proprietor of the bridge over the Big Hole River. The " second Mrs. Welsh" spoken of, is Mrs. S. J. Jones, of Helena. She came to Montana a Presbyterian, lived at Unionville, near Helena, started a Sunday-school and did the best sort of missionary work in it, and in 1875 was confirmed by me. " Bishop Tuttle

Curtis " died in 1890, at the age of fourteen. Rev. Mr. Lewis wrote me about his death. He says of him: " He was a great hand for a book, studious in his way, though as yet he had had few opportunities. He was a good boy, never needing but a word to keep him right, and always anxious to avoid the wrong. So he was a comfort to his mother when the other harum-scarums worried her."

" *Salt Lake City, Utah, September 21, 1876.*
" REV. AND DEAR SIR :

" Once more, and for the tenth time, I have visited Montana. Three and a half months were consumed, and I held services at twenty-nine different places, baptized seventeen, confirmed thirty-nine and administered the Holy Communion to one hundred and thirty-two communicants.

" In Montana, this year, one hundred and six, all told, have been baptized.

" I left home June 5th. Roads were bad, and streams swollen. It was a time when we needed the most steady and experienced of stage horses. What a helpful thing is discipline ! Don't armies know it ? And don't schools know it ? And don't stage-coach travelers know it ?

" But ours were four undisciplined steeds, named broncos. And so, in crossing the Big Hole River, which had overflowed deeply beyond its bridge, each individual bronco wanted to stem the waters his own way, and didn't want to obey orders, and finally two didn't want to go at all, and wouldn't be persuaded. Therefore in a swift-running stream, deep to the wagon bed, two men of us, and two women and three children, were left to the study of hydrodynamics for two hours, until the driver could go back and get American horses to pull us out. As we

were waiting, a churchman, late from Rochester, New
York, who had a letter to me, came along on horseback,
and we shouted the salutations of first acquaintanceship
amid the roar of the waters.

" At Deer Lodge I found Rev. Mr. Gilbert in his hired
log cabin. And young as he is, I found him an already
loved and trusted pastor. His committee (or vestry) are a
Campbellite, a Presbyterian, a Baptist, a Quaker and an
Unknown. But they all believe in him, and are loyal to
him. And this is the way our mountain work is done.
Everything at first depends on the man. If the people
like the minister as a man, and gather around him, then
the step is taken on the way that, under God the Holy
Spirit, will lead them to be churchmen and churchwomen.
If they do not like the man, not much, humanly, can be
done.

" Mr. Gilbert gives one Sunday a month to Butte, a
vigorous mining town, forty miles distant. He may want
to build a church there by and by. Besides, he looks
after Blackfoot, and Philipsburgh, and Missoula, and, in
fact, all Deer Lodge and Missoula Counties, a region half
as large as the State of New York.

" In Missoula I spent two Sundays. The people learn
about the Church only from Mr. Gilbert's occasional visits
and my yearly one. Yet four adults were baptized by
me. Two, husband and wife, had been reared among the
' Second Adventists,' and felt they must be immersed.
Accordingly on Sunday morning, in the Rattlesnake
Creek, I baptized the four ; two first, on the shore, by filling my pocket font from the stream and pouring upon their
heads ; then the other two by immersion. And a
Roman Catholic citizen of wealth consulted me about the
education of his boy ; and next year, probably, under my
advice, he will send him to Shattuck School, Faribault,

This is the way it works. The Bishop of Montana, it is felt by all Montanians, belongs to them. They consult him, he influences them. This feeling of local loyalty is very strong. And so the bishop of any territory, ringing all the door-bells of that territory, and making cordially the acquaintanceship of all people, by this and his annual visitations, gets to be regarded, in a remarkable degree, as the pastor of all. And this feeling should be carefully taken account of and utilized by the Church.

" The feeling was curiously expressed one evening at a reception that I attended in Helena, given to a Methodist bishop who had come for a day or two to preside over the conference. A coterie of gentlemen in a corner were saying kind things about the fine-looking, dignified ecclesiastic whom we had gathered to honor. ' Yes, but,' said one, ' he is not as—and as—as *our* bishop.' And the speaker was a prominent Jew merchant, at whose house and upon whose excellent family I always call.

" One Jewess and three daughters of Roman Catholics we have sent from Utah to St. Mary's school, Knoxville, Illinois.

" At Helena the four Montana clergymen came together, and the meeting cheered us all. The Rev. Mr. Toy presented twenty-six for confirmation. My heart was filled with gratitude to the Holy Spirit for His goodness, and to the faithful pastor and his people. To one helper among them, specially loving thanks are due. To those who know the work at Frankford, I can say she is a second Mrs. Welsh. Without cant or obtrusiveness, in earnestness and simplicity and Christian zeal, with pleasant voice and in untiring ways, by visiting the sick, calling at the houses and showing interest, teaching in and out of the Sunday-school, she wields among quartz miners and mill workers a power, winning men and women and children to Christ and His Church, which the most admirable pulpit eloquence would vainly reach after.

"Mr. Toy went with me to Fort Shaw and Fort Benton, one hundred and forty miles distant. At Shaw we found many anxious wives whose husbands were in the field against the Indians, and had been so for five months, under General Gibbon. Fort Shaw is General Gibbon's headquarters. Montana has this summer been more or less troubled in all its borders about the Indians.

"At Bozeman, Rev. Mr. Dickey, in an absolutely new mission station, is doing excellently. He has a church built, having done largely the work upon it himself. A gentleman of Brooklyn gave me five hundred dollars, and by this help the building is all paid for, and in it a parish school is held.

"When Mr. Dickey and I were holding evening service at Hamilton, twenty miles distant, I was quite put to the blush.

"While I was preaching I saw that a ranchman and his wife and four little ones came in and sat near me; so after service closed I went to them and shook hands, as I had in previous years seen their faces, but could not remember the names. Then I spoke to the children and patted the baby on the head—a bright and handsome little fellow. The father bashfully said something about naming the child, and I patted again, and he said something about 'Bishop Tuttle,' and I smiled and patted again.

"Then I turned away, but soon Mr. Dickey came to me and said, 'Those people want the baby baptized.' 'Ah!' I said, and added to the congregation, 'Those of you who wish to stay, please be seated, and the sacra-

ment of holy baptism will be administered.' Then proffering my services as godfather, and asking Mr. Dickey
to baptize, and pressing upon the parents that all the
children should be baptized, I took out my diary and
wrote down the names of the first three. Coming to the
baby for its name they said ' Bishop Tuttle.' I smiled
assent and began writing my name for it ' Daniel Tuttle.'
But no, the father bashfully, but pertinaciously, insisted
on ' Bishop Tuttle.' I couldn't resist longer, and when,
as godfather, I handed the baby into Mr. Dickey's arms,
and was asked for the name, I had to give ' Bishop
Tuttle.' So a ' Bishop Tuttle Curtis ' is growing up in
Montana. God make him a better man than he whom
he is named after, for the Saviour's sake !

" At Virginia City I spent two pleasant weeks with
Rev. Mr. Prout. He is the senior pastor in Montana,
and one whom I lean on. One of his communicants
walked ten miles to come in to attend services each Sunday that I was there. In St. Paul's church, Virginia
City, is the old cross that, in my seminary days, was on,
or over, the altar of old St. Paul's chapel, New York City.
Friends kindly sent it to us when changes were made in
the latter chapel. It seemed to greet me as a friend, for
once I was the superintendent of the New York City
Sunday-school."

How individuals come trooping into my memory:
Ferd Kennett, of Missoula, Montana, an earnest Pres-
byterian, but for years, whether on the official committee
or off, one of my wisest counselors and best helpers;
Nat Stein, of Corinne, Utah, a Quaker in gentleness and
integrity and purity; Ed Maclay and Judge Blake, of
Virginia City; Con Kohrs and Ed Larabie and Granville
Stuart, of Deer Lodge; A. J. Davis, and Hyde, of Butte;
Eastman and Perault, in Boise; Captain Hooper and

Bishop Sharp, in Salt Lake; Hauser, Kinna, Floweree and Murphy, in Helena; Power, in Benton; Kelly, in Pioneer, and hosts of others, the express mention of a few not intending at all to exclude these! The people I speak of were Roman Catholics, and Mormons, and Agnostics, coming to church almost never at all, yet faithfully co-working with me for years in founding and supporting the church.

My old friends the stage drivers, with their loyalty and good will, come into my memory. Once I was starting to go from Kelton to Boise. The stage was full of express freight. The agent (we were starting at midnight) asked me if I could ride on the outside. I laughingly replied, " Oh, yes, I'm used to it! Anywhere! "

We started out, the driver and I alone. Snow and sleet were driven by the keenest kind of a wind hard into our faces. I sat still and endured it. By and by, after twice or thrice looking over my way, the driver said: " Ain't you cold? Perhaps we can put a robe over you some way." " No," I said, " I can get along all right." Then came another silence. At last, whipping his hands vigorously over his chest, he broke out with: " You'd 'a' made a good stage driver, sure, if you'd 'a' started young enough! "

Another one drove me often between Market Lake and Sand Hole, a villainous stretch of road on the route from Salt Lake to Montana. I knew him by sight and to talk to, but not by name. In after years I got a letter from one " Robert Buchanan," who was employed at some military post, I should think as a teamster. He asked from me the right translation of three neatly written lines of Greek poetry. I answered him, not knowing at all who " Robert Buchanan " was, in my answer calling attention to a blunder in the Greek and giving the

desired translation.   Subsequently, when in 1899 I revisited Salt Lake, Buchanan called upon me and showed
me the letter that I had written him.   I recognized him
as my old stage-driving friend and asked him: " Who
wrote that Greek?"   He answered, " I did."   With true
stage-driver reserve he had never told me when I was
sitting beside him on the box that he was a college
graduate.   Nor when he called on me in Salt Lake,
though he looked seedy and worn, did he ask for any
favor or help.   He seemed merely to come for the sake
of old comradeship and to show his loyalty and good
will.   How my heart, even in these later days, goes
strongly out to the good, faithful old friends of the box
and the whip!

I cannot forbear quoting a letter from Rev. Geo. H.
Davis, who was for several years rector at Boise City,
Idaho:

" *March 16, 1894.*

" MY DEAR BISHOP:

" For a moment this morning I was almost startled
into the belief that I was back in old Idaho.   As I came
out of the post-office the salutation came to me, ' Where
is Bishop Tuttle now?'   I turned, and there was a typical
frontier stage driver, Mike Hall—' three fingered Mike.'
We had quite a chat and he told me of the times he had
driven you over the mountain roads of Montana and
Idaho, and of your inviting him on sundry occasions to
go to church.   He also remembered me in Boise, although I must plead guilty to having forgotten him.
He has drifted back towards Eastern ' civilization,' but
had not apparently been improved by it.   He is still the
same rough fellow you would expect to see on the ' box '
in the far West, redolent with poor whiskey, but with an

element of manhood in him which always appealed to me in even the rudest of those old fellows. It warmed my heart to talk with him, and I know it would have done you good, and given you cheer amid your cares, to have heard the kind words he had for you as the memories came back. What a place you have in the hearts of all those people of every class! It seems to me it's worth a man's whole life to gain such affection and esteem."

In the account of my first winter in Virginia City I told of my meeting with Jack Langrishe, the actor, and Mrs. Langrishe. Many times subsequently we met as we went about our respective duties. I called on them always when I could. They always came to church when they could. Seeing in later years, after Mr. Langrishe had become a newspaper man and an Idaho legislator, a notice that he and Mrs. Langrishe had gone by stage a hundred miles to present a play at an entertainment got up to help build an Episcopal Church, I wrote a grateful and loving letter to Mr. Langrishe expressive of my friendship and esteem for both him and his wife. The following letter from his pastor, Rev. A. J. Holworthy, tells of the death of Mr. Langrishe. Play actor, to the world, he was. Very well, he tried to be an honest and faithful play actor. To me he was a friend, esteemed and loved, and I want to lay this little tribute of my friendship upon his mountain grave.

Jack Langrishe, the play actor! A bishop grown old in the service pays his tribute of tears of affectionate remembrance to thy honest friendship in the mountain days of long ago.

" Holy Trinity Rectory, Wallace, Idaho,
" December 4, 1895.

" MY DEAR BISHOP TUTTLE :

" Here, working in the field where the imprint of
your footsteps is so plainly visible, I have always felt
strangely drawn towards you in affection and reverence.
Often when visiting the boys in their cabins on the
lonely hillsides, especially in Murray, does your name
come up, and they remember you with affection and
esteem.

" And it is with a deep personal feeling of regret that
I write to tell you of the passing away of your old and
dear friend, Judge Langrishe, who died very suddenly at
his home in Wardner on Saturday last (I have mailed
you papers containing an account of his death and
funeral). Mr. Langrishe had been quite sick for several
weeks but was feeling much better during the ten or
fifteen days preceding his last and fatal attack. He had
heart trouble and suffered very much, always hiding his
pain whenever possible for his dear wife's sake. During
the last two weeks he was very busy and got his paper
out as usual and walked home on Saturday evening, feeling somewhat tired. He lay down on the bed, and after
resting there awhile asked Mrs. Langrishe to sit down
in a chair where he could look into her face. He smiled
several times, seeming very happy, and without any sign,
without any apparent pain or struggle ; his head fell back
and Mrs. Langrishe realized that he was dead. Poor soul,
it was really heart-rending to see her for several hours
afterwards, but she finally became calm and bore up
wonderfully well on the day of the funeral. While she
spent the last few moments looking for the last time on
earth on the face of him who had for half a century been
her faithful companion and protector it was my privilege

to be alone with her, and try to comfort her as well as my own deep sorrow would allow, for he was one of my warmest friends and more like a father in his attachment to me. Grand old man, he is sleeping the sleep of the just (for he had so many, many virtues that if he had any faults they were more than covered by his noble qualities) up on the lonely hillside where he has toiled many a time to pay the last tribute of respect to a brother man, more than once reading the beautiful service for the burial of the dead, where no minister could be had. There he has been laid to await the final summons, and God grant the blessed reward for all his faithfulness in many kind and generous deeds, which, if a cold unfeeling world has only carelessly noticed, have not escaped the eye of his heavenly Father, who was his comfort and support in his last illness.

"When I went East a few months ago, he said to me one afternoon in the church, where he was regularly to be found, 'Mr. Holworthy, you may see Bishop Tuttle while you are away and if you do, tell him,' and then he broke down and cried like a child. I soothed him and told him I knew what he wanted me to say—for he had read me a letter some months ago which you had written him, and which he wanted to answer so much. He had told me that several times he took out the letter from the drawer where he kept it, intending to sit right down and reply to it, but each time he was so very much affected that he had to give it up and it worried him so much for fear you might think him unkind and unappreciative of your thoughtfulness of him and the kind sentiments expressed in the letter. During his last sickness, while sitting with him and talking of you, we agreed that as soon as he was quite well again he should tell me what to say and I would write the letter for him. Now

I am writing to tell you how much he loved you, and
that he, poor fellow, will never be able to tell you so
himself."

Professor Shoup, an educator in the state of Iowa,
came out to visit Colonel Shoup of Salmon City, now
United States senator for Idaho. In the *Overland
Monthly* of July, 1888, the professor tells of his visit. I
make some extracts:

" Here (at Challis) we met Bishop Tuttle of Salt Lake
City, who had annually for many years made the rounds
of the towns and mining camps of this whole region,—
preaching to the people, baptizing their children, and
doing what he could in every way for their spiritual welfare. The roughest men we met had nothing but words
of unstinted praise for this noble-hearted and self-sacri-
ficing man. They knew that he voluntarily gave up, for
their good, the comforts of his pleasant Salt Lake home
and the society of his cultured wife and family; and this
appealed most strongly to their better natures. If they
never had any other Sabbath they were sure to have one
the Sunday Bishop Tuttle was in town; and they made
it a point of honor to turn out and hear him preach, no
matter what their creeds might be.

" The bishop has a fund of good stories which he enjoys telling, especially when the laugh happens to be on
himself. There are two good Methodist brothers who
travel through certain parts of this region occasionally,
doing what good they can in their humble way. They
are men of no great literary attainments, but they are
quick-witted and ready with retorts. One day while
crossing the mountains with one of his clergy, Rev. Mr.
Stewart, in a one-horse buggy, the bishop happened to
meet these two ministers jogging along in a comfortable
carriage with a fine span of horses. They stopped to

greet each other, when the bishop said in his good-natured, bantering way, ' Stanley, how is it that you Methodist preachers can ride after spanking teams in two-horse carriages while we poor Episcopalian bishops and parsons must travel in one-horse buggies?' Whereupon one of the disciples of Wesley retorted, ' Why you see, bishop, we're none of your one-horse preachers.' The bishop, good-humoredly accepting the home thrust made, said quickly to Stewart at his side, ' Drive on, Stewart, drive on.'

" But while the bishop preserved a cheerful exterior, he fully appreciated the seriousness of his work. In conversation with him one day, I referred to the hardships he must necessarily endure while making his long annual tours of the mountains. He sat in a thoughtful mood for a moment, and then said, ' Yes, it is very fatiguing, but I have been blessed with unusually vigorous health, and have thus far been able to bear it; and I trust to exert an influence for good over these people; but there come times when I feel myself shrinking from the work with a dread lest I break down and lose my power over them. I am forcibly reminded of the story of an actress, who, though she had drawn large houses night after night—came forward one evening to the footlights and stood silent and motionless as if listening to some one a long way off; she then turned to the manager and said in a loud stage whisper, " Don't you hear them hiss me?" She had been living at too high a mental strain and now suddenly felt her power giving way, and she realized that her influence over the public was going from her. So I, when starting on these long tours of the mountains, sometimes find my intellectual nature responding to the promptings of my soul with " Don't you hear them hiss me?" ' '

" How many of us have had such feelings of our own,—
a fearful looking forward to a possible time when our
powers shall have given way, and we are doomed to see
our work pass from us—when we have outlived our day
of usefulness ? "

Many a year I have ridden over that horseback trail of
sixty-five miles from Salmon River to Challis; sometimes
alone, and not seldom with one of my sons in company.
Once Arthur and I encountered an immense black bear
on the trail. But he seemed as much in a hurry to get
away up the mountainside from us, as we, having nothing but pistols, were anxious to get away from him.

Colonel Shoup tells the story of an encounter with a
grizzly on the same trail :

" Some years ago I had a large herd of cattle ranging
in this region, and in order to collect them it became
necessary to search all the little cañons which run back into
the mountains. Going up one of them for some distance
and finding the way badly obstructed, I tied my horse to
a bush and pushed on afoot. Reaching a clump of
bushes I stopped and shouted, to drive out any of the
wild cattle that might chance to be there. I soon heard
a great commotion in the brush, and, to my amazement,
instead of cattle an old she grizzly bear was coming directly towards me with open mouth. I turned and ran
at my utmost speed for a bunch of black birch bushes,
accidentally dropping one of my gloves on the way.
The bear on reaching this stopped long enough to rend
it into shreds, during which time she was joined by her
two cubs. Knocking one of these to the right and the
other to the left with her maternal paws, she again came
on. I had by this time reached the bushes and climbed
up as far into one of them as its slender and highly
flexible stem would support me; but as the old bear

rushed at me with open mouth, and uttering most savage grunts, I saw plainly enough that when she should rear up my feet would be within her reach. With a yell of despair I threw my other glove to her, hoping to divert her attention for a few minutes at least. While she tore this her undutiful cubs again came running towards her, when she made a rush for them knocking them right and left to drive them back into the bushes.

"During this brief respite I noticed two other bushes a little larger than the one I was clinging to, and so near together that I hoped, should I succeed in reaching them, their united strength might support me out of reach of those horrible claws; so dropping to the ground I made a break for them and had just succeeded in drawing myself up between them when the infuriated brute again arrived. I was out of reach of her claws, but so slender and flexible are these whalebone shrubs that I felt perfectly confident she could bend them over as soon as she reared against them. I remember two thoughts that were very prominent in my mind as she came rushing at me; first, how long would it take her to finish me when she got hold of me; and second, whether my friends would ever succeed in finding my mangled remains in that wild and out-of-the-way cañon. As she reared up I threw my cap with all my force right into her face, whereat she stopped to rend this as she had done with the gloves. But now her cubs again came on the field, and noticing this, her outraged maternal feelings so far overcame her that she again left me and went for those badly trained youngsters, this time chasing them so far back into the bushes that I seized the opportunity and ran for my horse,—probably just a little faster than ever I had run before."

In the summer of 1897 the Presbyterian church in

Bozeman, Montana, celebrated its twenty-fifth anniversary. I was kindly invited to the celebration. In the letter of invitation occurred the following sentence: " One of our members recently said, ' We always looked upon Bishop Tuttle as the people's bishop and felt that he was one of us.' "

This remark is suggestive of my relations to the whole field. I never hesitated to administer the holy communion to " all Christians by whatever name they call themselves, who will come in penitence, faith, and charity to receive the pledges of the blessed Lord's love and gracious help."

A printed letter of mine contains the following:

" To be hailed lovingly as a friend all through the mountains ; to be greeted cordially as a pastor by people of all sorts and conditions, and indeed religions, and asked to baptize their children ; to see, as I can see, the healthy knowledge root itself and grow, that the simples and substantials of Christianity are belief in and obedience to the Creed, the Lord's Prayer, and the Ten Commandments ; and to find year by year, as I do, more ready and earnest use of the responsive parts of our public worship, by those who can witness our service only when I come; these are circumstances to make a man soft-hearted and grateful, and a bishop enthusiastic.

" Nine yearly visits I have made. In consequence numerous are the scattered families looking to me as their only pastor. Not a few are the children that I have baptized (one hundred and fifty-three in Montana) some of whom I am now beginning to confirm. And year by year men and women who had rarely or never heard the ritual of our public worship have learned to know it, and many of them to like it and join in it."

I have no regret or self-reproach for having spent so

much of my time in the early days in meeting people, and talking with people, and visiting people. Access to their hearts was obtained in that way. Love and sympathy in my own heart, the best and strongest forces for influencing people, best grew in that way.

It was after the railroad had reached my region that the incident in the following printed extract occurred. Weather-worn and dust-covered from a long stage-coach ride I had entered the cars some distance up the line. Rev. Mr. Bleecker had come from Logan, farther down, to meet me. It was in August, 1883. " In the Wood River region, I was rejoiced to find the Rev. Mr. Osborn in restored health vigorously at work. Once we held services together in a theatre, once in a dining-room, and once in an abandoned restaurant. He is trying to build a church at Hailey. It will be the first Protestant church building in the town. In faith that some other one will be, under God, the one to fulfil, I have been the one to promise him $500 towards building.

" About one hundred miles of my tour I have made on horseback, and eleven hundred by stage-coach. In many towns I gave the only religious services that they had had for a twelvemonth. The church wins the hearts of many strange and scattered people by thus giving them a pastor in the missionary bishop. In these pastorless places I baptized twenty-six.

" Rough journeyings are not best made in rich attire. Most of our mountain people know me even with my traveling suit on. The newcomers do not. One of the latter was usher to the passengers to direct them to their breakfast the other morning. A clerical brother in suitable coat happened to be with me. The guide pointed him promptly to the better table. But touching me by my gray and dusty coat he said, ' Sit here.' I obeyed, though my table companions were not of the upper sort. We both kept quiet over it. People who knew me were much amused. The clerical brother wanted, he said, to get the usher's ear and say that really he would have no objection to the other man sitting beside him.

"But insults, or even disrespect, I never meet with even among the most worldly and the most wicked of this far away region. Personally there are valued and loved friends to help me everywhere. May God bless them all. Only would that more of them, under His guidance and blessing, would be as good to their own souls, and as thoughtful for their own better selves, as they are to me!

"Our schools are all to open next week. Hard work is the order of the day now. God help us to do it with a will, and from the heart, and for Him. In thanks for the past, and hope for the future, and a courage that the merciful Lord keeps bright for us thus far, we say, ' All right; we are ready to take hold and do for the best.' "

It once fell to my lot to minister to two murderers under sentence of death. One was a young man in Salmon City, Idaho. Spending a Sunday in the town I visited him in jail and prayed with him. He was to be executed on Wednesday. I could not stay because my public appointments of the week compelled me to leave Salmon on Monday, but I assured him I would find some Christian man to come to be with him. And I begged him not to talk much at the last, but try to be content with leaving himself in penitence and faith in the Saviour's merciful hands with earnest, repeated supplication of the inner man, " God be merciful to me a sinner." In going up the Lemhi Valley next day I stopped at the blacksmith's shop of a good old Methodist friend of mine and got his promise to go to Salmon and be with the condemned man on the scaffold. And I gave him a Prayer-book to help him in his ministration.

The other case is mentioned in the following extract from one of my letters of 1884. This was an older man. He had been raised a Lutheran. In the carriage on the way to execution we urged upon him the same reticence on the scaffold. But he did not heed us, nor did he seem to realize the awfulness of his position. The latter part of the letter calls attention again to the cheering help always rendered to me by the officers of the United States army.

"August 1st a murderer was executed at Hailey. With Mr. Osborn I visited the man in his cell, and accompanied him to the scaffold. Thank God for the guidances and helps that the wise church provides for such an awful occasion. And thanks, too, for her constantly implied teaching that a grave reserve and reverent silence from 'professions' and 'expectations' best become the time and place. The condemned man was grateful for our attention, but seemed indifferent to his fate. From the scaffold he gave a disjointed recital of the facts attending the shooting of his victim, with a claim for self-justification. While Mr. Osborn was reading the commendatory prayer, he was engaged in striking a match to light his cigar. The binding of him immediately after, the adjusting of the noose, the throwing on of the black cap, the touch of the fatal spring, and the drop of the man in awful suddenness out from our sight into eternity are to me now as a strange, painful dream. The sheriff's duties were discharged with admirable method and wisdom. The six hundred men and three women, who came two or three miles out from town to the appointed place to witness the execution, were sober, silent and reverent. The stern majesty of the law in its supremacy and sacredness impressed itself, I think, upon all.

"After leaving Hailey, accompanied by my son Herbert, I went to towns and regions where almost no religious services of any kind are ever held in the twelve-month elapsing between my visitations. If in our weakness and infirmity we missionary bishops are accomplishing little else, this sort of work for the Master is precious and blessed. It is to go out into the highways and hedges, and seek and do good to and gather in the neglected. And His gracious approval surely attends the church which in trusting love sends us forth to be shepherds, where none else are, to these His ' little ones.'

"My last appointment in Idaho was at a garrison post of the United States army, Fort Cœur d'Alene. No army chaplain is within hundreds of miles. Yet at the celebration of the holy communion on Sunday morning there were ten communicants, and two more are in residence. The commander, the colonel of the regiment, reads the church services every Sunday morning, and quite a little congregation steadily attends. This was my first visit to this post, and I greatly enjoyed it. Bishops Morris and Paddock have visited it for me in previous years.

"Here again I beg to call attention to the way in which missionary bishops' services count for the best. No small number of our brave defenders of the army are scattered in the frontier posts of our missionary districts. Our visits of once a year, if we cannot make them oftener, relieve somewhat the spiritual forlornness of these seemingly banished and certainly scattered men. Personally unworthy though we are, our services and the sacraments that we are permitted to offer to them are without doubt of great value to the Master and His cause, to the coun-

try and her flag, and to the army and its sons ; and never
is anything but a cordial welcome and a helping hand
extended to us wherever we go among the army people.
Let the church who sends us to them and supports us
know of this great good done."

I have tarried long with this thought, that the church
is " the mother of us all," and that the missionary bishop,
as her representative, is to be the guide and helper of
all, and specially the pastor of the pastorless.   St. Mark's
hospital throughout its history, under the bishop and by
the side of the bishop, has stood for this thought.   By
its motherly care, its Christlike work and its unrestricted
beneficence, it has won universal commendation.

CHAPTER XVI

SETTING APART MONTANA, 1880

THE field to which I had been assigned was indeed a large one in area. It extended, in round numbers, over 340,000 square miles. If it had been only to visit churches that I was sent, that would have been an easy matter. St. Michael's church, Boise City, Idaho, it will be remembered, was the only one listed. But I tried to go wherever there were communities, and when I looked round I found fifty-two places for me to visit in Montana, fifty in Idaho, and nineteen in Utah. I could not well go about in winter, there were no railroads and the distances were very great. My first winter was spent in Virginia City, my second in Helena, and all the others in Salt Lake. As communities increased to the one hundred and twenty-one mentioned, I found that it took me all the time, from May to November of every year, to get around. That was not the worst of it, I could not fully get around. There was the northern part of Idaho, the town of Lewiston, the first capital of the territory, and the region thereabout that I lacked the time to visit. Bishop Morris of Oregon most kindly made a yearly visit for me, and his clergymen, Rev. Dr. Nevius and Rev. L. H. Wells, supplemented with missionary work. There were many other towns in Montana, especially in the Yellowstone country, that I could not reach. Troubled at not being able to do the full work needed, I began as early as 1876 to plead that Montana should be set apart as a missionary district, that it might have a bishop of its own.

In my Tenth Annual Report to the Board of Missions
(1876), I said: "Of late years I never come home from
Montana without having it borne in upon my convictions
that this territory ought to have a bishop of its own. It
it sure to be a prosperous and populous region. The
Church has already a hold upon the people that is really
remarkable. It is not too much to say that it is looked
upon by them as eminently their religious guide. Rills
upon rills flow churchwards now. And now is the time
to place right there the watchful superintendent to see to
it that no obstructing bars or deflections of current be allowed. So, God guiding and time lapsing, shall the rills
naturally swell to steady river courses of healthiest church
growth. It would be a failure in duty if I did not say
strongly to the whole American Church, Montana ought
to have a bishop of its own."

In the bishop's address to the Fifth Annual Convocation (1878), held in Salt Lake City, I said:

"In October I attended the General Convention and
the meeting of the Board of Missions in Boston. By a
committee appointed by the convocation of last year I
was requested to present to the House of Bishops their
memorial concerning the division of this missionary district. I am obliged to confess that I did not present the
memorial. There did not seem to be any opportunity.
It was plainly evident that those wishing it need not
hope, and those not wishing it need not fear, any division
of the district at present. From the dearth of funds in
the missionary treasury, or from a growing feeling that
the American Church is moving too fast in its multiplication of bishops, or for other reasons to me unknown,
there was, I thought I discovered, quite a fixed intention
among leading members of the present House of Bishops
not to divide the missionary districts further.

" And yet I am unchanged in my conviction that Montana ought to have a bishop of its own. The real good of Church work loudly calls for this change. Until it can be made I must serve the three territories as best I can. I am grieved at heart that I am not well serving them. No one will say that I ought not to do more in Utah; yet no one traveling over it and knowing of the large continuous immigration will say that I ought to do less in Montana. And with the Salmon River country settling up and the Utah and Northern Railroad pushing on, I ought to do more in Idaho. It is hard to know and realize, as I do, what for the best good of the Church ought to be done each year, and yet to have only the inadequate three hundred and sixty-five days thereof wherein to do it. May I ask of the clergy to supplement all they can my sad lack of service. Get interested in the towns round about you, and visit them if possible; and so be to the bishop, unwillingly neglectful, eyes and voice for prosecuting missionary activities."

To the Seventh Annual Convocation held in Helena, August, 1880, in the bishop's address I said :

" Eight months of the twelve, from May 1, 1879, to May 1, 1880, I was traveling in the field upon Episcopal visitations. Nor by that much activity could I get over it all. Park, Echo, Bingham, Alta, Provo, Beaver, San Pete and other towns in Utah, I have not visited for divine services, though each and every one ought to have a visit. Also Malad, Oxford, Blackfoot, Challis, Bonanza, Wood River, Quartzburg, Middleton, Payette and Jordan Creek in Idaho have gone unvisited. Rocky Bar, Atlanta and Albion only received a visit after long neglect. And Lewiston and Northern Idaho have never been seen by me, being dependent for Episcopal care upon the kindness of my good brother, the Bishop of

Oregon. And in Montana there is a larger list yet of places, and important places, that I do not get to. Miles City, Fort Keogh, Fort Custer, Stillwater, Coulson, Fort Assinaboine, Chestnut, Martinsdale, Chico, East Gallatin, Bedford, Meadow Creek, Fish Creek, Silver Star, Twin Bridges, Terminus, Frenchtown.

" Facts and feelings co-work to force upon me conviction of the truth ; experience of the past, knowledge of the present, forecast of the future agree in pressing deep the conviction ; that the Church, while suffering three territories to be the charge of one bishop, is not laying hands for guidance as she should upon the sturdy infancy of these vigorous and intelligent populations.

"And my opinion remains unchanged, that, leaving Utah and Idaho perhaps at present together, Montana, rapidly and substantially developing as it is, should have a bishop of its own. And what I say to you I shall feel constrained to say in New York City this fall, with such strength as I can, to the House of Bishops and to the General Convention which is now the Board of Missions of the Church."

Our aggressive attack for relief was made upon the General Convention of 1880, sitting in St. George's church, New York City. The committee appointed by convocation sent in their petition, on the second day of the session ; the presiding bishop, Bishop Smith of Kentucky, presented it to the House of Bishops, and after that it was referred to the Committee on Memorials. This committee, consisting of Bishops Clarkson, Huntington, and Gillespie, on the fourth day made the following report :

" The Committee on Memorials, to whom was referred the petition of the convocation of the missionary district of Montana, Idaho and Utah, asking that a division of said district be made, on account of its great size and its constant and rapid growth, beg leave to recommend that said petition be referred to the committee of this House on the domestic missions of the Church.

"In making this reference, your committee take the liberty of expressing their opinion that the prayer of the petitioners should be granted."

The Committee on Domestic Missions, consisting of Bishops Whipple, Neely, Vail, Doane, and Jaggar, on the sixth day made the following report: "The Committee on Domestic Missions, to whom was referred the memorial of the convocation of the missionary district of Montana, Idaho and Utah, respectfully recommend that the prayer of the memorialists be granted, and that Montana be set off as a separate jurisdiction."

On the ninth day the report came up for consideration in the House and the *Convention Journal* recites that, "The Bishop of Montana offered the following resolution, viz.:—'*Resolved*, That the House of Bishops consent to the division, and do hereby divide the missionary district of Montana, Idaho and Utah into two missionary districts of which the territories of Utah and Idaho shall constitute one, the territory of Montana the other; which was adopted.'"

On motion of the Bishop of Montana, it was

"*Resolved*, That the present Bishop of Montana be assigned to the charge of Utah and Idaho, and be styled the Bishop of Utah with jurisdiction in Idaho."

The Bishop of Utah then offered the following resolution:

"*Resolved*, That this House will proceed as the Order of the Day to nominate a missionary bishop   Montana, on Thursday next October 21st, at 12 M."

On motion of the Bishop of Quincy, it was, as a substitute for the foregoing, "*Resolved*, That this House will consider the question of the nomination of a missionary bishop for Montana, on Tuesday next at 2 P. M."

The consideration appointed for that Tuesday, the twelfth day of the session, October 19th, resulted in the nomination by the House of Bishops to the House of Deputies of Rev. L. R. Brewer for Bishop of Montana. On the thirteenth day, October 20th, the House of Deputies elected unanimously Rev. L. R. Brewer to be Bishop of Montana.

Bishop Brewer was consecrated in his own parish church, at Watertown, N. Y., December 8, 1880. His own diocesan, Bishop Huntington, presided, and I preached the sermon. At Bishop Brewer's request, I retained the charge of Montana for him, to January 1, 1881.

At the time of present writing (1902), Bishop Brewer has been at work in Montana for more than twenty-one years. And his work has been done industriously, unselfishly, devotedly, with single aim and with signal success. He has won for himself and for Montana a place of high honor and of much influence in the church. The statistics of the diocese are eloquent. The seven clergy, 487 Sunday-school scholars, and 368 communicants left by me have been multiplied into twenty-five clergy, 2,141 Sunday-school scholars, and 2,555 communicants.

It will have been noticed that in the House of Bishops I offered the motion that the present Bishop of Montana be assigned to the charge of Utah and Idaho and be styled the Bishop of Utah; and that immediately afterwards the Bishop of Utah moved to proceed in the business of securing a bishop for Montana. Between those two motions, immediately after the first one was declared adopted, I ceased to be Bishop of Montana and became Bishop of Utah.

Singular change, rapid accomplishment, of what we had been planning and working for during five years! Before that time, I had come to the conclusion with sad reluctance that I must give up Montana. There were two strong reasons for my retaining Montana. (1) When I was baptized into the Episcopate the name Montana had been given me. Jurisdiction in Idaho and Utah was merely appended. I wanted to keep the name given, I was used to it, I was fond of it, I was proud of it. (2) Without disparagement of other kind friends, the people of Montana seemed specially near and dear to me. I knew them almost all by name and face. I visited all the towns and hamlets of the territory save the few that in later years grew up in the Yellowstone Valley. I was gratefully touched by the affection and loyalty of all the people towards him who bore ecclesiastically the name of their own noble territory.

But on the other hand, there were two strong reasons why I should give up Montana. (1) In my home were four children, between five and fourteen years of age. The Montana schools were not yet first-rate, while in St. Mark's school, Salt Lake, we had an institution of our own to meet the needs of those children. (2) The work among the Mormons was plainly difficult. I did not think it would be right in me to flinch from it. I had had thirteen years and more of experience in it. I did not think it would be right or wise to turn it over to inexperienced hands. And, indeed, I had strong reason to doubt whether the House of Bishops, with whom would rest the ultimate decision, would approve of my withdrawing from Utah.

So with a heavy heart, but clearly conscious of doing

right, I stepped down and out of Montana. My last
service in it as its bishop was on Sunday, September 5,
1880, at Bannack, where in the Methodist church I held
services and preached, and also baptized three young
girls who presented themselves, Mary Helen Peabody,
Montana Elizabeth Nay, and Mary Helen Nay. I did
not know the service was my last. I could not know
what the House of Bishops in the coming convention of
October was going to determine. From May to September I visited thirty-seven towns of Montana, planning
for the next year, the same as usual, and with no expectation in the people's hearts or indeed, I may say, in my
own, but that I would be among them the coming year.
Never, however, since that night at Bannack, have I seen
Montana again as its bishop, though twice I have looked
upon it with my eyes; once, in November, 1881, when I
was present at Helena at the consecration of St. Peter's
church and preached the sermon, and at Butte, at the
opening of St. John's church, and preached the sermon;
and once, in the summer of 1899, when I spent the
month of July in the state.

In my sermon at the consecration of Bishop Brewer I
gave utterance to a little of what was in my heart:

"Your field! right reverend fathers, reverend brethren,
and brethren all, pardon an outflow of natural weakness
in a personal direction. If you will grant me, I will have
a few words as it were alone with him. They are not of
St. Paul to Timothy; but they are of a retiring bishop to
the newcomer whom he gratefully hails and to whom he
lovingly bids Godspeed.

"Montana! my brother, I have been for thirteen years
the bishop so named. The illimitable mountain pasture
ranges of that territory, its broad valleys yellowed with
grain harvests, its cattle upon a thousand hills, its abound-

ing herds of rich-fleeced sheep, its exports of robes and
furs, the uncounted and almost uncountable treasures that
lie stored in its numerous mines of copper and silver and
gold,—of all these I know; and out of that knowledge let
me say into your ears, what I am sure your own mouth
will echo back to me by and by, ' The American Church
has indeed been wise in her generation, and alive to her
privilege and her duty in giving now to that territory a
bishop of its own.'

" From the first you will find your heart and mind and
hands full in the effort to meet the fresh abounding life
of the incoming migration, and to bring to bear upon it
the moulding influence of the church. You will need
gifts constant for sustentation, from the home church at
the East. But your great work you will find to be to
evoke and direct and administer in the best way the
influences and energies and help ready at your hands
among your own people here.

" I make bold to tell you, Montana is to be a great
state; one of the greatest at the West, and in no far off
time either.

" Stay, then, right among your people. Identify yourself through and through with them. With all your
vigor as a man, and with all the power of your office,
seize the growing empire for Christ. Everywhere in the
infant hamlets and nascent towns plant church influences,
plant, water, enrich, watch, train, prune. God will give
the increase. And the typical life of that wondrous new
region will, under Him, get at your hands a Christian
mould and a churchly set that shall be a blessing to
the dwellers there, an honor to you, and a help to the
Master.

" All that loyal fidelity of loving pastorship which
has been yours here, and which has so grown and

strengthened here that your people's hearts are agonized
and breaking over our coming to-day to disrupt it,—take
all that with you there and make it to abound yet more
and more.

"To tear up by the roots these outgrowths and in-
growths of the bonds of the old home, and these ties of
a long and affectionate pastorship,—I know what it costs
the life and how it wrings the heart. But what is torn up
cast you not away. Not even any little of it. The
manly faithfulness, the unswerving devotion, the tender
love, O pastor of souls, transplant all of it there with
you; and fasten whatever you can of soft home earth to
the exposed roots, that they may take kindly to the
transplanting. Never have a doubt that souls there are
to be fed and a flock there is to be led, in numbers and
needs such as to call out all the loving guidance and helpful strength you have to give.

"My brother, you will not seldom wander where I
have trod. You will be a kindly voice to say good-by
for me to not a few men and women and children that
were mine in the gospel, and whom I love almost as the
fruit of mine own loins.

"I, too, to-day break up a loving pastorship. We are
brothers indeed. And as I have said for you to your
people now some good-by words, so you will, will you not,
say for me the tenderest good-by to my people there.
Bid them for me serve the Master, stand by the Church,
set their affections above, reaching out for the HOME
there. 'Hold up the weak, heal the sick, bind up the
broken, bring again the outcasts, seek the lost.' I was
told solemnly to do that. I have honestly tried so to do
it. You are soon to be told to do it. Do it in yonder
mountain field. Hold up the weak, heal the sick, bind
up the broken, bring again the outcasts, seek the lost.

"In doing it, if sometimes you come across my footsteps I beg you be to me a helpful brother indeed and cause that my weaknesses and mistakes, ay and sins, shall not go and grow to be harm to the precious work. Do right where I went wrong. Make good the losses and wastes that I neglectfully allowed to come. So save you some of my work, and almost some of me, from being destroyed as by fire. And for each loving-kindness my heart will thank you and my life shall honor and help you evermore.

"The robes of the Bishop of Montana, I lay them down. Yours, my dear brother, they now are.

"God's blessing make them with you more unstained and pure, of a more shining whiteness before Him and a more saintly power among men, than ever they were with me."

By my ignorance of what was coming I had been saved from the saying of tearful good-bys in the summer of 1880. Therefore, from Watertown on the day of the consecration, I sent my written good-by, as follows:

"*Watertown, N. Y., December 8, 1880.*
"*To the Clergy and People of Montana:*

"DEARLY LOVED FRIENDS:—In an hour or two the Rev. L. R. Brewer is to be consecrated your bishop. There is made over to him the name I have always been proud of and have loved, the ' Bishop of Montana.'

"It becomes me to say my good-by. My heart, torn with sorrowfulness at this rupture, tells how you are imbedded in it. Precious memories crowding themselves upon this hour witness how lovingly good you have been to me.

"Let me say out my sadness. The valleys and hillsides, the very nooks and crannies of your territory, are dear to me from association, your clergy and men and women and children and homes more dear from ties of fond affection. I were a stone statue could I speak this farewell unmoved. Sad indeed sit I now to write it.

"Sadder settles the feeling at this hour, when my oversight of you ends, that I have not done for you and among you as well as I ought and might. I have done things that I ought not to have done, and have left undone things that I ought to have done. You have over and over said kind words to me about my diligence, and, as you were pleased to see and call it, my faithfulness. Love prompted these words, and my heart is touched at recalling them. But God knows how, to Him and me, this your picture of me is marred by selfishness and earthiness. The book of my pastoral stewardship of your souls closes itself now unto the one only opening of the last Great Day. I am praying, God forgive me the debts and lacks the wastes and losses and sins of unfaithfulness in that record, for the merciful Saviour's sake!

"But saddest comes the thought that many of you whom I dearly love and who have been tenderly kind to me have not placed yourselves freely and fully on the Lord's side as earnest communing Christians. Dear, dear friends, I beg you, I pray you, turn you to God in faith and prayer and obedience, and in holy baptism and holy communion. Seek ye the kingdom of God and His righteousness. Be grateful to your Saviour and kind to your own souls. Warring life has no real happiness in it for you and me, and coming death no well-founded peace, without Christ.

"But be my closing word one of gladness; Montana has a bishop of its own. 'Tis the right thing for Montana to have. 'Tis high time for her to have him. Let us

' thank God and take courage,' you with me, I with you.
I beg you love and help him as you have loved and
helped me. Give him your full confidence. Stay up his
hands. Cheer his heart. Under him, prayerfully, make
you the Master's cause grow, and the church's life strong.

" Brethren beloved, good-by! That means, God be
with you. He will helpfully bide with you if you trustfully lean on Him. My love and prayers are yours.
With an almost bursting heart I lay down my pastoral
staff as Bishop of Montana. God help me. Amen!"

For thirteen years and eight months I had charge of
Montana. I wandered over the territory widely, and
never for a single mile upon a railroad. In fifty-one
places I held services: Argenta, Bannack, Bear Creek,
Belmont, Bishop's schoolhouse, Blackfoot, Boulder, Bozeman, Butte, Centreville, Clancy, Corvallis, Deer Lodge,
Diamond, Etna, Fish Creek, Fort Benton, Fort Ellis, Fort
Logan, Fort Shaw, Gallatin, Glendale, Hamilton, Harrison, Helena, Jefferson, Madison Valley, Marysville,
Meadow Creek, Missoula, Nevada, New Chicago, Newman's Ranch, Philipsburgh, Pioneer, Poindexter's schoolhouse, Pony, Radersburgh, Red Bluff, Sheridan, Silver
Bow, Skalkaho, Sterling, Stevensville, Summit, Sun
River, Unionville, Virginia City, Whitehall, White Sulphur Springs, Willow Creek. Of these, only seventeen
are rated as parishes or missions in the published list for
Montana of the present year (1902). Some, I dare say,
have ceased to exist. Perhaps Diamond, Nevada, Pioneer, Summit; certainly Fort Ellis, Fort Logan (earlier
known as Camp Baker), and Fort Shaw. Some have
changed their names. For instance, the " Hamilton " of
my list (known earlier as Morse's store, and Potter's
store) was in the Gallatin Valley. The present " Hamilton " is in the Bitter Root valley. The " Centreville " of

my list was in Meagher County. The present "Centreville" is near Butte. Some, as Bear Creek (Gallatin
County), Bishop's schoolhouse, Etna, Fish Creek, Meadow
Creek, Newman's Ranch, Poindexter's schoolhouse, and
Willow Creek were only farming neighborhoods. And
many towns I am sure Bishop Brewer still visits, where it
is not thought wise or well to organize as yet a parish or
a mission. In my thirteen years of service there were in
Montana 781 baptisms, 300 of which were performed by
myself, 239 confirmations, 142 marriages, and 216 burials.

I have never hesitated to predict a bright and prosperous future for Montana. In most respects, and specially
in the matter of giving, and in Sunday-schools, she is at
the very head of the twenty-one missionary districts of
our church. And it will not be very long before she will
knock at the door of the General Convention for entrance
as an independent diocese.

In writing the record of my official severance from
Montana my memory is crowded with associations and
experiences of my life lived there. There were the men
I met, stalwart, fearless, kind, generous. W. F. Sanders
I have spoken of before. In critical early days no one
man stood with more courage for Montana's true interests than did he. It was meet and fit that he should be
one of the first to represent the new state in the United
States Senate. In 1899, when I revisited Montana and
the old-timers insisted on gathering to meet me at Butte,
Colonel Sanders, with his wife, came over from Helena
that he might introduce me. The trouble he took was
of a piece with the unvarying kindness which he and his
good wife showed me all through my mountain life. The
president of the evening was Hon. W. A. Clark, then
United States senator elect. He is now among the men
of greatest wealth in all the world. I met him first in

Helena in 1869, when he was disposing of a stock of groceries he had brought in. I met him again in Deer Lodge, in a bank; then I saw him in Butte. In Deer Lodge he fitted up a vacant cabin near his own with chemical and furnace appliances and spent such time therein as his busy life allowed in reducing and assaying samples of ore. He soon made himself so expert as to be able independently to determine the worth or worthlessness of mines, and sagaciously to pass upon questions of buying and selling. Intelligent, alert, self-controlled, courteous, temperate, resolute, painstakingly industrious, and indomitably persevering, success with him has been the natural outgrowth of forces set in action. His wife and sister were confirmed by me in Deer Lodge, and he himself, in Deer Lodge and in Butte, was for years a member of our parish committee or vestry.

The old-timers gathered on the evening I have alluded to, comprised all sorts and conditions of men. It was a comfort to look into their faces again. Sobered, furrowed, saddened, doubtless they were—for it was thirty-two years since I had first come among them. But their hearts were unchanged. And hand-clasps after the meeting were not a whit chilled or weakened.

Lee Mantle was telegraph operator and stage agent at the home station known as "Pleasant Valley," on the confines of Idaho and Montana, on the old stage route from Salt Lake to Virginia City. It was here that in June, 1870, I married my stage driver friend, David Allerdice to Mrs. Hall, the housekeeper and eminently good cook of the hostelry. Young Mantle was active, diligent, trustworthy, faithful in his duties. He, too, became a United States senator.

Geo. A. Baker was a merchant at Fort Benton. In the early days Fort Benton, as the head of navigation, was the centre of an immense freight and forwarding business. This business was controlled by two large commission firms, Conrad & Baker, and T. C. Power & Co. After some years Baker went to St. Louis, Mo., taking some money and much experience. Mountain life, as in many another instance, had strengthened, not ruined the good in him. He became the president of a bank in the city. He was a leader in the Methodist Church. A very embodiment of Christian manhood he lived to be, useful, helpful and good. He died crowned with the respect, admiration, and love of the entire community.

D. W. Tilton was my first host in Montana. He was proprietor of the *Montana Post*, the pioneer paper of Virginia City. He gave me up one corner of his log cabin to sleep in. I married him. For years he was a helpful committeeman or vestryman at Virginia City. In my last visit to Butte, spoken of above, as a citizen there he was again my kind host, though not putting me this time into a corner of a one-roomed log cabin. I found him a faithful warden of St. John's church, having been confirmed by Bishop Brewer.

James H. Mills was editor of the *Montana Post* when I came to Virginia City. A clear, keen, clean pen he wielded. His own paper of after years, the *New Northwest*, of Deer Lodge, was a power in Montana. He, too, was my good helper as vestryman for many years. He became secretary of the territory and has filled many federal positions.

Phil Lovell of Bannack and Beaver Head is one of the earliest of the pioneers; he is eminently good-natured yet sleeplessly sagacious. Every time I was anywhere in the Beaver Head country he would come miles and miles to service. He was of church stock in the old country. During my last visit, in 1899, I was at his ranch. There were anecdotes, laughter, dinner, prayers, and tears. Some time afterwards he was confirmed by Bishop Brewer.

Another, among the first of the pioneers, is Frank H. Woody of Missoula. Forty years in the mountains have not worn away the culture and charm he acquired in his old Maryland home. He, too, was a vestryman for me for years, though like many another of my vestrymen, not extraordinarily diligent in coming to church. But they all did the business duty they undertook for me, straightly, squarely, kindly, helpfully, and my heart is still full of loving gratitude to them.

Another of these vestrymen was General L. S. Willson, one of the early settlers and makers of Bozeman. His wife, skilled in music, Presbyterian though she was, seconded me heartily and splendidly in the services every year I came to Bozeman. His brother, Davis Willson, was one of the few devout men of the early days who helped me keep the spiritual side of my nature from going to rack and ruin. He has since become a Presbyterian minister.

Granville Stuart of Deer Lodge and Con. Kohrs were among the oldest settlers. Both were good and helpful friends. Yet I cannot remember that I ever saw either of them before me in a church service. The former, of superior intellect and scientific accomplishment, served, however, as one of my " vestrymen," and was particularly kind in guiding and helping me to take up and fence in the Deer Lodge church lot in early days.

A. M. Holter of Helena was one of my generous standbys, though he came little to church. His son Norman was baptized as an infant by me in February, 1869, in Helena. He, in turn, is now one of the staunch supporters of the church in Montana.

John Ilow had been mayor of St. Louis and a millionaire. Reverses came and he migrated to the mountains. In the '70s I often met him in Virginia City, and I never met him without profound admiration for his manliness, courage, resolution and energy. He worked hard, driving an ox-team, hauling ore, developing a mine, running a mill, in strong and stern effort for recuperation.

Major John Owen, the sturdy old pioneer after whom Fort Owen in the Bitter Root Valley was named, I did not come to know till he had sunk in the sloughs of self-indulgence and dissipation. Nothing remained above water but his amiability of disposition and his gentlemanliness of manner.

There were the homes I had. I know that on the frontier every house is always a home to any wanderer, the duties and privileges of hospitality are nowhere so free and unlimited as there; yet I had special kindness shown me. The homes that were kindly opened and made inviting to me were so many as to be altogether impossible of enumeration.

One of these was the log cabin, in Deer Lodge, of W. A. Clark, when Mrs. Clark was herself maid of all work, and cook for her guests. Another in the same town was the house of Dr. Higgins. Mrs. Higgins, staunchest of churchwomen, never deemed any trouble too much to take for the comfort of her bishop on his yearly visits.

My sojourns in Missoula were always eminently restful. The mail with its exactions came in only three times a week. There were only about a dozen families to be visited. I usually remained nearly two weeks in order to give a Sunday to the Bitter Root Valley. On my first visit I stayed with Mr. and Mrs. Harvey Lent.

Mrs. Lent was one of the most intelligent and best informed churchwomen that I had anywhere met.   Once,
also, in a subsequent home they had at Gird's Creek in
the Bitter Root Valley I stayed with them.   But in most
of my visits in Missoula William Kennedy and Mrs.
Kennedy took care of me in their hotel.   And excellent
care it was.   The letting up of the tension of duty, the
comforting kindness of the Kennedys, and the peacefulness and restfulness of the far away hamlet, as in these
days it was, made my yearly visits to Missoula special
seasons of refreshment and invigoration.   The parish at
Missoula was named the Church of the " Holy Spirit."
My college classmate, Mr. Elbridge T. Gerry, of New
York, so named it when giving me five hundred dollars
for its help.

My chief home up the Bitter Root was at the farm of
the Bass Bros.   The " Pine Grove," the babbling mountain brook of sweetest water, and the splendid fruit farm
made it a most restful place.   The wives of the brothers
were sisters.   Both of them were confirmed by me.
The younger couple I married in the home, in June,
1876.   Across the river from the farm were old Fort
Owen and Stevensville.   In 1877, when I came along on
my visit, the Nez Perces war had broken out in Northern
Idaho.   And the old Nez Perces trail came down the
Lo Lo into the Bitter Root only a few miles from the
Bass farm.

Some days after my visit, the Nez Perces came over
the Lo Lo; marched up the valley past Stevensville, and
camped at the head of the valley, on the divide between
the Bitter Root and the Big Hole.   Here General Gibbon,
with 182 men of his Seventh Infantry from Fort
Shaw, and reinforced by settlers, overtook them and,
August 9th, fought the battle of the Big Hole.   The

Indians cunningly set fire to the dry prairie grass to the
windward of the general, and it would have gone right
hard with the forces of the latter, had not the wind suddenly and strongly changed its course. As it was, the
general lost three officers, seventeen men, and four settlers killed ; and five officers, thirty-six men, and five
settlers wounded. He put the Indians to flight, however,
and they hurried past Bannack and Horse Prairie on
their way over to the Yellowstone country. On Horse
Prairie they killed several citizens, passing dangerously
near another of my Montana homes, viz., the home
of Mr. and Mrs. Martin Barrett. These friends of
mine were Roman Catholics, but they would come over
to Bannack, year by year, for our services, and then take
me home with them to stay all night. In the morning
they would send me on to Red Rock to take the down
stage for Salt Lake. Mrs. Barrett's father was Captain
Cook, who, with Mrs. Cook, kept a most delightful hostelry for stage passengers at Boulder Valley. Another
daughter married E. M. Pollinger, once a division superintendent of the old stage line. Four of her children I
baptized at " Governor " Pollinger's Ranch, which he
called " Alaska," in June, 1879. Still another daughter
married William T. Sweet, a mountaineer, bluff and jolly ;
and their three children I baptized at Boulder Valley, in
August, 1874. The father has been confirmed by Bishop
Brewer.

One officer killed in the battle of the Big Hole was
Lieutenant Kendrick, who a little more than two weeks
previous had kneeled before me in the service of the holy
communion at Fort Shaw. One of the citizens killed
was Lynde Elliott, a noble man and to me a dear personal friend, one of a colony of " Second Adventists "
settled near Skalkaho, in the upper Bitter Root. After

the battle, my dear young brother, Rev. Mahlon N. Gilbert, sprang on his horse at Deer Lodge and galloped off to the battle-ground to be of what use he could in caring for and bringing in the wounded.

Besides Indian troubles, the year 1877 brought sadness to me. My own dear father died in Windham, New York, at the age of eighty. A telegram reached me in Virginia City in August that he was failing fast, and asking if I could not come to him. My letters to Mrs. Tuttle tell why I could not go.

"*Virginia City, M. T., August 18, 1877.*

" I do not forget that you were born this day into this world, and dear little Kitty into the next. I have kneeled and prayed God to bless you and to help us both that we may go one day to the pure and restful home to meet her. And so with prayer and love in my heart and tears in my eyes I start my letter to you.

" I am much hurried. I have just finished my report, and in an hour Mr. Prout and I must be off to Madison Valley. To-morrow, after morning service there, we must ride in, twenty miles, and then have service here. So I write this for to-morrow's letter. Whether it will reach you directly I know not. News comes that the Indians have attacked and burned two stage stations. Perhaps our mails will all be stopped. And my heart is sad anew for the death of Mr. Lynde Elliott, a dear good soul of Skalkaho, Bitter Root, where Mr. Kirby and I stayed all night. He was killed while serving with Gibbon.

" This town is filled with women and children in refuge from ranches. But General Howard is now near Bannack, with six hundred men, and we will doubtless be protected. Do not worry."

"*Virginia City, M. T., August 21, 1877.*

"The blow is falling. Your telegram just received. I have just telegraphed mother: ' Telegram just received. Duty keeps me here.' God comfort mother. Ask dear father's dying blessing on me. I must not leave my work. But I now recall dear father's last good-by. With tears and sobs, kissing me he said: ' I shall not see you again in this life.' Dear old father ; good Christian saint! I fear it will be so. Please write, dear, that we mean to be in Windham as we said, September 15th, and that from convictions of duty we do not see how we can get there earlier. Besides, the Indians have now stopped all the mails and it is dangerous to go through to Salt Lake. I have prayed God's peace and help to aid me to be cheer-ful and faithful in meeting duty.

"Pray for me, darling. It is very, very hard. In an hour I must take stage with Mr. Prout to Sheridan, to hold services.

"God's will be done! But if only once more I might have met dear father! It is well for him, but sad for me. If only I can live so good a man and die so hopefully as he! Poor dear, dear mother! The half of her own self going, too! I can have only the glimmering of a hope that it may still please God to spare him till I come.

"Your telegram, however, sent the 17th, has only just come through the Indian blockade. So my fears are great that father cannot last. God's will be done! I will try faithfully to go on.

"If I dared, I would think of taking stage to-night to come to you and to go on home. But I dare not so throw duty behind me. My dear, true, old, Christian father himself would say: ' Don't do it, my son. Fulfil your task. If not now, we shall, please God, meet by and by in the Home. ' "

In the year 1877 the General Convention met in Boston.
I reached my old Windham home, September 14th. During the long journey from Salt Lake I had indulged the
hope that my dear father might yet be alive. But at
Catskill I met my brother-in-law, who was to drive us
the twenty-eight miles over the mountain to Windham,
and he quietly said to me, " Father was buried three days
ago."

My tribute to my loved father need not be set down in
words. If my life has been of any worth, be that life the
tribute. He was a blacksmith in the days of my boyhood; and in later days a small farmer. He was an
honest man, kind, true, clean, good, with a goodness
universally recognizable, so that he was " Uncle Daniel "
to all the countryside. Once and again he was elected
the supervisor of his town. He was a leader in the
Methodist Church, an every-day saint, an all-days Christian. My mother, who survived him only a year or two,
was a dear, faithful Christian mother, a Methodist too,
loving and lovable. But in my case, the mightiest human
influence to start me right and keep me straight were the
family prayers, the daily example, the benevolent simplicity, and the stainless character of my dear father.
He lived by faith, he worked through love, he died in
hope, and he left me to tell out through tears my love
and gratitude on his fresh made grave.

I have often administered the holy communion to my
dear parents, though they were not confirmed. And I
have had the blessed privilege of laying my hands in
confirmation upon the heads of my brother, my brother-in-law, my two sisters and their five children, and one
grand niece.

I have been led into digression from the story of my
Montana homes. Mr. A. F. Graeter, of Bannack, opened

one such to me. He was a miner and ditch-owner, and remained one of the truest and sturdiest of friends all through my Montana life.

Mrs. French, first of Bannack, afterwards of Argenta, was one of the best of my kind hostesses. In Bannack, in July, 1868, I baptized her five children. In Argenta I stopped, year by year, for services when the place was almost deserted, because Mrs. French was there. She was postmistress and landlady. Devout in faith, of cheerful temper, kindly disposition, refined taste, and unselfish life; her housekeeping most attractive, her hospitable comforting blessed my life immensely. When she died, I said, " an every-day, practical, common-sense saint, of utmost helpfulness, has gone home."

In Beaver Head Valley was a coterie of friends. Mr. and Mrs. Poindexter took care of me more than once. They were, I think, South Methodists, from Missouri, but in their home, and in the schoolhouse near by, I held some of the most earnest of our church services.

Gallatin City was a hamlet of some half dozen houses at the Three Forks, where the Jefferson and Madison and Gallatin Rivers unite to form the Missouri. Major Campbell's cabin here was my home. Dear Mrs. Campbell made it a most comfortable home, spite of the dreadful onset of the pestiferous mosquitoes. Two married daughters lived in the neighborhood, Mrs. Gallaher and Mrs. Dunbar, whose children all, I think, I baptized. The son, Gurdon, an unusually intelligent and well educated man, though in body somewhat deformed, was the merchant of the place. After the death of the mother and father, the third daughter, Miss Fanny, was my hostess. The following letter to Mrs. Tuttle tells of Gallatin City, and also tells of the kind and amount of work that a missionary bishop often finds upon his hands.

"*Gallatin City, M. T.,*
"*Monday, 10 A. M., August 13, 1877.*

"I am in a house where I was never entertained before. Miss Fanny Campbell, my long time hostess, is absent in Chicago, so Mrs. Thomas, the wife of the miller here, has kindly taken me in. After most sensible fashion she is leaving me in her 'front room' alone to write my letters. I arrived here about nine o'clock, and first had to look into the question of ways and means for getting to 'Pony' to-morrow. After I have finished letters (eight or ten of which I have to write), I hope to be able to go down and have a swim in the Madison River, before dressing to make some calls and getting ready for the evening service at the schoolhouse. I do not at all feel so tired as I expected to, and am wondering at myself. Yesterday at Bozeman I had eight services alone, and last night I got little sleep.

"At 9 A. M., at Mrs. Beall's, I baptized two Kruger children. At 10 A. M., at Mrs. Spieth's, I baptized a child. At 11 A. M. I had services at church, with the holy communion (communicants, twenty-one; offerings, $24.95). At 1 P. M. I opened the Sunday-school and baptized four children. At 2 P. M., at Mr. Perkins', I baptized a child. At 3:30, at Fort Ellis, three miles distant, I held services. At 4:45, at General Brisbin's, I baptized a child. At five I dined with Mrs. Brisbin, and at 8 P. M. held services in St. James' church. After services I met my church committee and gave them my report; then I had to go to Mrs. Beall's to pack up and bring my valise to the hotel. At the hotel I got to bed at 11:45 o'clock, and at 1:45 was called to take the stage hither.

"The new Presbyterian minister, Rev. Mr. Richards, fresh from Union Seminary (New York City), was at my

three services and. at holy communion. We are going
to lend St. James' church to the Presbyterians for the
present."

In Butte Mr. and Mrs. John Noyes took care of me;
and Mr. and Mrs. Clinton H. Moore. So, too, did
Mr. and Mrs. Richard S. Jones. Mrs. Jones' first husband was John Rogers, whom I buried at Deer Lodge,
in July, 1874.

My home in Blackfoot was with Mr. and Mrs. Charles
G. Birdseye. A wonderful place was that Blackfoot
log cabin, for comfort, invitingness, and repose.

In Benton I stayed with Mr. and Mrs. Jo Hill. I confirmed Mr. Hill, and married him, and subsequently confirmed his wife and baptized their children. A typical
American business man Mr. Hill was, laborious, energetic,
resolute, reticent, obliging, sincere.

My Helena homes were with Judge and Mrs. Chuma-
sero, Mr. and Mrs. T. C. Groshon, Mr. and Mrs. Paynter,
Mr. and Mrs. W. G. Bailey, and Mr. and Mrs. S. J. Jones.
From the time that they came to Montana, living first at
Unionville, three or four miles from Helena, Mr. and
Mrs. Jones were helpers to me of the best sort.

In all the homes my good, strong health enabled me to
enjoy to the full the hospitable comfort which people invariably extended to me. That story of good health has
only a few interruptions. One such is told about in the
following letter:

" *Boulder Valley, M. T., July 27, 1876.*
" Mr. Toy sits in the room reading. It is ten o'clock
in the morning and about noon we expect to start back
to Helena. It threatens to be an intensely warm day.
My own darling, I have sadly wanted you the last two
days. Monday night when I went to bed I felt my left

lower jaw grumbling some, and soon found that little or
no sleep was to be mine that night.   It was a clear case
of neuralgia, such as I had at Boise, where it prostrated
me for two or three days, bringing me to my bed.   I
rose Tuesday morning, blue enough and homesick.   But
my appointments were out for Jefferson and Boulder and
I thought I must try to meet them.   At seven o'clock,
therefore, Mr. Toy and I took the stage and I rode in
agony to Jefferson.   There I put myself in Mrs. Mason's
hands, one of the kindest of little women, and she put me
to bed and covered me up and made me take a real sweat
and would not let me go out to make calls or do anything
all day.   At night I went to the schoolhouse and
preached.   Her vigorous treatment did me good.   Tuesday night I slept well and yesterday had only a few
twinges of the enemy."

Montana experiences taught me a good many things.
One of these was, to reprove or rebuke with thoughtful
premeditation, not on quick impulse.   In Virginia City
one of my congregation had a good heart and a fair voice
but no ear.   In our singing his pedal bass was a distress.
So one day in giving out the hymn I blurted out: "May
I suggest that those of us who are not gifted with voice
and ear for music leave it to others to sing for us, we
praising with all our heart."   Note the consequence.
The person aimed at never suspected the intention of my
remark and went on vigorously as before; while two or
three of my best sopranos (Mrs. Sanders being of the
number), stopped singing to my great dismay.   I never
afterwards undertook to interfere with the church music,
save in the utmost privacy and by tactful individualizing.

Another lesson I learned was not to lose my temper.
I was obliged, as I have said, to circulate subscription
books and collect funds for ministers' salaries in Virginia

City, Helena, Deer Lodge, Missoula, the Bitter Root, Butte, Bozeman, Fort Benton, as well as in many towns in Utah and Idaho. Even in this matter people of all sorts were good to me. But twice, once in Helena and once in Salt Lake, I lost my temper and said biting things about what I thought and called stinginess. Note the consequence. I lost my hold on two men and so injured my cause. Besides, I forgot that no one man can righteously and equitably set himself up as a judge of what another man ought to give. He cannot know all the private, family and charitable claims upon that other's purse.

I learned also that one ought to put up cheerfully with disappointments and to give and take good-naturedly. On not a few occasions the committees or vestries of my parishes, in spite of all my arguing and reasoning would not vote as I wanted them to. I remember once, particularly, in the Helena committee I was beaten after as vigorous a fight as I knew how to put up. My practice on such occasions was invariably to yield without sulking. Note the consequence. Further time, the revolution of a year perhaps, would make a change and I would find my aim pleasantly and fully secured. Ministers are not trained to the habits of " give and take " as lawyers and business men are. If we will persistently require that our own chosen way be taken in everything, little and great, may I commend to my brethren and myself the consideration of two short mottoes :   " She stoops to conquer," and " He rides to ruin."

To preserve one's equanimity under misunderstandings is another lesson I learned. If a man's life is in any sense before the public such things are sure to arise. I do not claim to be a total abstainer, but I hope I have been temperate. A lady once said to me: " I hear something very bad of you, if it is true. A man told me, and I told him the next time I saw you I should ask you about it, that once riding near Diamond you offered a man some brandy, and on his telling you he was a Good Templar, you made light of it and begged him to drink; you said 'twould do him good,—and that that man has since gone back to his gutter drunkenness." I answered, " I may have offered a man brandy. I have several times done so aboard the stage if men were sick. I have a flask of brandy with me now. But all the additional part about the Good Templar, etc., is a fabrication." Then she said, " I've also been told that at Bannack you refused to hold services in the Good Templar hall for your bitter hate to the organization." " Not a word of truth in that, madam!" I said. " I appreciate and am thankful for the good the Order has done in these mountains." So she let me off, after my warm commendation of her course in coming direct to me.

Speaking generally, I learned that to put a little brandy in the drinking water in the alkali regions was wholesome. But I learned also that I could best endure hot days and long dusty rides by drinking infrequently. So my practice became that of passing philosophically by the creeks and stations, and drinking only three times a day with my meals. I was never as much a sufferer from thirst as were my fellow passengers who flung themselves down at every stream we crossed. When covered thick with alkali dust, at the meals I would only wash my lips and mustache, leaving my dust plastered face quite undisturbed till we should get out of that region. So I saved my face from becoming roughened and sore.

Montana! It is not a rough word. To my ears it is melody and strength combined. I ask not that any may play upon it for me. It sings itself. The sound of it goes to my heart. The memory of it touches my inmost life. It has been a lover's task to recall my wooing of thee in the days of my youth and of thy youth, a generation ago.

Montana! I never hear the word but my heart beats quicker with love and thanks and pride. Dear old friends of Montana, not a few have gone the way of all the earth. Peace to them and rest! Ye living ones of the old friends, the greeting of a grateful friend of the long ago, who has never let the love of you go out of his heart, runs with warmest flow into these written words. Memory holds me a willing captive, and my hands, my heart, my thanks, my love are yours.

Montana scenes; Montana friends; Montana kindnesses! Ye shall be remembered till this heart of mine cease its measured earthly beatings, and the floodgates of its activity be lost in the great ocean of eternal rest.

CHAPTER XVII

SECOND CALL TO MISSOURI, 1886

As I sit down now (July, 1904), to write the last chapter in these reminiscences many thoughts press upon me. It seems to me I ought to give utterance to some of them. In July, 1889, my dear wife urged upon me this sort of writing. But for her I should never have dreamed of entering upon it. She had thoughtfully preserved my early letters as material. I therefore promised her to do as she requested. But my life has not been one of leisure and I could only devote to the writing promised the Julys and Augusts of my resting time in summers. This I have done for fifteen years, except in the summer of 1897, when we went to London to the Lambeth Conference, and of 1899, when I went on a visit to my old Rocky Mountain field. During this visit, as I have shown, my wife, who had remained in St. Louis, on the 18th of August, her fifty-eighth birthday, passed to the rest of Paradise.

It may well be understood that it has seemed a sacred duty for me to press this writing to completion while my own life should be mercifully spared.

How I have been shrinking in the area of my work,—though I hope, not shrinking in the doing of it,—for these thirty-seven years! In 1867, Bishop of Montana, Idaho and Utah, a field of 340,000 square miles. In 1880, Bishop of Utah and Idaho, 195,000 square miles. In 1886, Bishop of Missouri, 70,000 square miles. In 1890, Bishop of Missouri (West Missouri having been set apart as a diocese), 32,000 square miles,—but whatever

456

shrinking I have done, the areas themselves have not shrunk, and the work done in them has not shrunk. In my original field three bishops are now working, Bishop Brewer in Montana, Bishop Wells in Northern Idaho, and Bishop Funsten in Southern Idaho. Besides, Bishop Leonard was in active duty in Utah for sixteen years. Seven months ago he died. By the canons of the church his vacant field fell to my charge as senior bishop, until another bishop can be chosen. So once more, after eighteen years of absence, it falls to me to be the acting Bishop of Utah. This is one among the strange happenings that have come to my life. In the seven months I have made two visits to Utah. St. Mark's school I have found closed and its property sold, because of the growing excellence of the public schools. Rowland Hall and also St. Mark's hospital, however, I found in excellent condition.

It will be remembered that in Montana, Idaho and Utah, when I was made bishop, there was not even one clergyman of the church. Now in the same field there are four bishops, forty-nine clergymen, and 4,887 communicants. And Montana has been erected into a diocese and will knock for entrance at the doors of the General Convention at its meeting in Boston, in October next. Surely there has been no shrinking of work or shirking of work in the old Rocky Mountain region.

I have told of my going in 1899 to revisit the scenes of my early labors. I may be permitted to set down some extracts from my letters to Mrs. Tuttle during that summer.

" Helena, Montana, July 3, 1899.
" God's goodness to me touches me to the heart. He has preserved me in safety and strength, and permitted

me to look with my own eyes once more on the mountains and the old region where thirty years ago I tried to
do work for Him. It fills my heart with abounding
gratitude.

" I went down to Jackson Street. The place where we
lived and where Herbert was born is now occupied by a
big brick business house called the ' Pittsburgh Building.' Then I walked the whole length of Rodney Street,
trying almost in vain to find the old land marks. In the
main the former houses of wood are replaced by brick.
Mr. Paynter's house, corner of Rodney and Broadway,
where I used to be a guest, was almost the only one I
recognized.

" At church, both morning and evening, there were
large congregations. In the morning I preached a
written sermon and celebrated the holy communion.
Bishop Brewer was with me. Mr. Love had gone to
Butte to take Mr. Blackiston's services, the latter being
quite broken down by his daughter's death. There were
about one hundred communicants. In the evening
Rev. Mr. Hunting of Evanston, Wyoming, was with us
helping. He has come from Bishop Leonard to drum
for Rowland Hall among Montana girls. After each
service I came down into the isle and greeted old friends.
The Rumseys were there. Lottie is, Mrs. Jones says, a
most loyal and helpful church girl. Mrs. Holter, with
the sweetest countenance and manner, greeted me.
Norman Holter, whom as a baby a little older than
Herbert I baptized, is one of the vestrymen. " China "
Clarke, the former head of the firm of Clarke, Conrad
and Curtin, sent word he wanted to see me. I went in
the afternoon to see him. He is eighty years old now
and confined to his house by weakness. He thanked
me for coming, with tears. I had prayers with him. He

is a South Methodist. He was kind enough to say my visit did him a great deal of good. It touches me that the older friends have such deep honest desire to see me. God bless them all!

"Helena now has 15,000 people or more, and has eight excellent large public schools beside the high school. Also two Lutheran churches, two Methodist, a Presbyterian, a Campbellite, a Baptist, a Jewish synagogue and two Roman Catholic churches are here besides our own.

"I was at Bozeman for Sunday, July 9th. Bozeman then had about 6,000 people; and Methodist and Presbyterian and Baptist and Campbellite and Lutheran and Roman Catholic churches, besides our own. The Presbyterians the strongest, and we next. We have by all odds the handsomest church, of stone, substantial and beautiful. The Rev. Mr. Lewis has been the faithful pastor there now for twenty-five years."

I visited also Deer Lodge, Missoula, Bass' "Pine Grove" farm, and Dillon. At Deer Lodge Rev. E. G. Prout was rector. Previously for years he had been rector of St. Paul's, Virginia City. There he succeeded his father, Rev. H. H. Prout, who had gone to Salt Lake City. These were son and grandson of the old senior warden of my native parish at Windham, New York.

I want to pause here to write about two men from Windham. First, of the Rev. Thomas S. Judd, the rector of the country church in Windham, the home of my boyhood; second, of the Rev. H. H. Prout.

The Episcopal church being in the country near my home and the Methodist church, to which my father belonged, being in the village two miles distant, I attended the Sunday-school of the former. In the district school on a certain Friday afternoon when we were "speaking"

pieces, Mr. Judd was present. I spoke. The next week
he asked my father if he might give me lessons in Latin
and Greek. I was then a little over ten years old. So,
without interfering with my district school tasks, for
nearly three years Mr. Judd steadily and judiciously in-
jected Latin and Greek into me. This describes the
matter. I did not take to the process with much fervor,
nor take in the linguistic food with great delight. Mr.
Judd persevered. I dutifully obeyed. In the autumn of
1850, when I was thirteen, he paved the way for me to
go to Delhi to enter Delaware Academy. I was to live
with a Mrs. Sherwood, a widow. Mr. Judd had once
been a teacher in Delhi and I think also a pastor. He
had been engaged to a daughter of Mrs. Sherwood who had
died. I was to pay my way at Mrs. Sherwood's by milk-
ing the cow, working the garden, and " doing chores."
I stayed three years. The last year the principal of the
academy, Mr. McKoon, made me a pupil teacher; and
while I was studying Livy and Homer and trigonometry
I was teaching Virgil and Anabasis and algebra and
geometry. Mr. Judd had known Rev. W. W. Olssen
when the latter had been a clergyman at Prattsville, a
neighboring town to Windham. So in the autumn of
1853, when Mr. Olssen wanted a teacher to assist him in
his school at Scarsdale, N. Y., Mr. Judd advised my going there. After I had been a year with him, Mr. Olssen
paved the way for me to go to Columbia College, he
himself being a graduate therefrom. I entered the
sophomore class.

Mr. Judd was my second father. He loved me. I
loved and revered him. He did not stay in Windham
during all my course at college and seminary, but was
in one and another parish in Connecticut, his native
state. After I had been in Morris for about a year he

came to the charge of Gilbertsville, the parish nearest
to me. He served it for a year and died there in
March, 1863, at the age of sixty. I was with him at the
last, alone, on my knees, holding his hands and afterwards reverently closing his eyes. He lies buried by the
side of the Rev. Mr. Foote, in Hillington Cemetery,
Morris. To him more than to any other man save my
own father, I am indebted for character and attainments.
In loving gratitude I pay this little tribute to his sacred
memory.

The Rev. H. H. Prout came to Virginia City, Montana,
in the autumn of 1871. His father was the senior warden
at Windham, N. Y., during all the years of my boyhood.
He came to my help direct from a rectorship at Windham. He was in Virginia for about two years, and then
in Salt Lake for five or six years, part of the time having
special care of Corinne. He was nearly sixty years old
when he came to me. I was thirty-seven. I buried him
in the cemetery at Salt Lake in 1879. I owe him much,
and want to pay a grateful tribute to his memory. He
was a saintly man, but with a saintlikeness quite other
than that of weak and mild-mannered sentiment. He
faced duty bravely. Once or twice in a kindly but sturdy
spirit he rebuked me. He said he was glad I was popular,
but he said also that along with the winning of men's
affection and allegiance to the person of the bishop, he
could not but earnestly desire that I would not forget will
and effort to win them to be repentant sinners and God's
children and Christ's disciples.

He was an accomplished English scholar, and his was
a chastened literary taste. To him redundancy and ver-
bosity were qualities sorely grievous. He courageously
faulted more than once the multiplication of adjectives in
my own written sentences, and urged upon me the truth

that loud voiced superlatives are in most cases weaker
things than plain and quiet positives.   No college lessons
in rhetoric helped me so much as did his gentle and courteous strictures.   He could not help being gentle and
courteous, it was his nature.

He was a trained theologian and an unflinchingly
loyal Prayer-Book churchman.   But with him, strength
of loyalty and breadth of wisdom and depth of charity
made a threefold cord.   Time and time again with his
soft voice, in his sweetly persuasive way, when we were
thrown together, he pressed upon me thoughts about the
Church *versus* Episcopalianism.

Isms, in the nature of the case, he would say, are
narrow, fragmentary, partisan, excluding things.   The
church ought not be partisan, must not be so, and, I
think, under God's blessing, as time goes on, will not be
so.   In America at the close of our Revolutionary War
the Church was in a state of sore depression.   Suspected
of sympathy with the British cause, deficient in equipment as having had no resident bishop for the one hundred
and seventy seven years of her history, weakened from
within by consequent lack of godly discipline, and set
upon from without by those alien to her ways and
prejudiced against her order, she was in no condition to
make claims, or to assert and explain her reason of being,
or her philosophy of life.   She must needs be content
with the liberty to exist, and must busy herself with
marking time to get breath, and with the use of the
simplest plans and readiest means to nurse herself into a
position of independence.   No wonder that she did no
more than call herself the " Episcopal Church," or the
" Protestant Episcopal Church," merely aiming to gird up
her loins and gather her forces together to build herself
into the steadiness of organized existence.   She is now

well organized after American methods, she is acclimated
to the American atmosphere, she is rooted deep and
strong in the American soil.   Now, it is not untimely
nor unfit to give thought to her reason for being and to
her philosophy of life.

The Church is the body of Christ.   Holy Scripture so
witnesseth.   All the baptized, in the gracious covenant
of adoption, are members of that one body.   The fulness
of the Blessed Saviour's grace and mercy and love is
ready to flow into the heart of each and every individual
of His body, unless that individual set up bar or ban
against it.   Narrowness, exclusion, demarcation, delimi-
tation are not in order.   We have so far been busy with
nursing Episcopalianism, and protecting Episcopalianism,
and providing it a rooting to give life and room for
organic growth.   Doubtless we have done well.   There
is a time for all things.   The Church has had its rightful
day to challenge our loyalty and evoke our support because of circumstances and necessities.   But Episcopalianism must be rated a stepping stone; and there
comes a time when upon the stepping stones of our dead
selves we are to rise to higher things.

If our thought is well founded and on the right line
some conclusions of a practical nature may be mentioned.

1.   The Church Militant is to represent and embody,—
so far as her natural elements, of the earth, earthy, will
allow,—the fulness of grace and mercy and love of her
Head, the Lord and Saviour Jesus Christ.   She must
not, then, count it right to limit to the list of her own
membership her succors and benefits and benedictions.
The Saviour by His death is the Redeemer of all mankind.   In His Incarnate Life He is the loving Brother of
all mankind.   His representative, the Holy Ghost, now

here on earth, pleads with all mankind through the
reason, the conscience, the inner life. The Church, His
representative, also indeed His body—ought then to have
no lower aim than to touch and help and bless all men.
Solicitude must not be limited to her own members.
Sinners, the unbelieving, the disobedient, the unrepentant,
should not be regarded as outside her thought and care.
And an all-pitying love and a never despairing patience
should be characteristics of that care.

2. He who has been rating himself as the Episcopalian
minister or priest must recast his thought and take it into
his heart that he is an ambassador of Christ, and is to be
the messenger and minister of His all-embracing mercy
and love. Wherever in America he is settled he will
find hosts of people who profess and call themselves
Christians, but who would stoutly decline to be enrolled
as Episcopalians. These he is to consider as in the
Church. They are baptized. They love the Lord Jesus
Christ in sincerity. They obey the Holy Ghost. They
study and reverence and follow the Holy Bible. They
walk worthy of the vocation wherewith they are called.
In his town he probably finds half a dozen religious
organizations other than his own, each under its own
pastor. As a gentleman he will take pains not to interfere with the rights of those pastors over their own flocks,
nor to cross unkindly their paths, nor to mar their work.
Nay, more, he can consider that they are doing Christian
work with him, and even for him. For by the laws of
the primitive Church he is set in that town to be, under
the bishop, in spiritual charge of all the souls therein.
All living there,—if we except just now the Roman
Catholics, the question of jurisdiction in their case falling
along other lines,—are under his pastorship. Theoretically, or philosophically, or historically, as you please, but

anyway in a sense, they all belong to him. He is responsible, spiritually, for them all. Practically he cannot reach them all, or be in touch with them all. But the other pastors do that work for him. However sad and wasteful the seeming divisions among Christians are, may he not be honestly and heartily thankful to God's gracious Providence that the needed religious work is being done, and done quite efficiently too, in the town, and that the Church is upbuilded therein, even though he himself is by no means permitted to do it all ? If he can take this view, suspicion, envy, jealousy, bitterness, hatred about dissensions and divisions will have no room to grow in his heart.

Then the people who do not belong anywhere religiously, the unattached people, the worldly people and the wicked people in the town, how about them ? If he is a thoughtful man he answers : They are not Methodists, and my Methodist brother is not bound to look after them ; nor is my Baptist brother, for they are not Baptists, and so on through the list of the pastors. And they are not Episcopalians, and so as an Episcopalian minister I am not called to look after them ; but he adds quickly, I am not an Episcopalian minister merely, I am the spiritual care-taker of the Church for souls. I am the ambassador of Christ and must represent as fully as I can His mercy and love. These are His little ones, His wandering ones, His weak ones, His misguided and beguiled ones, His lamed and defective and lost ones. These sinners are indeed mine to see to. The Saviour and the Church love and try to save the sinners, though they hate and warn against their sins. Shame be to me if humbly and heartily I do not set myself to follow their lead. And the Prayer-Book says, " Hold up the weak, heal the sick, bind up the broken, bring again the out-

casts, seek the lost." God help me to try to do just that
faithfully!

3. The heart which is warm with good will to Christians of other names for their faithfulness and zeal in
saving souls and in building up Christ's kingdom on
earth, will be no less warm in fervent loyalty to the ancient
things of the Church, her charter, her commissioned ministry, and her historic continuity. Gratitude for the
breadth of the church and for her loving inclusiveness
need not impair in any way fidelity to the trusts committed to her, or unflinching devotion to whatsoever is necessary to preserve the validity of her ministry and the
integrity of the faith. And deep and strong and widely
pervasive will be our grateful appreciation of God's
gracious Providence in preserving to us that conspicuous
bulwark of protection, the Book of Common Prayer.

Dear old Mr. Prout! Your " memorabilia " sank into
my mind and heart and life. They did not remove all
perplexities and anxieties. But they diminished them.
They gave me a different view of things. And from the
changed view-point I became more thankful for the past,
more trustful in the present, more hopeful of the future.

In 1899 I went to Salt Lake, and then to Boise, Idaho.
From Boise as a centre I made excursions round about
to visit old places and see old friends. I went to Payette,
Weiser, Idaho City, and Placerville and held services in
all of them. I planned also to go to Silver City and to
Hailey.

Then God's Providence arrested further goings. A
telegram came of the illness of my dear wife and that it
was increasing. I left Boise for St. Louis on August
18th. On the 19th, at Granger, where the Oregon Short
Line connects with the Union Pacific, a telegram from
my son dated at St. Louis, August 18th, was placed in

my hand. It said: " Mother died peacefully this morning. Funeral to be on Tuesday." In my lonely grief,
along the plains and sand hills over which together we
had ridden in the stage westward thirty-one years before,
I was then borne swiftly eastward to stand by the open
grave to say the last of the earthly good-bys, many and
many of which we had been obliged to speak to each
other in our frequently separated, but lovingly and closely
united, missionary lives.

Now let me come to the subject of this chapter, " The
Second Call to Missouri." It will be remembered that I
was called to be Bishop of Missouri in 1868, when I was
in my cabin in Virginia City. The telegram was received
on June 1, and was as follows:

" St. Louis, May 30, 1868.
" You were unanimously elected Bishop of Missouri on
first ballot.

" M. Schuyler,
" President Convention."

I declined that call. Then Missouri elected Rev.
Charles F. Robertson of Batavia, N. Y., a graduate of
Yale College, and a classmate of mine in the General
Theological Seminary. For nearly eighteen years Bishop
Robertson served Missouri well, with constancy and
courage, with industry and zeal, with devotion and suc-
cess. He died May 1, 1886.

In the latter part of May I was engaged in a visitation
of Southern Utah. About noon of May 27th I rolled
into Silver Reef on the lumbering stage, sitting outside
with the driver, and covered thick with dust. As we
stopped at the Wells Fargo office before going to the
hotel, the agent, R. S. Gillespie, an old friend of early
Montana years, and himself a Missourian, handed up a
telegram to me. It was this:

"*St. Louis, Mo., May 26, 1886.*
"By unanimous vote of the diocese of Missouri you have been elected their bishop. Will you accept? Please answer.
" M. SCHUYLER,
" Pres't of the Convention."

I took no long time to think. When I had taken a bath and dined I sent Dr. Schuyler the following telegram :

" If still in session I beg you elect another man. I am needed here."

The next day came to Silver Reef the answer :

"*St. Louis, Mo., May 28, 1886.*
"Am ordered to telegraph you as follows :
"*Resolved,* that the convention is unanimously unwilling to change its choice and that the convention feels that Bishop Tuttle is needed here. Further particulars by mail.
" M. SCHUYLER,
" President."

I stayed in Silver Reef over Sunday, the 30th. It was a mining town, without a church of any kind in it. Nor, if I remember aright, was there a minister of any sort there. Sunday was a busy day for me. Besides holding in a hall the two regular services, morning and evening, at 9 A. M. in a house I baptized three adults, and at 7 P. M. in another, three children. At the morning service in the hall I also baptized a child, and I celebrated the Holy Communion with nine communicants. Mrs. Tuttle wrote me :

" *Home, Saturday Afternoon, May 29, 1886.*
" Some way I dread to write to you in the face of all this startling announcement from Missouri. We are in

sore perplexity and I realize it thoroughly. You know
the two messages, and I know your answer to the first.
Thank you for the thoughtfulness which sent me that
answer. My dear husband, I can say nothing. I feel it
not right for me now to offer advice or to express my
own wishes. My thoughts are prayers, and they bring
me often to my knees. It is a very critical period in
your life. God must guide you and direct you ; and may
He help and comfort you, and help us cheerfully to do
what seems to be His Holy Will. That first telegram
called me up in the middle of the night. You can think
how it startled and troubled me, and how when I did
sleep it was to dream of you, and to mix everything in
terrifying confusion. Your side of it all is the hardest
and my love and sympathy follow you each hour, as well
as my poor stumbling prayers. It is with great impa-
tience that I await your home coming next Wednesday
night. I think you need to be at home, and to have
some one to help you.

" Mr. Wallace says that if you must go to Missouri
they must have Mr. Kirby made their bishop. Docket
(Dr. Hamilton) says that he doesn't want to live here if
you go away."

I reached home June 2d. Letters poured in, some urg-
ing acceptance, and as many urging declination of the
Missouri call. I consulted with our senior warden, Mr.
George M. Scott.

I pause here to say somewhat about Mr. Scott. He
came to Salt Lake from California in the '70s. He had
gone to California early from his home in Northern New
York, and like all others had met rough experiences
there. But no roughening of his gentlemanliness had
taken place. No, nor of his gentleness either. He was
unmarried, but his heart and life were a home for the

sweet domestic graces. And his loved niece, Miss North, living with him helped to give air and sun and growth to the home virtues. Always firm in the right, yet ever kind and considerate in the method of it, he became one of our best business men and leading citizens. In after years he was the first, and I think has been the only, "Gentile" mayor of Salt Lake. In the spring of 1875, when the day for confirmation at St. Mark's Cathedral was approaching, I went into his office one day and asked him to give me ten minutes of his time. I said, "Mr. Scott, you are helping us in the church, you are trying to do justly to your fellow men, and you are, I believe, walking humbly with your God. You ought to be confirmed. Will you not come next Sunday and take your place in the inner circle of grace as is your duty and privilege?" He answered, "I do not think I ought to be confirmed. I am not fit. I have not thought enough about it. Business presses so that I cannot give it the thought I ought." I replied, "I wish earnestly to urge the step upon you. I shall put up my own prayers that God will move you to take it. You need not say yes or no to me to-day. But next Sunday if you think it right, and indeed I earnestly hope you will, come up with the others at the proper time and be confirmed. Thank you for giving me a hearing. Good-morning, Mr. Scott."

My prayers were answered. The next Sunday morning when those to be confirmed approached the chancel, Mr. Scott came among them. And for all these years nowhere could a more faithful and devoted servant and officer of the church be found, than the senior warden of St. Mark's Cathedral, Salt Lake, has been. He has now gone back to California to live, but his memories, his

love, his sympathies, his help, are with St. Mark's
still.

In my conference with him about the Missouri call Mr.
Scott would say but little.   Personally, I think, he wanted
me to stay.   But he was not clear in expressing his
thought of what it might be duty for me to do.   Then
came to me the following communication penned by
him :

> *" Salt Lake City, June 15, 1886.*
> *" Rt. Rev. Dan'l S. Tuttle,*
>   *" Bishop of Utah and Idaho,*
>
>   " DEAR FRIEND :—It having come to our knowl-
> edge, as wardens and vestrymen of St. Mark's Cathedral,
> that you have been elected Bishop of Missouri and that you
> are now considering the acceptance of the position, we
> wish to state that while we do not desire either to stand
> in the way of your removal to a larger and possibly a
> more tempting field of Christian work and duty, or to
> run the risk of allowing our deep personal esteem and
> love to place a barrier on what you may consider the
> path of duty, we do think this a proper occasion of ex-
> pressing, not only for ourselves as individuals but in our
> associated capacity as wardens and vestry of St. Mark's
> Cathedral, speaking the unanimous sentiments of its con-
> gregation, the abiding affection and love in which you are
> held, based upon long years of personal contact as
> bishop, pastor and friend, and the great, if not irreparable,
> loss the parish, missionary district and community would
> sustain in the severance of your present relations.   Your
> special adaptation to the work of the church in this re-
> gion, your unequaled devotion and vigor in its promo-
> tion, with your knowledge of the people of the whole
> district, and their love for and their confidence in you
> give the Church a vantage ground of great value which
> she would lose by your removal.   It would give us and
> all for whom we speak the greatest gratification if, con-
> sistent with your views of duty, you will still continue

those relations which in the past have strengthened the work of the Church by building it upon a strong basis of Apostolic service and Christian character.

"We are, dear bishop, your sincere and devoted friends,

> "GEORGE M. SCOTT,
> "GEO. Y. WALLACE,
> "HENRY STRATFORD,
> "C. B. DURST,
> "I. H. WOODMAN,
> "E. WILKES, JR."

And this letter from Ogden:

> "*Ogden, May 31, '86.*

"MY DEAR BISHOP:

"Your Ogden children are confronted by the dread of a great uncertainty. They, with all the others in two territories who look up to you with a great filial respect and love and in their heart of hearts consider and call you Father, are in much the same condition of a great fear for the future that the disciples of our Lord were in when the sad word had got abroad that spoke of His going away.

"We know that you will not leave us, unless you are very sure that the Lord wills and the call of duty is clear and plain. We shall be glad when the suspense is over and the matter is decided, and we shall not cease to hope and pray that the decision will be that you go not away.

> "Faithfully and aff'ly yrs,
> "SAM'L UNSWORTH."

I wrote to Mr. Kirby to ask his view. Before he received my letter he had written me under date of June 1. After receiving my letter he wrote:

> "*Potsdam, N. Y., 14 June, 1886.*

"Yours of the 29th May was received some days ago. I have not written before, partly because I have not known what to say, and partly because I had already written saying something on the subject of your letter. Of course you have already found that such a question as the one which has come before you will have to be decided by yourself, and that others cannot help you much. I imagine that, take it all in all, Missouri is a harder and more laborious field than the one you have. For that you would not care. From what I know of you I do not believe you would be as happy or work as freely in that diocese as you are and do in your present field. As far as the honor and reverence of others are concerned, I am inclined to think you will retain more of that by declining than by accepting this election. I feel that you deserve and merit an eastern diocese, but I am pretty sure that the average mind will go out to you more if you refuse to turn your face eastwards. It strikes me that the whole missionary work would receive something of a blow if you ceased to be known as a representative missionary bishop; and your Utah work would surely suffer immeasurably under any change of oversight during your lifetime. I have thought a good deal over this matter and feel, without being able to give good reasons for it, that it would be a mistake, as far as you are personally concerned, and an injury to the Church were you to yield to the pressure that will be brought to bear to draw you away from your own work. I say this the more freely as I do not believe you would find your home life more attractive and pleasant in St. Louis than at Salt Lake. It strikes me that the great argument for a change that might be brought forward by some is, your position among the bishops. It might be thought that one so far up on the list as you are, and not unlikely in the ordinary course of Providence to be presiding bishop, ought to be at the head of a diocese. How much force there is in

this I am not able to say. As for useful work for the
Church I believe you will do more of that where you are,
as long as your life is spared, than in any such region as
Missouri. I have made my own feelings pretty plain,
but have not put forth any reasons that ought to influence you, and I can't, and I do not believe any one can.
There are certain points where one's friends are not of
much help, and you have, I think, reached such a point.
You know what we say about the road to Colton. That
whichever one a person takes, he wishes before he reaches
the end that he had taken the other. So, however you
decide this question, there will be those who will feel
that you have not acted for the best, and you will have
to run the risk of feeling so yourself. For myself I shall
accept any decision you may make as the best for yourself and the Church, as I know you will only make it after
honest prayer and mature deliberation, and with all the
bearings of the question before you as they can come before no other. May God help you and bring you out of
your perplexities into a clear mind."

I wrote to Bishop Williams of Connecticut, and to
Bishop Lee of Delaware, the presiding bishop. Their
answers follow :

" Middletown, June 7, 1886.
" MY VERY DEAR BROTHER:
      " I have thought and prayed about you ever since
I heard from Missouri. Indeed it is a hard question to
settle; and I confess I am ' in a strait betwixt two.'
      " On the one side *you* could by God's blessing do what
Missouri so much needs; on the other who *can* do what
you are doing in Utah? So it shapes itself in my
mind.
      " And when the scale is evenly balanced, the place
where God's Providence has placed one should I think
turn it that way.

" So dear brother, while I should rejoice to see you
take poor Missouri in charge, I must own that in my
view Utah has the higher claim.

" I write in haste on the wing for my convention.
But the thoughts have been with me all along.

" The good Lord bless and guide you.

" Yr loving brother,

" J. WILLIAMS."

" Wilmington, Del., June 7, 1886.

" MY DEAR BISHOP TUTTLE :

" It is a very difficult thing for any one but the
individual himself to decide a question of duty. It depends so much upon circumstances and convictions of
which others know but little. I can only give you my
impression as an outsider.

" I cannot see that considerations of ' right and duty '
require you to resign your present position. Either in
Missouri or Utah there is a wide field of usefulness and
great work to be done. It does not strike me that there
is any such indication of a Providential call as to decide
the question one way or the other. If on the one hand
the diocese of Missouri offers a wider field, on the other
the work in Utah being of a peculiar nature can be
better directed by you than by any one likely to succeed
you.

" You have had a charge of special difficulty and hardship. If the change would bring you any relief from
toil and anxiety you would be, after your long service,
fully justified in embracing it. If your own feeling and
preference are in favor of remaining at your present post,
it does not seem to me that you are under any stress of
conscience to relinquish it. It is not a question of assuming the burden of the Episcopate presented to a
parish minister,—but of choosing between two important
spheres of usefulness, a somewhat embarrassing position,
but the decision of which I think depends upon your own
feelings. The church will be satisfied whichever way you
determine.

" Trusting that you will be rightly guided and abundantly blessed I am,
                    " Faithfully yours,
                        " ALFRED LEE."

It was evident that the decision was to be thrown
back upon myself, so I debated with myself as follows :

1. I do not desire to change. My home in the
mountains is dear to me, five of my children have been
born here, in my nineteen years here other children have
grown to be men and women round about me. The
roots of mutual affection between me and all my people
have struck deep and grown strong. They love me, I
think. I love them. I know I do not want to go. Besides, there are difficulties in this field, and some of them
peculiar. I have much experience and can best get
along with them. I ought not to withdraw, making that
experience count for naught, and in what seems a shrinking and shirking way. But

2. I am forty-nine years old. Utah and Idaho are
developing in settlement and increasing steadily in
population. Last year I held services in forty-four
places. In many of them I must stay several days at
a time to make it sure that all work may go on well. I
left home the middle of April and was wandering in my
visitations till the first of November. Engagements for
Utah and Idaho begin to crowd, as six years ago they
did for Montana, Idaho and Utah. Is it reasonable to
think that in the fifties and by and by in the sixties I can
cope with them as well as I did in the thirties? Is not
this a fit time, then, for me to step out and for a younger
man to be put into this widely scattered and vigorously
growing field? And,

3. I cannot now plead as once I did, that I am too

young and inexperienced to have charge of a diocese. Nor, if I should change can it be thought or said that a missionary bishop has disgracefully thrown up missionary work before even getting it well in hand. The history of nineteen years will prevent all that. And furthermore,

4. Is Missouri not to be considered? That diocese called me to be its bishop in 1868. After eighteen years of service rendered by the faithful and devoted Bishop Robertson, with a steadfast loyalty and unshaken confidence and a persistent love it has repeated to me that call. Is not its claim upon me an unusually strong one for considerate and kind treatment?

The outcome was that I felt it duty to listen to Missouri. On June 16th I sent to Dr. Schuyler notice of my acceptance of the call, subject of course to the consent of the bishops and Standing Committees of the whole American Church.

Dear old Dr. Schuyler! It fell to his lot as president of each convention to send me two telegrams, quite identical in text, with eighteen years lapsing between. He was seventy-two years old when sending the second. He lived ten years longer to work by my side in St. Louis, the wisest of counselors, the strongest of helpers, the kindest of friends. A more lovable and saintlike man, a more painstaking and successful pastor, I have never known.

Immediately after sending my acceptance of Missouri, I started upon the visitation of Idaho. I was gone six weeks, but I visited only nine places, whereas the year before I had visited thirty-three. It was a good-by tour, and I allowed myself to cut it short. I went to Boise, Silver, Idaho, and Placerville, the old towns that had been familiar to me for twenty years. And I took in five of the ones that were nearer to me, Emmett, Bellevue, Hailey, Ketchum, and Lewiston.

To be vanishing out of their midst was a sadness to me. To say the good-bys was not a pleasure to the mountain people. Witness the following communications:

> " *Boise City, Idaho, July 6, 1886.*

" To the Rt. Rev. D. S. Tuttle:

" As you are about to sever the official bond by which you have been so long united to the Church in Idaho, the undersigned, the rector and vestry of St. Michael's church, Boise City, Idaho, deem it but fitting that we should express the deep regret with which we have learned of your decision, and the affection and esteem in which you have been, and will ever continue to be, held by ourselves and by the Church we are privileged to represent.

" For nineteen years you have been, under God, the chief pastor of this people, and it is with profound gratitude that we bear witness to the unvarying fidelity with which you have labored in the discharge of your duties.

" In those hours of discouragement which have inevitably come to the church struggling to establish itself in a new country, you have ever faithfully stood by our side and encouraged and stimulated us by your words of faith and hope. By the integrity of your life, the frank and open honesty of your words, and your devotion to the Master's cause you have endeared yourself to this people in a most unusual degree. Your name is written upon their hearts and indelibly impressed upon the annals of the Church in Idaho.

" While we deeply regret that duty should seem to demand your removal from our midst, we assure you of our continued affection, and our prayers that God will bless you in your new field of labor, and that the Holy Spirit may guide you in the future as we feel sure He has guided you in the past, until at the end of your earthly stewardship you may be enabled to say with the apostle,— ' I have fought a good fight, I have finished my course, I have kept the faith; henceforth there is laid up for me a crown which the Lord, the righteous judge, shall give me at that day.'

"G. H. Davis, Rector,
"A. G. Redway, ⎫
"T. E. Logan, ⎬ Wardens,
"John Huntoon, ⎭
"A. L. Richardson,
"G. W. Brumm,
"Fremont Wood,
"S. H. Walker."

"*Hailey, Idaho, July 27, 1886.*
"Dear Bishop:

"At a meeting of the committee of Emanuel church, Hailey, held July 22d, the following was made a part of the record of the meeting:

"Whereas, In the Providence of God, the time has come when we as a committee of men representing Emanuel church, Hailey, must say good-by to our bishop,

"Therefore, be it

"*Resolved*, That we severally and collectively desire to express our sense of the deep obligation that we shall ever owe to his faithful labors in our own and the Church's behalf, acknowledging that to his Christian faith and zeal, his manly devotion and his patient love, is due the degree of success that so far has crowned our own efforts in Church work.

"And, although knowing that we cannot express by words the deep feelings of our hearts, we still ask that we may be allowed in this manner to record our gratitude and loving regard, and we promise our prayers for his welfare and success in the new field to which he has been called.

"I. T. Osborn, Rector,   "Alex. Willman, Treasurer,
"Texas Angel, Secretary, "E. C. Coffin,
"W. T. Riley,   "J. C. Fox,
"V. S. Anderson,   "Homer L. Pound.
"*To the Rt. Rev. D. S. Tuttle, S. T. D.,*
"*Bishop of Utah and Idaho.*"

I wended my way down to Southern Idaho and stopped at Soda Springs. Here Mr. Geo. Y. Wallace and Mr. Charles W. Lyman, of Salt Lake City, who had married sisters, had summer cottages. The former was our junior warden. The latter afterwards became and is now (1904) the treasurer of the diocese of Nebraska. Both were among my kindest and most generously helpful friends of the mountains. I rested for a few days, and there at Soda Springs, Idaho, on the morning of August 9th, I became the Bishop of Missouri.

That morning's mail brought me a letter from Mr. Charles Hofman, secretary of the Standing Committee of Missouri, certifying that a majority of consents of bishops and standing committees to my translation had been received. When I took the letter in hand to read I was Bishop of Utah, and after I had read it, as I understood the matter, I was Bishop of Missouri.

Strangely, the canons provide for no formal pronouncing or announcing to the man chiefly concerned the completed action of the transfer of a missionary bishop to be the bishop of a diocese; and therefore I was obliged to decide for myself that the reading of that morning's letter changed me on the spot from the Bishop of Utah to the Bishop of Missouri.

So, by the turning of a leaf in a small documentary letter, I ceased to be a missionary bishop. This was true in name, more than in fact, however. For Missouri itself was one great missionary field. And I did not know that for a year or more, owing to the declination of Utah by Mr. Kirby when elected bishop, and until Bishop Leonard should be consecrated in January, 1888, I would still have charge of "Utah and Idaho" under the presiding bishop; and that in the summer of 1887 I would be in the mountains again in discharge of that delegated duty. Nor did I know, further, that as time went on and the lamented death of Bishop Leonard supervened, I would be called upon to take charge once more for a year (1903–4) as bishop of " Salt Lake."

I was not worn out. By God's mercy and goodness my health and strength, save for a defect in hearing which was growing upon me, were wonderfully retained. I was not discouraged or depressed. Cheerfulness had always been blessedly ministered to me from above, nor was it failing me now. Missionary enthusiasm had not run dry. It began with me and roamed about with me and my dear faithful horse " Jersey " among the hills of old Otsego County. I entertained it in my heart and fanned it with my love into a steady flame. I remember how I induced James Lloyd Breck to come to my country parish of Morris, though we were forty miles from a railroad, to tell us about missions. He was the foremost missionary among us of that day, and his visit was inspiration and benediction. In after years (October 21, 1897), I had opportunity to pay grateful tribute to that faithful missionary, at the side of the grave at Nashotah in which his sacred remains, brought from California, were to be finally deposited. I said : " Amidst the russet of this gray autumn day, from out of the pressing activities of a busy session of our missionary council (at Milwaukee), many of us have come to help lay in their final resting-place the perishing remains of a brother who was also a man of work. What a contrast,—life and death, strength and weakness, sturdy courage and trustful submission ! Could he speak to us he would bid us not dwell on death, he would urge us to think of life and faith and work. Brethren all, then,—you older ones who, kneeling awhile ago at yonder rail, recalled the fact that with Breck thirty and forty years ago you were students and laborers here at Nashotah, and you younger men who are putting your armor on,—I bid you think, not of death, but of life.

" There was a Grecian race in which the runners were charged to care not for themselves, nor indeed for each other, but for the torch they bore.   As one and another, wearied and overcome fell by the way, he held aloft his torch, handing it to a comrade who seized it quickly and sped on.

"So with the torch borne by the Christian man.   It has a triple flame,—God's truth, Christ's love, men's good.   We are to hold it up and pass it on.   One or another of us is soon to fall in the hard-trodden, dusty path. But never mind us, it is dust to dust, though it may be sacred dust, that falls, and God will take care of it.   Do not mind us ; seize the torch, we pray you, and push on to the blessed goal.

" It is with thanks we leave these sacred remains here in the bosom of mother earth,—thanks for the life our brother lived, the faith he avowed, the work he did, outspringing from that faith.   And with hope,—the assured hope through Christ that after the communion of saints come the forgiveness of sins, the resurrection of the body, and the life everlasting.   And with peace,—the sighing and soughing of the wind through these trees shall utter peace ; the birds hiding under the leaves shall carol peace ; the green, fresh grass-blades springing upward to the sun and responding to the moistening dew and refreshing rain shall speak peace ; the sweet waters of yonder lake, never lashed to fury, shall whisper peace.

> " ' Life's race well run,
> Life's work well done,
> Life's crown well won
> Thanks, hope, peace, rest ! ' "

With good health and· missionary enthusiasm some
other things were of help in doing my work. May I
mention two or three?

Fidelity in fulfilling promises and punctuality in keeping engagements I put in the very forefront of practical
maxims to be observed; nor have I ever learned that
such rating of their value was in error.

Family prayers I urged in every way. Homes with
the fulness and sweetness of their real meaning were not
much in evidence in my mining communities. But
homelike hospitality I was offered here and there and
everywhere. And with my kindly host, even where
hostesses were not, it was my custom, whenever practicable and becoming, to have family prayer. The boyhood's memories of my own loved father's constant habit
came to me as benedictions. The child is father of the
man. Family prayer sows blessed seeds in the hearts of
the children. The plants grow up and bear fruit all along
the way of earthly life. I am convinced that no one
human thing will do more to ennoble citizenship, to
deepen and strengthen Christianity, and to assure the
salvation of souls, than will family prayer. A former
missionary of Idaho wrote me lately:

"Shall I ever forget that night we spent at Trotter's
Hotel, Rock Creek! A wilderness, just six houses on
the Kelton-Boise line, not counting the stock tenders'
stations. We were a mixed crowd that night; but the
bishop and his coadjutor looked as tough and dirty as the
others. Oh, my! I can see those great grizzled men
watching each other through their opened fingers as they
were kneeling down while you read family prayers. I
tell you I admired your nerve. That was work. But it
had its many compensations, and we shall both always
love to think of it. No doubt when we get Home we

shall see some—many—I hope all, of the old friends. I don't believe that even in Paradise we shall be too happy or too busy to talk over those dear old days that are no more."

I practiced the giving of the tithe. From the time I was eighteen years old I have done so. Putting into the " Lord's purse " one-tenth of my salary whenever it was received. And then taking out of the " purse " as needs and calls were presented to me. Not only is the setting aside of a tenth a practice which, as I think, brings down God's blessing upon it; but the giving a tenth is a habit which induces cheerfulness and promotes happiness. When the needs and calls come it is a genuine pleasure to take out of the purse the wherewith to meet such as commend themselves to your judgment. If nothing be found in the purse, the conscience cheerily acquiesces in your words to the applicant that he must wait for a more convenient season. It is the Lord's purse. It is happiness for you to put your tenth into it. And it is honest joy for you, as the Lord's representative, to take out of it wherewith to help His little ones. Anxious and perplexing thought as to what you can do and what you ought to do in giving is banished, or at least reduced to a minimum.

From Soda Springs I went to my Salt Lake home. But for a stay of only three weeks. On September 1, 1886, I took actual charge of the diocese of Missouri as its bishop. The process of vanishing from my old field of the mountains was a quick one now. I had served as missionary bishop nineteen years and four months.

I had baptized 117 adults and 757 children in that field, I had confirmed 1,203, I had solemnized 146 marriages, I had buried 117 persons, and I had held in all 3,783 services.

Personally it was in much anguish of heart that I withdrew. But officially I had no feeling of distress. Bishop Brewer, wise and strong, already had the vigorous Montana work well in hand. And this year (1904) he makes it a diocese with twenty-four clergy, thirty-two church buildings, fifty organized parishes and missions, ten unorganized missions, and 2,725 communicants. The Church, I knew, would not neglect the rest of the field.

The House of Bishops in October elected my dear old friend and helper, Mr. Kirby, to be Bishop of Utah and Idaho. He declined, so for one year more I was kept in charge. Then changes in area were made. Utah was put with Nevada, and in October, 1887, Bishop Leonard was appointed Bishop of Nevada and Utah. Afterwards, under another change of metes and bounds, Bishop Leonard became the Bishop of " Salt Lake," a missionary district comprising all of Utah, the east portion of Nevada, the west portion of Colorado, and a county of Wyoming. Actively and untiringly for sixteen years he did the hard work given him to do, and then lay down to his well-earned rest. At his lamented death the old field yet once more reverted to my hands and I have charge of it now and until a new bishop shall be chosen. Idaho was conjoined with Wyoming and there the buoyant and energetic Talbot served as bishop for eleven years. Then under still another change, the missionary district of Boise was constituted, comprising Southern Idaho and Western Wyoming ; and of this Bishop Funsten, clear-headed and loving-hearted, has charge. Northern Idaho has become a part of the missionary district of Spokane, under Bishop Wells, who won his spurs in earlier years as an active missionary in Walla Walla and throughout the great Northwest.

God be thanked for the good work going vigorously

on! God forgive me for seeming to have shrunk from it and shirked it! Coming to Missouri I shrank again. Bishop Atwill, diligent, loyal, true, stepped into West Missouri. But shrinking is now over. I am wedded to Missouri " for better for worse, for richer for poorer, in sickness and in health, till death us do part."

There is to be no change more till quietly I shrink from the activities of earth into the peaceful rest I hope for, through the Saviour, with the prayer written deep in my heart, if not spoken out by the lips, " God be merciful to me a sinner!"

On Sunday morning August 29, 1886, I said my good-by in St. Mark's Cathedral, Salt Lake City. Perhaps it may be permitted me to make that a good-by also to my present readers.

" How can thoughts other than of stewardship come over me and you to-day? The Providence of Almighty God hath thrown our paths together for near twenty years. The same Providence severs us now, bidding us part unto diverse ways. We stand on the divide a little while between the paths whence we have come and whither we must go, and we may have pardon for casting a look at each.

" On the morning of the 2d of July, 1867, after nearly a thousand miles of travel by stage coach I entered this city, my brother,[1] who is here in the chancel to-day, also being with me. Two months previous the Rev. Messrs. Foote and Haskins had come and had started regular services and opened St. Mark's school. We found three communicants. One of them[2] is here to-day. Not a Sunday has there been, I think, from then till now in which the regular services of the church have not been

[1] Rev. G. D. B. Miller.   [2] Mrs. J. F. Hamilton.

maintained. In this parish twelve ministers have served, —G. W. Foote, Haskins, H. L. Foote, Pidsley, Kirby, Turner, Prout, Fowler, Miller, Unsworth, Armstrong, Putman. Under them 1,274 have been baptized, 411 have been confirmed, and the three[1] communicants have multiplied to 324. In my missionary field 3,809 have been baptized and 1,203 confirmed. In St. Mark's school and Rowland Hall, 3,186 boys and girls have been taught. In St. Mark's hospital 4,776 patients have been cared for. The parish since it began to be, has given for church and charity purposes, $271,045.63.

"These are figures and facts. Who shall estimate spiritual meaning and moral forces underlying and overlapping them? I am proud of and thankful for the faithful work of all the pastors and teachers ; and for the faithful coöperation likewise of the men and women and children of the parish.

"I cannot undertake to say all my thanks. Words would fail. Manly strength would go out of my voice.

"The wardens and vestrymen—if man ever find brothers in men, I have found them brothers indeed to me, clear headed, warm hearted, strong helping. Truer brothers I never expect to find in the life that is left me.

"The ministers who have come and gone—three of them stand forth conspicuous, the founders, Foote and Haskins, and the dearly loved pastor, Kirby. Two[2] have been called from work to rest.

"Teachers in the schools,—there have been scores of them. I can myself remember the names of fifty-four, besides other scores and scores of Sunday-school teachers. What a blessed work all theirs has been! Two other

---

[1] Mrs. J. F. Hamilton, Mrs. T. F. Tracy, Mrs. Oliver Durant.
[2] Rev. Morelle Fowler, Rev. H. H. Prout.

kinds of work only are more valuable than theirs, the Holy Spirit's, and parents'.

"The physicians in our hospital,—we think too little of what real benefactors medical men are. Ah, in the hard stress of disease how lovingly and trustingly your heart turns to them! Let us not ungratefully forget that in the hospital ward and in serving the sick poor without earthly pay they are followers, in fact (would God they all were followers in heart), in the footsteps of the Great Physician so merciful to help and to heal.

"The singers who have done duty in this church,—my heart is full of loving gratitude to them. The praises in holy worship,—God asks for them and owns them as much as the prayers. Ye have been right loyal helpers.

"The mantle falls. The work is done. The change has come. The roll of stewardship for twenty years is closed up. God's mercy and forgiveness be upon it! Turn we from the past.

"In October, at Chicago, your new bishop will be chosen. You are going to welcome him cordially. You are going to hold up his hands sturdily. You are going to cheer his heart and help on his work generously. How do you know,—does any one ask? We judge of the future by the past and so I know.

"Then, let us say a cheery good-by. Cheery, because of deep and long-to-be remembered thanks with which our hearts are full this day. Cheery, because there is great, good work to be done yet by you and me for God, if He spare our lives. Cheery, because if ever a people ought with abiding trust in God's Providence, we ought now to 'thank God and take courage.'

"We will do it. Thank God and take courage.

"Dear brethren, so long valued and so loved, I beseech you let us kneel once more together in the Holy

Communion of our Blessed Lord and pray Him, ' not weighing our merits but pardoning our offenses,' to keep us in His ways, and hold us in His hands, and save us in His love, that we may be together again with Him by and by.

> " ' God of our fathers, by whose hand
> Thy people still are blest,
> Be with us through our pilgrimage
> Conduct us to our rest.
>
> " ' O spread Thy sheltering wings around
> Till all our wanderings cease ;
> And at our Father's loved abode
> Our souls arrive in peace.' "

INDEX

INDEX   **495**

Irishmen, 312; bishops, 313; Mountain Meadow's Massacre, 324; baptism, 337; confirmation, 338; Lord's Supper, 338; tithing, 340; missionary seal, 341; conference, 343; stage driver's testimony, 349; baptism for the dead, 351; woman suffrage, 352; Zion's Mercantile Coöperative Institution, 352; seagulls, 353
Morris, 1; call to, 2, 7; assistant minister, 14; elected rector, 15; Sunday services, 16; missionary work, 16, 20, 28; last sermon at, 35, 39, 77, 205, 360, 481
Morris, Bishop, 44, 302, 424, 426
Morrow, Col., 394
Moss, H. O., 34
Moulton, G. B., 388
Mount, Jane, 44
Mount, Misses, 44
Murphy, J., 411
Myers, Gen., 68
Mygatt, H. R., 32, 33, 54, 55

NAUVOO, 63, 305, 311, 352
Neely, Bishop, 29, 32, 208, 430
Nelson, Judge, 56
Nephites, 308
Nevill, S. T., 266
Nevius, Dr., 302, 426
New Berlin, 34
North Platte, 65, 75
Nowell, W., 388
Noyes, J., 481
Nye, Senator, 55

ODENHEIMER, BISHOP, 32, 41
Ogden, 44, 48, 52; first church service, 254; old tannery, 255
Olssen, W. W., 49, 358, 460
Omaha, 63, 64, 211
Orofino and Florence mines, 119
Osborn, Rev. Mr., 421, 423, 479
Otego, 31
Overland mail, 332
Owen, Major, 443
Oxford, N. Y., 32

PADDOCK, B. H., 219, 259, 261
Paddock, J. A., 424
Palmer, C., 52

Palmer, Frank, 79, 83
Park City, 106
Parochial organization, 11, 12, 13, 15
Pastor, influence as, 3, 18, 19
Paul, Mr., 276
Paynter, W. S., 218, 451, 458
Pearsall, Emily, 272, 396, 398
Perpetual emigration fund, 333, 341, 346, 348
Pidsley, E., 40, 266, 267, 389
Pierce, Rev. Mr., 104
Pike's Peak mines, 119
Plain City, 106, 377
Plummer, 121, 124
Poindexter, Mr., 449
Polk, Bishop, 23
Pollinger, E. M., 445
Polygamy, 308, 311, 321, 347
Pomeroy, Mrs., 33
Pony express, 332
Pope, F., 299
Pope, Rev. Mr., 136
Portlandville, 40
Portneuf cañon, 95, 96
Potter, Bishop H., 1, 2, 22, 28, 29, 32, 42, 52, 54, 187, 260
Potter, W. B., 52
Power, T., 411
Poxon, Ellen, 258
Pratt, Orson, 345, 354
Prayer-Book, used for burial service by laymen, 6, 12
Promontory, 243
Prout, E. G., 410, 446, 459
Prout, H. H., 400, 459, 461
Prout, Mrs., 401
Putnam, N. F., 391

RADERSBURG, 199
Railway, Union Pacific, completed, 105
Randall, Bishop, 24, 30, 32, 42, 55, 67, 77, 78, 85, 208, 210
Ravalli, Father, 166
Redway, A. G., 149, 479
Reed, B., 251, 261
Reed, superintendent, 74
Regeneration, declaration on, 41
Richards, Rev. Mr., 450
Richards, Willard, 325
Rigdon, Sidney, 327
Riley, Bishop, 52